NOFZIGER

LYN NOFZIGER

NOFZIGER

REGNERY GATEWAY
Washington, D.C.

Library of Congress Cataloging-in-Publication Data

Nofziger, Franklyn C.
    Nofziger / Lyn Nofziger.
        p.   cm.
    Includes index.
    ISBN 0-89526-513-3 (alk. paper)
    1. United States—Politics and government—1945–1989—Anecdotes.
2. California—Politics and government—1951– —Anecdotes. 3. Press and politics—United States—Anecdotes. 4. Reagan, Ronald—Anecdotes.
5. Nixon, Richard M. (Richard Milhous), 1913– —Anecdotes. I. Title.
E839.5.N57   1992
973.927′092′2—dc20   92-15908
                                                                CIP

Published in the United States by
Regnery Gateway
1130 17th Street, NW
Washington, DC 20036

Distributed to the trade by
National Book Network
4720-A Boston Way
Lanham, MD 20706

Printed on acid-free paper

Manufactured in the United States of America

10 9 8 7 6 5 4 3 2 1

For Susie
In Remembrance

Acknowledgments

I AM TOLD that all authors of all books of nonfiction and even those that might best be categorized as semifiction always run lists of names of people without whose help their masterpieces would never have been written.

Sometimes the author will have a list that runs into the dozens, or the scores, or even the hundreds. Some list only a few. My list is in the "few" category.

To start off, I want to thank everyone I've named in the book, friends and enemies alike. Without you this book would not be the book it is.

Second, I want also to thank all the people I've known during my political career, indeed, during my entire life, because you helped make me what I was, what I am, and what I may eventually be. For better or for worse you shaped me, you participated in my life, and without you this book would never have been written in the way it has been written. This includes my wife, my children, all the rest of my kinfolk, and everybody else out there who has impinged in one way or another on my life.

Finally, I want thank those people directly involved in whatever success this book may have. These include Maria Downs, my agent, who pestered me into writing it, Trish Bozell who edited it down to size and sharpened it up in the process, Al Regnery who decided to publish it even if he wouldn't publish my Western novels (You had your chance, Al), and Stanley Trettick who took the cover picture.

To anybody else who thinks he or she should have made the list and didn't I offer apologies both sincere and humble.

Lyn Nofziger

Contents

NOFZIGER

1

Politics and the Press

THE TELEPHONE CALL that changed my life came on a cold day in early January of 1966. The caller was Capt. E. Robert Anderson, USN (ret.), the chief aide to James S. Copley who owned the chain of newspapers for which I worked.

He came right to the point. "Jim would like you to take a leave of absence and come out to California and be Ronald Reagan's press secretary for his campaign for governor."

Thus ended my career as a newspaperman and thus began my career as a Republican politician. Before Andy's call I had been for eight years a reporter, editor, even a photographer on small California newspapers, and then for the next eight years a Washington correspondent and politics writer for the Copley newspapers, at that time a chain of sixteen small- and medium-sized papers in California and Illinois.

By the end of February I had ceased being a reporter. But even so, for the last twenty-five years I have worked with and observed those who are, and during that period I have noticed a vast change in the attitudes of the press and the way it functions both as a body and as a body of individuals. I think much of it has to do with television. The reporters you and I watch on television these days are not just reporters, they are performers, personalities, if you will. And that is true whether they are television reporters or merely print media reporters who are making an extra buck by appearing on one of the numerous public affairs shows that are carried on TV.

The aim of too many reporters today is not to cover a story but to get on television, there to show off their expertise in all things. They do not want to cover the news or write the news; they want to be part of the news. And who can blame them? Everyone can use an extra buck and most of us like the idea of being a celebrity.

Thirty years ago a reporter was given a byline for a feature, as opposed to a hard news story, or for a job exceptionally well done. Today almost every story, including obituaries, merits a byline. In fact, in some labor disputes, in order to punish management, reporters have withheld their bylines under the mistaken and fatheaded impression that readers care. The best that can be said about today's byline craze is that the subject of the story knows who it is who stuck it to him or misquoted him or just plain got his facts wrong.

At my age nostalgia sets in; the old days were indeed better.

In the old days being a reporter did not mean getting a chance to be important and famous, unless you went on to write a syndicated column like, say, Westbrook Pegler or David Lawrence or Walter Lippman. These days television has added an extra dimension to "important and famous." Today you can get to be important and famous—and rich—without having nearly the talent of a Pegler or a Lawrence. All that is needed is a pretty face and a dulcet voice laden with important inflections.

I spent my first eight years as a newspaperman working on two small Copley newspapers, the *Glendale News-Press* and the *Burbank Daily Review*, eventually becoming editor of the *Review,* which isn't saying much because it was a pretty small paper. But I've always thought you learn more working on a small paper than on a big one.

Big papers have more reporters than stories; small papers have more stories than reporters. As a result reporters on small papers write more and cover a bigger variety of news. During my eight years in Glendale and Burbank I covered every beat except the women's page, which in those days was always guarded zealously by its editor as the realm of women. I covered city hall, police and courts, and the board of education. I wrote sports and obits. I wrote features. I edited copy, wrote heads, assigned stories, and made up the paper.

I took pictures of wrecks, weddings, fires, whatever came along, first with an old 4 x 5 Speed Graphic, and later with a Rolleiflex because I tired of lugging around that heavy old Graphic.

In those days cameras used flash guns with bulbs that now and then exploded. I stopped a basketball game once to clean up the broken glass from an exploded bulb. Another time a bulb exploded with a loud pop while I was taking a picture of a pregnant woman who had been hurt in an auto accident. She thought she'd been shot and screamed. The gathering crowd muttered unhappily and I left quickly, without my picture.

There are problems with small papers. For one thing investigative reporting is difficult. They are understaffed; reporters are overworked and seldom have the time or resources to do the digging that investigative reporting ordinarily requires. Worse, the publisher is a part of the community, usually active in civic affairs and often in politics as well. He is not always eager to take on or attack in his newspaper those with whom he works and socializes. As a result reporters often are discouraged from digging into areas where, were it a metropolitan paper, they would be given carte blanche.

Then there is the matter of advertising—the lifeblood of all newspapers. A large newspaper can withstand the threat of a major advertiser pulling his ads; for a small paper one major advertiser can be the difference between profit and loss. So when a big advertiser in a small paper threatens to pull out if a story is run, or for that matter if a story is not run, the publisher is forced at least to listen. The idea of a free press is wonderful, but it is possible for a small paper to exercise its freedom right into bankruptcy.

At the *Burbank Daily Review* Christian Scientists were big with the implied threat that their business people would pull their advertising if one specific demand was not met. It had to do with obituaries. In the newspaper business people don't pass away or pass on; they die, and obituaries are written accordingly. But when a Christian Scientist in Burbank died a member of the church almost always came in to remind us that Christian Scientists don't die; they pass on and it would behoove us so to note. The conversation was always civil but always with the implied warning that we needed them more than they needed us. Which was true. Thus, in the *Daily Review*, while everyone else died, Christian Scientists passed on.

There are other problems with working on a small newspaper. Mainly, the pay is poor. After five years I was making $100 a week. Even in 1955 that wasn't much. The hours were long, with no overtime. Expense accounts didn't include buying drinks. You got drunk on your own or someone else's money, but not the paper's.

Going from a small newspaper to the nation's capital is like jumping from high school baseball directly to the major leagues. That was true even for the Washington of 1958, which had a much smaller infrastructure, whatever that means, and a much smaller press corps, and a much different set of rules.

I went to Washington to work in the Copley Bureau in January of 1958 and checked in at the Willard Hotel across the street from the National Press Building. The room rate was $14 a night. I arrived carrying one bit of advice from Hoyt Cater, the *Daily Review* publisher, regarding Robert Richards, the Copley bureau chief.

"Don't," he said, "try to drink with Bob Richards. He has a hollow leg."

That was a scary piece of information because in those days the Copley people prided themselves not so much on the quality of their product as on their ability to hold their liquor. I fit right in. But as far as Bob Richards was concerned, I quickly learned that Cater was right. Richards, a little man with a loud, snarly voice to go with his hollow leg, owned a corner of the men's bar in the National Press Club which, in those good old days, had no women members. Three drinks at lunch was minimum for Richards, but he always filed copy in the afternoons, even if it meant writing a new lead on a wire service story and filing the whole thing as his.

Five years after I arrived Richards died from a massive stroke, but he died the way he would have wanted to. He was at a cocktail party and had just announced, "I think I'll get another drink," when he crumpled to the floor.

In those days the Copley Bureau was on the twelfth floor of the National Press Building, one floor down from the National Press Club and therefore thirty seconds from a drink, less if you were really thirsty.

It was on the southwest corner of the building, overlooking 14th Street on the west and the Washington Monument on the south. In those kinder, gentler days presidents rode around in open cars, and about the only places with any security were the White House, the Defense Department, and the CIA. And even there it wasn't very good.

The Old Executive Office Building, the departments of government, the halls of Congress were among the places you would wander in and out of at will.

Even after Puerto Rican terrorists shot up the House of Representatives in 1954 nothing much changed. Only a few people still remember that incident, but I do because of an anecdote Frank (Jeff) Macomber, a longtime Copley reporter, used to tell concerning an old Alabama congressman named Frank "All for Love" Boykin. Boykin was on the floor of the House when the shooting began, but he got out of there in a hurry. As he rushed for an elevator someone stopped him and asked where he was going.

"To get my gun," he yelled.

"Where is it?"

"At home," he called back, hurrying off.

I also remember when Nikita Khrushchev came to town. President Eisenhower went to Andrews Air Force Base to greet him and ride with him into town. From the Capitol to the White House the two leaders rode in the back of an open car. As they went past the Press Building I could easily have dropped a sack of water on them. Lee Harvey Oswald could have done even worse. The two men were sitting ducks.

Security at the time consisted of someone from the government coming around to our office, among others, asking if anyone had a gun and when we said no, going away. Yet on that same trip those in charge wouldn't let Khrushchev go to Disneyland, for reasons of security. Too dangerous, they said. You figure it out.

During the Cuban missile crisis security wasn't much better. Much of the news was coming out of the Pentagon and a lot of reporters wanted to cover the briefings being held there. Trouble was, only a relatively few reporters had Pentagon passes. To make it easier on everyone some high muckamuck decided that temporarily anyone with a White House pass would be admitted. A couple of days after this brilliant decision someone discovered the man from Tass, the Soviet news agency, wandering around the building at will. He had a White House pass. And he, like most Soviet reporters abroad, was probably a member of the KGB. Today you can't even get into the Department of the Interior without a pass, whether or not you're a member of the KGB.

If you work on a paper in any small city it's easy to think that covering Washington is just like covering city hall, but bigger. Wrong. Nothing compares. Not city hall, not the state capital. Washington is much bigger, much more spread out, much more complex. People are harder to find, harder to know, harder to deal with. They think they are more important and they bask in their own importance. They have bigger staffs and more people to interpose between them and you. Personal secretaries are more possessive and more resistant.

The tragedy of Washington for a good reporter is not that there aren't enough stories but that there are too many. No news organization covers the town thoroughly; none can. And even if one could it wouldn't matter because even a paper that may brag that it carries "all the news that's fit to print" couldn't crowd it all in. Anyway, it doesn't really matter. Most reporters want to cover just the big stories, the ones everyone else is covering, which means you can have fifty reporters on one story and none on another that's almost as good.

One of two things, sometimes both of them, happens to too many reporters who come to Washington. One is, they get lazy and find it easier to write the stories that everyone else is writing. Another is that they become self-important and only write the stories that they and other "important" reporters think are important. Add these two problems to the herd instinct that infects most human beings and you wind up with that news media syndrome best exemplified in Washington: Pack journalism.

Everybody wants to cover the same story. Everybody wants to make sure he doesn't miss the lead or the important quotes. Before tape recorders reporters gathered around to check their notes to make sure their quotes were accurate. When you were lucky enough to find a reporter who took shorthand, like Don Irwin of the *New York Herald Tribune* and later the *Los Angeles Times*, you made sure he got up in front so he could hear, then you checked your notes against his shorthand.

Today everyone has a tape recorder. So now, especially out on a presidential campaign, all the reporters gather around, listen to the tape, try to figure out what it was the candidate meant when he said what he said, and then they all go write the same story. Reporting in most places is a highly individualistic trade. Not so in Washington.

When I came to Washington Dwight Eisenhower was just starting the second year of his second term as president. Every now and then he held a press conference, but it wasn't like it is today. There were no television cameras, for one thing. For another, reporters were told by Jim Hagerty, the president's press secretary, that they could not quote the president directly, they had to paraphrase him. The reason for that, I think, was that Ike was nearly incoherent when he spoke. He wasn't when he didn't, however. When he did say something reporters wanted to use verbatim they compromised; they quoted him directly, they just didn't use quotation marks.

John F. Kennedy was the first president to hold regularly televised press conferences. Kennedy had a matinee star quality about him that made him a natural for television and he and his people took advantage of it. But even as late as 1964 television reporters were still not always treated as members of the regular press corps. That year Nelson Rockefeller, running for president, held separate press conferences, one for the writing press and one for the electronic reporters.

I went to Washington as a regional reporter, primarily covering news of interest to the eight Copley dailies in the Los Angeles area and sometimes helping Jeff Macomber, the reporter covering for the two Copley San Diego papers. There was a lot of truth to Bob Richards' belief that Washington affected the people back home more than city hall.

I covered the offices of half a dozen representatives and two senators, and wrote about the tuna fishing industry and the aircraft industry and the defense industry. I wrote about the navy and the air force and the Congress. I covered the 1960 political conventions and the Nixon and Kennedy campaigns. And I rewrote Helen Bentley.

Helen is a congresslady or congressperson or some such thing these days but back then she was the very good maritime reporter for the *Baltimore Sun*. I didn't have time to cover maritime matters so in lieu of that I read Helen faithfully.

And when she wrote something my papers would be interested in I rewrote her and put what I'd written on the wire, and thereby for a short time gained a reputation as a good maritime reporter. For those who wonder if using the material someone else dug up was ethical the answer is heck, yes. Everybody used to do it and, despite some recent phony fusses about the ethics of the practice, I hope they still do. News is where you find it, even if someone else found it first.

Political conventions are not the easiest things in the world to cover, principally because so much of little importance is going on at the same time. The reporter's job is to make the inconsequential seem less so and the important seem earthshaking. The only incident that sticks in my memory from the Republican convention of 1960 is Nelson Rockefeller's seconding speech for Nixon which he closed by shouting, "I now give you our next president, Richard E. Nixon." Nixon's middle name is Milhous.

The Democratic convention wasn't much more exciting. I remember mainly that the liberals, supported by Eleanor Roosevelt, made a run at nominating Adlai Stevenson again, as if two losses weren't enough.

When I asked Eleanor's oldest boy, James, a California congressman, who was backing John F. Kennedy, if his mother had changed his mind, he replied, "No, Lyn, she hasn't," thereby keeping his priorities straight.

I remember more about John F. Kennedy's campaign for president in 1960 than I do about his opponent's, Richard M. Nixon. Maybe it's because the Nixon campaign was smoother and better organized. Maybe it's because I spent only three weeks with Nixon while I spent five with Kennedy. Maybe it's because the atmospheres in the two campaigns were so different. There was a swagger to the Kennedy campaign that was missing from the Nixon campaign, a kind of enthusiastic amateurism that overcame misspelled names—Jerry ter Horst of the *Detroit News* was once identified on a roster of the traveling press as Chief Two Horse while Charlie Cleveland of the *Chicago Daily News* became Jolly Cleve—lost luggage, shortages of hotel rooms, and sundry other inconveniences.

There was one other major difference between the two campaigns: Pierre Salinger, the Kennedy press secretary, took care of the friendly press, and Herb Klein, the Nixon press secretary, took equally good care of the Nixon-hating press. Of course, these two groups were one and the same. I have always thought that Klein thought that treating the Nixon-haters nicely would neutralize them. I learned from that; it never does. Still, it was the worst of both worlds for a Republican reporter working for a chain of avowedly Republican papers. Klein wouldn't let me talk to the candidate because I was a friend; Salinger wouldn't let me talk to the candidate because I wasn't a friend.

When a lot of reporters are covering a story, sometimes there isn't room at a certain event or in a certain situation for everyone. So a pool is formed, consisting of a few reporters representing the rest of the media. The pool reporters, having covered a particular situation, put out a "pool report" which is made available to all the reporters who were left out. On a campaign, pool reporters are rotated so that every reporter viewed as a regular on the campaign has an opportunity to cover a pooled event, because being there obviously is better than getting the story secondhand.

On the Kennedy campaign I was never a pool reporter. Eventually I found out why. Don Wilson, an assistant to Salinger who handled the pool assignments, took my name whenever it became my turn and moved it to the bottom of the list. If that gambit could have worked for me when I was press secretary for Ronald Reagan I might have done the same thing. But it wouldn't have. Too many Democrats in the press; not enough Republicans.

There were three debates between Nixon and Kennedy in that campaign and I covered all three. But it was the first one that is remembered best because it gave Kennedy the opportunity to measure himself against the older, more experienced Nixon. The Kennedy boys—Jack, Bobby, Ted—shared at least one trait besides their obsessions with pretty women; each prepared thoroughly for any public appearance that pitted him against another politician.

Kennedy was totally prepared in that first debate, as was Nixon, but all of us watching in person, like most people who watched on TV, went away convinced that Kennedy had beaten Nixon rather soundly. It wasn't what they said, it was the way they said it. Kennedy seemed confident and sure of himself, not at all nervous. Nixon, as always, perspired profusely and was fidgety. It was a victory of style over substance, and an early and serious indication of how television could and does affect national and big state campaigns. Because, while Kennedy won the debate on TV, persons who heard it on the radio have told me they thought Nixon was the clear winner. On television body language speaks louder than words.

Kennedy started out slowly in that campaign, drawing small crowds, and at one time seemed in danger of losing his voice. But as the weeks rolled by his voice got stronger and his appeal, especially among young people, grew rapidly. Girls watching his motorcade pass by or standing in a crowd would jump up and down and scream, just as they had done in an earlier day for Frank Sinatra. I have always thought that the Kennedys learned from their singer friend and paid some of the first jumpers, hoping their antics would catch on. If they did, it worked.

On one of the last nights of the campaign I was standing in the back of a large Kennedy rally in New York. When Kennedy appeared the young woman standing next to me started jumping and screaming. I thought she was going to wet her pants. Tired and irritable, I snarled at her to shut up. She wasn't offended.

"I've been waiting here for three hours," she said. "I left my baby at home with my husband and they haven't had dinner."

"I hope he beats you when you get home," I muttered.

"He probably will," she replied, still not offended. "It'll be worth it."

Which maybe is why Kennedy was elected. I have never had a woman of any age tell me it was worth a beating to see Richard Nixon.

Four years later, in 1964, Barry Goldwater, with the help of F. Clifton White and his band of right-wing outsiders, stole the Republican party from such moderates as George Romney, Nelson Rockefeller, William Scranton, and Charles Percy. Goldwater, as we know, lost to Lyndon Johnson, but nevertheless wound up playing the role of a political John the Baptist to the man who was to follow, Ronald Reagan. To his discredit, Goldwater always seemed to resent being superseded by Reagan and refused to support him in either 1968 or 1976 and wasn't exactly his chief cheerleader in 1980.

This, although Reagan had been the most effective of all those who campaigned for Goldwater in 1964. Probably Reagan was too effective from Goldwater's point of view because Reagan, not Goldwater, emerged from that campaign as the conservative hero.

I don't know why any Republican wanted to run for president in 1964. Nobody was going to beat Johnson who was running on the coattails of the assassinated John F. Kennedy, and everyone knew it. Nixon, eager as he was to be president, was smart enough to wait four more years. But along with Goldwater, the moderate four—Scranton, Rockefeller, Romney, and Percy—all decided to make a run at the Republican nomination, as did Harold Stassen and, in a kind of half-assed way, Henry Cabot Lodge.

Romney fouled out early when he said publicly that he'd been brainwashed on a visit to South Vietnam. Percy never was a factor except in his own mind. He tried to mount a late campaign by train but no one paid much attention. And Scranton, the governor of Pennsylvania, proved to be too much of a Hamlet to be an effective candidate.

There was still another candidate, Harold Stassen, the one-time boy governor of Minnesota and not yet a national laughingstock. Carl DeBloom, then the Washington correspondent for the Columbus, Ohio, *Evening Dispatch*, and I were standing on a street in Manchester, New Hampshire, one cold winter evening in early 1964 when we spotted a couple of men handing out Stassen buttons to the occasional passersby.

What goes, we asked, and were told that Harold Stassen would come by shortly to make a speech. Sure enough, in a few minutes a sedan pulling a flatbed trailer drove up and stopped by the curb. A man jumped out and hooked up a microphone. Then Harold Stassen in person got out, climbed on the trailer, and made a rip-roaring speech promising to put stay-at-home mothers on social security just like everyone else. After the multitude of a dozen or so had dispersed, he told the attending press—both of us—his plan.

This was just the beginning, he said. He wouldn't win New Hampshire but he would gather momentum and wind up winning California in June. Then, he would go to the convention and claim the nomination. He made one slight miscalculation, however. He was never able to gather enough names on a petition to get on the California ballot.

The Goldwater-Johnson campaign was not nearly so much fun to cover as Nixon-Kennedy even though it was the first one in which the candidates flew around in jet aircraft. One reason probably was that from the beginning Goldwater never had a chance. Another, for me, was that Jim Copley personally assigned me to full-time coverage of Goldwater, which should not happen to anyone, but Jim wanted to be sure Goldwater got fair treatment and he worried that his other political reporters were anti-Goldwater.

For the most part, the traveling press in 1964 seemed to have little use for either candidate, although by a large margin they preferred Johnson. John Averill, then a reporter for the Associated Press, explained to me one day in a bar why he was going to vote for Johnson.

"Johnson's a crook but Goldwater is crazy," he said.

Another day I asked Clark Mollenhoff of the *Des Moines Register* and *Tribune* why he, a liberal, was supporting Goldwater. "Because Lyndon

Johnson's a crook," he growled, "and I hate crooks." He didn't say how he felt about crazy people.

No matter how hopeless their cause and how clear in the beginning their recognition of this fact, candidates and those around them usually end up thinking the miracle will occur and victory will be theirs. The Goldwater people were no exception.

At campaign's end they just knew that their Barry was going to win. After all, hadn't he drawn big crowds and, besides, as the Goldwater slogan said, "In your heart you know he's right." (Once the Democrats' dirty tricks artist, Dick Tuck, hired a helicopter to carry a sign over a Goldwater rally in Los Angeles that read, "In your guts you know he's nuts." In those days liberal reporters thought such "pranks" were funny. So did I.)

As the 1964 campaign wound down Goldwater headed for his home in the hills above Phoenix while the press contingent following him was lodged in the Camelback Inn in adjacent Scottsdale. On election night Goldwater's staff and members of the press gathered in a large room at the inn to await the results. The reporters to a man—or woman—knew Lyndon Johnson would win. But the Goldwater people were expecting the miracle. The first results came in from a remote and tiny New Hampshire precinct. Goldwater, as expected, won it handily. Denny Kitchell, his campaign manager, sidled up to me and muttered, "I told you we were going to win."

But, as they, or at least I, say, "In politics one precinct does not an election make."

As I look back, the eight years I spent as a reporter in Washington were the best years of my working life. Aside from the conventions and campaigns, I covered Kennedy's last trip abroad, the sinking of the nuclear submarine, *Thresher*, the Kennedy-Macmillan summit meeting in the Bahamas, and the Kennedy and Johnson inaugurations. I spent a day cruising the Atlantic on the nuclear attack submarine, *Skipjack*. I was in Berlin two weeks after the communists began building the wall. And I covered the Cuban missile crisis. For eight years I could watch firsthand and up close, and sometimes write about, the events that were making history. It was an exciting time.

On occasion it was also a frustrating time. Reporters in Washington who work for other than metropolitan papers, the wire services, or the networks have to work harder to get at high-level people. Even though I don't like it, it makes sense. Say, for instance, that I'm the secretary of defense. I have only so much time to talk to reporters on a one to one basis. Who am I going to talk to? The *New York Times* or the Copley newspapers? The answer is easy.

So what does the Copley reporter do? He works harder. He cultivates the people around the secretary or the president or the candidate. And he winds up with some pretty good stories that are all his own, mainly because the important reporters were too important to go looking for stories that the other important reporters also weren't bothering to cover.

Then comes the second frustration. You send your exclusive story out to your papers. Half of them don't use it. The other half bury it back by the classified ads. Then, one day or one week or one month later, the AP finds the same story and puts it on the wire. And, bingo! It's on page one in the papers you work for. Maybe it's even a banner headline. And you wonder why the hell they bothered to send you to Washington in the first place.

The problem with too many news editors out in the sticks is that they are wire service-oriented. It isn't news until the wires have carried it. And their story is always right, even when it isn't. On occasion the reporter and the wire service file the same story at the same time, but the facts are different. So whom does the news editor call and complain to? Not the wire service, but his own reporter, whom he doesn't quite trust.

Despite the news editors, being a Washington correspondent is still a great job. And once in a while it does happen that you get to interview the secretary or the candidate or even the president.

As a result of my press background I have, for the last twenty-five years, worked primarily in the press/communications area of politics. And even when not, I have found myself by choice dealing with reporters and others in the news media and, frankly, enjoying that part of politics the most. After twenty-five years away from the business I can still on occasion look back at it with nostalgia and wonder in my heart if I made the right decision by abandoning it. But in my head I know I did. As a politician and briefly, from time to time, a public servant, I've been able to have an impact here and there; I've been a participant in events and activities that have affected California and the nation.

Reporters, on the other hand, even though they can have an effect on government, basically are observers. As the *Washington Post*'s political writer, David Broder, once put it, "We are voyeurs."

Some are also prima donnas, experts in their own minds on all matters, self-important, above criticism, and members of an elite group that arrogates unto itself unique and broad-ranging privileges not available to the average citizen, for whom they pretend to write. No wonder I sometimes wish I were reporting again. Or at least writing the kind of column that would demonstrate my superior intellect, wide range of knowledge, political judgment, and common sense. Maybe, even, a few people would read me. Just like they do Evans and Novak, Germond and Witcover, Jack Anderson, Dave Broder, and sundry others.

Broder is a nice man and he writes a political column for the *Post* and sometimes hard news. He does both well enough that somewhere along the line he picked up a Pulitzer Prize.

In 1987, Dave wrote a book, *Behind the Front Page, A Candid Look at How the News Is Made*. Dave was gracious enough to send me a copy.

But as I read the book I found myself several times in disagreement with the author. One issue I want to take up since it involves me.

He quotes me at length and I would like to repeat that quote here. It stemmed from remarks I made at an American University forum after the 1984 presidential election. What I said was without bitterness or rancor—just a statement of fact from someone who had seen presidential campaigns from the reporter's side and the press secretary's side. I had been Ronald Reagan's press secretary in all or part of three presidential campaigns and had covered two others. As a reporter I had perhaps failed the other members of my craft by not delving deeply into the philosophy of why reporters write stories, or by not viewing myself as advancing or at least trying to advance the greater good through my stories.

I never gave these things a thought. And I never hid behind the phony complaint that if the subject of my reporting wouldn't talk to me he was interfering with the people's "right to know." The main reason I was trying to get a story was because it was my job and it was a job I really liked. And if I did it well I might even get a raise. Anything else I always looked on as self-serving and kind of phony pious.

I had the same sort of attitude as a press secretary and it was this attitude that Dave Broder found, if not offensive, at least indicative of my lack of understanding of what it is that makes this country great. What I said was this:

> The media would like us to run a campaign . . . that makes it possible for them to write stories and cover things. For example, the media will demand a press conference. They will demand that maybe you have a new speech every week . . . and they do not understand that they have a job to do, which is to cover a campaign, but the people in the campaign also have a job to do and that job is to win an election. . . . And winning an election does not mean catering to the press. Winning an election means doing the things and having your candidate do the things that he can do most effectively and that will influence the most votes.

Broder flat-out rejected the "Nofziger thesis," which, to my way of thinking, is kind of like rejecting the law of gravity. In his view, "The campaign is not the candidate's personal property. It is the public's hour of judgment."

That's beautiful writing; I wish I wrote that well. But I would like to point out that a campaign is not the news media's personal property either, although some reporters think it is.

In my view there is only one valid reason for running for office, and that is to win. If you wish to educate the public go write a newspaper column or be a schoolteacher. If you wish to protest the state of the world go picket the White House or buy an ad in the *Washington Post*, which no one will read.

But if you want to run for office, run to win. You owe that to your supporters, to your contributors, to your family, and to yourself, most of all to yourself. It matters a lot if you win or lose, but it matters almost as much how you play the game of politics.

Running to win means you cannot let the news media direct your campaign or set its direction or interfere with the direction you as the candidate and/or campaign manager have determined it must take. You are not trying to win the approval of reporters, you are trying to win the votes of a majority of those in the electorate who bother to vote.

You do this by adhering to your plan, not by knuckling under to the demands of the press.

When I was Candidate Ronald Reagan's press secretary I was often accused of thrusting my ample belly (the longer the campaign the ampler) both literally and figuratively between the candidate and a reporter, any reporter. I plead guilty. Most candidates have a compulsive urge to answer a question. It was my job, it is always someone's job in a campaign, to keep the candidate and the campaign on track. Otherwise the other guy wins.

Let's look at a hypothetical case. This week the candidate wants to emphasize national defense. At every stop he will talk about national defense. The schedule has been set up carefully. He visits a naval base, an air base, a shipyard, a missile base. He makes a speech to the American Legion and another to the Reserve Officers Association.

After a couple of days of this the press grows bored. And the questions start coming—about the candidate's health, or what he thinks of something his opposition has said, or about anything else that is irrelevant to the topic of the week.

Broder and other reporters would have the candidate answer those questions even though to do so would detract from the point the candidate has been trying all week to make, not to the reporters but to the voters. As for me, I am not going to let him answer their questions if I can help it. I'm going to stand between the candidate and the reporters and shout, "No questions," or "This ain't no press conference," or something similar. And they will write that Nofziger won't let the candidate answer questions. But the fact is, nobody except the reporters cares. The average reader or viewer recognizes a self-serving journalistic whine when he sees, hears, or reads it.

Frankly, the members of the press, or at least the Washington press and those related to it, largely along the Eastern seaboard and in Los Angeles, have gotten to be awfully self-righteous. They—the reporters, columnists, anchormen, and editors—have set themselves up to be much more than they are. And almost as much as, down deep, they think they are. A lot of them, but not all of them. Some still remember how it was and how they were before they became important.

What they are, believe it or not, is plain, ordinary citizens with the same rights and bound by the same laws as us other ordinary mortals. They do not have any special privileges, despite the attitudes of some gutless and/or fuzzy-minded public officials. They do not, for instance, have a special "right to know" even though some would like the rest of us to think they have.

Any member of the media who talks "right to know" is talking absolute crap. Nothing in the Constitution or in any amendment to it guarantees anyone the right to know. By implication it guarantees the right to find out and to disclose what you find out. But all citizens have this right; they merely do not have the wherewithall—a radio or TV station or newspaper or magazine—to get their facts and views disseminated.

Oh, it's true the media get some privileges that most of us don't have, like press passes issued by cops, the Congress, the White House, and sundry other government agencies. These allow them to cross police lines, harass congressmen and, on occasions when the press secretary permits it, talk to a president. The theory is, and on the surface it is valid, that these privileges allow them to pass on news to the masses, which is necessary in order to have a well-informed electorate that can then elect men and women of integrity and wisdom and vision to all the elective offices in the land. And if you don't believe that isn't, in the words of George Bush, a lot of doggy doo-doo, take a look at some of the fine folks who represent you in the Congress of these United States. Anyway, that's mainly what's behind the "right to know" pitch.

But despite their superior status, reporters have no more right to break the law than anyone else, although many seem to think that stealing information or accepting stolen information is all right for folks of their special rank. It isn't. Ethics is ethics and honesty is honesty and stealing is stealing, no matter what your job or profession. But don't try to tell that to some journalists.

Twenty years ago Daniel Ellsberg stole the "Pentagon Papers" and passed them on to the *New York Times*. There was general approval in the media. In contrast, in 1980 someone stole a briefing book belonging to Jimmy Carter and passed it on to the Reagan presidential campaign. A year or so later, when the theft became public, the media almost unanimously criticized the Reaganites. Who says you can't have it both ways?

It may surprise some Americans to learn that reporters don't have a right to press conferences, either. They have a right to demand them, just as they have a right to ask questions, but that's about as far as it goes. The decision to hold or not to hold a press conference is made by the person the press wishes to question. That person also makes the decision whether or not to answer a reporter's question.

I've watched reporters at press conferences insult and browbeat a person into answering questions he didn't want and didn't need to answer. And I've always felt sorry for the victim for not having the gumption to tell the interrogator to go fly a kite. Clark Mollenhoff was one of the great browbeaters of his time. I think it was because he instinctively didn't like public servants, although he eventually put in a short stint working not for the public but for Richard Nixon in the early years of his presidency. Mollenhoff was an ex-football lineman, big, with an arrogance to match. I would never have told him to go fly a kite.

I'm sure Broder and most of his cohorts disagree with me on my approach to press conferences, too. They say—I don't know what they really think—that presidents and other public figures have an obligation to hold press conferences so that they can be questioned, and their answers and their goofs (the in-word these days is "gaffes") and their appearances and their attitudes can all be printed or broadcast and interpreted, and from all of this the American people can, if they wish, but they probably don't, and won't, form their impressions of the person who holds the press conference.

But the average reporter, at least before he becomes a pundit and/or television celebrity, is really more interested in getting a story than he is in making sure the people are well informed. At least he ought to be. That's what he's getting paid for. Sometimes, to be sure, he also wants to embarrass the person holding the press conference or make him look bad. Incidently, most reporters I know will deny that last statement, which, of course, only lends it credibility.

The only practical time for a public figure to hold a press conference is when it serves his purpose. Media spokesmen, usually self-appointed, will say, "How terrible." But that is because they don't wish to believe the truth, which is that holding a press conference just to satisfy the press isn't very smart.

Now this doesn't mean your average public figure should never or seldom hold press conferences. In my opinion, Ronald Reagan as president didn't hold nearly enough press conferences. He often went for months without one. George Bush is doing much better. In saying this I purely have Reagan's interests in mind. I think any president or anyone else, with the exception of political candidates, who is covered regularly by a gaggle of reporters should hold frequent press conferences.

These do several things for a public figure. They convince the media that he's not afraid of them and that he may even, perish the thought, have their best interests at heart. They mean any person holding frequent press conferences doesn't have to remember so much or have to be briefed so thoroughly before each press conference. They mean the media have fewer topics about which to ask which again means the public figure has less to be concerned about. They mean that the public figure can more frequently make his points with the media and thus with the voting public. And again, the only reason a public figure should hold a press conference is to make his points.

Finally, if the public figure handles the press well, handles questions well, appears knowledgeable, and keeps his cool the media will come to respect him—or her—and that respect will show up in the ways they write or air their stories.

When Ronald Reagan was inaugurated governor of California in 1967, we, primarily me, determined that he should hold a press conference for the large Sacramento press contingent once a week. As a result, he was always sharp, usually knowledgeable, and generally effective. It also meant that he dealt better with individual interviews and that on the occasional times he went on a national interview show he did very well.

I recall the late Bill Lawrence, a *New York Times* political reporter who later reported for ABC, saying admiringly after one interview show with Reagan, "We never laid a glove on him."

I'm confident that would not have been the story if he had been holding press conferences only once every two or three months the way he did as president. Unfortunately, when Reagan entered the White House many of those around him, including his chief of staff, James Baker, and his longtime aide, Michael Deaver, seemingly had no confidence in his ability to handle the press. For that reason they scheduled as few press conferences as they thought they could get away with. As a result Reagan never handled the Washington press corps as well as he had the one in Sacramento.

Of course, every president or, in Reagan's case, every president's staff, must decide how frequently he should meet with the press. George Bush, who I thought was pretty inept at handling the media when he was vice president, has come on as president to deal with them superbly well. One reason for this, I'm certain, is that he meets with them frequently, sometimes oftener than once a week. Another reason is that he puts up with no nonsense, insisting that they follow his rules of press conference conduct.

Campaigns are a different matter, however. As I said earlier, a press conference held just to be holding a press conference can change the tenor of a campaign and indeed put the candidate on the defensive, sometimes for lengthy periods. It can cost him votes, or an election, or a career.

A press conference, held in a fit of pique and frustration, almost cost Richard Nixon his political career. It was a press conference his press secretary, Herb Klein, didn't schedule, didn't want, and didn't expect. It occurred in 1962, the morning after Nixon lost the race for governor of California to Edmund G. (Pat) Brown.

Nixon appeared unexpectedly at a press briefing Klein was holding and among other things declared that "You won't have Dick Nixon to kick around anymore." His enemies never forgot it.

The most stupid press conference I know of was called by William Scott, a Republican senator from Virgina. Irate after the capital press corps voted him the dumbest man in Congress, Scott called a press conference to reject the honor. Scott was a well-meaning man but he lacked the political perspicacity one needs to survive and advance in Washington. In 1976 he generously offered himself as Reagan's vice presidential running mate "if you can't find anyone else." It turned out that things in the Reagan camp were not that desperate.

The news media has grown increasingly more arrogant since Watergate. The success of the *Washington Post*'s Carl Bernstein and Bob Woodward encouraged every young reporter not only to want to be an investigative reporter but also to want to bring down an important public figure. What began as constant, detailed investigations into the public lives of public figures has led to the investigation of private lives, including sexual peccadillos and alcoholic capacity, of public figures.

Former Democratic Sen. Gary Hart of Colorado was one of the

first prominent politicians to feel the bite of the new press morality. When asked about rumors of his extramarital activities he challenged the press to follow him around. The *Miami Herald* took the dare, found Hart socializing with a young thing, printed what it found, and ran Hart right out of the race for the 1988 Democratic presidential nomination.

One wonders what would have happened if Gary Hart's name had been Jack Kennedy. My guess is, probably nothing. Kennedy cultivated the press and in turn was liked by it. Many members became his social friends. Hart didn't have many friends in the media. Whatever his faults Kennedy was looked upon as a man of integrity; to many, including me, there is a certain phoniness about Gary Hart.

But just as Watergate brought about an era of investigative reporting, so Hart may well be responsible for a new era of peephole reporting by the so-called responsible press, a unique legacy, indeed, but probably better than any he might have left as president.

The great, gray *New York Times* was among the first members of the media to rise to the new challenge to poke publicly into politicians' private lives. In 1987 it sent a letter to all those it deemed possible candidates for president asking, along with the usual information such as income tax returns, for the right to pry as far into their personal lives as its reporters wished. The *Times* would then in its wisdom decide what and what not to print.

The *Times* asked each candidate to waive his right to privacy to any FBI or other government files. It wanted the same total access to medical files. It also wanted the names of each candidate's closest friends since high school as well as names of political advisers and major fund-raisers.

At the time I was serving as an unpaid political adviser to the incipient and ultimately abandoned presidential campaign of Paul Laxalt, a former Republican senator from Nevada. Naturally I urged him to ignore the letter. Laxalt's political director and longtime associate, Ed Allison, and I worked out a statement for the senator that said in part that the First Amendment does not give newspapers a hunting license and that he would not comply with the request.

Some of the other candidates did much the same while others settled for sending the information ordinarily supplied. Only two or three knuckled under completely. I would not want any of them for president; they are gutless wonders.

Even the *Times* had second thoughts. Executive Editor Max Frankel, in an internal memo and in a masterpiece of understatement, said as how the paper had gone "a bit too far."

He added that "Their lives, their personalities, their finances, their families, friends and values are all fair game for fair reporting." And, of course, he was right. But the key phrase in his memo was "fair reporting." Reporting can be, and sometimes is, less than fair or objective. In fact, these days, many reporters as well as some editors scoff at objectivity. They prefer "interpretive reporting," another term for subjectivity. At least one news magazine, *Time*, appears to have abandoned any effort to be objective.

Throughout the profession reporters and editors have come to believe that facts are not enough, that the average reader cannot judge accurately what is behind a story unless the reporter interprets the facts for him. Intellectual arrogance today is the rule, not the exception among reporters, at least in the nation's capital, and among their editors.

In his book Broder notes that high officials "can bend the truth out of shape." He says Joe McCarthy, the senator, not the baseball manager, taught this to the press. That is an incredible statement, when you consider that high officials have been bending the truth out of shape for at least as long as there have been high officials. And while reporters haven't been around that long their own record is not exactly lily white.

To some reporters, as well as to some politicians, the truth is what they want it to be. How many times, for instance, have reporters or columnists written that the first time I left Reagan's employ was because I had been fired at the demand of Nancy Reagan. The fact that Nancy denies it, that I deny it, that Reagan denies it makes no difference. It's a lot more titillating to have me be Nancy's victim than just to have quit.

I recall an argument with a political reporter, Lou Cannon of the *Washington Post*, during the 1976 Reagan campaign over Reagan's failure to hold a press conference. I explained that it didn't suit our purposes and gave him the line that just one could change the direction and tenor of the campaign. Cannon, who had to know better, wrote that we were afraid to let Reagan face the press. I always figured that since he couldn't have his way he settled for sticking it to us. That's hardly objective reporting.

In the early days of the first Reagan presidential administration some reporters covering Nancy were less than fair. They wrote nasty and dishonest stories about how she was redoing the White House living quarters. They failed to mention the expensive redecorating job done twenty years earlier by Jackie Kennedy. They minimized the fact that the work was financed by private contributions and that the "new" furnishings were not new at all but were rescued from General Services Administration warehouses where they had been stored after having been given to the government by generous and public-spirited citizens who were seeking tax write-offs.

Shortly before I left the White House in early 1982 the Reagans thoughtfully invited Bonnie and me and Paul and Carol Laxalt, he was then the junior senator from Nevada, to a private dinner in the White House. After dinner Nancy showed us through the living quarters. She explained that among other things some of the plumbing had had to be replaced because it was literally rusting out. Damp in some of the walls called for replastering. The floors hadn't been refinished since President Truman had rebuilt the White House in 1950.

After the tour I asked Nancy if the redecorating was complete.

"No," she replied ruefully.

"Are you going to finish it?" I asked.

"I don't dare," she said sadly. "There's just been too much fuss."

Such is the power of the press, a press that on that occasion conveniently forgot that the White House belongs to all the people and should be a showplace of which all the people can be proud.

Nancy also was criticized by the press for buying a new set of china for state dinners because there wasn't enough left of the old set to go around. Once again most stories neglected the obvious. One, that the china was donated by a tax-free foundation, thus costing neither the government nor the taxpayers a cent. Two, that the china was manufactured in the United States and thus the purchase was a boost to American industry. And, three, that the greatest nation in the world ought to be able to entertain foreign heads of state appropriately.

These are just a few examples of the press bending or ignoring the truth. There are more, to the shame of its members. The arrogance and self-righteousness found in many members of the media today stand up under even semiclose scrutiny no better than the record of the average politician.

One final word on how newspapers from time to time insert their editorial policy in their news columns. In 1966 when Reagan was running for governor of California, the *Sacramento Bee*, one of the most unabashedly Democratic newspapers of the nation, instructed its political writer that whenever he began a story with Reagan's name he was to add a qualifying phrase so that the lead would read: "Ronald Reagan, the Goldwaterite candidate for governor. . . ." Whoever handed down that order underestimated Goldwater's popularity in California as well as the people's ability to detect bias.

It boils down to this: Most newspapers are relatively honest and accurate; and, for the most part, reporters also try to be honest and objective. But almost all of them are a little more holier-than-thou than they ought to be. They love to air other folks' dirty linen and point out other people's mistakes and shortcomings and transgressions; they do their collective best, which is very good, to hide or deny their own.

2

Farewell Copley,
Hello Ronnie

THE FIRST LESSON I learned about politics is, if you don't want to get involved stay away from the candidate's brother. I didn't, and it cost me. It cost me a good, if not outstanding, reporting career, most of the rest of my hair, and hundreds of dollars for the purchase of antacids. The only reason it didn't cost me my wife, like it has so many others, is because she is more patient, more stubborn, and more forgiving, especially more forgiving, than many political wives.

Neil Reagan is Ronald Reagan's older and only brother, and when I met him in 1964 brother Ron was not yet a candidate for anything. All he was was an alternate delegate in the California delegation to the Republican National Convention, which in 1964 was held in San Francisco. I covered that convention but never ran into him and never thought to look for him. In those days he had yet to excite the members

27

of the conservative movement with THE speech on television on behalf of Barry Goldwater.

He was only a conservative actor who was having a tough time getting roles in the liberal Hollywood film industry. But he was on television, hosting and occasionally playing a lead role in the Western anthology series, "Death Valley Days." The series was sponsored by U.S. Borax whose advertising agency was McCann Erickson for whom Neil Reagan was the West Coast vice president.

Reagan's denigrators, of whom there are a few for almost any topic on which you might wish to denigrate him, love to sneer at his acting ability and career, which makes him madder than sneering at his politicking. But an objective look will find that the man was a professional in the field of acting, just as he became one in politics. He's not the only good actor who never won an Oscar.

Up to 1965 Reagan had always said publicly and probably privately that he was not interested in seeking public office. And it's likely that he wasn't—at least consciously—although, even before the famed speech for Goldwater, he was being eyed by Republican political pros as a possible future candidate.

In very early 1962 a delegation of conservative California Republicans that included Rep. H. Allen Smith of Glendale visited Reagan and urged him to run for governor that year against the Democrat incumbent, Gerald (Pat) Brown. Reagan, who grew up as a New Deal Democrat and had only recently become a Republican, turned them down. Probably just as well because shortly thereafter the job was wanted by Richard Nixon as a springboard to a second run at the presidency. Nixon eventually won the Republican primary, but lost to Pat Brown in the general election.

By not running that year Reagan lucked out. Not only did he not get bloodied in what almost certainly would have been a primary race against Nixon, but he also came up to 1964 as pure politically as the driven snow and with that one great speech behind him. Without question that speech propelled him into politics as a gubernatorial candidate which led eventually to the presidency.

But a lot happened between 1962, when he refused the invitation to run, and mid-1965, when he finally agreed to give it a try. Two of the things were that I met Neil Reagan and Ronald Reagan met me. It's hard to say today which was the bigger disaster. I suppose it depends on your point of view.

When Neil Reagan and I first met, he was Goldwater's television adviser. In those days, unless you had a black, Nixonesque beard, Neil's assignment meant little more than occasionally powdering the candidate's glistening brow. I was the national politics writer for the Copley Newspapers owned by James S. Copley, an unabashed Republican who, unlike so many of today's owners and publishers, never relinquished editorial control of his papers.

Jim Copley's flagship paper in 1964 was the *San Diego Union*, and the *Union*'s editor was Herbert G. Klein. Klein had been Nixon's press secretary in the 1960 presidential campaign and had worked for him and with him since Nixon's first run for the Congress in 1946. He was a member of the Nixon inner circle. He was also a dichotomy in the business of politics, a Nixon Republican who was liked and respected by the Washington political press. Indeed, he still is.

Almost too nice a man to be in politics, Klein was ignored when the boys were plotting the Watergate break-in and the ensuing cover-up. He was the White House director of communications at a time when other top Nixon staffers had little use and much contempt for Klein's kind of man—decent, honest, ethical, and honorable. I was one of those who thought he ought to be meaner, tougher, less willing to play by the rules. I was wrong.

There are some people, including me in retrospect, who think if he had been kept on the inside and listened to, all that nonsense would not have happened. The voice of reason—his voice—would have prevailed. Which brings up another tenet of politics. It's all right to have the hard chargers and risk takers around—you need them—but don't ignore the voices of experience, the men who remember that for every upside there's a downside. It's easy to be overly cautious in politics, but it's dangerous to be overly bold.

In any event, it is now 1964 and Ronald Reagan becomes uniquely involved in politics and takes his first unknowing step toward the presidency. And I am covering the Johnson-Goldwater presidential campaign.

It was on the Goldwater campaign plane—one of American Airline's first 727s—that I met J. Neil (Moon) Reagan, a delightful man with a whiskey voice and a sense of humor. We became good friends and I allowed him as often as possible to buy my lunch or dinner. We huddled together the way minorities usually do and, believe me, we were members of a distinct minority—Republicans sitting in the press end of the Goldwater campaign plane.

Besides myself I knew only one reporter who was supporting Goldwater, although it turned out later that there were at least two. The one I knew about was Clark Mollenhoff, a big, hulking man, a fine investigative reporter, and winner of a Pulitzer Prize. He was a liberal but, more important, he was a man who believed that elected officials and public servants had a duty to be honest and principled. He thought Lyndon Johnson was neither, and worked so actively on behalf of Goldwater that he might as well have been working for his campaign instead of covering it.

Years later, Clark and I worked in the Nixon White House, but before long he left, pretty thoroughly disillusioned. If you work in any president's White House it is likely that you will have to make excuses for what goes on there and Clark was not very good at making excuses for the kinds of things and deeds he had spent years as a reporter uncovering and criticizing.

The other reporter on the campaign I learned later voted for Goldwater was Sam Donaldson who went on to stardom as a White House reporter for ABC-TV. He confessed as much to me at a party at Victor Gold's house on the New Year's Eve that ushered in 1965. Sam was young in those days and didn't know any better. Gold had been Goldwater's assistant press secretary and later was Spiro Agnew's press secretary and still later wrote speeches for George Bush, articles for *Washingtonian* magazine, and off-beat books.

One of the good things about political campaigns is that you always make a batch of new friends. One of the bad things is that after the campaign is over everyone disappears into the hazy yon ("How misty grows the hazy yon"—Walt Kelly) and you never see most of them again and if you do you can't remember their names. And if you do and they do, you wind up wishing you hadn't, because the guy you knew in the confines of the campaign plane, the guy you drank with, complained with, and shared notes with is not always the same guy you run into later on at the bar of the National Press Club.

But Neil Reagan was different. We became and remained good friends even though it is he, along with one Stuart Spencer, whom I blame for dragging me into politics.

I think my troubles began on the Goldwater campaign plane in the fall of 1964.

"We're going to run Ronnie against Tommy Kuchel no matter what Kuchel runs for," Neil told me one day.

Memory is a selective thing. Sometimes it's difficult to remember what someone told you yesterday, especially when you get older. But certain things seem to stick all through your lifetime. That statement by Neil Reagan has stayed with me from the day he made it, as we sat conversing on a flight between nowheres. Brother Ron's name had come up naturally. He was the famous brother.

Tom Kuchel was California's senior senator and the Republican Whip, which made him the number two Republican in the Senate. He was a nice man, earnest, sincere, and well liked in the Senate.

But by 1968 Kuchel was in trouble in California. His problem was that he was an Earl Warren Republican in a state where the Republican party majority had moved far to the right of Warren. The Reagan brothers were part of that rightward movement. Ron, in fact, was already on its cutting edge.

The dream of the state party's right wing was to beat Kuchel in a primary whether he ran for reelection in 1968 or for governor in 1966. Ultimately, Kuchel decided not to run for governor, so the right wing didn't get to beat him until 1968, which it did in the primary. But it was a man named Max Rafferty, not Ron Reagan, who did it, because Reagan had already been elected governor and was not interested in being a senator.

The conversation with Neil Reagan made one thing clear—brother Ron was coming around to the idea of seeking office himself. He was no longer satisfied with just campaigning for others.

In early June of 1965 when I first met brother Ron he was claiming he was still not sure he would run, and even in August when I met him for the second time there was no definite decision. But I didn't believe him and wrote a story saying he would probably run. Public disclosure that he would run came in the late fall, and he announced in a prefilmed half-hour broadcast right after the first of the year. In the meantime he had spent much of the summer and early fall traveling up and down the state by car, testing the political waters to see if Republicans would welcome him as a viable candidate.

This precampaign campaigning was done under the watchful eyes of Stuart Spencer and William Roberts who ran a political public relations firm in Los Angeles and, with a man named Fred Hafner, another in San Francisco. Spencer-Roberts had been involved in Kuchel's 1962 campaign and had run Nelson Rockefeller's California campaign for the 1966 Republican presidential nomination. Rockefeller lost to Goldwater but the fault lay with him, not with Stu Spencer and Bill Roberts. Indeed, Goldwater was so impressed with the way Spencer-Roberts ran the campaign against him that it was he who recommended to Reagan's wealthy supporters that they be hired to manage any Reagan campaign that might materialize.

Reagan campaigned by car in those days because he wouldn't fly. He had flown before the war, but afterward he decided the odds were not good. He only began flying again when he was finally persuaded that he could not successfully campaign up and down the eight-hundred-mile length of California without flying.

But not until the Reagan children were grown would he and his wife, Nancy, fly together. They were fearful of leaving their two children, young Ron and Patti, parentless, which probably wouldn't have bothered Patti at all. I suggested once that the Reagans could solve their problem by all of them flying together, on the theory that the family that flies together dies together. They were not amused.

Though Reagan did not announce his candidacy until early in 1966 he had made his decision to run by late 1965 and the pressure began building on Spencer-Roberts to put together a campaign organization. Among their needs was a press secretary. And, though he denies it to this day, I have no doubt that it was Neil Reagan who first recommended me for the job. Which is why I blame him for everything that has happened since. Damn good thing for Neil that I never went to jail.

I joined the Reagan gubernatorial campaign reluctantly. The job I had was a good one. In fact, aside from the salary, which was on the low side, Copley not being the biggest spender in Washington, I thought it was the best reporting job in the business.

Therefore, I had no trouble turning Spencer down when he first approached me about joining the Reagan campaign. I had no trouble the second time, either, even though the proposed salary about doubled what I was making.

Finally, desperate, Spencer turned to Reagan's rich supporters for help and two of them, Holmes Tuttle and Henry Salvatori, responded. Tuttle was probably the best Republican fund-raiser in the history of the California party. Salvatori, a wealthy oil man, was a big giver to the party and its candidates. They, along with Bill Roberts, went to La Jolla and met with Jim Copley. As a result, Jim had Captain Anderson contact me and ask if I would take a leave of absence and become Reagan's press secretary. Obviously, he didn't think much of Reagan's chances of winning the primary election in early June because he suggested that I return to my job immediately after the primary. I never did, sometimes to a slight twinge of regret.

I joined the Reagan campaign in late February of 1966. Reagan and Spencer and Roberts and others of the campaign entourage were attending the Republican state convention being held at the ancient Hotel del Coronado on Coronado Island in San Diego Bay. The Reagans had spent their honeymoon there fourteen years earlier, but they weren't enjoying it much this time. Reagan had the flu.

By this time Reagan and I were buddies. We'd met three times.

I first met Reagan at a fancy farm several miles outside of Columbus, Ohio, on June 8, 1965. I remember the day because it was my forty-first birthday. By the time Reagan arrived I was not sober. The event at the farm was a cocktail reception in Reagan's honor and he was late, very late. In fact, most of the invitees had gone by the time Reagan showed up. And this noninvitee would have been better off if he, too, had left.

Reagan and I were in Ohio for basically the same reason. The next night there was to be a series of dinners around the state honoring Ray Bliss, the Republican national chairman and former Ohio Republican chairman. Reagan was to speak in Cincinnati. I was to cover the main dinner in Cleveland where former president Eisenhower was the speaker.

When Reagan arrived at the farm there were only a few of us still partying so I had no trouble introducing myself to him as a friend of his brother. We talked briefly but it was clear that he was not greatly enamored of inebriated reporters, so we soon parted. I saw him later that evening at the auditorium after he had spoken and again we exchanged pleasantries. Unfortunately, when he spoke I was still not sober and what notes I took were indecipherable the next day. I never did file a story, but it didn't matter much; it was THE speech.

Two months later I interviewed Reagan over lunch at the Hollywood Brown Derby and from that interview filed the story predicting that he would run for governor.

I had been called to California for a meeting with Jim Copley, Captain Anderson, and others at the La Jolla headquarters. Knowing I would be in the area I called Neil Reagan and asked if he could set up a meeting with his brother, which he did. We were to meet at noon on a day in August 1965. Neil would buy. He and I arrived about on time. Brother Ron strolled in fifteen minutes later, which was prompt for him.

I stood to greet him and as Neil introduced us I said, "You may not remember, but we've met before."

"Yes, I do," he replied, looking down his big nose at me. I quietly sat down and quickly changed the subject.

It was a pleasant lunch, with Reagan denying that he had decided to run for anything. He said he was still exploring the possibility. I didn't believe him, however, and of course I was right, even though it was four months before he announced. Over the years, despite the urgings of staff and friends, Reagan always waited until the last possible moment to announce his candidacies, even when there was little doubt in anyone's mind, including his own, about his ultimate decision. He had an instinctive feeling about what was right politically for him and it was almost impossible to budge him once he had made up his mind. So he announced pretty much on his timetable, not the campaign management's, not even an astrologer's.

The third time I met Reagan was at his home in Pacific Palisades. I had already signed on to his campaign, but was not coming aboard officially until the end of February 1966. But I agreed to attend a strategy meeting early in the month at the Reagan home. I was greeted at the door by a tiny, very attractive woman who turned out to be Nancy Reagan. She welcomed me graciously and ushered me into the Reagan living room.

There were seven people at the Reagan house that night. Ron and

Nancy Reagan, Bill Roberts, Bob Mardian, Tom Reed, Henry Salvatori, and I.

Mardian, a lawyer and savings and loan president from Pasadena, had in 1964 been one of Barry Goldwater's Arizona Mafia. He had been selected to be Reagan's state chairman. Mardian was an experienced politician but he made one large mistake that eventually forced him out of the campaign. He thought that, as chairman, he should be involved in the decision-making process, a logical assumption. But, in fact, the decision-makers were Spencer and Roberts and Holmes Tuttle and, to a lesser extent, Henry Salvatori. By the first of April Mardian was only a figurehead and he resigned as chairman well before the June primary.

Tom Reed, a wealthy young businessman from San Rafael, had had a part in building the first hydrogen bomb. After Reagan was elected governor he became California's Republican national committeeman. He was/is one of the smartest, ablest, toughest men I have met in or out of politics. He was serving as Reagan's Northern California chairman.

A young lawyer named Phil Battaglia eventually was named southern California chairman and, after the primary, state chairman. After Reagan was elected he served for seven months as his executive secretary or chief of staff.

In area California is the third largest state, behind Alaska and Texas. Because of its size, people running statewide campaigns traditionally break it into northern and southern regions with a chairman in each. Six years later, in 1972, when I was running the Nixon reelect campaign in California I went a step further and broke it into four regions: the San Francisco Bay area, the San Joaquin/Sacramento Valley and the mountain counties, Los Angeles County, and the southern counties aside from Los Angeles. That was a mistake—you've just added a layer of campaign bureaucracy and increased expenses and the chances of dissension.

One thing you quickly learn in politics is that, while the United States is a democracy and must be, campaigns cannot be. Somebody has to be in charge and the fewer who think they're at least somewhat in charge the better off the campaign is. And in all honesty, campaign chairmen and cochairmen and regional chairmen and all the other chairmen you appoint in big campaigns are not in charge. They are supposed to do what they are told. It is the campaign manager who is in charge and even he is subject to the unreasonableness and ignorance of at least three people: the candidate, the candidate's wife, and, if he's good, the person who raises the money—the finance chairman.

The candidate, by rights, should have the last word. He is the person with his neck on the line, the person with the most to lose. But a candidate who interferes too much in his campaign is like a lawyer who represents himself—he may well have a fool for a client.

Reagan was the best candidate I have ever known because he instinctively knew what a candidate's role should be, just as later he instinctively knew the proper role of a president. He interfered only when these same instincts told him someone was making a wrong decision. And on those occasions he was almost always right. There are those who say he usually didn't interfere because of his years of taking direction as a film actor. But I think it went beyond that, because if he felt he had to he did interfere. Whenever, which was rarely, Reagan refused to do something or insisted on doing something he always made one point: "I know what's good for me." And generally he did.

The candidate's wife has a lot at stake, too. There's nothing so embarrassing personally and sometimes financially as being married to a loser. So most of them are there, peering over the campaign manager's shoulder, offering brilliant suggestions, demanding changes, insisting that someone be hired or fired, second guessing.

But in fairness, most of them also work hard, campaigning with their husbands or separately, putting up with press interviews, which they secretly love, going to teas, standing in for their husbands, and just being there. When a woman is the candidate, husbands generally do the same, only not so well. The "little woman" as a rule is a lot more effective with the voters than the prince consort.

The third person the campaign manager answers to can be the most difficult of all. The finance chairman is truly indispensable if he's any good.

"Money," Jesse Unruh, California's renowned politician, once intoned for the ages, "is the mother's milk of politics."

Every finance chairman knows or at least suspects that this is so and each is determined to see that not one cent is wasted. And that's understandable. Money-raising is hard and grubby, even if you are working for the best of candidates. It's hard to convince yourself that you're not begging. It's hard to convince others that they're being offered an opportunity to participate meaningfully in the political process. And it's hard to have your best friends turn you down, or worse, give you twenty-five bucks when you've asked for twenty-five hundred. Finally, you learn quickly that he who gives money in any significant amount sooner or later will want something in return—money for his pet project, the right to meet and advise the candidate or the campaign manager, help in getting a job or an appointment after the election has been won.

But in making sure that money isn't wasted finance chairmen, who usually know nothing about running political campaigns, too often decide they must have a major say in where and how the money is spent. Therefore they and the campaign manager are often at loggerheads. Who finally wins depends on several things, such as whose side the candidate takes, or the candidate's wife, or how serious the finance chairman is when he threatens one more time to quit.

A troika of wealthy men had decided that Ronald Reagan, with the proper backing and the proper management, could be elected governor. They were Tuttle, Salvatori, and A.C. (Cy) Rubel, who had retired in 1965 as president and CEO of the Union Oil Co. of California. Rubel died that same year, leaving Reagan in the hands of Salvatori and Tuttle. A little later others entered the circle of rich supporters and advisers, including Jacquelin Hume of San Francisco, Reagan's one-time agent Taft Schreiber, and Ed Mills, a business associate of Tuttle. But Tuttle and Salvatori were dominant.

Justin Dart, who headed Dart Industries, despite what has been written by persons who don't know, never became part of Reagan's so-called kitchen cabinet until after the first victory had been won. Leonard Firestone was another latecomer to the group but he left in a huff when Reagan decided to challenge Gerald Ford for the Republican presidential nomination in 1976. He had never been what one might call a tireless worker on Reagan's behalf, anyway.

As a team Tuttle and Salvatori never hesitated to use their wealth and fund-raising capabilities to get their way in the gubernatorial campaign, but in all fairness they did not interfere as much as they could have. Once, however, early in that first gubernatorial campaign Salvatori went so far as to threaten to pull out and recruit former Gov. Goodwin Knight to enter the primary against Reagan and his two serious primary opponents, former San Francisco Mayor George Christopher and businessman William Penn Patrick.

Salvatori was not happy with the way the campaign was being run, and he had concluded, besides, that Reagan was not smart enough or stable enough to be governor—this latter after Reagan lost his cool one Saturday afternoon in early March 1966 at a convention of black California Republicans.

The blacks, meeting at the Miramar Hotel in Santa Monica, asked Reagan, Christopher, and Patrick, to address them and take questions from the audience. All three were on the podium at the same time.

Reagan was not up to snuff that day. He was tired, having been on the road for three days and still recuperating from the flu bug. In fact, that flu and its aftereffects bothered and debilitated him during the entire campaign, leading many reporters to conclude that he was either lazy or shy on stamina. It wasn't until the presidential campaigns of 1976 and 1980 that they came to understand what a healthy horse Reagan really was.

Among the three candidates Reagan was the recognized conservative. During the session both Christopher and Patrick needled Reagan constantly, implying that he was a bigot and a racist. Finally, Reagan could take no more.

"Sons of bitches," he muttered angrily, but loudly enough to be heard in the audience. Then he crumpled a piece of paper he was holding, flipped it into the audience, and stalked off the stage, muttering oaths under his breath. I had been sitting in the audience and I caught up with him as he strode down the aisle. We walked out of the auditorium and into the parking lot where, along with one of the campaign researchers, Ken Holden, we stopped to take stock.

Reagan's car, driven by a former Los Angeles policeman named Bill Friedman, was waiting, and we decided that Reagan should go to his home in nearby Pacific Palisades while I stayed behind and tried to figure out our next move. That day I could have used Spencer or Roberts, but neither one was around. As Reagan drove off, a prominent black Republican named Jim Flournoy came out of the auditorium.

"Where is the candidate?" he asked.

"He's gone home," I said.

"I think it would be a mistake for him not to come back. People here think he walked out on them," he remarked.

I explained that Reagan was not angry at the blacks but at Christopher and Patrick for their sly innuendoes that he was a racist. Flournoy understood but he iterated that Reagan ought to return.

I drove to Reagan's house where I found him and Nancy ruefully discussing the episode.

"We've got to go back," I said. "They're having a cocktail party and they're expecting you and if you don't show they'll think either that you don't like blacks or that you're afraid to face them."

Reagan didn't argue, nor did Nancy. They saw immediately that he had to return. So back he and I went. The greeting he received was friendly and for the most part understanding. Any ruffled feathers were smoothed. Neither Christopher nor Patrick showed, and their absence also helped.

That might have been the end of it except that the *Los Angeles Times* had a reporter at the afternoon session named Paul Beck. I later hired him as my assistant in the governor's office, but at this time he was writing politics for the *Times* and spending a lot of time covering Reagan. Beck wrote a factual but rather lengthy and lurid story about Reagan's walkout and, probably out of ignorance, did not mention that he had returned for the cocktail party. It was Beck's story that set Salvatori on his ear.

A cartoon by the *Times'* Pulitzer Prize-winning cartoonist, Paul Conrad, didn't help either. Conrad is one of the earliest and most dedicated Reagan haters. They have only one thing in common, they are both anti-abortion, but in 1966 Right to Life vs. Choice was not yet a major political issue and Reagan, like most people, had not yet formed any strong views on the issue.

Conrad's cartoon was devastatingly funny. Reagan had recently published an autobiography called, *Where's the Rest of Me?* The title was taken from a line of his in *King's Row*, his favorite of his fifty movies. In one scene he was lying in bed after awakening from being operated on by the film's villainous doctor who had just amputated both his legs. He looked down and seeing that both limbs were missing, cried out in anguish, "Where's the rest of me?"

Conrad, correctly implying that Reagan had lost his head when he walked out of the black meeting, had drawn a caricature of a headless Reagan holding his head under his right arm and asking plaintively, "Where's the rest of me?"

Reagan had not been in politics very long and his skin, which never did develop any callouses, was still very thin. When he and Nancy saw the cartoon they blew their respective tops. By the time I arrived at their home they were fuming. Reagan was threatening to call Buffie (Mrs. Norman) Chandler who was the queen bee of the Chandler/Times-Mirror dynasty, and demand that Conrad be fired.

I explained that it would do no good: she wouldn't do anything anyway and Conrad would be pleased to know that his arrow had hit the bullseye.

"What you ought to do," I suggested, "is write or call Conrad and ask him to autograph the original and send it to you."

We compromised. He never called Mrs. Chandler, but neither did he ever contact Conrad, which I still think he should have done.

It took more than a year but Reagan finally got even, at least temporarily, with Conrad. I say temporarily because you never really get even with the man who wields the pen in the public print, either as an artist or a writer. He always has the last word, or picture, which is why it is best to shrug off the cartoon or column or comment that sticks it to you. Reagan learned that sooner than most, but underneath, the ridicule, the belittling, and the self-righteous contempt of those who will never get as far as he still get to him.

Reagan got even in a way that must have left Conrad angrier at the *Times* management than at Reagan. In fact I've wondered why Conrad didn't quit in disgust.

What happened was this. During the early days of the Reagan administration Conrad and many other editorial cartoonists were taking regular potshots at Reagan, but Conrad's were the meanest, most pointed, and least humorous and Reagan was constantly upset by them. Then one day Carl Greenberg, the senior *Times* political reporter, asked for an interview. He was a good reporter, an honest reporter, and a genuinely decent man. When I cleared the interview with Reagan I suggested that he take the first part of it to bitch like hell about Conrad's "unfair" cartoons.

When Greenberg arrived, Reagan lit into him nonstop for about ten minutes. Greenberg was stunned. He tried vainly to defend Conrad but Reagan was loaded for bear and finally he just sat and listened.

Afterward he did what we hoped he'd do but really didn't expect. He carried the message back to the *Times'* editors. As a result the paper began running a notice under its editorial page masthead to the effect that only the written editorials on the left side of the page represented the *Times*' opinion, nothing else did, not the columns and not the cartoons. Conrad was left hanging out there all alone. To top it off the *Times* moved his cartoons off the editorial page and onto the adjacent OpEd page. After a few months someone at the *Times* realized that this was no way for a major newspaper to act and the notice was withdrawn. But Reagan, for a little while, had his day.

But in March of 1966 the Beck story and the Conrad cartoon had an effect that Conrad, Beck, and Greenberg could not have anticipated and that, fortunately, none of them discovered. Not only did Reagan react but so also did Salvatori, and in a manner that could have destroyed Reagan's political career before it ever really got started.

I learned that Salvatori was upset when Reagan and I were at a Republican gathering at a fairgrounds near Placerville, a small Sierra foothills city east of Sacramento. Somebody gave me an urgent message to call Mardian. I called him; he was frantic, and with reason.

"You've got to get down here right away and talk to Henry Salvatori," he said. "He wants to dump Reagan and run Goody Knight."

"You can't be serious," I said.

Goodwin Knight had been governor of California for one term and part of another in the 1950s. He had served as lieutenant governor under Earl Warren and when Dwight Eisenhower named Warren chief justice of the United States Supreme Court, Knight moved up to governor. He was elected on his own in 1954 but was less fortunate four years later, when he ran for the United States Senate and lost to Clare Engle, an obscure Democratic congressman from the Northern California cow counties.

Mardian was insistent that I had to "get down here right away and talk him—Salvatori—out of it."

I told him I couldn't leave Reagan and that we would be home the next day. He said he would set up an appointment with Salvatori and let me know.

Two days later on a Sunday afternoon the three of us met at the Salvatori home. He had decided that Reagan's walkout on the black Republicans showed he was unstable and not a good candidate. He indeed wanted to run Knight in Reagan's place. I argued that out in the hustings Reagan was proving to be a very good candidate and was being well received wherever we went. I explained to him that Reagan had been exhausted at the black meeting, that he didn't walk out on the blacks but on Christopher and Patrick, and that he had gone back in the evening, something that the *Times* had not reported.

It took all afternoon but we finally managed to persuade Salvatori that he was stuck with Reagan. To my knowledge Reagan was never told of this incident. He did learn, however, that at a small private dinner at his inaugural festivities Salvatori drank a toast to "Ronald Reagan, the next president of the United States."

It was quite a change of heart, although, like some of the rest of us, Henry missed by fourteen years and during that period he had deserted Reagan at least one more time, when he supported Gerald Ford in 1976.

My memories of the 1966 campaign start with my talk with Bill Roberts after coming back from an early trip with Reagan. "There's something out there," I said. "I don't know what it is but there's something between Reagan and the people. He's going to be elected governor and someday he might even be president."

Bill looked at me pityingly with his big bulgy blue eyes. He must have wondered what kind of a naive nut he had hired.

"Oh Lyn," he remarked, "what will the poor soul do if he's ever elected governor!"

It was easy to see that Reagan had never inspired any great feeling of confidence in Bill Roberts. Bill was a good day-to-day campaign manager, as good as anyone I've ever known, maybe better. But like a lot of moderate Republicans he looked on Reagan as a not very smart right-wing actor. The Reagan campaign was a job to Bill Roberts, a job that paid well, and if he and Stu pulled off a victory, a job that presaged many more jobs in the future.

In any event, Bill never had the same sense of inevitable victory that I had, which certainly is just as well because, as I learned over the years, there is no such thing as inevitable victory in politics.

But there are always exceptions that prove the rule and this primary was one of them, because Reagan clobbered Christopher badly with Patrick running a weak third. Reagan's victory embittered Christopher almost beyond reason. Christopher, because he had run for lieutenant governor four years earlier and lost, thought he had earned the right to the Republican nomination for governor, and when the race began it looked as if he was right because he was odds-on favorite in the media, with the Democrats, and with the moderate Republicans. But he also learned a lesson that year: While the party leaders may support a candidate for his dedication to and work in the party, most persons who vote in a primary don't give a hoot about the wishes of the party leaders. They want somebody who they think represents their views and will serve them well. In 1966 that man was not George Christopher.

Many things have weakened the party system in this country over the years, almost none of which is ever addressed by the liberal reformers, most of whom don't really understand politics. One so-called reform that has hurt the two-party system is the selection of party nominees through the primary ballot rather than through the party caucus or convention.

In a convention or caucus state, of which there are now only a few, party workers and activists, those who've been involved at all levels of the party from the precincts all the way up to the state committee, have at least an indirect voice in picking the candidate. As a result the candidate generally represents the mainstream of party thinking. He— or she—may not be the most exciting or the most brilliant candidate but the odds are he's paid his dues, he knows the way the game is played, and he understands the role of the candidate. In other words he is truly representative of the party and it is easy for the party to coalesce around him.

Not so with primaries, as George Christopher, who should have known it all along, found out. Along with party activists, primaries bring out the radicals on both the left and right. They bring out the people with axes to grind, the single issue people, the right-to-lifers, the gun owners, the ERAers and NOWers and gay rights activists and zealots of all stripes. And the great middle-of-the-road who are bored with all this and seldom think about elective politics until the World Series is over, stay home. That is, unless some issue has arisen that threatens their peace of mind or gives them a chance to really stick it to the rascals in power.

During that 1966 campaign nobody had more confidence in Ronald Reagan than Ronald Reagan. The people who persuaded him to run for governor did so for one main reason. They thought he could beat Pat

Brown and they didn't think Christoper could, and they very likely were right. Even Pat Brown had more pizazz than George Christopher. I don't think the initial Reagan backers—the Tuttles and Salvatoris— ever gave much thought to whether Reagan had the ability to govern effectively. They assumed that it would just happen, or if it didn't, time enough later to rectify the situation. For the nonce they were more interested in a winner than in a governor. Besides, they didn't know any more about governing than he did.

Spencer and Roberts also had their qualms and rightly so, but they were qualms about Reagan as candidate, not Reagan as governor. Reagan, after all, was a novice candidate and a novice politician. He had spent his entire adult life either as a radio announcer or a movie actor. He knew almost nothing about the worlds of politics or governance. Only his activities in the Screen Actors Guild had any relationship to what he would come face to face with over the next twenty-five years.

He had never been through the rough-and-tumble of a campaign. He had never dealt with the political press or with political hecklers or with the caliber of political opposition he was to face in both the primary and the general elections of 1966.

But none of this bothered Reagan. From the beginning he was serenely confident that he could handle himself in the political arena. His reasoning was simple. In his mind party politics could not possibly be as tough as the union politics he had been involved in as president of the Screen Actors Guild for six years, much of it while the Communist party was attempting to dominate the film industry.

While Bill and Stu had their doubts about Reagan's ability to think on his feet, Reagan had none. And he was proved right. From almost the beginning of his campaign, to the initial dismay of his managers, he insisted on opening himself to questions from the audience. His ability to answer questions and handle hecklers first surprised Bill and Stu but eventually laid their minds to rest. Surprisingly, the smug Brown people, as well as many in the press, ignored Reagan's ability to handle himself. Brown, in fact, made it clear throughout the primary that he hoped to run against Reagan, a dumb actor and therefore the easiest to beat.

When he eventually did lose, like George Christopher before him, he could never understand why. And, like Christopher, he never quite got over either his bitterness at losing to that actor or his contempt for Reagan's apparent lack of knowledge of the detailed workings of government. This was the first but certainly not the last time Reagan benefited by being underestimated by both his opposition and the media.

Reagan's insistence on answering questions allayed another Spencer-Roberts fear, the fear that he might not understand the issues and, even if he did, that he wouldn't be able to explain them. In fact, about all they really knew about Reagan was that he had given a speech in the Goldwater campaign that had electrified the nation, that he had great name recognition, and that he was still, in most people's eyes, a MOVIE STAR. What they didn't know, but worried about, was that he might not be just a conservative but, instead, a real, genuine, right-wing kook.

He was not. Right-wing, yes. Kook, no. He managed to sidestep, duck, or explain away earlier stands that otherwise would have hurt him with many California voters. He denied he wanted to make Social Security voluntary, although he had implied as much in the Goldwater speech. As an old union man he was, at that time, truly against right-to-work, although the leaders of the AFL-CIO refused to believe it or give him credit for being the only union member—he still belonged to SAG and had a lifetime membership card to prove it—running for governor.

When I asked him about his pro-right-to-work position he said, simply, that he saw nothing wrong with an employer signing a contract with a union regarding who would work for it. Later on he changed his mind and by the time he ran for president he was a strong believer in right-to-work.

He also got away with denying that, in referring to efforts to preserve California's famed and endangered redwood forests, he ever said, "A tree is a tree. How many more do you have to look at?"

My secretary, Judith Kernoff, had it on tape, but that was something we didn't tell him or anyone else, so he was free to do one of the things he has always done best—convince himself that the truth is what he wants it to be. Most politicians are unable to do this, but they would give their eye teeth if they could.

What Reagan turned out to be was the most manageable candidate one could possibly hope for, a candidate who instinctively knew what the role of the candidate should be and who interfered very little and only occasionally in the other areas of the campaign.

Spencer and Roberts, for their part, proved to be adept campaign managers, dealing well, if not always successfully, with the real campaign prima donnas—the Holmes Tuttles and Henry Salvatoris and Taft Schreibers—and with Nancy Reagan whose deep concern for her husband and his political future, along with a lifetime tendency to worry, made her sometimes difficult.

Once, a campaign headquarters switchboard operator who had had difficulties with Nancy made a blunder that could have cost the operator her job. Nancy had called campaign headquarters looking for Roberts, and the operator, having gotten him on the line, said, "That bitch is on the phone"—realizing too late that she had left the line open and Nancy probably had heard. To Nancy's credit she never said a word to Roberts or anyone else, and the operator kept her job.

Reagan himself was a jewel. In only a few instances did he exert the candidate's perogative and demand that things be done his way. In one case he very naturally and very firmly stated that brother Neil's advertising agency, McCann Erickson, would handle campaign advertising.

It may surprise some people, but I don't know who, to learn that Ronald Reagan is no genius. His IQ probably doesn't match Jimmy Carter's, which may have been a blessing for the nation. Carter is so smart he knows every tree in the forest, what kind it is, when or if it sheds its leaves, what kind of fruit it bears, if any, and what its wood is used for. (He'd make a fine carpenter.) He can tell you how high and how old each redwood is. But he can't see the forest.

Reagan, on the other hand, sees mainly the forest. He can't tell one tree from another, nor does he care, which may be part of the reason for his infamous remark about the redwoods. I've been accused from time to time of inventing that line and planting it in Reagan's all too receptive mind, but it's not true. Reagan invented and recited it all by himself.

But, while Reagan may not be as smart as Jimmy Carter or Richard Nixon, he's smart enough and certainly he's smarter than some presidents of recent and not so recent vintage. In addition, he is a quick study. You don't have to tell him something very often for it to stick. And sometimes something sticks when you wish it hadn't. A general rule for those around Reagan was never say anything in his presence that you didn't want repeated. Reagan has a great "in" button but his "out" button sometimes sticks on "open."

Despite an occasional blooper, Reagan's retentive memory has stood him in good stead over his career, both as an actor and a politician. It was that memory, plus a unique "access to information" system invented by a couple of behavioral psychologists named Stanley Plog and Kenneth Holden that in 1966 helped Reagan confound both George Christopher and Pat Brown with his broad knowledge of state issues. The system put information on all important state issues at Reagan's fingertips in the form of brief but carefully indexed position papers that Reagan carried with him in loose-leaf binders.

A sloppy staff can make a candidate or an officeholder look bad. A good staff can make that same person look better than he is. Reagan, all through his political career was notoriously dependent on staff, although I don't think he thought so. I think he thought he could handle whatever came along, with or without staff. He leaned on staff because it was there and because staff, not having the confidence in him that he had in himself, expected to be leaned on.

There's nothing wrong with leaning on staff. President Eisenhower, fast rebecoming an American hero, did so heavily. Reagan's opposite in this area also was Carter, who liked to attend to details himself. He was a man with a limited understanding of the proper role of the president in a large and highly complex government. In his early days as president he is alleged to have gone so far as to keep track of who was to use the White House tennis court. He also worried about who his senior staff hired as secretarial help.

This devotion to detail was probably responsible for his wondering publicly whether the job of president might not be too big for one man. It was a good wonder, but the presidency in one way is like every other job: it depends on the man.

Reagan never indulged in that wonder. He always knew he could handle the job because he instinctively knew his job was not to count the trees but to guard the forest. It boils down, I guess, to Carter being a micromanager while Reagan was a macromanager, and sometimes almost no manager at all. This may explain why one of his favorite foods is macromoni, and why he is a believer in its holy bonds.

That style, whether natural or cultivated—with Reagan it was natural—is absolutely dependent on good staff. And over the years Reagan unconsciously attracted good staff people. He didn't seek them out; he didn't have to. They fought for the chance to serve him, and only once in a very great while did staff fail him. It is easy today to point to the big failure—the Iran Contra affair—as an example of Reagan's flawed management style. But other presidents whose management styles have not been subjected to the same criticism have had disasters as big or bigger.

Jack Kennedy's Bay of Pigs fiasco with its loss of lives, prisoners, and face was worse by far than Iran Contra. His idea of hiring Mafia hit men to assassinate Castro wasn't much better. And the steps he took to move American troops into a fighting role in Vietnam makes Iran fade in the shade. (Thank you, Jesse Jackson.)

One wonders whether a president relying on a competent staff for advice and counsel as heavily as Reagan did would have gotten into these sorts of trouble. But nowhere, surprisingly, have these world-class blunders been blamed on Kennedy's management style. In fact, the press and Democrat-controlled Congress were relatively sanguine about the demonstrable lack of good judgment of this immature president and the clique around him.

Bad staff work comes in big and little doses. Of course, the minor snafus are usually not transcribed into the pages of history books, but many are fun to recall and some that seem minor at the time turn out to be otherwise. Like Watergate, for example, whose cover-up effort was a case of staff running amok in what most of us thought was a tightly disciplined, carefully controlled environment. The ensuing panic and the old cover-your-ass syndrome turned what should have been an easily controlled staff screw-up into a disaster that changed for all time the way the nation is governed and how the government is reported by the news media.

Reagan was the occasional victim of bad staff work aside from the Iran Contra affair. Once, in 1966, when he was touring the boondocks of Northern California he stopped for an outdoor rally in Lake County which, as a matter of fact, is all boondock. There he was, talking to maybe a hundred farmers, ranchers, and townsfolk and taking questions as was his wont.

Came a voice from the crowd, "What will you do about the Eel River project if you're elected governor?"

Quick as a flash Reagan asked, "Where's the Eel River?"

Just as quickly the voice shouted back, "You're standing on it."

In March of 1966 Reagan's campaign for the Republican gubernatorial nomination got underway in earnest and it was then that he made the decision that whenever he made a speech he would take questions from the audience.

Roberts and Spencer tried to talk him out of it. They were political pros and they knew that wrong answers or controversial answers or nonanswers to questions thrown from left field or right field or deep center could literally destroy a candidate. This was especially true in the case of Reagan who already was being attacked both by Democrats and liberals within his own party as a dumb actor who did well only when he had his lines memorized. Bad answers to tough questions could only enhance that belief.

This lack of faith by his own people annoyed Reagan and made him even more determined to prove what in his heart he already knew—that he could think on his feet, could speak without memorizing lines and, for the most part, did understand the issues of the campaign. Over the course of the campaign he did surprisingly well, too, for several reasons.

First, he had a quick and retentive mind which had been honed by years of studying lines for movies and television. Second, he was much better informed than people wanted to think he was. He had been for years an omnivorous reader of current periodicals and daily papers. Third, he studied constantly the Plog and Holden issues books, which were frequently updated.

But even though Reagan did well, his contenders continued to label him a dumb actor who had no business running for governor. Christopher was particularly outraged, viewing Reagan as an interloper. But interloper or not, Reagan had a lot more going for him than Christopher did. He was a much more charismatic candidate. In Stu Spencer, Bill Roberts, and Fred Hafner he had much better management—was much better organized and had better media. And, of course, he had a better press secretary. Finally, his money people, largely Holmes Tuttle and Henry Salvatori and Ed Mills, outraised Christopher's people handily.

And there was one other factor. During and after World War II California's power and population centers had moved from northern California and San Francisco to southern California and Los Angeles. As a result, by 1966 it had become much more difficult to win a statewide nomination or election if you were from northern California. Today, twenty-five years later, even though the increasingly effective use of television has made geography less important, every governor since Pat Brown, up to and including Pete Wilson, has been from southern California. It should be noted that Pat Brown's two victorious gubernatorial campaigns were against Sen. William Knowland and Richard Nixon. Knowland, like Brown, was from Alameda County in northern California and ran a lousy campaign. Nixon, though a southern Californian, had been gone for eight years and was viewed by many as an opportunist looking for a new base from which to run for president rather than as a man who wanted to do things for California.

None of this meant anything to Christopher and he spent the general election sulking, giving only a cursory endorsement to Reagan. In fact, his antagonism toward Reagan lasted until the presidential primary campaign of 1976 which pitted Reagan against incumbent-but-never-elected President Gerald Ford. Christopher, a Greek-American, had no use for Ford's policy toward Greece vis-à-vis Turkey so for that reason alone he supported Reagan.

In 1966 Christopher's antagonism had little effect on the general election, largely because, immediately after the primary election, Reagan personally invited all of Christopher's top campaign people into his campaign in leadership positions. Reagan, the dumb actor and right-wing kook, was smart enough to know that it would take a united Republican party, as well as about a fifth of the state's registered Democrats, to beat Brown.

Actually he had taken the initial step toward unity much earlier. He had adopted the so-called Eleventh Commandment: Thou shalt not speak ill of another Republican.

Although the news media usually give Reagan credit for coming up with the commandment it was actually thought up and spelled out by a California politician named Robert Walker, who was then working for the California Republican party chairman, Dr. Gaylord Parkinson, perhaps the most effective in modern California political history.

Parkinson, although publicly neutral as befitted a party chairman, was a secret Reagan supporter and he quickly seized on Walker's proposed commandment to keep other candidates from attacking Reagan for his lack of experience and party background. So at the February convention he announced the commandment and demanded that all candidates abide by it.

Reagan, quick to see its advantages, adopted it immediately. It allowed him to run a positive campaign, one bent on convincing the voters that he knew and understood the issues, that he was not a right-wing kook, and that he was competent to govern.

As for his competence, the Plog-Holden briefing books were key to Reagan's ability to convince the electorate that he was on top of the issues and had some answers for the state's problems. He also used his six-year presidency of the Screen Actors Guild as proof that he had executive experience that would serve him in good stead in the governor's office.

The right-wing kook accusations, however, were a bit of a problem. The liberal bogeyman of the period was the John Birch Society, the Boston-based right-wing organization whose members believed that everything bad was the result of a red plot; under every bed lurked a communist. And American liberals, if not communists, were communist tools. The Birchers meant well and most of their relatively few members were earnest, God-fearing, loyal Americans. They just didn't think other people were.

The discovery that America was infested and infected with Birchers gave the American left wing, long accused of communist sympathies, its own dog to kick. And kick it did, to the point where to be a member of the John Birch Society was a little like having leprosy, only worse. Two competent California Republican congressmen were defeated in 1962 when it was discovered they were Birchers.

The two, Edgar W. (Eck) Hiestand, now dead, and John Rousselot, were really a couple of pretty decent people. Rousselot eventually was reelected to the House, where he served honorably for another four terms. In 1982, he was gerrymandered out of his seat.

But in 1966 Rousselot, between congressional stints, was not only an active Bircher but also a Birch official, handling public relations for the organization. But he refused to accept that he was a pariah in his own party and sought to continue as a normal, decent human being. That made it difficult for his friends, such as I, who were engaged in trying to elect someone and were afraid some of his pariahness might rub off on our candidate. On a couple of occasions he attended events where Reagan was speaking and sought to come up afterward to shake Reagan's hand. Having spotted him, I sent people out to block his way while I did my best to hurry the candidate to his car. It was a shameful thing to do, but the last thing Reagan needed was a picture in the paper with a cutline that read: Birch official greets Reagan.

I was surprised that Bill Roberts, a bona fide liberal Republican, didn't feel as strongly about the situation as I did. One day I discovered that Reagan was to attend a campaign fund-raiser at the home of a Birch member. I told my fears to Roberts who insisted I was making a forest out of a Birch tree. I pestered him for two days before he finally agreed to move the event. It was a victory for right, if not for the far Right.

Reagan himself had no trouble accepting support from Birch members. His stock answer to the question, "Why are you accepting the support of those dirty Birchers?" was, "If they're supporting me they're accepting my philosophy, I'm not accepting theirs."

It was a good enough answer so that neither the Democrats nor the news media was able to tag him with the Birch label. It may surprise many Democrats, liberals, and reporters but one of the traits that attracts people to Reagan is that he is a genuinely nice man. It isn't something he has to work at. More important, it's a trait that stayed with him as he moved along from country boy to actor to governor to president. It's amazing to me that somewhere along the line he never got a fat head or became arrogant or lost the human touch, but he didn't. He didn't but some of the people around him did.

From the time I first met him I thought that here was a good guy, the kind of person you would like to have as a friend. But it was several months after I went to work for him before I learned that not only was he a nice guy, he wanted other people to be nice as well.

It was the early summer of 1966, after Reagan's victory in the June primary but before the fall campaign had begun. We— Reagan, Art Van Court, who was his security man, and I—had flown into Los Angeles International Airport, where we were to have a press conference before Reagan went off to his home in Pacific Palisades. As we entered the terminal I found that my wife and two teenage daughters were waiting to take me out to Chatsworth in the northwest corner of the San Fernando Valley where they were staying with my parents for the summer. They had come out from our home in McLean, Virginia (we moved there before it became posh and once we left we never went back; poshness is not my thing), a week or so before. I said something to the effect that they would have to wait for me until after the press conference and went on about my business. And thought no more about it.

Several days later Reagan and some of the campaign leadership were at a large cabin at Lake Tahoe where Reagan was undergoing a briefing session on important issues in the fall campaign against Governor Brown. Evening had come and we had stopped for cocktails and dinner. Several of us were having drinks on a large deck overlooking the lake when Reagan wandered out and joined us. After a moment he drew me to one side.

"Lynwood," he said in that gentle voice of his, "you've got to be nicer to your wife and children."

"What in the hell are you talking about?" I asked, not a little surprised, and more than a little indignant.

"The other day at the airport," he explained. "You were pretty rude to them."

"I was busy," I said. "They understood."

"Nevertheless, you should be nicer to them," he insisted. "Take it from an old married man."

"I've been married longer than you have," I said, truthfully.

"Not if you count both my wives," he said, grinning.

We both laughed and that ended that conversation. But from that moment on I quit beating my wife.

That was not the only time Reagan showed his thoughtfulness. In the early days of his first term as governor—in fact, all during his time in public office—Reagan tried to leave his office around 5 P.M. or shortly thereafter. If there was nothing important on his schedule he refused to hang around just to impress people with how hard he was working. He instinctively understood that that wasn't why he was elected. From the beginning he knew that the drudge work and the minutia were someone else's job; that his job was to set policy and make the big, important decisions.

Also he was not then and never became a politician's politician, the kind who likes to sit around after hours, or all night for that matter, with his feet propped up on the desk, talking politics. He preferred to go home, put on his pajamas, eat supper, romp with his son, and either read the papers or watch television. Nothing wrong with that, especially if you don't demand any more from your staff. And Reagan didn't.

The governor's office in the state capitol in Sacramento is known as the corner office because it is located in the southeast corner of a quadrangle, which is located in the southeast corner of the capitol building, which is located in the middle of a good-sized park through which the squirrels and legislators roam and it is hard to tell which is which. In the center of the governor's quadrangle is a patio, and down each side of it are the offices of the governor's staff—his chief of staff, press secretary, legislative aids, legal counsel, and the like.

Often in those early days, as he was preparing to go home, Reagan would stroll down the hallway and poke his head into the various offices. Instead of saying goodnight, though, he'd say, "It's getting late, fellas. Why don't you go home to your wives and children?"

Our replies would be, in effect, "Who's going to get the work done if we go?"

"It's not that important," he'd insist. "Go home." And he'd follow his own advice.

But not us. We were all very important in those days, all very impressed with our jobs and with the knowledge that government could not run without us. So we'd stay and let dinner get cold or, more likely, let our wives and children eat by themselves.

But the fact is, Reagan was right. Almost everything we were doing those late evenings could have waited. Much, if it had never gotten done, would never have been missed. And even when it was done it would never, if the truth were known, have any particular effect on the state of the state, the nation, or the world. Reagan instinctively knew that, and acted accordingly. We, either because of our self-importance or our insecurity, didn't. Which probably is one reason why he was elected governor and president and none of us ever will be.

3

A Taste of Governance

BEFORE HE WAS elected president Ronald Reagan liked to boast that he was the first governor of California to be elected by a million votes and four years later by nearly a million. It sounded impressive, but it wasn't quite accurate. He was elected in 1966 by nearly a million votes and reelected in 1970 by a little over half a million. The margins were nothing to be ashamed of. After all, in 1966 he was running against a popular two-term governor in a state that had five registered Democrats for every three Republicans. Four years later his opponent was one of the shrewdest politicians of his time, Jesse Unruh, then the Speaker of the California State Assembly.

In both elections, once victory seemed assured, Reagan went all out to help elect other Republicans. In 1966, pleading, "Don't send me to Sacramento alone," Reagan campaigned for the other members of his statewide ticket, with emphasis on Robert Finch, a protégé of Richard Nixon, who was running for lieutenant governor. Spencer and Roberts even changed Reagan's radio and TV spots, as well as his billboards, to help Finch.

The strategy worked. On election day Reagan's coattails proved strong enough to elect Finch, along with the Republican candidates for state comptroller, treasurer, and secretary of state. And the right-wing Republican, Max Rafferty, was reelected to the nonpartisan office of Superintendent of Public Instruction. Ironically, Finch, the man for whom Reagan campaigned hardest, ran slightly ahead of Reagan, something the Finch people wrongly took to mean that Finch would have won without Reagan's help.

The biggest fluke of the election was the victory of Houston Flournoy, the Republican candidate for comptroller. Flournoy, a member of a little coterie of liberal Republicans, ran only because he lost the toss of a coin in a four-way gamble to see who would run in what he and his friends thought was a no-win race against the incumbent, Alan Cranston. The victory propelled Flournoy eight years later into a race for governor, a contest he lost to Pat Brown's eccentric son, Jerry, better known as Governor Moonbeam.

In 1970 Reagan devoted a lot of energy in an attempt to have his old acting buddy, George Murphy, reelected to the United States Senate. In vain. Reagan could not overcome the charge that Murphy had unethically and perhaps illegally taken expense money from the Technicolor Corporation while a senator.

Long before election day in 1966 I was confident that Reagan would win. I still thought I smelled that indefinable something between Reagan and the people, or at least most of them, that something I had mentioned to Bill Roberts nearly eight months earlier. After all these years I have not yet figured out just what it is, but it may be that he is an eternal optimist. Reagan, who is also a great raconteur, used to tell a joke that, whether or not he knew it, epitomized his own attitude. It was about two little boys—twins—one of whom was a terrible pessimist, the other a confirmed optimist. Their parents called in a child psychiatrist to see if he could bring more balance into their lives.

To cure the pessimist the psychiatrist took him into a roomful of new toys and told him, "These are all yours." The boy burst out crying and, when asked why, wept that the toys might break or be lost or someone might steal them. Nothing could comfort him.

The psychiatrist then took the other twin into a room piled high with horse manure. The kid let out a joyful whoop and began burrowing into the pile. When he was asked what he was doing he replied, "With all this manure, there has to be a pony in here somewhere."

Reagan is like that kid. He always figures there's a pony in there somewhere.

With his actions and looks and bearing and words Reagan exudes confidence, not only in himself, but also in the people. They seem to sense that confidence, his belief and trust in both himself and them. And they respond. More than this, he comes across as one of them, which perhaps is a remnant of his childhood days when he grew up poor, the son of, economically at least, lower-middle-class parents. Whatever the reason, he has, more than any public man I know of, managed, in Kipling's words, ". . .to walk with kings nor lose the common touch."

Of course, some people voted against him, common touch or not, those who hated him or were contemptuous of him and what he stood for. But still, in all his elections, he never lost many Republican votes and he always picked up a lot of Democrats, most of whom never dreamed they would ever vote for a Republican until they actually did.

As the 1966 campaign drew to a close it became obvious to us, if not to the Brown people, that Reagan was going to win. So about three weeks before the election Phil Battaglia and Bill Clark, our Ventura County chairman, detached themselves from the campaign to plan for the transition from a Brown to a Reagan administration.

By this time I had decided that I would like to be part of a Reagan administration, but I didn't want to ask for a job, so I waited for Reagan to ask me. Later, I learned that you don't do that sort of thing to Ronald Reagan. If you're on the team he expects you to come aboard and for the most part he figures "the fellows," of which you are one, will agree among themselves who will do what. But this was the first time around for all of us, including Reagan, so he was forced to go through the formality of naming Battaglia as his executive secretary, a.k.a. chief of staff, Clark as his cabinet secretary, and Tom Reed as his appointments secretary, which in this case meant being the man who served as administration headhunter.

Because in my case working for Reagan meant bringing my family from McLean, Virginia, to Sacramento I asked Reagan to write my wife Bonnie explaining that it would be helpful if she would agree to the move. He did. It was a great letter because Reagan is the world's greatest letter writer. If somebody dies get Reagan to write to the survivor. If someone is sick get a letter from Reagan. Ditto if someone needs advice or counsel. Reagan is better than Abbie and Ann combined.

A lady named Helene von Damm (who is a story in herself, but she has written her own book) was once Reagan's personal secretary. She had a wonderful idea for a book—Reagan's letters. Letters to strangers, letters to his children and other people's children, letters to the living and to the dying, to the rich and the poor, to the important as well as to the unimportant. They are a better insight into the real Ronald Reagan, the Reagan behind the invisible veil, than any book yet published, including both of his autobiographies.

Helene's idea became a published book, in paperback only, in 1976 under the title *Sincerely, Ronald Reagan*. It was never promoted and not much read, mainly because Reagan at the time was a has-been actor and one-time governor of whom the pundits and seers never expected much more. Only a few people, fools such as myself, still thought he could be president. The book which was printed to sell for $1.25 never made its way into many book stores and I don't recall ever seeing it on the paperback shelves of the airport newsstands either.

Conspiracy? Probably not. More than likely a misjudgment on the part of paperback distributors who, generally speaking, are more attuned to sex and violence than to politics.

Reagan's handwritten letter to Bonnie and the girls made her feel good and me feel better than good. It allowed me to do something I really wanted to do without feeling guilty about uprooting my family. It read:

> I know how disappointed you must have been when the election was finally over and done with and the one you've been missing these many months didn't come home. I'm sure you have some thoughts tending toward the swift elimination of a recently elected Gov. and I can't say that I blame you. However let me state my case and while it won't make you miss him less perhaps you will all understand better why he didn't come home.
>
> You see part of this is his own fault. Without him I might very well not have been elected and there'd be no problem at all. Believe me it could have been a different campaign without his knowledge, experience and wise counsel. I owe him a great debt of gratitude and you even more for

sharing him and for doing it in such a way that he was truly effective. The days ahead are frightening at best but they would be impossible without him.

He's told me he'll be with you for Thanksgiving and I'll see that he's there for Xmas if I have to get a court order and have the Sheriff run him out of Calif.

I'm grateful to all of you—And your missing Husband and Father is of such help there are no words to really express my thanks. Just know that I do thank you from the bottom of my heart.

Reagan's victory over Brown brought the inevitable question: What do we do now?

Reagan, as usual, delegated the job of doing what had to be done, namely finding people to serve in his administration and arranging for the transition of authority from the Brown administration to the Reagan administration.

Surprisingly, or maybe not so surprisingly, Reagan knew what he wanted when it came to picking cabinet heads and other top officials. He had campaigned on the claim that he was not just another politician; he was a "citizen-politician," which in a way was kind of funny. When asked if he was a conservative Republican or a right-wing Republican or any other kind of Republican his stock answer was that he was an unhyphenated Republican. But he was perfectly willing to hyphenate what kind of a politician he was. His intent was clear in both cases. As an unhyphenated Republican he sought to unite the Republican party behind him. As a hyphenated politician he sought to divorce himself from the epithetic picture that "politician" unhyphenated brings to mind.

Pat Brown was a "politician" pure and simple and proud of it, but to a lot of people labeling a person a politician is like calling someone a "used car salesman." Ronald Reagan, on the other hand, was a "citizen politician" which was supposed somehow to connoted honesty and integrity and sincerity and any other virtue that might come to mind.

And Reagan believed this. He believed there was a big difference between career or professional politicians and people who entered politics as a public duty, such as he felt he had done.

At the same time he didn't believe that people, at high levels at least, should make careers of government. His ideal public servant was a business executive or professional person who would go into government for two or three years, bringing his business or professional expertise with him, and then leave, turning his post over to another business or professional person and taking his newly won government expertise with him.

It didn't always work the way Reagan envisioned but it did work after a fashion. True, while some people came and left, others came and stayed, but the approach did bring a surprisingly large number of competent people, with little or no prior government experience, into his administration.

While Clark and Battaglia and others worked on the transition, the campaign fat cats formed themselves into an executive search committee. Tuttle and Salvatori made a Los Angeles lawyer, William French Smith, from the firm of Gibson, Dunn and Crutcher, the committee chairman. Smith was their boy.

After Reagan's primary victory they had sought to bring Smith into the campaign as Reagan's traveling companion and their information link to Reagan, but to my great relief Battaglia successfully fought the effort. He viewed Smith as a potential spy, a person who would block access to the candidate, and an unessential adjunct to what so far had been a successful campaign. I never talked to Reagan about the idea but clearly if he had been eager to have Smith with him he could have. But he never protested when Smith left the campaign.

For myself, I didn't want Smith in the small traveling party for several reasons. Although at the time I wouldn't have admitted it even to myself, the fact is he would have diminished not only my access to but my influence with the candidate. I was afraid he would be second-guessing what the candidate and I each were doing, would be critical of my work and of what Reagan was saying, and in other ways further excite the already excitable duo to whom he reported.

I was probably wrong. Smith, now dead, was really a very decent sort. And while some of us early on unfairly viewed him as a lightweight he turned out to be an effective and innovative attorney general during Reagan's first term as president. Regardless, Battaglia won the fight and Tuttle and Salvatori settled for making Smith Reagan's personal attorney, an integral part of Reagan's "kitchen cabinet," and eventually head of Reagan's presidential executive search committee.

Reagan was sworn in as California's thirty-third governor one minute after midnight on January 3, 1967. Our official reason, and as far as I know the real reason for that unusual time, was that Reagan wanted to be sworn in as soon as legally possible so that Brown could not make any further "deathbed" appointments, especially of judges, just before stepping down. But the argument doesn't hold water. Brown had made about all the appointments he could make in the two-month interval between election and inauguration. Neither was he the kind of man deliberately to embarrass or antagonize Reagan on his inauguration day.

Certainly the midnight ceremony was a good publicity gimmick, if that's what it was, but I was not included in the decision as normally I would have been. This leads me to wonder about the old rumors that it had something to do with stars and zodiacs and that sort of thing. But in her memoirs Nancy says astrology had nothing to do with it and sticks to the appointments story. And who am I to doubt Nancy? But, still, I wonder. What were the stars saying that night?

As Reagan settled into the governor's office only one member of his senior staff knew anything about how government really worked. He was Vern Sturgeon, a former state senator who had been redistricted out of his seat. He became the liaison between the governor's office and the state senate. The liaison to the state assembly was a businessman named Jack Lindsey who was as ignorant as the rest of us. Nevertheless, the senior staff consisted largely of smart, able, and energetic men who learned rapidly and were not afraid.

There were no women in the highest part of the hierarchy. Just men, a couple of whom, it turned out, not only were men but appeared to like men. It isn't that we were deliberately sexist, just that we were naturally sexist. This was true not only of the staff, but also of the governor; all of us would have denied the charge then and would do so today.

But the fact is, the only senior staffer who had a woman working for him above the secretarial level was me. I had brought on board a woman named Nancy Reynolds, a San Francisco television reporter who had done a horseback—literally— interview with Reagan during the campaign.

Toward the end of Reagan's first year his scheduler, who nominally reported to me, departed and I was able to promote his assistant, another smart lady named Pat Gayman, into his job.

While on the general subject, there also were no blacks, Jews, or Mexicans in that uppermost echelon. It was a 100 percent WASP outfit, if you can call Italian Catholics Wasps. This is not a criticism, merely a statement of fact. There was no deliberate effort to keep women or minorities out; it just happened that way. Reagan is certainly not a racist or a sexist or a bigot in any way.

His wife is not only the love of his life but also a significant part of his political and public lives. He appointed the first woman member of the Supreme Court and his first ambassador to the United Nations was the redoubtable Jeane Kirkpatrick. His agents, Taft Schreiber and Jules Stein, were Jewish, and Schreiber until his death was a member of Reagan's "kitchen cabinet" as was another Jew, Ted Cummings, who also served as Reagan's first ambassador to Austria. And his first combination driver and security man was a Jewish ex-cop named Bill Friedman.

One of the smart things I did in the early days was to get Reagan to agree to a weekly press conference. As I said earlier, it assured us of regular coverage by the large capital press corps, kept Reagan on top of his game, and pleased the reporters because they had regular and frequent access to the governor. Washington reporters like to think of themselves as the cream of the crop, but capital reporters in California are every bit as good. And they had one rule that made their governor's press conferences in a way even tougher than a president's—questioners stayed on a single subject until all questions on that subject had been exhausted. In contrast, Washington reporters scattershot their questions, each one asking the question he thinks he can write his own lead on or that makes him look smarter or tougher or meaner than anyone else.

We also, and this was Nancy Reynolds' idea, began filming short— one to one-and-a-half minute—film clips (there was no video tape then) of Reagan saying something important or at least newsworthy. We'd make a transcript of what he said for the writing press, tapes for the radio press, and send film clips directly to the television stations. This upset some reporters. They thought we were going around them, which we were. I explained to them that we were trying to get some of the governor's views to the people unfiltered through reporters' typewriters. Somehow they thought this was unfair, but we continued to do it anyway on the grounds that the governor's office was not there merely for the benefit of the news media.

Reagan proved to be adept at press conferences, making few of the alleged gaffes the Washington press loved to accuse him of in his first years as president.

Reagan has been accused of a lot of things, but cowardice is not among them. During his campaign for governor he unhesitatingly bearded the student lions in their campus dens. And as governor he faced down dissident mobs outside and inside the capitol and on the state university campuses.

Once, at the beginning of a press conference, a belligerent group of Cesar Chavez's farm workers gathered outside the pressroom door. Reagan's security man, Arthur Van Court, now the U.S. marshal in Sacramento, came to me and suggested that after the press conference we take him out a back way. I agreed. As soon as the press conference ended Art and I hustled him out a back door. We had gone just a few steps when he stopped.

"Why are we going this way?" he demanded.

I shrugged, "Just a change of pace."

"That's not it," he answered. "Why are we going this way?"

I broke down and told him.

"I'll be damned if that bunch is going to scare me off," he said, turned around and headed back to the pressroom. Without hesitating he pushed his way through the milling mass, which parted to let him through, and strolled on back to the governor's suite, undeterred by the wrath of the grapes.

Another time a crowd had gathered on a Saturday to protest cuts in the state budget. Reagan was in his office with a few of his senior staff, preparing to leave town on a speaking engagement. The crowd demanded that he appear while Reagan's staff urged him to sneak off without making an appearance. But Reagan, refusing to appear a coward, went to the front steps of the capitol, stepped up to the microphone, and began: "Ladies and gentlemen" and in an aside, "if there are any." Some reporters heard and duly reported what he had said, but they were impressed with his courage, as were many in the mob.

In the beginning Reagan attended all meetings of the Board of Regents of the state's university system which include the great campuses of Berkeley and UCLA. The dishonest gentlemen who ran the system were stirring up faculty and students by charging that Reagan was trying to cut their budget, which was a lie. He was merely trying to reduce the size of a proposed budget increase. But neither the faculty nor the students nor, for the most part, the press, bothered to differentiate between the two.

Once, after a lunch break at a regents meeting at the Santa Barbara campus, Reagan was walking back to the meeting room. The way led across campus and the sidewalk was lined with students giving him the silent treatment. As he approached the building in which the meeting was being held Reagan turned, put his finger to his lips, and said, "Shhhh."

The nearby students broke out laughing and Reagan smiled and waved and entered the building, the clear victor.

But Reagan got off to a rocky start in his dealings with the university. These were the early years of the free speech movement, of unrest and violence on campus, the years of hippies and marijuana and LSD, of long hair and long dresses and dirty bodies and dirty clothes, of free sex and communal sex. They were the years of the Black Panthers and the Student Nonviolent Coordinating Committee (Snick) and the Weathermen and the motorcycle gangs.

Reagan, for reasons unfathomed on campus, was opposed to what was going on—school takeovers, sit-ins, book burnings, and those sorts of things. Old-fashioned, he thought college was a place to go for an education and objected to using taxpayers' money to pay professors and subsidize students who thought differently. He placed much of the blame for the educational chaos on the university president, Dr. Clark Kerr, best remembered (by me at least) for the bumper sticker that read: "Freedom Under Clark Kerr," with the first letter of each word in red.

During his campaign Reagan made it clear that one of his objectives as governor would be to persuade the regents, of which as governor he was to be the president, to get rid of Kerr. So when he went to his first regents meeting the press expected him to make a run at Kerr. But he had already decided he wouldn't, reasoning that doing so would make him look both rash and vindictive. He still planned to get Kerr, but later.

However, in a private meeting with the regents Kerr demanded a vote of confidence. Instead they voted to fire him. Kerr, and the media, publicly blamed Reagan for what he, Kerr, had done to himself. But the public was on Reagan's side; they thought he had done what he really hadn't.

Many years later Kerr came by my office in Washington to get my recollections on the matter. He freely admitted that Reagan had not done him in, and I just as freely admitted that it had been just a matter of time.

Government turned out to be somewhat different from the way Reagan had envisioned it. In the first place, he found that cutting the size of the bureaucracy wasn't so easy. In the long run he was unable even to cut the size of his own staff, though he had criticized Brown for the size of his. He discovered that to control the bureaucracy, and for that matter, the activities of his own cabinet officers, to deal with the legislature, and to deal with the public and the special interests took more rather than fewer people. He was unable to reverse the growth of government; the best he could do was to slow it.

More than any other elected officials, the governors of California and New York automatically are viewed as potential candidates for president. So when Reagan was elected he joined Nelson Rockefeller, the governor of New York, as a possible candidate in 1968. Rockefeller had already made a serious run at the Republican nomination in 1964, losing out to Barry Goldwater. There was also a third possible candidate who had never been a governor lurking in the weeds—Richard Nixon. A crafty politician, Nixon had spent 1964 and 1966 campaigning for anyone who would have him and putting together the same kind of effective political machine that Reagan was to put together between 1977 and 1980.

Although Nixon had a near lock on the Republican nomination well before the 1968 convention, in December of 1966 nobody had locked up anything, or so a few of us around Reagan believed. Thus in early December a meeting convened in the Reagan residence to discuss the possibility of making the governor-elect, who had yet to serve a day in public office, the next president of the United States of America.

The perpetrators of this affair were Tom Reed and I. Others present were Reagan, Battaglia, Tuttle, Salvatori, Taft Schreiber, and Ed Mills, Tuttle's business associate. The outcome of the meeting was that the fat cats agreed to let Reed enlist the aid of F. Clifton White to survey the situation and, if it seemed at all reasonable, to begin to put together some sort of a draft organization.

White already was a political legend. In 1963 he had pulled off a draft-Goldwater movement that had won him the Republican nomination in 1964. Goldwater repaid him for that classically successful effort by shunting him to one side during the disastrous general election in favor of Dean Burch, a member of Goldwater's "Arizona Mafia." Goldwater had Burch named Republican national chairman, a post White had long craved, and in a blooper of rather large proportions put his campaign in the hands of the Republican National Committee.

Although a genuine conservative, White had grown up in politics as a member of Tom Dewey's New York State political organization. A near genius in putting together the mechanics of conventions, he understood, participated in, and prevented for his side the shenanigans that often go on in such conventions. And he surrounded himself with some of the party's best regional politicians from all areas of the country. He also controlled the conservative wing of the national Young Republican Organization. He was the ideal person for what Reed had in mind.

As a result of the December meeting a low-key, unofficial, and easily deniable "Reagan for President" organization was hatched that functioned all the way to the 1968 Republican National Convention in Miami Beach. There was only one problem: The candidate wouldn't cooperate. Although he had approved hiring White and putting out feelers, in his mind he was not, as he later admitted, ready to be president. But that was something Reed and White and Nofziger didn't believe, didn't care about, and didn't want to hear. And in retrospect we, not Reagan, were right. When you look at the presidents and the presidential nominees of both parties in the twentieth century the Reagan of 1966, despite his innocence, fares pretty well.

While White and Reed plotted the making of the president that never came off, Reagan settled down in Sacramento to learn how to be governor in his own low-key, laid-back, let-the-staff-do-the-heavy-lifting style. It worked well for him over the years, with only a couple of glitches, but mainly because he attracted top flight staffers and cabinet officers who had his best interests at heart and who subordinated their own ambitions to work on his behalf.

Unfortunately, that style got him off to a bad start. His first executive secretary/chief of staff was Phil Battaglia who, hardly seven months later, was forced to resign. But before the roof began falling in on him, those early days in the governor's office were truly exciting. What could be more exciting than Battaglia changing my title from "press secretary" to "communications director," as far as I know, the first "communications director" ever? I thought the title a little highfalutin' but Battaglia felt that "press secretary" was beneath what dignity I had.

Still, even though I had a press secretary, Paul Beck, working under me, I was always a little embarrassed when I had to state my title, so I usually lied and called myself press secretary. Later, in the Nixon administration, Herb Klein took and legitimized the communications director title.

But other exciting things were happening too. Edwin Meese III, a highly regarded young attorney from Oakland, had come aboard as clemency secretary, but Ed quickly changed that title to legal affairs secretary and, without protest, took on new responsibilities commensurate with the broadened title. It was a good move, good for Meese and good for Reagan. In those days of racial unrest and campus violence Reagan needed a tough law and order attorney on his staff and Meese, under his Yale undergraduate veneer and Boalt Hall legal training, was a cop at heart.

And what could be more exciting than the invention by Cabinet Secretary Bill Clark of the mini-memo that became Reagan's standard one-page briefer on any issue brought officially to his attention? Though not the soul of wit Clark was a great believer in brevity. Later, when he was serving as a justice on the State Supreme Court, Clark became famous in legal circles for the conciseness and astuteness of his opinions. Obviously, a rare combination.

What could be more exciting? Well, over the twenty-one months I served in the Reagan administration in Sacramento, several things.

For one, the dream of making Reagan president, a dream I'd had almost from the beginning. I didn't know then that it was going to take fourteen years to make that particular dream come true. It seems like a long time until I remember that some folks go all their lives without a single important dream ever coming true. In fact, some people never even have a dream.

My feeling was that Reagan had to strike while the iron was hot, to put it tritely. I was afraid that if he waited too long, like, for instance, until 1972, it would be too late—if a Republican were elected president in 1968 Reagan would have to wait until 1976 to run. And by that time, after two terms as governor if reelected in 1970, he would be wearing ten years worth of political scars. He would also be sixty-five which, in my innocence, I thought a little old to be seeking the presidency. In contrast, in 1966–67 he was a hot political figure, the natural successor to the aging and irascible and forever defeated Barry Goldwater.

So throughout the turmoil of the next nineteen months, some positive, some distinctly negative, I managed to keep my eye on the goal I had set for my leader—the presidency. Tom Reed, who stayed only briefly in the governor's office, although he remained close to the governor and the senior staff, was the driving force in the effort, along with White.

White's group of conservatives from the Goldwater campaign for the most part rallied to the new cause or, rather, to the new leader of the old cause. Among them were a couple of old political hands from the West: Frank Whetstone of Cutbank, Montana, known as "Uncle Frank," and Anderson Carter of Lovington, New Mexico. Each was a bear of a man, well over six feet and burly. Each was a political power in his home state. Carter, like Reagan, was a former Democrat who had seen the light in time to run for and lose a U.S. Senate seat twice. He drank George Dickel whiskey and smoked innumerable cigarets. Both he and Uncle Frank had enough money to indulge in their joint hobby, which was politics.

We worked well together. As they politicked through the West they would drop the word that Reagan was running for president. Local reporters would call me in Sacramento, all excited at their scoops, and ask me if it were true. I would deny it, and they would write stories saying Reagan was going to run for president, even though his spokesman, Lyn Nofziger, denied it. I would then get hold of Frank and Andy, tell them they'd done good work, and urge them to keep it up. Which they did.

White (as in Clif) people in other parts of the country were doing the same thing—J.D. Stetson Coleman in Virginia, Sam Hayes in Wisconsin, Cy Joley in Maine, Roger Allan Moore in Massachusetts, Bill McFadzean in Minnesota. Non-Whites were also stirring, such as Ken Rogstad and Jim Munn in Washington, and Bob Hazen and Don Hodel in Oregon.

During this time Reed was doing his best to present Reagan to the American public as a knowledgeable and responsible conservative leader. He arranged for Reagan to deliver an Alf Landon lecture at the University of Kansas and as early as April 1966 to address the prestigious Detroit Economic Club. Reagan also spent several days at Yale as a Chubb Fellow, which won him coverage in the national news magazines.

And he showed up at every governors conference—national, regional, Republican—much to the dismay of the other governors because Reagan clearly dominated the meetings, not so much with his knowledge of government as with his personality and celebrity status. Worse, he charmed the other governors with his wit, his store of stories about the movies, and his treatment of them all as his equals. Though they may not have liked his conservative views, even such liberal Republicans as Tom McCall of Oregon found him hard to dislike.

I am surprised that no one has written a book on McCall, who was a good governor but also a maverick and an oddball. Over the years he and I got to be pretty good friends. Once, attending a national park dedication, he picked up a flat rock, on one side of which he printed "Genuine Oregon Petrified Turd," only he spelled it "petfried." On the other side he wrote, "To Lyn Best wishes" and signed it "Tom McCall." It still rests among my souvenirs.

The best story I ever heard about McCall involved his mother who lived in Boston, Tom's hometown. The old lady thought her son had been neglecting her but was unable to get through to him on the phone. One night in frustration she put in a call to the White House and, for reasons still unexplained, got through to the president. After hearing her out he put in a call to McCall in the governor's mansion.

When Tom came on the line, he ordered, "Tom, this is Lyndon Johnson. Call your mother."

Despite all our efforts Reagan remained adamant about not running for president. In all the time I've known him it was the only time he really meant it, but I didn't believe him even then. His resolve was strengthened by Bill Clark, who in August had succeeded Battaglia as executive secretary, Meese, and other goo-goos (good government advocates as compared to politicians) around Reagan. These people had the nonsensical belief that just because Reagan had been elected governor he should concentrate on being a good one. Which he did and was.

In private Reagan did talk of being willing to accept a draft, and at that stage in his career he even believed that such a thing could be legitimate. He had some other beliefs, too, that I'm not certain he ever got completely over. He believed that if God wanted him to be president He would see that it got done. He believed that the cavalry does come charging over the hill at the last moment. And finally, he believed that right really does triumph.

I have never figured out whether all this was naivete or mysticism or excessive optimism. Whatever it was it shouldn't be scoffed at because it saw him through some tough times and eventually took him to the presidency, much to the surprise of a lot of people, including Jimmy Carter.

Whatever Reagan's thinking or believing, from time to time he agreed to do something that might help his chance at the nomination. One of those arose in early 1968 when I had what I thought and still think was a brilliant idea, even though it came to nothing.

I suggested to the governor that he go to Washington and make a speech on domestic issues with emphasis on the welfare problem. In this way, I reasoned, he could prove he was a thoughtful governor with concern for all the people, could show himself to be the kind and gentle man I knew he really was and not the heartless, uncaring right-winger the Eastern news media portrayed him as being. He liked the idea and I arranged to have him address the Women's National Press Club.

Everything went just fine; I only made one mistake, but that one did it for us. I picked the wrong date—April 5, 1968. I myself went to Washington on April 3 to make certain everything went as planned. When the Reagans arrived in Washington the next afternoon, I met them at the plane with the bad news.

"We're going to have to go through with this," I told them. "But we're not going to get any publicity. Somebody has shot Martin Luther King."

While a panicky city and an incredibly short-sighted White House sat passively by waiting for the predictable black riots, Reagan spoke as planned and then—damn fools that we were—we headed for Southeast Washington, a largely black area, to meet with a group of militant black leaders. The meeting had been set up by Ed Gillenwaters, our man in Washington, as part of the master plan to soften Reagan's image.

The blacks we met with were angry, barely civil. After talking with them for only a few minutes, a cop poked his head in the door—Gillenwaters had been smart enough to tell them where the governor of California would be.

"The city's going up," he said quietly. "You'd better get out of here."

We left without a civil good-bye on either our part or theirs. The police led us as far as the Capitol, but there they stopped and told us they had to stay in their precinct. That left us to fight our lonely, nervous way back unescorted to the Madison Hotel at Fifteenth and M streets Northwest, where Californians always seemed to stay in Washington.

There were five of us in that car. Dale Rowley, a California highway patrolman and the governor's Sacramento driver, was driving. Piloting him in the other front seat was Gillenwaters. In the back were Reagan, Art Van Court, his security man, and I, the guy largely responsible for this mess.

As we drove you could almost taste the panic as people attempted to flee the city. And we saw some other things, too. At one intersection we saw a man in a business suit stepping out to direct traffic. At another corner we saw an elderly white woman stumble and fall, and two black men help her to her feet. And we saw young blacks smashing windows and grabbing their contents.

We were still four blocks from the hotel when traffic gridlocked. After sitting for about five minutes, I suggested that we leave the car and walk the rest of the way, all but Rowley who opted to stay with the car. As we started to get out Van Court pulled out his dark glasses.

"Here, governor, wear these so they won't recognize you," he urged.

Reagan refused. Van Court reurged. Reagan rerefused.

Finally I said something like, "For cripes sake, Ron. Put 'em on. Let's get out of here!"

Grumbling, he put them on. Across the sidewalk from us, leaning casually against a building, were two tall blacks. One of them spotted us and said, "Hey, man, there's Ronald Reagan."

As Reagan tells the story, they then asked him for his autograph. But that isn't so. What happened was that he yanked off the dark glasses, and we strode unmolested and unrecognized back to the Madison. About five minutes later Rowley joined us, car and all.

Once there we went up to a penthouse and watched as fires began breaking out. Before dark we decided to make a run for it, so we piled in the car—Rowley, Ron and Nancy Reagan, Nancy's aide, Nancy Reynolds, who really worked for me, Van Court, Gillenwaters, and I. It was a bit crowded. We drove out New York Avenue headed for Friendship (now Baltimore-Washington) Airport just south of Baltimore. On the way out we met convoys of the National Guard coming in. A welcome sight.

A couple of days later we got the clippings of Reagan's speech from both the Washington papers, the *Post* and *Star*. In both cases, about three paragraphs, way inside. So much for the best-laid plans.

By June of 1968, when it was much too late, Reagan began to be nibbled by the presidential bug. He had agreed to become a favorite son candidate in California which would allow him to run unopposed in the primary. His stated reason for running—and he believed it—was to avoid a divisive California primary fight between Nixon and Nelson Rockefeller. Others of us wanted him to run as a favorite son because it would give him a significant block of delegates if he ever decided to become a real candidate.

As a favorite son Reagan began to draw a little interest from others involved in presidential politics. A delegation from Texas, including Anne Armstrong, the national committeewoman, visited him in Sacramento to urge him to support Nixon. Reagan was at his noncommittal best that night and they went away emptyhanded. Later, Gov. Spiro T. Agnew of Maryland came to see him and said he would support a Reagan-Rockefeller or Rockefeller-Reagan ticket, either way. Reagan remained noncommittal and Agnew, too, went away.

Perhaps the most memorable meeting Reagan had was in South Carolina with Sen. Strom Thurmond, then in his late sixties. "Young man," Thurmond said prophetically to the fifty-seven-year-old Reagan, "you'll be president someday but not this year." Thurmond, like Goldwater, was solidly in Nixon's camp and worked hard and successfully to keep Southern delegates with Nixon even though in their hearts they wanted Reagan.

The June primary marked an end to the carefreeness of national presidential campaigns for the foreseeable future. A nut—or paid assassin?—named Sirhan Sirhan shot and killed Sen. Robert Kennedy the night he won the California Democratic presidential primary. Shortly thereafter, President Johnson decreed that the Secret Service henceforth would provide protective services for any person deemed to be a legitimate candidate. Reagan was so deemed, and within a short time he had a full-fledged, around-the-clock team of Secret Service agents guarding him at home, at the office, and on the road.

The two agents in charge were a couple of New England Irishmen named John Simpson and Edward Hickey. They made a hell of an impression on the guardee. Hickey later resigned from the Secret Service to take charge of all security for the Reagan administration in Sacramento. In the Reagan White House he handled travel logistics, liaison with the military, and communications. Later Reagan named him chairman of the Federal Maritime Commission. He died of a massive heart attack in 1986 and was buried with full military honors in Arlington National Cemetery.

John Simpson remained in the service, and one of President Reagan's early actions was to name him its head.

When I think of Simpson my mind's eye always pictures one minor incident that indicates the kind of no-nonsense approach he had to his job. Reagan had arrived in Miami Beach and was walking into his headquarters hotel when a man, probably a fan, started to move toward him. Simpson saw him out of the corner of his eye and without stopping or turning his head stuck his arm out sideways, put the palm of his hand in the man's face and pushed. The man stumbled backward and Reagan and his entourage kept moving forward, for the most part unaware of the incident. I suppose that if something like that were to happen today some civil rights lawyer would end up filing suit against the Secret Service in general and Simpson in particular.

At the convention Clif White and his men tried valiantly to pry some Nixon delegates loose and recommit them to Reagan. Reagan himself, though still a professed favorite son candidate, met with anyone White considered might switch from Nixon. And some wanted to but either were bound by their state's unit rules or else were fearful of retribution.

On nomination day the late William Knowland came to me with an idea. Knowland was a former U.S. senator, a one-time Senate majority leader, the publisher of the *Oakland Tribune*, and a man who had seen his own presidential hopes dashed when he lost a gubernatorial race to Pat Brown in 1958. At the moment he was a member of the California delegation.

His idea was simple. Reagan should announce that he was no longer just a favorite son and throw his hat in the ring in earnest. I said, let's go see Reagan. We did. Reagan liked the idea and made the decision without further consultation. It was dumb of me to take Knowland to Reagan without bringing in White or Reed or any of the others. And it was dumb of Reagan not to call in White and the others. After all, Knowland had proved in 1958 that he wasn't the smartest politician around. But the decision was made and Reagan became a full-fledged candidate, nearly a year too late and well over a dollar short.

The announcement made no difference in the convention's outcome or in Reagan's vote count. It did anger Reagan's political mentor, the short-tempered and sometimes irascible Holmes Tuttle, who raised all kinds of hell. Reagan, knowing he had goofed, knowing Tuttle had a right to be angry, and not wishing to destroy a friendship, let Tuttle have his say. For my part I was glad Tuttle was unaware of my part in the fiasco.

It also put Reagan's friend and fellow governor, Paul Laxalt of Nevada, in an awkward spot. Even though he was pledged to Nixon, Laxalt had agreed to second Reagan's nomination as a favorite son candidate, but when Reagan announced he was running in earnest Laxalt came to him and said he could no longer second him. It was the proper thing to do but his decision upset the people around Reagan.

The day after Nixon was nominated Reagan told me what he apparently was to tell a number of people in the ensuing two or three weeks, namely, "I'm not disappointed that I didn't get the nomination. I wasn't ready for it."

And that was what had bugged him all along, that was why he had fought becoming an active candidate until he finally got caught up in the excitement of the convention, and that was why he was able to campaign enthusiastically for Nixon and go back to his governorship a happy and relieved man.

A few weeks later I left the governor's office, my dream of making Reagan president in ashes. Fortunately, however, like the Phoenix bird, it kept rising, and a mere twelve years later it hit paydirt. Some dreams don't die easily. Others don't die at all.

In some ways I was lucky to be around for that first run at the presidency. The year preceding the convention had been a rocky one, so rocky that in retrospect it's surprising that I wasn't fired or didn't quit. Either action would have served the governor well.

As background: Ron and Nancy Reagan had spent much of their adult lives in Hollywood, where dwell and work a significant number of homosexuals. As a result, both were tolerant of this sort of aberrant sexual behavior. Indeed, when Reagan was president, Nancy's interior decorator, Ted Graber, and his "significant other" were overnight guests in the White House.

But public attitudes in 1967 were not nearly so sexually liberal as in the 1980s; the closet was a lot more crowded then. Once, at a 1962 press conference, a reporter asked Reagan if he would approve of a homosexual group distributing flyers at a county fair. The usually verbose Reagan gave a curt no.

But Reagan had been in the governor's office barely six months when a problem, that later became a scandal, arose involving alleged homosexuals in high places on his staff. Reagan's first executive secretary (Ed Meese later changed the title to "chief of staff") was Phil Battaglia, a pudgy, balding six-footer in his early thirties who chewed his fingernails to the quick. He was married and the father of two toddlers, both adopted.

Shortly into the Reagan administration Battaglia began to view himself as more than just the chief of staff. At the very least he considered himself the deputy governor, and, as such, often made decisions for the governor without bothering to consult him. His egotism and aggressiveness paralleled in many ways that of a much later Reagan chief of staff, Don Regan. But whereas Regan stuck close to Reagan's side, Battaglia moved out in front, seeking, perhaps subconsciously, to outshine his boss.

As far as I could tell, Reagan was not put off by Battaglia's executive style until his alleged homosexuality was brought to his attention. Battaglia was forced to resign but, in truth, he would have had to go anyway, for in trying to control the governor's office he had lost control of himself, as well as the respect of his peers in the administration.

An innocent victim of the almost hysterical way that Battaglia performed was a young man working as an intern in the governor's office. His name was Jack Kemp, and in the fall and winter he was a professional football player, starring as a quarterback for the Buffalo Bills in the National Football League. Before being traded to the Buffalo Bills Kemp had been the quarterback of the San Diego Chargers. When not playing football he worked for the *San Diego Union*, the flagship of the Copley newspapers, as a public relations representative.

Kemp also was a friend of the *Union*'s editor, Herb Klein, and a conservative Republican already looking down the road to a career in politics. In 1964, when I was covering the California presidential primary race between Goldwater and Rockefeller, Klein sent him to travel with me for a few days so he could get a close-up view of what a political campaign was all about. But in 1967 Klein, a part of Nixon's inner circle, didn't have much direct clout in the Reagan organization so it was another San Diegan, Gordon Luce, Reagan's secretary of business and transportation, who arranged for Kemp to intern in the governor's office in the spring of 1967.

Battaglia was immediately taken by the intelligent, articulate, and handsome football hero. He took Kemp under his wing and had him accompany him whenever he left Sacramento, which was frequently.

Kemp and I later discussed the situation. He had been, he admitted, naive. He was excited, understandably so, when Battaglia made him a kind of personal aide, and in doing so, gave him a firsthand look at the inside workings of the governor's office in the biggest, richest, and most complex state. The two became friends, but nothing more. At times Battaglia cried on his shoulder, disclosing his fears and frustrations, but not his desires, if he had any.

Kemp accepted the trips to Washington and elsewhere as a learning experience, unaware that Battaglia was attempting to keep his presence secret, unaware, too, that the close relationship was causing talk and breeding suspicion in the governor's office. And he compounded his mistakes by going in with Battaglia to buy a cabin at Lake Tahoe. Later he sold his half back to Battaglia, but not before the Washington political gossip columnist, Drew Pearson, had written a completely false column charging that members of Reagan's staff had used it for a homosexual orgy.

This seemed to confirm rumors that Battaglia and a third young man named Richard (Sandy) Quinn, Reagan's scheduling aide, were involved in homosexual activities. The talk had centered around Quinn before Battaglia; ironically, I had discussed the Quinn rumors with Battaglia—which he pooh-poohed.

I am not a homophobe, though I would not want my daughter to marry one, nor my son either, if I had one, but I had two serious concerns about the possible presence of homosexuals or a homosexual ring within the governor's office. To repeat, in 1967 most homosexuals were still in the closet and for good reason. Those on the outside were pretty thoroughly ostracized, except in the arts and entertainment circles. Neither Gary Studds nor Barney Frank, avowed homosexuals, could have been elected to Congress in those years, even from Massachusetts.

My concerns were purely political and they had to do with Reagan. I wanted him to be elected president and I was certain it would hurt his chances if the voters, especially conservatives, who were his base, thought he had surrounded himself with "queers." Because he came out of the Hollywood scene, where homosexuality was almost the norm, I also feared that rumors would insinuate that he, too, was one. In those days that would have killed him politically.

Therefore, with the help of Art Van Court, who was then in charge of the governor's security, an investigation was begun. I discovered shortly that Bill Clark, the cabinet secretary, had heard the rumors and that he and Tom Reed, back in civil life, were also looking into them. We decided to hold a meeting of Reagan aides we knew were heterosexual, trustworthy, and loyal to Reagan. Attending were Clark, Reed, Meese, Van Court, Curtis Patrick, who worked with Van Court, Gordon Luce, and Ed Gillenwaters, who represented California in Washington. I had known Gillenwaters, who initially informed me of the situation, for several years when he was administrative assistant to Rep. Bob Wilson of San Diego, and, in fact, had persuaded Reagan to appoint him to his current position.

We agreed to investigate. We did. And we made the Keystone Cops look good. When Van Court went to investigate Quinn's apartment, he couldn't get in. We tried and failed to bug Battaglia's office. We sent a man to tail Battaglia and Kemp and he lost them even though they didn't know they were being followed. We searched out their room arrangements in a hotel in San Francisco and discovered they took separate, nonadjoining rooms and slept in them all night. Despite Drew Pearson's columns to the contrary, we never took pictures—we could find none to take—and we never taped the sounds and sighs of an orgy—we heard nothing to tape.

But still, we were convinced. We knew in our minds, though no place else for sure, that there was hanky panky; we just couldn't prove it. In August we decided that we would approach the governor with our suspicions. I drafted a report outlining what we thought we knew and what we suspected and what we had heard. Put together, they made a convincing case. Even more convincing, as far as Reagan was concerned, was the fact that the report was presented by men in whom, for the most part, he had developed a great deal of confidence.

The Reagans were staying at the Hotel del Coronado on Coronado Island in San Diego Bay. They had gone there to let the governor recuperate from a prostate operation he'd undergone two weeks before. Eleven of us barged in unannounced. Nancy, who had just finished showering, at our insistence joined us wearing a terrycloth robe with a towel wrapped around her head. Naturally, the Reagans were curious.

I handed each of them a copy of our report. We waited silently as they sat side by side on the sofa in the living room and read. Nancy finished first and gave us a quizzical look. In a moment he too had finished.

Looking up, he quietly asked the old question, "What do we do now?"

The discussion lasted for nearly an hour. At the end Reagan agreed that Battaglia and Quinn would have to go. Kemp, the victim of circumstances, had already left to begin football practice. He would not return.

Despite his innocence, for more than twenty years Kemp was dogged by the rumors, but he faced them down and moved ahead with his career: three more years of football, nine terms in Congress, a run at the presidency, and, at this writing, secretary of housing and urban development. During these years the scandal was resurrected from time to time, but Kemp rode it out with courage and an absolute refusal to let it ruin him, his family, or his career. I have done what I could to help; the hurt done to him and his family perhaps was unavoidable, but on my part it still is a matter of tremendous regret.

After our meeting with the Reagans, those of us who headed back to Sacramento celebrated by getting drunk at the airport and drunker on the airplane, or at least trying to. I know I succeeded pretty well. The recent weeks had been filled with tension and misgivings. We had won a great victory, not only for Reagan and his political future but also for ourselves. But the cost to the three men involved had been terrible. That should have been the end of it, but it wasn't.

Reagan—then and forever after—didn't have the stomach to fire people, Battaglia included. Instead he arranged for Holmes Tuttle and Henry Salvatori to summon Battaglia to a meeting at Tuttle's home in Hancock Park, a rich man's enclave near downtown Los Angeles. There, acting in Reagan's name, they demanded and got Battaglia's reluctant resignation without ever explaining in detail why they wanted it. Battaglia sought to make a deal, a judgeship in turn for his resignation, but it was no dice. No judgeship either.

Meantime, as far as the press and the public were concerned Battaglia had resigned for personal reasons. The ever-compassionate Reagan was determined to do nothing and say nothing that would hurt wives, families, or careers, even if it meant telling one or two white, or at worst, light gray lies.

The Reagans returned to Sacramento on the weekend following our meeting. On Sunday I was contemplating calling him to recommend that he name Clark to succeed Battaglia, when he phoned. He sounded a bit embarrassed, but he plunged bravely ahead and said he thought Clark would be the best person to be executive secretary. I think he was afraid that I wanted the job and didn't want to hurt my feelings. But he wasn't the only person who thought I wasn't qualified for the job; their name was legion, and I was among them.

I told Reagan truthfully that I was as pleased as punch, that Clark was my choice, and that I had been prepared to recommend him.

Clark's laid-back, low-key style quickly brought calm to the governor's office, but for several days it was a nervous place. Upon our return Clark, acting on Reagan's authority, immediately sealed the governor's office as well as Battaglia's. The few Battaglia loyalists, namely Lee Holt, his executive secretary, and Paul Beck, my deputy whose title was press secretary, tried to plot a countercoup, but to no avail. Nobody else wanted to revolt.

A few days after Reagan returned to work I spoke to him about what I considered to be Beck's disloyalty and said I was thinking seriously of firing him (I don't suffer from the Reagan syndrome; I can fire people), but Reagan was reluctant.

"There's been enough upset around here for now," he said. "I think you should keep him on and see how it works out."

Which I did, and it worked out well, with Beck succeeding to my job when I resigned thirteen months later.

Within weeks after leaving, Battaglia was back in town using his Reagan contacts and Reagan's name on behalf of clients. Because we had not put out the word that he had been fired, he was taking advantage of the situation. His continuing presence around the administration was an irritation to those of us who knew the whole story. Nancy was among them.

One day in my presence she asked in exasperation, "Why doesn't someone do something about Phil?"

The question was directed to no one in particular, but clearly she was upset because she thought Battaglia was trading in on what people still believed were his close ties to the governor.

Being a damn fool, I took it upon myself to rectify the situation.
Had I left it alone it probably would have gone away. But maybe not.
Drew Pearson had picked up rumors somewhere and had written several columns, lacking in truth and fact, but certainly titillating. He did
what I thought no reporter or columnist would do in those days,
because nobody that I knew of had—he wrote about a homosexual
scandal. A real ground-breaker for one of the great scandalmongers of
our times.

But before Pearson wrote his columns I had contacted half a dozen
senior California political reporters individually, sworn them to secrecy,
and told them the story. My purpose was to destroy Battaglia's credibility as a member of the Reagan team. I did not think they would have
written the story anyway. Nor did they until it broke elsewhere, which
speaks well for them and for my judgment of them, if not for my
judgment. One, the *Los Angeles Times'* Carl Greenberg, laughed when
I told him my story.

"I wondered how long it would take you guys to find out about
Battaglia," he said, adding that the rumor had been around for years. It
was reassuring to have just a little bit more confirmation.

The summer and fall of 1967 stand out in my memory for three
reasons: our homosexual scandal, Reagan's prostate operation which I
will return to, and the cruise of the *Ship of Fools*, about which ditto.

The cruise, the brainchild of Governor Rockefeller, was a floating
governors conference. It began in New York and ended in the Virgin
Islands. New York is where I discovered that our little scandal was
making the rounds. My friend, Karl Fleming, informed me as the cruise
got underway that he was aware of it and that something would appear in
"Periscope," *Newsweek*'s rumor and scandal page. That didn't make me
feel very good since I knew he hadn't gotten it from me, meaning that
somebody else was talking.

Still, I was denying to one and all that there was any truth to the
rumors when an old friend, David Broder, took me aside.

"Lyn," he said, "you told me about it."

I was flabbergasted. Dumbfounded, too. I didn't remember having
done so then; I don't remember now.

"I couldn't have," I gasped.

"You did," he insisted.

I knew he wasn't lying. I don't think he has a lie in him.

"If you say so," I conceded.

That worried me. If I didn't remember telling Broder, whom else had I told? I still don't know. But I do know that I was talking too much in the naive belief that no one would write the story.

By the time we returned to Sacramento the story was out, but Reagan, a genuinely kind man, was determined not to give it credibility, even if he had to lie. And lie he did until it finally went away. But before that happened I got caught in the lie and I was in trouble, not so deep with Ron but real deep with Nancy, who believed that I had damaged her husband's credibility and, perhaps, even his career. And she could well have been right.

Drew Pearson's so-called expose ran on October 31, 1967, the day of Reagan's weekly press conference, the Nofziger innovation of which I was very proud, but which we could have done without for once. The press homed in on the Pearson column. Reagan denied there was any validity to the rumors, then turned to me.

"Want to confirm it, Lyn?" he asked.

I didn't hesitate. "Confirmed," I lied, quickly joining Reagan in a significant loss of credibility. It seems to me still, after all these years, that Reagan and I, all of us, would have been better off if we'd followed a basic dictum in dealing with the press, one that I knew and preached: If you can't tell 'em the truth, don't tell 'em anything.

That night Reagan had to fly to Los Angeles and I went with him. We were in a chartered business jet that landed at the Santa Monica municipal airport. The press was waiting for us. Before getting off I asked him, "What are you going to say when they ask you about the Pearson column?"

He replied lightly: "If Drew Pearson comes to California he'd better not spit on the sidewalk."

"Ha ha," I said. "Funny. Just don't say it out there."

He said of course he wouldn't and we got off the plane and went to meet the press. The first question was about the Pearson column.

And once more I died, as Reagan snarled, "If he ever comes to California he'd better not spit on the sidewalk."

For those too young to remember, you used to be arrested for spitting on the sidewalk. Today, spitting on the sidewalk is probably protected ᴖendment on the grounds that it is a form of artistic

ᴖne questions off as soon as possible, but the stories the next
ᴖudn't do our case any good. Still, the story eventually did go away,
mostly because in those days the media, with the exception of the
scandalmongers, were loathe to deal with the subject of homosexuality.

I don't think most reporters would hesitate today. And that is too bad.
A certain amount of kindness and compassion in the news business has
all but disappeared, largely since Watergate. Reporters and columnists
and editors, for the most part, no longer seem to care if they hurt people.
Indeed, many of them seem to go out of their way to do just that.
Somehow, they have come to believe that mean and cruel reporting is
better reporting, that the ruination of careers and the destruction of
families and family relationships are acceptable parts of the game. In
this book I have used names because those names are generally known.
I have treated those involved as fairly as I know how.

Though the story had pretty much disappeared by late fall Nancy's
anger at me continued to burn brightly into the new year. I knew that
both she and Reagan's fat cat friends, including Tuttle and Salvatori,
were leaning on him to fire me. So was Stu Spencer. Stu had brought me
into the Reagan campaign, but he now worried that I had lost my
effectiveness and credibility and, besides, he wanted to put a close
friend of his in my job.

The friend, also a friend of mine, Travis Cross, had worked for
Oregon Gov. Mark Hatfield and was one of the fine press secretary/
politician types in the Republican party. He quickly made it clear that he
didn't want the job at my expense. And Reagan refused to budge despite
the constant prodding of Nancy and friends, and because, among other
reasons, Bill Clark and Ed Meese continued to support me strongly.

But finally I'd had enough, enough of the stories and rumors saying I
was about to be fired, enough of the behind-my-back attacks by Nancy
and the others, enough, period. I drafted a letter of resignation, which
merely said that it was time for me to return to my job at the Copley
Newspapers, and took it to Reagan. He read it and looked up.

"This isn't the real reason, is it?" he asked. I learned later he had
been forewarned by Clark.

"If you must know, no," I conceded.

He waited for me to elaborate. So I did.

"I'm tired of Nancy cutting me up," I said. "It isn't doing me any good and it isn't doing you any good. It just isn't worth it."

As usual he was totally loyal to her. "She's not doing that," he remarked.

"Yes, she is," I insisted.

"Well, if she is, she won't anymore," he promised. And added, "I don't want you to go."

We talked a little longer and I told him what I really wanted was to stay on until after the election of 1968, but then it would be time for me to leave.

Those who think that Ronald Reagan is run by Nancy should know that almost immediately I ceased hearing about demands that I be fired. In fact, it wasn't long before she and I were back on speaking terms, where we have pretty much remained ever since. But months later, when I finally did leave, stories appeared saying that Nancy had had me fired. I knew better and she knew better and everyone knew better, but some members of the press didn't want to know better.

In the summer of 1967, as our investigation into Battaglia and friends continued, disaster of another sort struck Reagan. The after-effects of the flu that had felled him at the beginning of his campaign for governor in late February of 1966 dogged him for the next year and a half, giving rise to two false rumors. One was that he was lazy, which he wasn't, although at times overt boredom gave that impression. The other was that he lacked endurance, which during the flu period was true enough, but thereafter was nothing but a figment of reportorial fiction. Indeed, in the presidential campaigns of 1976 and 1980 Reagan kept to a schedule that wore out and surprised large numbers of much younger press and staff. It did not surprise those who knew Reagan well. For years he had exercised daily, swum frequently, and on his ranch, cleared brush, chopped wood, and ridden horseback.

But in 1966 the flu not only laid Reagan on his back in February but a lingering urinary tract infection sapped his strength during the entire campaign. The truth is, we didn't give him enough time to recuperate and we ran him too hard when he resumed campaigning. Exhaustion led to the few mistakes he made that year—when he walked out on the Negro Republicans, when I was forced to cut off a small, informal press conference because he was becoming confused, and when he evinced irritation and short temper so unlike his usually placid and easy-going self.

In April of 1966 Tom Reed and I accompanied Reagan to Detroit where Reed, who, like me, was already viewing Reagan as a possible presidential candidate, had arranged for Reagan to address the Detroit Economic Club. An effective speech before this prestigious group would do much to counter the all-too-common belief that Reagan was nothing but a dumb actor, and it would generate contributions to the campaign.

Reagan was due to speak at noon the day after we arrived. As usual he went to bed around 10 P.M, but he awoke a few hours later in serious discomfort, roused Reed who found a doctor, and he in turn gave Reagan some pills and told him to stay off his feet. Which, of course, Reagan couldn't do because he had a speech to give. And give it he did—impressively, despite more than a little pain.

Over the years, as a politician, Reagan always reacted well under pressure. This was the first instance I had seen, but I soon came to expect it.

After his speech we bundled him onto the business jet and hurried him back to his bed in Pacific Palisades where he spent the week recuperating. But he never entirely shook the bug, and by August of 1967 his doctor was recommending a procedure that was in effect a prostate operation. Due, apparently, to the lingering infection the prostate had become enlarged, thus narrowing the outlet from the bladder. In addition, tiny, seed-like bladder stones were further impeding the outflow.

There was no sign of malignancy and the doctors were confident they could handle the medical problem. But they had handed me what I perceived to be a political problem—the term "prostate operation."

To me a prostate operation was an old man's operation. Young men, vigorous men, didn't have them. I didn't want the public to think of Reagan as an old man which would hurt his chances of winning the Republican presidential nomination in 1968. Since Nancy was not yet mad at me I discussed the matter with her and found she was in complete agreement. She was with me when I explained my problem to the doctor.

"Give me as detailed an explanation of this as you can without ever using the word 'prostate,' " I pleaded.

He did and it stood me in good stead. Reagan was operated on at St. John's Hospital in Santa Monica. During the week he spent in the hospital I explained Reagan's operation to the press in great and knowledgeable detail. I told the truth but I never once used the word "prostate." The major papers such as the *Los Angeles Times* and the *New York Times* never bothered to assign a medical reporter to the story. Why, I don't know, but, for sure, I didn't push for one.

All went well until the day Reagan checked out of the hospital. That day I took a call from a reporter on the *Ventura Star-News*, hardly a major newspaper. He wanted to talk about the operation, so I went through my spiel.

When I had finished he asked, "Well, isn't that a prostate operation?"

I gulped, muttered "Oh, shit," and said, "Not exactly."

Surprisingly, he let it go at that. I never did see what he wrote, but if he wrote "prostate," it never caught anyone's attention. And Reagan emerged from the hospital still a young man.

I viewed it then, and now, as a great victory. After all, anyone can lie to the press, but confusing them with the truth is an art I am proud to have mastered.

By early fall Reagan was well enough to attend the annual National Governors Conference, hosted each year by a different governor. In 1967 the host was New York Gov. Nelson Rockefeller.

There tends to be a rivalry among governors when staging events that will be attended by their fellow governors. The fancier or more one-of-a-kindish the better. Rockefeller's was both fancy and unique. It was held aboard the cruise ship USS *Independence* which sailed from New York City to St. Thomas in the Virgin Islands.

Reporters accurately, if somewhat self-consciously, dubbed the vessel the *Ship of Fools* from the novel of the same name. The fools consisted of governors with wives and families, staff members, special guests, lobbyists, hangers-on, and, of course, a large contingent of the press, who somehow thought the term did not apply to them.

Governors meet frequently among themselves, all fifty of them, or in smaller groups, such as the Republican governors or the Western governors. The meetings are largely excuses to get out of town for a while at the taxpayers' expense, and reporters who attend on expense accounts write anything they can get hold of to justify their presence. Thus, great oaks from little acorns grow.

I do not attend meetings, except under duress. Bill Clark, on the other hand, being a good government man and conscientious besides, not only goes but also pays attention, as does Ed Meese. In those days Clark also was charged with occasionally nudging the fellow sitting next to him to keep him awake. The governor of California did not then or ever suffer boring meetings alertly.

Late in the morning of the first day's first meeting I strolled in to see what, if anything, was happening, knowing full well that nothing was. Clark beckoned me over and handed me a two-and-a-half page cable that I saw immediately was from President Lyndon Johnson and addressed to Price Daniel, a Democratic former governor of Texas who was serving as Johnson's representative to the governors. He had a reputation as an honest man which always bothered me because it never gave me the opportunity to ask what would be a fitting question about almost any politician: "What Price Daniel?"

"Where'd you get this?" I asked.

"It came in this," he explained, showing me a large manila envelope with Reagan's name on it. "Read it."

I scanned it hurriedly. It was largely a rehash of Johnson's Vietnam policies. I handed it back.

"I don't see anything exciting," I commented.

"Read the last couple of paragraphs," he urged.

I did. And now it made sense. Johnson was instructing Daniel to go into the governors' den and line them up in support of his Vietnam actions and policies. It was a bit of a surprise and it showed desperation on the president's part because a smart pol like him should have known it's virtually impossible to get governors to agree on anything, even if constructive.

"Why would they give this to you?" I asked.

"It was probably a mistake," he admitted.

"Before you give it to Daniel let me make a couple of copies," I said. "I might want to do something with it."

Late that afternoon a reporter approached me. "Clark says you have something that might be interesting," he said hopefully.

I fished out a copy of the cable. Other reporters gathered around, wanting to know where I had gotten it. I played coy and refused to say. They found Daniel, who charged with phony righteous indignation that we'd stolen it. I denied it and finally admitted it had been delivered to

Reagan by mistake. But it was too late. The press didn't believe me. It made a better story if I were perceived to have stolen it.

Clearly, they didn't know that I'd have been afraid to steal it, afraid of being caught. Besides, I didn't learn until the next day where one went if one were looking for a cable to steal. Actually, the press should have been grateful to me. I'd given them the only decent story to come out of the conference.

In the meantime, despite the distractions, the business of government went on, thanks to the good work of the goo-goos—Bill Clark, Ed Meese, Alex Sheriffs, the education secretary, and a slew of others. But don't ask me what they were doing; I was too busy trying to make Reagan president and to extricate myself from one self-inflicted jam after another.

The first time I quit Ronald Reagan's staff was on October 1, 1968. I had worked for him for thirty-two months all told, including the 1966 campaign, the transitional phase between his victory over Pat Brown and his inauguration, and close to two years while he was in office. It was long enough.

I walked out of the governor's office and into Max Rafferty's dying campaign for the United States Senate. Rafferty was an easy man to dislike. For one thing, he was not only a demagogue at heart, but an effective one. For another, like a lot of overly bright people, his judgment wasn't on a par with his intellect. Finally, if you hadn't gotten to know and understand him, he appeared arrogant and sometimes even rude. He was, in fact, both a good deal of the time.

But I liked him. Most of the time. And at one time I had high hopes that he could be elected a United States senator. Not that I thought he'd be a great senator. He was too much a maverick for that and too outspoken. And then, as I said, there was the matter of his judgment.

But Rafferty was the best rabble-rouser I have ever known, better than Reagan, better than most television evangelists. He could bring an audience to its feet cheering, or he could bring tears to your eyes, or he could start a riot. And I've seen him do all three. I visualized him not as a statesman in the Senate but as a great Republican money raiser.

Rafferty won the California Republican senatorial nomination in June of 1968. At the time he was state superintendent of public instruction, elected in a voter rebellion against the state's liberal education policies. He had upset the incumbent, Sen. Thomas Kuchel, a two-term moderate, largely because the conventional California Republican party no longer existed; it had been taken over by (gasp) conservatives. Kuchel was serving as Senate Republican Whip when he lost to Rafferty, which goes to show how much an in-house title is worth to an electorate that most of the time doesn't pay much attention to government and even more of the time doesn't understand how it works.

By the time Rafferty decided to run for the Senate he had become the darling of his party's conservative wing, now in decline but then in full blossom. It had beaten Nelson Rockefeller with Barry Goldwater in the 1964 presidential primary and had come back two years later with Ronald Reagan to take control of the party and the state government. In 1968, it fully expected to send Rafferty to Washington where he would join California conservative Sen. George Murphy, another former movie star turned politician.

But during the summer and early fall the Rafferty campaign had gone awry and by October it was in desperate straits. It was broke and its campaign manager, Bob McGee, had been fired. There were other problems, too, not the least of which was that Max was being beaten about the head and feet from two different sources for two different reasons.

In late September someone had prepared a speech for him that he gave without reading in advance. What it said, or implied, was that his opponent, State Comptroller Alan Cranston, was a virtual communist. A good politician, Cranston seized on Rafferty's speech and went up and down the state beating his breast and claiming that Rafferty had called him a communist outright.

The news media, which for the most part despised Rafferty, smelled blood and jumped into the fray. Rafferty denied he'd called Cranston a communist, said he hadn't meant to call him a communist, said he wasn't a communist, said whatever came to mind. Nothing helped— perhaps because he insisted that anyone who'd called for an end to the bombing of North Vietnam, as Cranston had, "came perilously close to treason."

About the same time, the *Long Beach Independent* ran a series on Rafferty's nonservice in wartime. He had flat feet and was 4-F, but the *Independent* said his feet weren't really so bad and that Rafferty had carried a cane until the war ended, whereupon he had thrown it away. Unfortunately, Rafferty didn't have much in the way of an answer.

At any rate, when I joined up on October 1 the Rafferty campaign had been stalled for a good part of September and generally was in bad shape. In fact, that is why I joined it. I should have done so earlier and could have because the little group that jointly chaired the Rafferty campaign had approached me in August, but I had turned them down. Like most people, at the time I thought Rafferty was a shoo-in, as he should have been. Besides, I didn't really know him and what I did know led me to believe he was a jerk—our jerk, to be sure, but still a jerk.

But in late September Tom Reed, by now California's Republican national committeeman, went to see Governor Reagan with the results of a poll he'd had taken. It showed Rafferty losing by twenty-five points which was bad enough, but it also showed he was hurting Republican chances of making gains in and perhaps controlling the state legislature, something Reagan with still two years to go on his first term dearly wanted.

By this time I had submitted my resignation effective September 30, which wasn't very smart because I had no job and no money while I did have a wife and two children. But I was tired of government (I tire of government easily) and I had come to believe that Reagan would never get to be president. And I guess I figured the Lord would provide, which, unsurprisingly, He did.

So, when Reed, after talking to Reagan, approached me and said they would really appreciate it if I would join him in trying to make sense out of the Rafferty campaign, I unhesitatingly agreed.

I think it was Ring Lardner who once wrote about the baseball players who "could have" made it to the major leagues, but somehow never did. Well, Max Rafferty could have been elected U.S. senator but somehow never was.

He wasn't, I think, because Reed and I got to the Rafferty campaign about a month too late. Too many things had gone wrong and there just wasn't enough time. The men running the campaign by committee, Dick Darling, Frank Adams, John Bohn, and Ed McCoubry, were truly glad to see us. They were fine men and good conservatives and they knew they were in a real bind.

To our dismay, we discovered right away that they had never invited

Kuchel's supporters into the campaign and, consequently, they were sitting on the bench sulking. Many of them were planning to vote for Cranston (and many probably did) out of spite, out of frustration, and out of a feeling that Rafferty would probably be the worst and most dangerous senator the state had ever produced.

Liberals often feel that way about conservatives and vice versa. Some were scared to death that a Senator Rafferty might some day wind up a President Rafferty, a scary thought indeed. But Rafferty's conservative backers were on a holy mission and they thought they could win the general election the same way they had won the primary—they wanted nothing to do with the moderate Republicans they had just whipped.

In contrast, two years earlier, the day after Reagan had won his primary race big against George Christopher, he and his people were on the phone inviting the Christopher leadership into the campaign in positions important enough to heal wounded pride and instill new enthusiasm. As for the Rafferty campaign, though we tried, it was too late to reunite the party.

From October 1 to election day was an exhausting five weeks. But exhilarating. I'd been aboard less than a week when I screwed up pretty good. Retired Air Force Gen. Curtis LeMay, then one of the great heroes of the political Right, was an inactive member of the Rafferty Advisory Committee. But in early October he agreed to be the vice presidential running mate of George Wallace, the candidate of the American Independent party.

I immediately put out a press release in Rafferty's name throwing LeMay off the Advisory Committee. The only thing was, I forgot to tell Rafferty who was campaigning somewhere out in the great California boondocks. When the press asked him about the announcement he rightly said he didn't know anything about it. Needless to say, he wasn't very happy when he found out what, according to Lyn Nofziger, he had done.

Fortunately, the blame fell on me and not on him, but it briefly made the campaign organization look even more disorganized than it was. After that I determined to travel with the candidate and keep in touch with the campaign by phone instead of the other way around.

Very early on I asked the candidate to throw away the five speeches he had prepared during the summer to give throughout the campaign.

"But I get standing ovations," he objected.

"You're preaching to the choir," I replied.

"What will I talk about?" he asked.

I told him there were two things the people were interested in: violence on the college campuses and Cesar Chavez's grape boycott, a symbol of labor unrest.

"I don't want you to talk about anything," I stressed, "except these two things and I want you to do it extemporaneously because you are the best extemporaneous speaker I've ever heard." Which was true.

"But, Lyn," he protested, "these are not national issues."

I told him that I didn't care and that the voters didn't care—they don't differentiate between state and federal issues, they just know what makes them mad. I added that if anyone questioned him on the subject he could say he would introduce legislation making them federal issues. He did what I asked him to do and he was most effective.

Very quickly the perception of him began to change from demagogue to concerned citizen, worrying about the same things that were worrying the average voter. My proudest moment was the day we took him into Santa Barbara County where the Republicans were mainly liberal. He spoke off the cuff and with great sincerity and when he was through they gave him a standing ovation and on election day he carried the county.

But time ran out on Rafferty. On October 1 he was more than twenty points behind in the polls. On election day he lost by four points. Close, but no cigar. Anyone who's ever been in politics can tell you of the one or two races they should have won, but didn't. This was one of mine.

There are a couple of incidents in that campaign that still stand out in my memory. One was when Richard Nixon, once again the Republican candidate for president, came to Los Angeles and agreed to do a television spot for Rafferty. We prepared him a script but he didn't want it; he would do it extemporaneously. It was a one-minute spot. He stood before the cameras concentrating on what he would say and when he was ready he gave the go-ahead to begin rolling. On his first try he ran a few seconds long. The second time he was a few seconds short. The third time he was right on the money. Most politicians don't do that well reading from a timed script. But most politicians are not as disciplined as Richard Nixon.

And another moment. When Rafferty was on the road campaigning it was not unusual for members of his small traveling party to gather in his room after the last event of the day to have a drink or two. He primarily drank brandy on ice and since that usually was all that was available so did the rest of us. It is not a bad drink, if that's all there is.

Rafferty, who was nothing if not erudite, loved to show off his knowledge of literature and poetry, especially high-falutin' poetry such as Shakespeare.

One night he turned to me and said, "I'll bet you can't name the saddest poem in the English language."

I didn't have the vaguest idea, figuring it was something by Browning or Keats or Shelley. But having nothing to lose I made a quick guess.

"Little Boy Blue," I said, pulling Eugene Field's tear-jerker out of thin air.

Max's jaw dropped. "That's right," he said, almost as amazed as I that I had stumbled onto the answer. "But I can recite it."

"So can I," I said, and promptly did.

There is one other incident I remember from that campaign. We were in San Diego and Rafferty spoke that night to a crowd of about two hundred. In the back of the room a small group of Vietnam war protesters began heckling. It was their mistake. Max stood at the podium and began taunting them, giving much better than he was getting. Finally, a big young man could take it no more and charged the podium. Max just stood there and waited for him and I was sure there was going to be a fight, in which Rafferty would have been thoroughly whipped.

But the big kid, who claimed to be a marine Vietnam veteran, failed to reckon with a man named Norman Moore, a retired Los Angeles policeman who was serving as Rafferty's bodyguard. He was about five feet, nine inches tall, about five inches shorter and thirty pounds lighter than the ex-marine.

Moore was standing smoking a cigaret as the young man rushed toward Max. Without taking the cigaret from his mouth he grabbed the young man as he charged by, flipped him onto the floor on his stomach, yanked his arms behind his back, and clamped handcuffs on him, all in about five seconds. When it was over he was still calmly puffing on his cigaret, the ash undisturbed.

After he lost the Senate race Max went back to being state superintendent of public instruction. In the spring of 1969 he decided that the following year he would run for a third four-year term. He asked me if I would run his campaign. By now I had set up in Sacramento a political public relations firm in partnership with a former and future Reagan advance man, Bob Tuttle.

This is a different Tuttle from the Bob Tuttle, the son of Holmes Tuttle, who became head of personnel in the Reagan White House. To avoid confusion I refer to them as Real Bob and White House Bob. Real Bob is a lawyer by profession but a politician by preference which is a good thing because I don't think I would want him to be my lawyer.

Real Bob and I, along with one of my secretaries from the governor's office, Karen Hanson, now Karen Munro, the wife of the secretary of state of the state of Washington, had set up offices on the ninth floor of a downtown Sacramento office building. We had so little to do that Bob and I spent many hours sailing doughnut-shaped pieces of paper out our windows, watching the drafts carry them sometimes clean out of sight and once all the way around the building. Great fun but no mon.

So when Rafferty offered us the chance to run his reelection campaign we leaped at it. But a few months later I was in Washington working as a deputy assistant to President Nixon for congressional relations leaving Tuttle to run the Rafferty campaign. I felt badly about leaving but Rafferty was gracious about it.

"You've been summoned by the president of the United States," he said. "You cannot turn him down."

My leaving made no difference. Rafferty's time was past. He was no longer a conservative hero. And he had never really been a member of the Reagan team, partly because he had never been a Reagan sycophant and partly because those around Reagan thought he was a bit of a kook. Which he was.

And as the California conservatives rallied to the Reagan reelect campaign 1970 Rafferty was left pretty much on the outside. In addition Reed and his protégé, Paul Haerle, who along with Spencer Roberts were running Reagan's reelection campaign, refused to respond to Tuttle's pleas for help or to involve Reagan in any way in Rafferty's campaign. But it didn't really matter.

Regardless, and even though I was working in the White House, I was irritated because I thought they were—and they were—abandoning both Rafferty and Tuttle. After the election Reed came to Washington and asked me to have a drink with him at one of the world's dreariest mausoleums, the Metropolitan Club. His purpose, it turned out, was to warn me that if I tried to get even with him or Haerle for refusing to help Rafferty "I will make sure that you never work in California again."

That was a good joke and I laughed, which I think didn't surprise him. Today, more than twenty years later, we are still friends.

After he lost, Rafferty accepted an offer from Gov. George Wallace of Alabama to become dean of students at Troy State University where he stayed until his death in 1982. I still look back on Rafferty's defeat by Cranston with regret. The world might not have been the better if he had won but it couldn't have been the worse.

4

Working for Nixon

IF RONALD REAGAN is responsible for my entering politics, Bryce Harlow taught me that politics can be an honorable and decent profession. Harlow was the man who brought me into Richard Nixon's White House in the summer of 1969 and remained my friend until he died on February 17, 1987.

I missed his memorial service because of airplane misadventures but consoled myself with the knowledge that I had seen him a few days before and had made it a point to visit him from time to time at his home at Harper's Ferry, West Virginia, after he could no longer come down to Washington. When Bryce died he'd had emphysema for nearly ten years, the result of smoking three packs of cigarets daily for close to forty years. But smoke and tar had been unable to touch the greatness of his heart or the sharpness of his mind. We knew he was dying, but that knowledge, while perhaps making his passing easier on friends and relatives, did nothing to lessen the sense of loss.

If anybody who knew Bryce Harlow had to name the three nicest men he had ever known Bryce would have been one of them. Unequivocally.

If anybody who ever knew Bryce Harlow had to name the three wisest men he had ever known Bryce would have been one of them. Unequivocally.

If anybody who ever knew Bryce Harlow had to name one of the three wittiest, smartest, sharpest men he had ever known Bryce would have been one of them, too.

He was only five feet four inches tall, and I suspect he had to wear shoes to get that high, but in any country where they measure men from the neck up he was a giant.

I loved Bryce Harlow, as did hundreds of others in both parties who work in the vineyards of politics and government that lie in and surround Washington. He brought me into the Nixon White House, but I loved him anyway. Over the years I have found it amusing that he, one of the world's nicest men, brought in both Lyn Nofziger and Chuck Colson, although I concede that the original Chuck Colson made me look like a softy.

Bryce worked for both Eisenhower and Nixon and also served as an unofficial counsel to Jerry Ford whom he had known from his first days in the Congress. At one time he considered Ford among his closest friends.

The tragedy of Bryce Harlow is that he never wrote a book. He didn't believe in it. He was a gentleman in the truest sense of the word. He believed things said and things done in confidence should be kept that way.

The book Harlow could have written would have been a book of marvelous insights into the characters and deeds of the prominent men of our times. It would have been a book of anecdotes, of funny and illustrative stories, a book that would have shed new light on the politics and the political figures of our time.

I first met Harlow in 1958. I had come to Washington as a correspondent for the Copley Newspapers, which in those days were unabashedly, unashamedly, and overtly Republican, as were Bob Richards, the bureau chief, Frank Macomber, and I. Periodically, Richards had lunch with Harlow, Jerry Persons, and other members of Eisenhower's White House staff, and it was through Richards that I met Harlow.

During the Republican out-years of 1961 to 1969 I would see Harlow from time to time but we were not close. But when we bumped into each other at the Kentucky Derby in 1969 he greeted me like an old friend. I was, I discovered, the answer to one of his problems. It was only by chance that either of us was at the Derby. I was handling the press operation for a meeting of the Republican Governors Association that was being hosted by Louie Nunn, a rare Republican governor of Kentucky.

I had left the Reagan governor's office in October of 1968 and was involved in a not-very-successful political public relations business in Sacramento. Reagan that year was chairman of the association and Tom Reed, who was handling political chores for him, was nice enough to throw a bone my way. As a result, I was in Lexington helping Nunn's man, Jim Host, put the finishing touches on preparations for the meeting. The highlight of the affair was to be the attendance of the governors at the Derby, for whom a special box had been set aside. As icing on the cake the country's new Republican president, Richard Nixon, was invited and decided to attend, the only president ever to do so.

Nixon came with a full entourage, including Secret Service men, advance men replete with walky talkies and ear plugs, and some of his senior staff, including Harlow. I had banned the working press from the governors' box so I could enjoy the races and talk to friends and acquaintances.

President Nixon, whom I had known as a reporter since 1958, was friendly and gracious. So was Harlow, and before long he took me to one side.

"What are you doing these days?" he asked.

"Political public relations," I replied, not mentioning that my clients were few and far between.

"Does this mean you're out of politics?" he asked.

"I hope not," I said. "I hope it means that I'm right in the middle of it. Why?"

"The president has a job he wants done. It's an impossible job but he's told me to find a man to do it. I think you might be that man."

"What is it?" I asked, intrigued or, rather, excited. I had been asked by others, notably Herb Klein and Bob Finch, if I were interested in joining the Nixon administration. A bit arrogantly I had said I was not interested in being the press secretary to the secretary of agriculture or anything like that, but if they had a job that was exciting and challenging I might be tempted. And now here was Harlow talking about just such a job.

The president, he explained, didn't think he was getting enough vocal support out of the Congress. He wanted someone who could change that, someone who could get members to praise him when he said or did something worth praising, defend him from his attackers, usually but not always Democrats, and attack his enemies, again usually but not always Democrats.

It was indeed a difficult job but I quickly said I'd like to give it a try. After an exchange of calls and letters it was decided that I would go to the White House. Then one day he called me with concern in his voice.

"If you come back here will you have to talk to the president?"

Aha, I said to myself, if I tell him yes he's not going to want me because he'll think the president has better things to do than talk to me and that I'm a prima donna or at least a fathead besides.

"No," I said. "As long as I can talk to the person who talks to the president." By which, of course, I meant Harlow.

That seemed to satisfy him because shortly thereafter I was summoned to Washington for what turned out to be a two-hour meeting with Harlow and Bob Haldeman, Nixon's tough, bullyish, but competent chief of staff.

I had known Haldeman from California. When Reagan became governor Haldeman, a UCLA graduate, was president of the University of California Alumni Association and as such sat as an ex officio member of the university Board of Regents along with Reagan and the lieutenant governor, Robert Finch.

Finch, a liberal Republican, and Reagan were not close, but he and Haldeman were buddies and when a vacancy opened for a full term on the Regents, he wanted Haldeman to fill it. The trouble was, Finch didn't have any real friends in the governor's office. In desperation he came to me and I, in turn, told the governor we ought to appoint Haldeman.

My reasoning was simple. I wanted Finch to owe us. I didn't want him cutting Reagan behind his back and creating problems for us with the liberal Republicans in the legislature. And in fairness to Finch, he had asked for almost nothing else.

I explained all this to the governor and assured him that Haldeman had pledged that we could have his vote at Regent meetings if needed. As a result, despite the objections of other staff members, including

Alex Sheriffs, the governor's education aide, Reagan appointed Haldeman to the board.

Although I never said anything to him I always figured Haldeman
knew how his appointment had come about and, perhaps because of
this, all during my time in the Nixon administration he treated me better
than most people, which some old Nixon staffers will say doesn't mean
much. But I even liked the man.

At the conclusion of the meeting with him and Harlow, Haldeman
said one thing I will always appreciate.

"The FBI will be doing a background check on you so if there is
anything in your past you don't want anyone to know about just tell us
you don't want the job and nobody will think any the less of you."

"Have at it," I said.

And in mid-July I arrived at the White House as a deputy assistant to
the president for congressional relations, reporting to Harlow. Titles
meant little in the Nixon White House. In the congressional relations
shop deputy assistants outranked special assistants but there were special assistants all over the White House who outranked me in terms of
real influence and their ability to deal directly with the president.

One of the things I've discovered is that out in the real world there is
something special about the term "special assistant." It has a more
important ring than just plain "assistant" and nobody ever heard of a
deputy assistant. I've been introduced to dozens of audiences as a
former "special assistant" to either Nixon or Reagan, even though I
have never held the title. Nothing "special" about old Nofziger, or so
I've been told.

Three things happened that month, two of which had a major impact
on the world, the other on me. Teddy Kennedy had a disastrous cookout
at a place called Chappaquiddick. Neil Armstrong went moon-walking.
And I went to work at the Nixon White House. My job, however, was
not the usual lobbying job congressional affairs staffers are involved in.
It was a propaganda job. My assignment was to persuade members of
the House and Senate to praise the president when he did well, or even
when he didn't, to support him vocally in the things he was attempting
to do, and to attack those who attacked him.

Nixon knew better than any president in my time the need of a
president for vocal support. He also knew that a president who keeps

turning the other cheek to his political enemies will soon run out of cheeks to turn.

The week I arrived was the week a bright young fellow named John Sears departed, the loser in a power struggle with Atty. Gen. John Mitchell. I felt sorry for Sears then. I understand Mitchell better now. I'm glad he won that one.

The word went around town that I had been brought in to bolster Nixon's conservative flank. And the word went around among the bright young men in the West Wing that the Reagan spy had arrived in the Nixon White House. I never really figured that out until it didn't matter anymore, but still, I was a little surprised that at the beginning I was treated a lot like Rodney Dangerfield. I got no respect.

And not much help or cooperation. Part of it was understandable. Harlow was extremely busy. I was not only a latecomer, but seemingly not really part of Harlow's staff. They were lobbyists, pushing administration legislation, and about the time I arrived their offices, all but Harlow's, were moved to the East Wing of the White House while I was quartered in the Old Executive Office Building, across West Executive Avenue from the West Wing and Harlow. And I was doing things that had almost nothing to do with what they were doing, which was fortunate, because lobbying is not one of my talents.

Harlow's other two deputies—I was the third—were Bill Timmons and Ken Belieu. Timmons was an old Young Republican leader whom I had known from my days as a reporter. He had worked on the Hill as well as in politics and campaigns. He was one of the class acts in the Nixon White House. Belieu was another. He had lost a leg below the knee in Korea and wore a prosthesis. I told him once he was the only man I knew who when he put his foot in his mouth got splinters in his tongue. He was kind enough to laugh. Harlow, an old friend, had brought him into the Nixon White House at the onset. Now, six months later, he and Timmons and their staffs were busy implementing Nixon's congressional priorities and were not—naturally—paying much attention to the new guy who had come aboard to do "different things."

Larry Higby was one of the young men in the White House who fetched and carried for Haldeman. He grew up to be a pretty decent sort, but it took a while. At the time of my arrival he was still impressed with his own importance. The White House does that to many people: it's the proximity to power, the being just down the hall or across the street from the Oval Office. Of course some people, Mike Deaver comes to mind, arrive already self-important, and the White House merely swells an already overblown ego.

Haldeman told Higby to take care of me. He did. He found me a dingy, much in need of paint, raggedy carpeted "temporary" office in the Old Executive Office Building. A day or two later he sent someone from the General Services Administration staff to swear me in. It was indeed an impressive ceremony, just him and me in a shabby, dirty room. Somehow it never made the papers.

By midweek, since no one had volunteered to help me, I decided I'd better find a secretary. So I called an old friend, James E. (Johnny) Johnson, the vice chairman of the Civil Service Commission. Johnny was/is very black, one of the most engaging, decent, gentlemanly people I have ever known, and a devout Christian. He later became an assistant secretary of the navy.

Johnny told me once his mother was part Indian and I said, "Yeah, Blackfoot."

He had been the marines' first black senior grade warrant officer. When he retired he sold insurance in Orange County, California, hardly a black ghetto, and shortly became a millionaire. The guilt complex of middle-class whites manifests itself in many ways including the purchase of lots of life insurance.

Johnson is that relative rarity—a competent, conservative, color-blind, black man. In 1967 he was just what the Reagan administration in Sacramento was looking for and shortly he was named head of the California Veterans Administration. Two years later he was just what the new Nixon administration was looking for—a competent, conservative, color-blind black man and shortly he was named vice chairman of the Civil Service Commission.

As an aside and knowing it will offend old-line Nixon haters, the Nixon administration had a policy of seeking out and appointing blacks, including such quality individuals as Gloria Toote, John Wilks, and Arthur Fletcher. Gloria Toote, a New York lawyer, later had the courage to defy Vice President Nelson Rockefeller and New York Republican Chairman Richard Rosenbaum and second Ronald Reagan's nomination for president at the 1976 Republican National Convention. She did the same in 1980.

Even so, and though he let it be known he wanted her, she never was given a major role in the Reagan administration. Reagan did not follow through on personnel matters, the one area of government in which he was uncomfortable and even a bit timid. At this late day I still wonder if the sneaky, snakey hand of the Republican party's Eastern liberal establishment managed to pull enough strings to keep her out.

When I called Johnson I told him, "Johnny, I need a secretary and I want to confound all these libs who think all right wingers are racists so find me a good Negro secretary." This was 1968, when blacks were still calling themselves Negroes.

"I'm going to send over half a dozen secretaries for you to talk to," he called back a few days later. "They're all very competent and qualified but there's one you are going to take. You'll know her when you see her."

Well, I did. The ladies came over one at a time. They were all nicely dressed, well spoken, skilled at secretarial duties, and presentable. Any one would have been more than adequate. And then Geneva came in, Geneva Curry, in a white summer dress and white gloves, all the above, dignified, and beautiful. I learned over time that she had a husband, a young daughter, an interest in a high-fashion boutique, and a penchant for getting speeding tickets in her new AMC Gremlin. I hired her on the spot. When she left I called Johnny back.

"You didn't have any doubts, did you?" I asked.

He laughed. "The only reason I sent her is because I couldn't hire her. My wife insists I keep my blond secretary."

Geneva turned out to be even more competent than she appeared. She had been in government for several years and knew how to handle the bureaucracy and how to throw my weight around. Actually, nothing much happened during the next two weeks. With a secretary I was able to begin doing what I was hired to do, but we were still in the same shabby office, and Higby showed no inclination to make things easier. I stopped him once on one of his incessant scurryings from one place to another to ask how we were coming along.

"I'm very busy now," he said and zoomed off.

Then overnight, literally, everything changed. I was given a permanent office, told I could hire a second secretary, interviewed by the interior decorator to make sure I had drapes I liked, walls the color I wanted, and furniture compatible with my tastes.

I was easy to please—pale blue walls, blue paisley drapes to match, and "Somewhere in the bowels of this place you must have an old rolltop desk."

It turned out that they didn't. No rolltop anywhere in the government warehouses.

"But we can buy you a new one for about $800," the man from GSA said.

Being a fiscal conservative, I decided to help retire the national debt instead. That year, by the way, was the last year the federal government had a balanced budget. I was pleased to be able to do my part. For the next year and a half I got along nicely with a fancy hardwood, flat-topped desk big enough for Shirley Temple and George Murphy to dance a number on.

It wasn't until a couple of weeks later that I discovered how this had all come about, why all of a sudden I had became a part of the Nixon team.

In the Nixon White House, at least in my days there, almost everyone worked on Saturdays, some because they had work to do, others because they wanted the people they worked for to think they had work to do. Harlow met with his congressional relations staff every Saturday morning in his office in the West Wing. So on my third Saturday in the Nixon White House I found myself attending Harlow's weekly staff meeting.

There was an oval table around which eight of us sat in no particular pecking order, except that Harlow sat at the end of the table, facing the office door. I had taken a seat opposite him, with my back to the door. Harlow began talking about something of great moment, because that's what everybody talks about in White Houses. Suddenly I heard the door open and saw Harlow and the others scrambling to their feet. It hit me that someone important must be entering so I, too, stood and turned.

Lucky for me because the somebody important was Dick Nixon. It was the first time I'd seen him since Derby Day.

His first words were, "Well, good morning, Lyn."

That shook up some people. It wasn't everybody's name he knew around Harlow's table.

"Good morning, Mr. President," I replied, fighting an urge to curtsy.

We shook hands briefly and then he walked quickly around to Harlow. It so happens that neither Nixon nor Reagan is a bone-crushing handshaker. You always get your hand back with flexible fingers. If they ever were bone crushers they have learned to conserve their right hands since they occasionally need to shake hundreds of hands in a short period.

I had known the president casually since 1958. I had covered his losing 1960 presidential campaign, had seen him from time to time during the ensuing eight years, and had been with Reagan when he met with him in San Diego after the 1968 Republican National Convention, so I was not surprised when he addressed me by name. I wasn't but some others were.

The president made a few remarks, noted that he was to depart momentarily for the summer White House in San Clemente, then went around the table shaking hands and saying a few words to each of Harlow's staff, two or three of whom had to introduce themselves. Then he came back and put his arm around my shoulders. Again, I fought an urge, this time to snuggle up.

"How are things going?" he wanted to know.

"Fine," I said, feeling he would not appreciate the truth.

We chatted for what seemed like five minutes but probably was thirty-one seconds. Then he left, and as he went out the door he turned and said, "I'll give your regards to the people in California."

Our meeting resumed and we went back to discussing momentous issues and making urgent decisions and I thought no more of what had happened except to bask in the warm glow of having been singled out by the president.

But a couple of weeks later I was in Harlow's office talking to one of his secretaries, a pretty and friendly young woman named Toni Etcheparre, who just happened to be the daughter of Wyoming's biggest sheep rancher. She was the kind of girl you'd like to gather wool with.

She said casually, "They're still talking about the time the president put his arm around you."

And suddenly I knew why things had changed. The president wasn't just being friendly that day. He was making a point much more effectively than he could have done by memo or directive. The point was a simple one: Nofziger is not the Reagan spy in the White House, he is a full-fledged member of the Nixon team. That's all it took. If, in Nixon's eyes, I belonged, then I belonged.

I hadn't been in my new office with its pastel blue walls and paisley drapes very long when I received a call from Harlow. He explained that at a party the night before he had been buttonholed by Martha Mitchell, the wife of the attorney general. It hadn't yet become clear that she was off her rocker, so she was treated as if she were sane or almost so. It helped that John Mitchell was her husband; everybody figured John was too smart to marry a nut.

Having latched onto Harlow's buttonhole, she sought his help, explaining that she was getting too much publicity, was being pestered by the press and, please, could he tell her how to change this. What Harlow should have done was send her to Herb Klein. Instead he called me and said to expect her call and to be sure and see her. I did.

She called, made an appointment, and came in. She was perfectly lovely. I spent an hour with her, explaining that she didn't have to go on television and she didn't have to talk to reporters or submit to interviews. She could say "no comment," she could refuse to take phone calls, she could be noncommittal.

She thanked me profusely and went out and did everything I told her not to do. She even hired a press secretary. At first she got great publicity, but over a period of three years she went downhill and downhill and downhill, finally destroying her relationships with the administration and eventually with Mitchell himself. So much for my advice.

I had only been at the White House for a couple of months when Nixon named Arthur Burns, a highly respected conservative economist, to head the Federal Reserve Board. Burns had initially been named counsellor to the president with cabinet rank, but had immediately made a serious tactical mistake. Instead of settling for a smaller office in the West Wing with its close proximity to the president he opted for a huge office in the Old Executive Office Building. In the White House proximity is everything. Being fifty yards and across the street from the Oval Office and the hub of activity is too far—by a thousand miles. As a result, as far as I could tell, Burns, a thinker and contemplator, did not play as great a role as expected, or as he might have hoped, in the aggressive, activist, impulsive, combative Nixon White House.

But he did me a great favor. In moving on to the Fed he vacated his basketball court-sized office. And for some strange reason, it was reassigned it to me. And I didn't ask why for fear they would take it back. It was a great office, facing onto 17th Street with a little balcony from which, as time went on, I reviewed the unwashed, pot-smoking rabble that marched from time to time in protest of the Vietnam War, set off not by their hand-picked enemy, Richard Nixon, but by their hero, John Kennedy.

It was a great office but Burns had had it painted a suffocating, claustrophobic kind of battleship blue gray. I saw it first on Friday; I was to move in the next Monday. I said to the man from General Services who was showing it to me that over the weekend I would like it painted my favorite pastel blue.

"Sorry," he said, "we can't do it over the weekend. We'll get to it in two or three weeks."

"Fine," I said, "I'm going home now. Let me know when it's painted and I'll come back."

You couldn't have kept me away, but he didn't know that, and when I came in on Monday the office had been repainted Nofziger blue.

The advantage of a big office is that visitors think you are important; therefore, because it was a very big office I was viewed by some as being very important. A few little accessories helped. Somebody, Haldeman probably, decided that my work was of such a nature that secrecy should be ensured. So they sent in a file safe with a combination lock on it, gave me a special key, and told me to lock my office door when I left. The cleaning people only cleaned my office when someone was there. God knows what they might have stolen. The icing on the cake came with a memo proclaiming that because of the nature of their work, the following eight people will be provided with shredders. Glory be, I was on the list. And this wasn't just an ordinary shredder. It shredded paper into little teeny pieces.

So there I was sitting there in my big office the day Joe Coors and Paul Weyrich came to see me. Weyrich was the press person for a Republican senator, Gordon Allott of Colorado. But he was also an emerging leader of the emerging New Right, who later founded the Committee for the Preservation of a Free Congress, a terrible name for an effective conservative political action committee.

Weyrich had this bright idea, but it was going to take a lot of money to get it going and he had latched onto Coors, a man with a lot of beer, a lot of conservative principles, and a lot of money.

Weyrich wanted him to put up a bundle to help establish a nonprofit foundation that would make research and information available in a timely manner to congressmen and others who supported conservative issues or opposed liberal ones. He had asked me if he could bring Coors to my office where, if I would, I could tell him of the need for such an organization.

Of course I would. There was a desperate need. There was and is a conservative-leaning organization in town, the American Enterprise Institute, then run by William Baroody who had played a prominent role in the Goldwater campaign. AEI did and still does good work, but it usually published too late to be of help in any fight over a current issue. I said as much to Coors. He believed me and went ahead and put up the money. Shortly thereafter there came into being a new organization called the Heritage Foundation, today one of the two or three leading conservative think tanks in the nation, for which I take a small bit of credit.

The fact that Bill Baroody never really forgave me is almost beside the point.

In some ways the Nixon White House was a strange place to work. Unlike Ronald Reagan, President Nixon kept a close eye on events and decisions that might in any way affect him. He wanted to make sure he got credit when things went well, since he knew that success breeds success. He also knew that failure breeds failure and foul-ups breed contempt. He could stand not being liked; he couldn't stand not being respected.

One day, a few weeks after I had arrived, I received a call from John Ehrlichman who was with the president at the summer White House in San Clemente.

"The president wants you to get the word out to the press that it was his personal leadership that was responsible for Senate approval of the MRV [multiple warhead reentry vehicle]."

Ehrlichman at that time had the title of legal counsel to the president, but along with Haldeman he was one of the White House Big Two, also known in the liberal press as "the Germans," code words for "the Nazis."

Being a new boy on the block I was loathe to argue with him, but nevertheless I cautiously reminded him that I would be intruding on Herb Klein's turf. I didn't want to upset Klein, an old friend, and besides he had the resources, the prestige, and the contacts to do the job—he was known as one of Nixon's top men—and I wasn't certain I did. Outside of California I wasn't much known, period.

But Ehrlichman was adamant. "The president wants you to do it," he repeated.

"Okay," I said.

It took me a couple of weeks, but I did it in such a way that (1) the president was pleased and (2) it was not traced to the White House.

I did it with the help of Les Arends, the House Republican Whip, an old-timer from Illinois, a Nixon loyalist, and a good old man. At my request Arends wrote a "dear colleague" letter to all the Republicans in the House praising the president profusely for his leadership in getting the MRV bill passed in the Senate. As soon as the letter was sent I arranged for another old friend, Vic Gold, a good friend of columnist Jack Anderson, to leak the letter exclusively to Anderson. Anderson ate it up and devoted an entire column to it.

The president loved it. I loved it. And I never told Herb Klein how it came about.

During Nixon's first term there was still considerable unrest and violence on college campuses. The war in Vietnam was the ostensible cause, but I've always thought the real reason was the draft, the selective service law. It was a bad law, as are most laws the Congress passes. But this one was particularly bad because it made young men from nineteen to twenty-seven eligible for the draft. That meant that for a period of eight years young men were unable to plan their lives or their futures, and young women weren't much better off. Who wants to marry a guy who shortly may be sent off to fight in the stupidest war in American history?

Unable to look ahead with any degree of certainty many rebelled. Unrest and violence were the result, much of it abetted by antiwar, anti-Nixon faculty members and by outsiders who came on campus to foment trouble. It seemed more than coincidence that the campuses quieted down almost immediately after Nixon, every liberal's favorite devil, abolished the draft.

In early May of 1970 trouble was brewing on the campus of Kent State University in Ohio. Gov. Jim Rhodes sent in the National Guard. Students threw rocks at the green troopers. In panic, some fired back. Four young people were killed and others were wounded. Unrest grew among young people across the nation.

The president did what presidents usually do in time of trouble. He appointed a blue ribbon commission, the Commission on Campus Unrest. He left the naming of commission members to Ehrlichman, a grievous mistake, because while Ehrlichman may have been a smart man and was certainly a Nixon loyalist, his political instincts left almost everything to be desired. To prove this he loaded the commission with liberals and Nixon-haters.

The chairman was William Scranton, a former Pennsylvania governor, but hardly an ironclad Nixonite or a pillar of strength. In the early 1960s when Scranton was debating running for president, the quip running around political circles was, "If only Bill Scranton were half the man his mother was." Scranton's mother had been a power in Pennsylvania Republican politics a generation earlier.

The staff director was a liberal democrat who happened to be a friend of Ehrlichman named Matt Byrne. Ehrlichman later tried and failed to have him named director of the FBI but did succeed, over my screaming protests to Haldeman, in making him a federal judge. The number two staff person was John Vandecamp, who later became California attorney general and an unsuccessful Democratic candidate for governor.

The commission had been going about its duties for a couple of weeks when I received a call from Haldeman.

"I'm calling on the personal instructions of the president," he said. "You are to kill the Commission on Campus Unrest."

"It's the president's commission," I protested, flabbergasted.

"These are the president's orders. He wants it killed," Haldeman repeated.

"Whatever you say."

Well, of course there was no way to kill a presidential commission. It's not like, say, firing a special prosecutor. The best we could do was attack it and discredit it. And we did.

Everything bad we could find out about commission members or how they were conducting their investigation we fed to friends in the press. We prepared anticommission remarks for congressmen and persuaded them to use them. Colorado Sen. Gordon Allott, at my request, delivered a speech on the floor of the Senate attacking the commission. It was written by a bright young speech writer named George Will who later became a pundit, a baseball fan, and Nancy Reagan's favorite columnist.

Finally, the commission compiled its report and Scranton gave an advance copy to the *New York Times*. I was informed of this by a Scranton aide named Dick McCormick who went on to bigger and better things at the State Department and elsewhere. I told him that Scranton had to get the copy back, that it was not proper for the *Times* to get it before the president. Scranton, bless his not-too-bright little heart, got it back. When the report was finally released, nobody paid much attention to it, at least partly because we had done a pretty good job of discrediting the commission.

Nixon's effort to kill his own commission, if known, would have raised an outcry from the news media. It would have been analyzed and reanalyzed by every pundit, columnist, and editorial writer in Washington from the point of view of what they wanted to believe about him. But I have never thought that members of the news media ever really get to know the people they cover, even though they may think they do. Sure, reporters who cover a public figure over a long period get to know the public man, or woman, very well. They see the warts, they watch for and find the idiosyncrasies and the personality flaws. They'll find that a Richard Nixon is uncomfortable around those he doesn't know well. They'll discover that a Ronald Reagan tends to simplify issues that they think should remain complicated. And they'll magnify the stumblings and bumblings of a Gerald Ford and misstatements of a Reagan out of all proportion. But few of them ever get to know the private person behind the public figure and when they do it makes their reporting less objective.

Many reporters became personal friends of Jack Kennedy before and during the 1960 presidential campaign, and you could read it or hear it in their reports. Almost none of them became friends of Richard Nixon, for a variety of reasons, and you could feel their antagonism in their writing, too.

Just as it's hard to tell whether the chicken or the egg came first, so too whether the antagonism of Nixon toward the press or of the press toward Nixon. All I know is that it began early and by the time I went to work for Nixon the mutual dislike bordered on mutual hatred.

I suspect that Nixon always had a thin skin when it came to press criticism that he thought unjustified or unfair. The press, on the other hand, had trouble with Nixon's victories over two superliberals, Jerry Voorhis, whom he defeated in his first run for Congress, and Helen

Gahagan Douglas, whom he defeated in his only race for the United States Senate.

Voorhis and Douglas, whiners like most losing liberals, complained that Nixon ran dirty campaigns against them, and the press generally agreed. Nixon's outspoken anticommunism as a congressman, which culminated in the trial of Alger Hiss, added to their dislike; his role as Dwight Eisenhower's hatchetman, when he was vice president, increased it; and, as previously mentioned, his "final" press conference in 1962, after his defeat for governor of California, at which he told the assembled reporters that "you won't have Dick Nixon to kick around anymore," was the icing on the cake. So by the time he had beaten the media favorite, Hubert Humphrey, for the presidency the unspoken but obvious feud was in full flower.

There were exceptions on both sides, of course. Herb Klein worked valiantly to keep the press neutral. Because he was honest and forthright he had earned the respect of most Washington reporters as no other Nixonite had. Most, of course, had never tried. To this day I've never heard a reporter who knew Klein say anything not nice about him, which is more than I can say for any other public or political figure I have ever known, including me.

Unfortunately, his friendliness with the political press, instead of being viewed as a plus was seen by many Nixonites as a sign of weakness when the White House was determined to tough it out.

In contrast to Klein, Haldeman referred to the press as "the snakes." He totally mistrusted them and it showed. Actually, I've always felt that members of the press in a way are like dogs. Dogs can smell fear in people, the media can sense dislike. In both cases dogs and media react in much the same manner—they attack.

Over the years Klein tried hard, maybe too hard, to make the press like Nixon. Sometimes it seemed that the more a reporter abused Nixon the easier it was for him to persuade Klein to give him an interview with Nixon. Unfortunately, the interviews never seemed to make friends for Nixon, only for Klein.

The Democrats have never had a need for a Herb Klein. Who needs to set up an interview between a Democratic presidential candidate and a Republican reporter (if you can find one) when most of the political news media are Democrats? Most of them preferred Kennedy over

Nixon, Johnson over Goldwater, Humphrey and McGovern over Nixon, Carter over Ford, Carter and Mondale over Reagan, and Dukakis over Bush. So much for the power of the press.

Nevertheless, if the media beat on a public figure long enough and often enough it will have an effect on how the public views him; it will also have an effect on the public figure and those around him. That was one reason why I was brought to the White House—to get Nixon's allies to speak out on his and his administration's behalf and hope that some of what they said would be covered by the media. Another reason was to feed derogatory material to the media about Nixon's enemies in the hope that some of that also would appear in print.

The advent of a Lyn Nofziger in the White House to run a propaganda operation was not some aide's bright idea, it was Nixon's. As was the idea of bringing in a Chuck Colson to rally businesses, industries, associations, and civic groups to support the president. In addition, Klein's shop was heavily involved in getting out the Nixon side of any story. Jeb Magruder, Klein's deputy, who also reported directly to Haldeman, regularly headed up ad hoc committees of White House staffers, who were given specific tasks to gain public support for whatever was important to the president at the time. I was always part of these groups.

A Saturday morning group also met in Klein's office, although Klein was seldom there, and Magruder usually presided in an informal way. Its members included Colson, William Safire who later became a *New York Times* columnist, Dick Moore who currently is President Bush's ambassador to Ireland, myself, and two or three others. Its purpose was to dream up ideas that would present Nixon in a positive light. I don't remember a single one that was adopted but there must have been a couple.

I do remember that Colson, that sly fox, suggested once that the meetings be moved to his office ostensibly so that we could work in a more businesslike manner, sitting around his conference table instead of Klein's coffee table, but really so he could control the meetings. Nobody around there was as smart as Colson but everyone was smart enough to know what he had in mind, so the meetings remained in Klein's office. Which didn't make any difference in the long run because by the time the Watergate stupidity destroyed the Nixon

White House Colson had gathered about as much power as one man could comfortably handle.

I belonged to one other White House group. It was made up of known conservatives, of which there weren't really all that many. Our little group consisted of Pat Buchanan, a speechwriter who has become, among other things, a presidential candidate; Harry Dent, a former aide to Sen. Strom Thurmond, who was a political operative in the White House; Tom Charles Huston, and I don't know what he did at the White House except think, ponder, and write memos; Clark Mollenhoff, a former reporter and future journalism professor who wasn't really a conservative; and Kevin Phillips, a bright young man from the Justice Department who went on to be a pundit and a critic of most things Republican. As I recall, the only idea we ever came up with was to try to persuade the president to bring William F. Buckley into the White House as an adviser to the president, thus reassuring all the doubting conservatives that Nixon was truly one of them. Nixon never bought it which is just as well because Buckley probably wouldn't have either.

The Nixon White House, probably more than any other, was geared to rallying public support behind the president. In contrast, it was difficult to convince either Reagan or his various chiefs of staff to do the same. They figured Reagan could do it all by himself. Colson's public outreach program was aimed at winning support for the president from special interest groups. In the Reagan White House, its purpose seemingly was to win presidential support for various special interest groups, just bassackwards from what it should have been.

The Reagan White House relied primarily on Reagan to win the day regardless of what the day was all about. The Nixon White House relied on everyone it could find. Regardless of Reagan's successes as president I'm convinced they would have been much greater if he, the Baker boys, Don Regan, and Ken Duberstein had understood the need to build active support bases in the White House and, through them, all across the country. Jim Baker, unfortunately, was more interested in keeping down the size of the White House staff, which would make him look good, than he was in doing whatever had to be done to make Reagan look good. His successors followed along.

Despite how much we tried, our efforts to popularize Nixon's agenda didn't always work. In the spring of 1970, Nixon appointed first Judge Clement Haynesworth and then Judge Harold Carswell to fill a vacancy in the Supreme Court. The Senate turned down both of them, Haynesworth, a fine judge, out of vindictiveness, and Carswell for cause— Carswell later was arrested for indulging in sexual improprieties in a department store rest room.

Harlow headed up the White House "save the judges" group that included me. Our job was to figure out how to get Haynesworth confirmed, and when that failed, Carswell. One member of our little group was an assistant attorney general named William Rehnquist. An observer representing Atty. Gen. John Mitchell attended but did not participate. He turned out to be the man with the perfect Watergate memory, John Dean, who later, to Nixon's everlasting regret, became White House counsel.

Aside from participating in these little groups I was left pretty much on my own. Harlow never bothered me and I only bothered him with an occasional pun in memo form. After he was promoted to counsellor to the president with cabinet rank, I worked primarily for Haldeman who also seldom bothered me. Bill Timmons replaced Harlow as assistant to the president for congressional relations and took over the day-to-day operation of the congressional relations staff.

Bill was/is my friend but he had this bright idea that I didn't think was bright at all. Since I was technically part of the congressional relations staff he decided he would bring me into his shop as the inside man. Handling legislation would not only have driven me crazy but it also would have revealed my total incompetence. I told him I didn't want to do it. He persisted. I resisted.

Finally, in desperation, I went to Haldeman and he quickly put an end to that nonsense and let me go back to defending the president and attacking Democrats while Timmons went about persuading the Congress to pass the president's legislative program without me there to foul it up for him.

After I had been at the White House a few months I began to realize that no in-house operation, whether mine or Colson's or both, could adequately present the president's side of every story to the public. I concluded that what was needed was an outside organization that could pawn itself off as a legitimate, or at least semilegitimate, news organization.

I sent a memo to Haldeman saying, "Seems to me the Haldemans and the Ehrlichmans and the Magruders and the etc's ought to give serious thought about setting up an outside agency, with outside money."

The memo went on to say that through it we "could distribute the stuff we need distributed that can't come from the Administration or the RNC. It would be a source of leaks, planted stories, etc. It could distribute editorials, columns, tapes, perhaps even TV clips.

"Done right we could build a viable propaganda agency that would be of immense help."

About now I can hear the screams of those who say such a proposal is undemocratic, unethical, and maybe even unconstitutional and just goes to show what terrible people the Nixonites were. Pooh!

And nuts! for several reasons. First, none of the media in the United States are government controlled which means that any information to come out of my proposed agency would have had to compete for usage with all the other bits of propaganda that vie for space and time in the media, propaganda from the various levels and agencies of government, from special interest groups, from business and industry, and from the news media themselves.

Second, information from the agency would have had to be factual, at least as factual as whatever the news media already was putting out, or nobody would use it. On second thought, maybe that's not true. The media use great gobs of phony material, such as propaganda about global warming and acid rain, scare stories about Alar and other alleged carcinogenics, and so forth.

Third, since no government funds would have been involved the people in the White House would have had only the amount of input that those putting up the money would have allowed.

Fourth, in about one year some reporter would have found out the connection and written a story. The stuff would have hit the fan, the White House would have panicked, the agency would have gone out of business, and the only reason I wouldn't have been fired is because I would have already left and Colson and Magruder could have been fired instead.

Regardless, Haldeman liked the idea and instructed Colson, Magruder, and me to refine it and find someone to run it. He told Alexander Butterfield, the man who later disclosed the existence of the Nixon tapes, to find the money. We talked to a number of people including Howard Hunt, leader of the Watergate break-in. At the same time, Butterfield decided to try to get $10 million from Ross Perot, the software billionaire. Perot, a smart man, was not interested. Not having any other handy billionaires, the whole idea just faded away. Another good idea shot to hell.

In the fall of 1969 Haldeman distributed a memo to senior staffers, one of which from time to time I was considered to be. The memo asked us to submit memos of our own to the president, through Haldeman, making suggestions about what should or could be done during the next year.

In my memo I said the problem with the administration was that it was filled with dull people, that nobody in the cabinet inspired anyone or could be viewed as a possible successor to the president. I sent it in and thought no more about it.

In early December I was talking with Jack Caulfield, who did special projects for Ehrlichman, and said, "Something is going on with John Connally."

"How so?" he asked.

"Look at the president's schedule," I said. "He met with Connally yesterday and is meeting with him again today. Presidents don't meet twice in two days with people who are Democrats and not close to the administration without a real good reason."

He agreed and a day or two later neither of us was totally surprised when it was announced that Connally had been named secretary of the Treasury, succeeding David Kennedy, a Chicago banker not known for his charisma. A week or so later I ran into Haldeman and remarked that the president was to be congratulated on naming Connally.

"You had a lot to do with it," he replied.

"I don't even know Connally," I laughed, forgetting that I had interviewed him once when he was Kennedy's secretary of the Navy.

"You remember that memo you sent to the president?" Haldeman asked rhetorically. "Well, the president read it. He talked about it for two or three days and then called Connally."

In his excellent book on the Nixon administration, *Before the Fall*, William Safire writes that in the fall of 1969 Nixon remarked to Ehrlichman, "Every cabinet should have at least one potential president in it. Mine doesn't."

I think I'll take credit for inspiring that observation.

Connally turned out to be an excellent appointment, earning Nixon's respect and admiration. In fact, in 1980, when Connally, by then a Republican, and Reagan were seeking the Republican presidential nomination, Nixon, though fond of Reagan, felt Connally would make the stronger president and supported him. Unfortunately, or fortunately, not very many people thought as Nixon did and Reagan blew Connally and several others out of the water that winter and spring.

As for politics in general, 1970 looked like a year in which the Republicans would make gains in the off-year elections, especially on the Senate side. It was not to be; they gained one seat instead of the half dozen they had hoped for. In political campaigns when things don't go the way the experts think they should, or when races are inordinately close, the experts tend to blame one incident or event. Usually this is nonsense, unless the event is of such overriding importance that it affects the entire voting population.

The first televised debate between Nixon and Kennedy was such an event. The foreign policy debate between Jimmy Carter and President Ford in which Ford insisted that Poland was a free country was another.

In the 1970 elections the pundits laid the blame for the failure of the Republicans to make significant gains on a taped election eve telecast that featured Nixon speaking for the Republicans and Sen. Edmund Muskie of Maine for the Democrats. The Nixon speech was on a videotape of poor quality and the president himself, it was generally agreed, had come on too strongly. Muskie, on the other hand, was laid-back, low key, and altogether "presidential."

Maybe that affected a few people but to say that by itself it changed the course of a nationwide series of state elections didn't make much sense to me then and still doesn't. The election was affected by a number of things: the unpopular war in Vietnam; the massacre by American troops at Mai Lai; the Kent State shootings; the preponderance of Democrats over Republicans; and the Democrats' refusal to let the Republicans paint them as soft on crime even though they were, thus taking away what the GOP had hoped would be a defining issue.

There was another factor, as there is in almost all elections. Don't ask me why, but Democrats as a breed are better politicians than

Republicans. With some exceptions, they are more willing to attack and they are better at putting the opposition on the defensive. They understand and relish the fight. Sometimes I wish I were a Democrat.

Beyond all this the Nixon administration had failed to rally Middle America to its side. A year before the election I had written a memo to White House political operative Harry Dent that said:

"The key to the hearts of the Middle Americans is only partly in what we do. The main thing is in the way we present it. I think we have to position the President and the Republican party in such a way that the Middle American thinks we are on his side.

". . . we have to position the Democrats as tools of the special interests. We—the administration—must become a part of and spokesman for Middle America.

"He [the Middle American] votes against probably more than he votes for. It is our job, then, to make sure he has more to vote against with the Democrats than with the Republicans."

Two years later, in the 1972 presidential campaign, the Democrats did the job for us; they fragmented their party into every special interest group they could identify and then gave us George McGovern to run against.

But in 1970 my office, at least, followed up on what I had written to Dent. I had been allowed to add a young man named Jim Hoge to my small staff and he worked mightily in the summer and fall of 1970 to find valid reasons for Democrats to vote against Democratic incumbents and candidates. One thing we did was put together a "radical-liberal index"—the brainchild of Pat Buchanan—in which we listed the key votes of thirteen liberal Democratic senators and one liberal Republican, Charles Goodell of New York.

With the help of Jack Caulfield we managed to chase down some rumors about various incumbent Democrats. We found that both Hubert Humphrey and George McGovern owned homes in Washington that had racial covenants in their deeds, a tidbit we, of course, leaked to the press. One fact: racial covenants had been outlawed by the Supreme Court and were therefore meaningless. Another fact: McGovern and Humphrey didn't even know they were there; who reads the fine print in real estate contracts? But we didn't care, because Democrats were always doing that sort of thing to Republicans. Besides, Democrats were the big civil righters who were always insinuating that to be a conservative was to be a racist.

We also found that Joseph Tydings, the incumbent Maryland senator, owned an interest in an apartment complex in Florida that allegedly was turning away Negro potential renters. We publicized that, too.

Early that fall a little group was put together inside the White House and instructed to see if it could make a difference in a few key campaigns. It consisted of Colson, me, Magruder, and the redoubtable Murray Chotiner, as well as a Washington public relations man named Paul Wagner who had been Barry Goldwater's press secretary in 1964. He was a partner in a public relations/lobbying firm while at the same time as much of an insider in the White House as an outsider can be.

Chotiner, who had run Nixon's campaigns for the House and the Senate, was a real Nixon insider. Because he had pulled no punches he had been labeled a dirty campaigner by liberals in the press and the Democratic party. He wasn't; he was a tough campaigner. He said something once that everyone who runs a political campaign should remember: "It is not a smear to tell the truth about a person."

The funniest thing I remember about Chotiner is that he, the man with the national reputation for dirty campaigning, became irate at something—I don't remember what—our little group discussed doing. When we persisted he threatened to pick up the phone then and there and call the president. We ceased and desisted. It wasn't that important.

Our little group was successful in at least one of the races we looked at. We beat Tydings with Rep. J. Glenn Beale, the son of a former senator and one of the nicest men in the House, but not one of the smartest. His campaign was floundering. I found him a speech writer, a press person, a man to handle the radio actualities.

More important, we put together a full-page attack ad that accused Tydings of everything he was guilty of, or that we thought he was guilty of. I wrote it. Colson found the sponsors for it. Wagner placed it. And the Democrats screamed bloody murder. After Beale won someone leaked that Colson was responsible for the ad and the liberals screamed bloody murder all over again. Colson, being a good soldier, accepted the blame, with the rest of us getting off scot free. (Beale turned out to be a one-term senator; we weren't there to help him the second time around.)

Earlier in 1970 I had an interesting visitor—Oral Roberts. Someone had sent him to see me because he wanted something very badly. He wanted to preach a Sunday sermon at the White House. President Nixon, a Quaker by church membership, had decided to hold frequent church services in the large East Room. Because of the Vietnam War Washington was the site of frequent demonstrations, not all of them peaceful, and for the president to venture out on Sunday mornings might not have been too smart. For certain the Secret Service would have been in a state of near panic.

And so, as an alternative, the president from time to time held services in the White House and invited prominent members of the clergy to preach. In those days the Rev. Billy Graham was a White House favorite. So why not Oral Roberts?

I don't know why he started out by coming to me. I told him I had nothing to say about the matter, but that I would look into it. Then I had a great idea. I knew that most television ministers had large mailing lists. I asked Roberts how many names he had on his list and he replied about six million.

My mouth watered. The people those names represented were basically conservative, Bible Belt, Middle America, Silent Majority types. They were patriots and were maligned as such by the antiwar extremists and Ho Chi Minh supporters. To those people "patriot" was a dirty word and they preferred burning the flag to saluting it. President Nixon's insistence on wearing a flag lapel button drove them crazy. But Oral Roberts' people were true believers and supported their beliefs with financial contributions, and if their financial contributions were small, being lower-middle income folks, six million smalls can make one very large.

I wanted a shot at that list for the 1972 reelection campaign which I thought would be tough. I could not foresee that the Democrats would be so kind as to give us George McGovern.

I told Roberts that faith healing would probably be a problem, but he assured me that he didn't do that anymore.

I asked how he got along with Billy Graham.

"Fine," he said. "We're friends."

Then I got down to business.

"I'll make a deal with you," I said. "If I can get them to agree to let you preach, in return I want a one-time use of your list for the 1972 reelection campaign."

He thought it over a minute and agreed.

I sent a memo to Haldeman telling him what I'd done. He sent back word that he'd turned the matter over to Harry Dent. Dent is a South Carolinian whom I had known from the time he had worked for Sen. Strom Thurmond. He was a devout Baptist who later became a lay minister. But at the time he was the White House political person.

A few days later he gave me the word. It was no.

"How come?" I asked.

"Billy Graham didn't think it was a good idea," he said.

Sadly I gave the message to Oral Roberts, not that Billy Graham had turned thumbs down, merely that I couldn't get it done. A week or so later the Roberts people came back with another proposal. How about letting the Oral Roberts Choir sing at the White House? I couldn't get that done, either. And somehow Oral Roberts never did offer to let me use his list.

The time had come for me to leave the White House. I'd been there for a year and a half, plenty long enough for it to begin to bore me. In fairness, I would probably be bored after a year and a half in heaven, were I ever to get there. Besides, there was another job I wanted. Sen. Bob Dole of Kansas was going to become chairman of the Republican National Committee—more on that later—and I wanted to go with him because I wanted to change the committee's communications operation into a full-fledged propaganda office. I went to Bob Haldeman and explained. He was pleased.

"The president and I have already been talking about sending you over there for just that purpose," he said.

We agreed that they would talk with Dole and work out a deal. I was careful not to ask him if this was a promotion or demotion; I chose to view it as the former. But in all honesty, with the emergence of Chuck Colson, brilliant, aggressive, a hardball player, and absolutely dedicated to the success of Richard Nixon, there was little need for a low key propagandist such as myself in the White House.

Colson could sense a power vacuum and move to fill it more quickly and effectively than anyone I have ever known. He was quoted once as saying he would walk over his own grandmother for Richard Nixon. Before his born again experience I'm confident he would have done as much for himself. Saul of Tarsus had nothing on Colson, and while Paul the Apostle may have had better contacts in high places, I'd be willing to bet he didn't put any more energy into spreading the Gospel than Colson has since his conversion.

When I finally got to the National Committee the salary was the same as my White House salary, $35,000 in 1971 pre-inflation dollars. From that standpoint the move was a lateral one. The title was about the same, too. At the White House I had held a high-ranking position as a deputy assistant to the president; at the RNC I was a deputy chairman.

But titles were really not relevant. What was important was that I was going to be able to operate a lot more freely than in the Haldeman-controlled White House. Both Haldeman and Colson tried to keep strings on me during the next months but I was a mile away down at the other end of Pennsylvania Avenue and in Washington that's like clear across the country. Besides, my ideas of what needed to be done and how I should go about doing it differed substantially from that of those in the White House.

Another benefit, though I couldn't know it at the time, was that this was the first of two steps that would take me clean away from Washington long before the Watergate storm broke. Looking back over the years, I have wondered if, had I stayed at the White House, I too would have been caught up in the events that led to Watergate. I'm confident that Rose Marie would have alerted me to anything that was extra dumb or a little bit illegal, but still. . . .

Even before I knew for sure that I was going to the RNC I asked my secretary, Rose Marie Monk, to go with me. She had replaced Geneva Curry six months earlier after Geneva had found it inconvenient to work on Saturdays. A genuine Texan, Rose Marie had great Washington experience, having worked several years for Sen. John Tower (R-Tex.) and for more than a year at the Pentagon. She was more than just a good secretary. She handled people well, she kept me somewhat organized, which is more than most secretaries have been able to do, and for the most part she kept me out of trouble. She also had excellent political judgment.

Before I left the White House I wanted to see the president, so I called Haldeman.

"I'd like to see the president for a couple of minutes before I leave," I said. "No reason in particular. I'd just like to tell him goodbye and thank him for the privilege of having worked here."

Haldeman made no commitment, but said he would see what he could do. A few days later he called.

"Come on over," he said. "The president wants to see you."

I went, figuring I'd get a couple of minutes, long enough for a handshake, a presidential golf ball, a quick picture, and a hearty good-bye. I stayed for half an hour, during which I had the most relaxed conversation I'd ever had with Richard Nixon. I even made him laugh. As usual he had some advice.

"Don't hire anyone over thirty," he said. "You need young guys who'll work hard and do what they're told."

As we were talking about the Democrats, he came up with one specific instruction. "Don't let them get away with any lies," he ordered, only half in jest.

"Mr. President," I kidded, "I'm not even going to let them get away with the truth."

He burst out laughing. Several days later my witticism was quoted in the *New York Times*. Fearful that the paranoids in the White House would think I had leaked it I called Haldeman to assure him that this was not the case. He told me not to worry, that the president had been quoting my remark to staffers and visitors, one of whom had evidently told a *Times* reporter.

I finally left the Oval Office, feeling guilty for having taken so much presidential time, but not before I got my handshake, my golf ball, and my picture.

The guilt feeling I had is long gone. As far as I can determine the only bustlingly busy president in modern times was Jimmy Carter and that's because he didn't understand the job. The others, including Nixon, bore the burden and responsibilities of the office without feeling the need to impress people with how busy they were while sneaking naps in the middle of their "sixteen-hour days."

The job of president is not to shuffle papers. It's not to get into details. It's not to worry about whom to name the next assistant secretary of agriculture. It's not to count the trees; it is to manage the forest. Ronald

Reagan understood this better than any modern president, which is why he aged less in two terms than Carter did in one.

Reagan always understood that the job of the president or governor is to decide the philosophy under which the government will operate, to set and define policy, and to make tough decisions. Somebody else can handle the details, somebody else can worry about the hiring and firing, somebody else can keep the schedule of use of the White House tennis court. Reagan's problems as president were not due to his philosophy but to the way others carried it out. Many came about because he allowed himself to be surrounded by persons who didn't really know him, didn't respect him, and didn't share his philosophy of government.

In mid-February of 1971 I sent Nixon my letter of resignation and on February 17 he sent me a cordial, though not overly long acceptance. I learned later that if you want a long, effusive letter from the president the best thing to do is write it yourself and then send it to the letter-writing office where, glad to be freed from the task, they send it on almost untouched for the president's signature, which may be personal but probably comes off a signature machine.

By March, after dickering with Dole over salary (I said I wanted what I was making at the White House, he said he couldn't afford it, I won), I was at the RNC where I stayed for the remainder of the year, sort of.

That was a good ten months. We, my staff and I, weren't as fancy as some of the people before us and some who came after, but we did what I went there to do—attack Democrats, along with a few anti-Nixon Republicans, and support the president actively and vociferously.

I assigned a young man named John Lofton to edit a weekly newsletter called *Monday*. John had come off the Republican Congressional Committee and before that had worked for William Loeb on the Manchester, New Hampshire, *Union-Leader* which, even though it is now run by his widow, Nacky Loeb, still ranks as the meanest newspaper of general circulation in the country. *Monday* never became a newspaper of general circulation but if anybody ever outmeaned the late Bill Loeb it was John Lofton. And John did it with facts, not name calling.

Lofton had enough gall to divide into three parts. He would call anybody on the telephone, drive his victim crazy with rude, blunt, unanswerable have-you-stopped-beating-your-wife-type questions, and print his frustrated, outraged, incoherent replies. Or note with glee that his victim had hung up on him. It was great fun for John and made great reading for Republicans, who for too long had seen their leaders on the receiving end of this sort of treatment.

We put out a press release weekly in advance of publication and mailed *Monday* to every political reporter in town. We got great results, with even the Eastern liberal press and the news services picking up his lead story almost every week. Dole's successor as national chairman, George H.W. Bush, then in the early part of his kinder and gentler stage, killed it. Too bad. It could have helped him as president.

Monday replaced a slick publication that reminded me of the old *Saturday Evening Post* which seemed to have no other purpose than to praise the leaders of the Republican party, to my mind a complete waste of time, talent, and money. In recent years I have noticed with regret that the RNC has regressed to that. It seems to me that the purpose of the RNC, or the DNC, is to help win elections. You don't do it by sitting around telling everyone how good you are.

In mid-1971 we began putting out a monthly magazine called *First Monday*, which existed for years afterward in one form or another. In the beginning it reprinted the best of *Monday* as well as some original material. Frank Leonard, a writer and graphics designer, designed a cover with a black background that Haldeman hated and that, for the sake of harmony, I eventually did away with.

One reason I wanted to go to the RNC was to work with Dole. After having served eight rather undistinguished years in the House, Dole was in the middle of his first Senate term. During his first two years he had grown greatly in political stature. He was, in fact, made for the Senate and the Senate was made for him. Under the rules allowing unlimited debate he was able to use his formidable debating skills and wickedly sharp wit in a manner impossible in the House.

At that time, many Republican senators were old. Others, members of a minority for more than a decade, had given up even though they now had a Republican president who relished a political battle and was prepared to take the fight to the Democrats. But Dole had been in office only a few months when he moved deliberately to become Nixon's man in the Senate. Newspapers talked about him "patrolling the floor," waiting for opportunities to join the debate on behalf of the president and his program. By the end of his second year he had become a force to be reckoned with as the senator who was always there when Nixon needed help. Although never personally close to Nixon, in many respects he was to Nixon those first years what Paul Laxalt was to Reagan during the eighties.

He also earned a reputation as a street fighter, so identified by the Democrats and the news media, neither of which was accustomed to a Republican who could and would fight using wit, sarcasm, and knowledge of how the Senate operated as his chief weapons. Once, after Dole had hijacked an issue the Democrats thought was theirs, Sen. William Fulbright, chairman of the Foreign Affairs Committee, arose to complain, "You have stolen our cow."

"No, sir," Dole replied, "we have only milked her a little."

After I'd been at the White House a little while Dole and I found each other and he would call frequently to suggest that I write him a short speech on a topic that had caught his fancy. I would also send him speeches on topics that had caught my eye. Between us we managed to build him his reputation as Nixon's hatchetman, a reputation with which he was never quite comfortable.

During the eighteen months I worked in the Nixon White House I wrote hundreds of statements and short speeches for dozens of Republicans in the House and the Senate, either to insert in the *Congressional Record* or to deliver on the floor. Some were serious, some pugnacious, some were witty as hell; all were aimed at supporting the president or attacking his enemies. One thing you learn in politics and government is that if you want someone to do something for you make it easy for him.

Dole quickly discovered that I was available to write on a moment's notice and that I could turn out a short speech in a hurry, thanks largely to sixteen years as a reporter, writing on deadline. Nothing beats covering police and city hall for a small newspaper as a speed course in writing quickly and concisely. Additionally, I had spent more than two years writing speeches and statements for Reagan and had learned some of the techniques of speech writing.

I had also learned that when you gave Reagan a speech he tended to soften and gentle up any tough language, even when it wasn't very tough, so I always wrote tougher language than I otherwise would have. That habit carried over into my time in the White House and some congressmen found my language a little too strong for comfort.

Earl Voss, a speech writer for Sen. Robert Griffin of Michigan, told me an anecdote about my speech-writing style. He had written a speech that Griffin did not think was tough enough.

"Make it more Nofzigerish," he ordered.

Voss toughened it up and took it back to Griffin who again told him to redo it.

"Too Nofzigerish," he pronounced.

Dole is a smart politician with good instincts and the drive to take full advantage of them. He has a crippled right arm from wounds suffered in combat during World War II. In all the time I have known him I've heard him mention his handicap only once, and just in passing. He's never sought sympathy, never asked a favor.

I knew a man in an army hospital named Granville Pearl Eads, who had lost an arm in combat in Normandy. The first day he was well enough to get out of bed he leaned over and pulled on his high top army shoes with the remaining hand. Then he laced them and tied them in a double bow. Bob Dole is that kind of man.

He is also ambitious. And thus, by the end of 1970, when it was clear that the ineffective Rogers C.B. Morton would step down as Republican national chairman, Dole wanted the position and began to campaign for it, calling friends inside and outside the White House to help. I was among them. I set out to do what I could to help him because I thought the committee, with Dole as chairman, would be a good place to practice the fine art of political propaganda.

A couple of weeks before the RNC was to pick a new chairman—actually it would ratify Nixon's choice—I had a call from one of John Mitchell's henchmen, Fred LaRue, a Mississippi politician of some note. Mitchell, although in a job allegedly above politics, was in charge of Nixon's political operations. A recent precedent was Atty. Gen. Robert Kennedy who was brother John's chief political operative (and inheritor of Marilyn Monroe).

LaRue, on behalf of Mitchell, informed me that Dole was to be the next chairman, but that it was too early to make his selection public. I was to stay in close touch with Dole because Mitchell didn't want him saying something he shouldn't. This was fine with me. I had a lot more confidence in Dole than Mitchell did and was confident he'd do nothing to hurt his chances.

In his book Dole relates how he was almost dumped as national chairman before he was even appointed. John Mitchell had committed the post to him, but at the last moment Nixon changed his mind, having been warned that Dole might be too independent. Instead the chairman would be Thomas Evans, a Delaware Republican and a Southern coordinator and fund-raiser in Nixon's 1968 campaign.

Dole fought back, determined to make Mitchell live up to his commitment. Finally, with the help of Harlow, a deal was worked out whereby Dole would become chairman and Evans cochairman, reporting directly to Dole. Very quickly Dole named another cochairman, Anne Armstrong, who had been the Texas national committeewoman. The Armstrongs lived on a ranch that was so big it had its own post office. I had met her early in 1968 when she and Sen. John Tower visited Reagan in Sacramento to try to persuade him not to run for president but to endorse Nixon.

Mrs. Armstrong did a fine job at the RNC, one that extended beyond working with Republican women, and was rewarded by being named ambassador to the Court of St. James somewhere in Britain. When the presidential campaigns of 1979–80 came along she joined the camp of her fellow adopted Texan, George Bush, thus keeping intact her record of never having supported Reagan. When Bush was picked as Reagan's running mate she was brought into the Reagan-Bush campaign as cochairman. When Reagan won, she was rewarded with the chairmanship of the President's Foreign Intelligence Advisory Board, better known as PFIAB, pronounced Piffiab. There, she began feuding with some old Reaganites including Marty Anderson, and eventually managed to have them thrown off the board. One tough lady. As usual the president did not get involved even though some, such as Anderson, had been key figures in his presidential campaigns.

Mrs. Armstrong had called me in 1978 (entirely on her own, she said) to see if I would be interested in working in a Bush presidential campaign. I told her I had no problems with Bush but that I felt obligated to wait and see what Reagan was going to do. What I didn't tell her was that if Reagan decided not to run my candidate in 1980 was the old high taxer, Bob Dole.

Mrs. Armstrong ran the women's end of the RNC while Evans, in effect, became the chief operating officer and Dole chairman of the board.

Both Dole and Evans left me pretty much alone to run the communications operation. What interference there was came primarily from the White House, meaning Colson. I am no longer critical of Colson for this because he did his job as he thought Nixon would have wanted him to do it if Nixon had known what he, Colson, was doing, which he probably didn't. But I was, then. He was not an easy man to work with. And, I guess, neither was I. After I had been at the RNC for several months Haldeman summoned me to the White House.

Colson had set me up. He had many complaints about my reluctance to do his bidding and he wanted Haldeman to lean on me. Haldeman also had a complaint: as mentioned, he didn't like the black background on the cover of *First Monday* magazine. Colson complained bitterly that I wasn't cooperative, which was true. He complained that I had responded nastily to some of his memos, which was also true. What he didn't know was that Rose Marie, without telling me, had not sent him the worst ones. He was unhappy, finally, because I had "crashed the phone" in his ear, thus ending abruptly an unsatisfactory conversation.

Clearly, I was not showing the proper deference to the resident genius in the White House. Trouble was, I had worked there and had worked with Colson and I was not impressed, or even believing, when he or one of his minions would call and say, "The president wants this done."

Self-important people in the White House use two gimmicks to let us know they are important. One is to have their secretary tell your secretary that "the White House is calling." The other is to say, "The president wants this done." Do not be impressed. The White House cannot speak and very few people speak for the president.

As it turned out, Colson and I had an even more basic disagreement than my disrespectful treatment of him. He—and Haldeman—thought I had been sent to the RNC to do what they wanted done. I thought I had been sent to develop an effective propaganda operation on behalf of the president. And I thought much of what they wanted done was counterproductive or ineffective. Besides, sometimes I worried about legalities and other minor details.

As the meeting was breaking up Haldeman said to me, rather bitterly I thought, "You'll go back there and not do any of the things we want done."

Magnanimous to the end, I replied, "I'll get rid of the black cover on *First Monday*."

Which I did, over Frank Leonard's protestations. It was an easy decision to make. Leonard worked for me; Haldeman, if he wanted to, could have me thrown out on my ear.

While I considered that incident a victory, I sure didn't win them all. One I lost was not very important but I still wish I had won it. As you know, the symbol of the Republican party is the elephant. A graphics artist named Jack Frost had drawn up an elephant logo that the national party had recently adopted. I hated it. I still hate it. I will always hate it. It looks like a loaf of bread with two stumps for legs and a hangy-down thing that could be a trunk, a tail, or some other appendage at one end. Along the top of the elephant are three stars that Frost drew upside down—one point on the bottom, two on the top. Everyone liked it but me.

As I look back, the logo really was a pretty good representation of what the Republican party was and too often is—fat, dull, and not knowing if it is coming or going. Nixon was determined to change all that, but Watergate got in the way there, too. In the beginning, Reagan was also determined to change it, but the Baker boys, Jim and Howard, along with Don Regan, got in the way that time.

Nixon's determination and willingness to take on the Democrats and to fight down at their level helped earn him the enmity and contempt of the liberal establishment, including the bleeding hearts of the Washington press. Among them was, and still is, Mary McGrory, a lady columnist who worked for the *Washington Star* until it folded, at which time the *Washington Post* snapped her up. She had always been a *Postie* at heart.

I have known her casually since 1960 when we covered the Kennedy-Nixon presidential campaign. She was a Kennedy lover. I was not. She was a Nixon hater. I was not. We don't have a hell of a lot in common. Once when she came out to California to do a piece or two on the Cranston-Rafferty senatorial campaign, I drove her from Los Angeles to Santa Barbara where Rafferty was speaking. Stanford was playing USC in football that day and Mary generously kept quiet until the game was over. I was and am grateful.

But during the Nixon years Mary was (and still is) less than kind to the president, attacking him at every opportunity and at other times as well. One day I thought I would have some fun so I wrote to her editor asking for equal space for the RNC whenever Mary attacked the president. He, having no sense of humor, wrote me a snotty letter in return. While it is all right to demand equal time from radio and television on the theory that the airwaves belong to all the people, it is not all right to ask for equal space in a newspaper unless you've been libeled. Newspapers, you see, largely belong to rich folk and are sacred to editors and other newspaper people who are hired by the rich folk.

Mary, likewise, was not amused. The next time she saw me she approached close and muttered low. I didn't catch all the words but I believe they were on the order of, "I'll get you, you dirty, miserable s.o.b. if it's the last thing I ever do."

But she didn't and, in fact, I think she eventually forgave me, for over the years she hasn't written anything bad about me. Or, come to think of it, anything at all. And she could have. Not only that, but she stuck up for the Salvation Army when the up-scale malls in the Washington area refused to let their bell ringers solicit donations one Christmas. For reasons going back to World War II I have a soft spot in my heart for the Salvation Army, to which spot I have now added Mary. But still, I'm glad I asked for that equal space back in 1971.

One other time Mitchell ordered me to babysit Dole and again it wasn't necessary. When San Diego was selected as the site of the 1972 convention Dole wanted his friend and political confidant, Huck Boyd, the long-time Kansas national committeeman, to organize and run it. The White House, meaning Mitchell, wanted Dick Herman, the national committeeman from Nebraska, to have the job and so informed Dole. Theoretically, it was the chairman's perogative to name the person to run the convention, and he hadn't even been consulted.

Dole spent half an hour complaining to me and threatening to appoint Boyd anyway, but then, good politician that he is, went out and named Herman.

Dole was the second successive chairman who was also a member of the Congress. His predecessor, Morton, served in the House until he was named secretary of the Interior. He was an able man, admired by Nixon for his political instincts, but like most congressional Republicans he had pretty well accepted that the Republicans would be a minority party for the foreseeable future. He was reluctant, therefore, to start any, to his mind, political fights. Which is why Nixon promoted him to Interior.

Dole, on the other hand, was a fighter as well as much more partisan than Morton. Those were the qualities Nixon wanted in a national chairman. Those were the qualities he saw in me.

But Dole had the same serious problem as Morton. He had a major conflict of interest. As chairman of the RNC his first obligation was to serve the titular head of the party, Richard Nixon. As the United States senator from Kansas his primary obligation was to his constituency. And as a senator he had a third obligation, to abide by the rules and traditions of the Senate. Had a Democrat occupied the White House or even a Republican president such as Reagan, who was indifferent to the workings of the RNC, Dole might have had little trouble blending his conflicts. But as chairman he worked for and was responsible to a very political president, one who understood that the RNC could and should be used to support him personally as well as the initiatives of his administration. Further, backing Nixon were Colson and Haldeman, two tough cookies who understood power and who were determined to use every available resource to bend the Congress to the president's will.

They were also determined that Dole, the chairman, and Nofziger, the propagandist, would follow their orders. Neither of us was very good at that. Dole was always wary of saying or doing anything that might bring the wrath of his Senate colleagues down on him, or worse, that of his constituents. Besides, his political instincts, like mine, told him that many of the things the White House or the president, *nee* Colson, wanted were ridiculous, counterproductive, or bordered on the unethical and even the illegal. A mile down the road Colson didn't have such worries. If the stuff hit the fan it would splatter not on him but on us. And we made enough trouble for ourselves by ourselves.

A couple of examples: In the days before Peggy Noonan, when speech writers were properly anonymous, somebody, not I, wrote a line in a Dole speech referring to the radical peacenik Democrat, Ramsey Clark, as a "left-leaning Marx-mallow." Dole used it. It was a good line and accurate. Clark, an attorney general under Lyndon Johnson, had swung way left and had become one of the most active and doviest of the doves. Liberals, who wait around for someone to insinuate they are communists so they can beat their breasts and shriek "McCarthyism," did exactly that. Dole allowed as how he should have said "marsh-mallow" and the liberals went back to beating on their chief target, the president.

The second example involved me, and what I did was worse in a lot of

Republican eyes, although not in mine nor, I'm convinced, in the president's. I had tired of Ted Kennedy self-righteously attacking Nixon at every opportunity, so I sent a memo to each Republican in the Congress, telling them they shouldn't let Teddy get away with this kind of thing. I reminded them of Kennedy's own record—Chapaquiddick, being tossed out of Harvard for cheating, multiple speeding tickets at the only school that would take him, the University of Virginia, and a few other odds and ends.

Somehow the memo found its way into the hands of columnists Rowland Evans and Robert Novak. They published it with many a tut-tut and dire warnings of how this sort of meanness would backfire.

Well, I did hear from a number of Republicans, who chided me for acting in an ungentlemanly, un-Republican manner. I wrote back, telling them that their attitude explained why Republicans were and likely would always be a minority party. I don't know why, but an awful lot of Republicans look on politics as the British look on cricket—as a gentleman's game. It ain't; it's more like mud wrestling. Democrats understand that and play accordingly, all the while pointing intimidating fingers at Republicans, many of whom are easily cowed.

Two of the places I never heard from in the matter of Teddy Kennedy were the White House and the chairman's office.

A third sector was also quiet; not one Democrat, not even Ted Kennedy, uttered a peep. One thing about Kennedy, and it grieves me to say anything good about him, he is not a whiner or a crybaby and he knows full well that if he is going to dish it out he is going to have to take it. It's hard not to respect him for that. Kennedy is tough, and a man who seems to love the game of politics. It is difficult to forget the night he chased Jimmy Carter around the platform at the Democratic National Convention in order to shake his hand and it is hard to forget Carter's broken field run to avoid him. Kennedy might have been a more liberal president than Carter, but he would have been a stronger one. He might have hurt the country more but it wouldn't have been from weakness or indecision.

Sometimes I wonder what history might have read like if a few prominent Republicans had had the guts to take on Teddy and a few of his roistering, heavy drinking colleagues during the fights over the appointments of Robert Bork to the Supreme Court and John Tower as secretary of defense. Kennedy and his ilk have generally enjoyed free rides over the years both from the Republicans and the national press.

By the fall of 1971, Jeb Magruder had left the White House and was heading up the preliminary effort to put together the Committee to Reelect the President, known later and unflatteringly as CREEP. One day he came to see me. He needed help with a project he had in mind in California. In California, if a minor party falls below a certain number of registered voters it is no longer eligible for the ballot. Magruder's project involved decertifying George Wallace's American Independent party. If Wallace could not run for president in California, the thinking ran, then Nixon, not the whoever Democratic presidential candidate, would get the Wallacite vote.

A disgruntled Wallacite named Robert Walters had come to Magruder and told him that for $10,000 he could switch enough registered Wallace voters to keep the AIP off the ballot. Magruder wanted me to find someone to monitor the project and serve as a go-between in the transfer of the money. Remember, these were still the days of freewheeling political spending and loose campaign election laws and money could be collected and spent with very little accountability.

In the Nixon camp money was no problem, and a lot of it was in cash. In fact, when the project came to light during the Watergate inquisition I was asked if one sum of $5,000 I had passed along was a check or real, honest-to-goodness money. I replied that "I didn't open the envelope but from the feel it was either cash or a mighty thick check."

After Magruder assured me that what he was asking was not illegal (the wrong man to rely on for legal opinions) I agreed to help. Magruder explained that for political reasons he didn't want it traced back to the Nixon campaign. It made sense to me, so I called Jack Lindsey, an executive and stockholder in a firm that packed and marketed olives, pickles, and other delicacies. I had helped him a couple of years earlier when he had run for Congress. He entered the race only after Barry Goldwater, Jr., assured him face-to-face that he would not run. But after Lindsey filed young Goldwater changed his mind, won, and became the only congressman in history to attend sessions of the House by riding his skateboard in the tunnels between his office and the Capitol. A boy his daddy could be proud of.

Although back in the olive business, Lindsey was at heart a political junkie and he agreed to take on the project. What he didn't know, what I didn't know, and what, I'm confident, Magruder didn't know, was that Walters, although he denied it, may have hired members of the American Nazi party to help him with the project. When the story broke the news media was all over us, attempting to link the reelect campaign directly to the Nazis. Poor Lindsey was named in the story which didn't do him any good, even though he, like me, was innocent of any dealings with Nazi party members. Walters never did succeed in getting the AIP off the ballot, but it didn't matter because a few months later, on May 15, 1972, Wallace was permanently crippled by an assassin's bullet.

My name came up one other time during the Watergate hearings. John Dean, Nixon's White House counsel and a star Watergate witness, testified that while I was at the RNC I had helped draw up a list of Nixon's political enemies. Of course he could not produce a list with my name on it because I had not done so nor had I been asked to do so. When questioned about Dean's charge by the press I replied that no good politician would have to write down a list of his or Nixon's enemies; he would have them all firmly filed in his head.

"I know a Nixon enemy when I see one," I said. And not many people doubted that.

Indeed, that attitude—that presidents have real enemies and that politics is a game for hardball players—helped endear me to Nixon, Mitchell, and other key figures as preparations began for the 1972 reelection campaign.

5

Reelecting the President

By October of 1971, the campaign to reelect the president was well under way. Magruder had left the White House and was busy putting together its various elements, with John Mitchell quietly overseeing the effort from his office at the Department of Justice. One of the problem spots was California, Nixon's home state, which he had to carry to win a second term. Any candidate for president who can't carry his home state is not only unlikely to win many others but will also be personally embarrassed. Even Walter Mondale and Mike Dukakis carried their home states.

Nixon had carried California in 1968, but not by much, and his loss in the 1962 gubernatorial race must still have rankled. Even though Reagan had won gubernatorial races in 1966 and 1970, California was still a swing state, as apt to go Democratic as Republican. It had two Democratic United States senators, Alan Cranston and John V. Tunney, and a Democrat was secretary of state. So Nixon and Mitchell were naturally concerned.

On the other hand, Reagan was in the first year of his second term as governor and he and his people thought he should have a lot to say about how the Nixon campaign in his state would be run and who would run it. Though Reagan had loyally supported Nixon and would continue to do so all the way to Nixon's resignation, the Nixonites and Reaganites had looked at each other with suspicion ever since the 1968 convention. The Nixon people had not quite forgiven Reagan for trying to wrest the nomination from their hero and the Reagan people still resented the hardball tactics the Nixonites had used to secure the nomination. In addition, the Reagan people never trusted some of the Californians in the Nixon administration, primarily Haldeman, former Lt. Gov. Robert Finch, and former Assemblyman Jack Venneman.

It was a foregone conclusion that Reagan would be Nixon's state chairman if he wanted the position, and he did. A governor always gets first shot at being his state's chairman for his party's presidential candidate. That's how the system works. As chairman Reagan would head the state's delegation to the national convention and would have much to say about its membership. Appointment to the delegation is one way to reward loyal followers, and rewards for loyalty and hard work are important in politics. Punishing disloyalty is equally important, although Reagan throughout his political career never found it in his heart to play consistent hardball with his political enemies. Fortunately, some around him, including his wife, didn't have that problem.

When, in the fall of 1971, Reagan suggested that I be named the working head of the campaign in California it seemed to solve the problem of finding someone for the position whom both camps trusted. John Mitchell had no objection to me from a loyalty standpoint, nor should he have had; I had no trouble then or now in being loyal to both Reagan and Nixon. Mitchell did wonder, however, whether I would be of more value at the National Committee or in California.

A couple of other questions also disturbed some in the Nixon camp. Could a person as disorganized and uncontrollable as Nofziger run a campaign in as big a state as California? And would he take orders? Only time would tell.

But I had some things going for me besides the loyalty factor. Having been one of them, I knew the national political press better than any of the Californians. I also knew the state and its Republican players, most of whom were friends and most of whom had more confidence in my ability to run a campaign than I did.

I was perceived as having done well in Reagan's first gubernatorial campaign, but that was as his press secretary, which was not a leadership position. I had also played an important role in his abortive run for president in 1968 and, along with Tom Reed, nearly pulled out a victory for Max Rafferty in his Senate race against Cranston. But I had done that more as the manager of a candidate than of a campaign.

I was not an organizer and I knew it, which was one reason I didn't jump for joy at the thought of going to California. But like Reagan, I was smart enough to learn from people who had more experience and know-how than I, and smart enough not to interfere with people who worked for me who knew their jobs.

But my competence or lack of it was not the reason for Mitchell's reluctance to send me to California. In late October he sent Bob Mardian to tell me he had decided I should stay at the National Committee. Mardian explained that Mitchell wanted me to "help keep a lid" on the committee, whatever that meant. But in Sacramento the Reagan people continued to agitate to bring me to California. As a result, only a few days after my meeting with Mardian, Mitchell called me to his office at the Department of Justice.

"Which would you rather do?" he asked.

"Don't put that monkey on my back," I said. "If I tell you I want to go to California and we lose it you'll blame me. If I choose to stay here and we lose it you'll still blame me. I'll go to Alaska if you want me to, but you make the decision."

He puffed on his pipe a minute. "Why don't you do both," he said. It was not a question.

"Okay, but I need one favor. Don't let Tom Reed in the state."

Reed had been a key player in both of Reagan's gubernatorial campaigns as well as his brief run at the presidency in 1968 and we were friends. But Reed, a man of unlimited energy, is about three times as smart as I am and has already done nine or ten things while I am still trying to figure out what to do about the first. He was overseeing a good chunk of the West for the reelect campaign and I knew if they let him into California I would spend most of my time wondering what he was doing and never getting anything done myself. Mitchell agreed.

For the next six weeks I tried to spend three days a week in California and three at the National Committee. It didn't work. I couldn't get on top of things in California and I couldn't stay on top of things in Washington. And I was exhausted. Finally, in mid-December I called Mitchell.

"It isn't working," I said. "I'm going to California."

But before that decision, I'd had one lucky break. At 6 A.M. one morning in my California hotel room the telephone rang. It wasn't my wake-up call, it was Peter Flanigan, a Nixon assistant, calling from Washington. He had a brother who, like all the Flanigans, wasn't poor, lived in nearby Pasadena, and wanted to get involved in the campaign. Would I talk to him? Of course I would.

John Flanigan turned out to be a big, hearty man in the midst of a second unhappy marriage who was looking for something to do. He would work full time as a volunteer. I hired him for that price and, wonder of wonders, he worked every day of the campaign, during which time he got a divorce and took up with a pretty coworker named Nancy Dunigan and eventually married her and, as far as I know, has lived happily ever after. He was a large reason for the success of our campaign organization.

Flanigan found us temporary quarters in a hotel near Los Angeles International Airport and later permanent headquarters on Wilshire Boulevard, traditionally L.A.'s street of political campaign offices—Reagan's headquarters in 1966, and Reagan's and Ford's in 1976. Even Democrats used the street. Flanigan also brought aboard a statuesque blonde named Patsy Von Schlagel, who added class to the campaign by driving to work in a borrowed right-hand-drive Bentley, and more class just by being there.

While I was commuting between Washington and L.A. Flanigan was making arrangements for insurance, interviewing potential campaign workers, and doing all the other things that had to be done so that we could run a campaign. Ours was the last great presidential campaign in California because it was the last with no limits on either raising or spending money. By the time the campaign was over we had close to two hundred people on the campaign payroll. Fifty would have been more than enough.

Flanigan drew up our first state budget and I took it back to Washington to explain and justify it to the national campaign higher-ups, including Mitchell and Maurice Stans, the campaign finance chairman and Nixon's first secretary of commerce. From sheer stupidity I left Flanigan in L.A.: he understood the budget; I didn't have the vaguest idea what I was supposed to be explaining. A rule of thumb is, show me a budget and I won't understand it. Stans, for some obscure reason, was upset at my ignorance. It may be that he thought that people in charge of spending large sums of hard-to-raise money should know what they were doing.

But Mitchell was not bothered that the operating head of Nixon's campaign in a major state didn't measure up to that standard. He laughed and sent me on my way and California wound up receiving about all the money we had asked for, something close to $3 million. And us without a candidate to support, without media to buy, or polling to do.

I split the state into four regions with a chairman in charge of each, theoretically reporting to Reagan but actually reporting to me. But, as I explained earlier, it was an error because it added another layer of bureaucracy to the campaign and gave me four more people who—mistakenly—thought they were in charge.

In Los Angeles County, a region of its own because of its huge population, Reagan named Dr. William Banowsky, president of Pepperdine University who later served as president of the University of Oklahoma. Bill had great political ambitions, but never quite screwed up the courage to run for anything; he wanted to be appointed, which happens to very few people, the exceptions being Gerald Ford and Nelson Rockefeller. Banowsky was nevertheless an able man, which he demonstrated by turning the drudge work of the campaign over to an aide, Dr. James Wilburn, who insisted on working hard and doing a good job. Banowsky eventually wound up as California's Republican national committeeman, but he blew his chances of going any farther by foolishly supporting Ford against Reagan in 1976.

The other southern California counties were overseen by a Riverside County supervisor and automobile dealer named Al McCandless, another man who took his politics seriously and who later was elected to the House of Representatives.

Up north, at my suggestion, Reagan asked David Packard, who had just resigned as deputy secretary of defense, to run the counties surrounding the San Franciso Bay. Packard, who stands about nine foot three in his shoes, ran his counties as fiefdoms, and answered to no one. I never told him what to do, I asked him, saying "please" and "sir" in the process.

The fourth region—about two-thirds of the land area of California and about one-tenth of the population—went to Bob Monaghan, the minority leader in the state assembly who had served a term as Speaker. Monaghan came from Tracy, in the heart of the California boondocks, so he was well qualified to take charge of the state's agricultural areas and such important cities as Sacramento, Stockton, Modesto, and Fresno. Monaghan later served a stint as an assistant secretary of transportation. He also brought in a smart young politician named Edward Rollins who later ran the political office in the Reagan White House and Reagan's reelection campaign in 1984.

Nixon was virtually unopposed in the presidential primary in California. On the Left, a congressman named Paul (Pete) McClosky had threatened to run. He was a marine veteran of Korea who vigorously and vociferously opposed Nixon's handling of the undeclared war in Vietnam. While at the National Committee I had managed to get the College Young Republicans to withdraw an invitation for McClosky to speak, and at my direction John Lofton did not treat him with kindness in *Monday*. Eventually McClosky, realizing that discretion was the better part of vanity, gave up any idea of tilting at the Nixon windmill, to everyone's relief, except for a couple of reporters who were writing books on Pete, the Nixon killer.

One congressman did take Nixon on—John Ashbrook, an Ohio conservative and one of the founders of the American Conservative Union, which had been organized after the Goldwater debacle. Ashbrook was still a relatively young man when he died of a heart attack. But while he lived he was a significant force in the resurgence of conservatism in America. Pretty good for a Harvard graduate.

In 1972 Ashbrook concluded—correctly—that Nixon was not a 100 percent true-blue conservative. But unlike most of his fellow conservatives, Ashbrook was not satisfied to sit and complain. He decided to run against him, for which decision I have ever since blessed him. It is difficult to put together and hold together a political organization when there is no opposition, nothing to occupy your troops. This is especially true in California, which, thanks to the late Hiram Johnson and other goo-goos, has a weak and ineffective party system, almost no spoils system, and therefore not many ways to reward loyal party workers and keep them busy between elections.

This means that in each election cycle campaign organizations have to be put together from scratch—not easy to do in a primary when a candidate has no opposition. Yet in the case of an incumbent seeking reelection it must be done in order to have an organization in place for the fall election.

What Ashbrook did for me was to give Republican activists a reason to join the Nixon campaign. They knew Ashbrook couldn't win but, still, they wanted to participate in handing him a beating. And I gave them a goal at which to shoot—keep Ashbrook under 10 percent of the primary vote, while never attacking him because we would need his supporters after the primary. Now, my grandmother could get 10 percent on a sympathy vote alone, especially since Nixon's national headquarters team determined to give Ashbrook a level playing field: it refused to provide us money for advertising or polling. National headquarters took a lot of polls that year but the White House was afraid someone would find out what was in them so they refused to make the results available to me and, I suspect, to those in charge of the other forty-nine states.

During all of 1972 I saw one campaign poll. It was taken in April, before the primary. And I saw it in July, a month after the primary. I never saw a poll pitting Nixon against the Democratic nominee, George McGovern. Late in the campaign the Democrats released their own poll claiming McGovern had narrowed the gap in California to about four points, but it was patently phony.

As it turned out, we needed no polls and no media for Ashbrook. We held him to just under 10 percent, a fraction behind my grandmother. In November things were almost as good against McGovern. He lost to Nixon by more than a million votes in California alone. The year 1972 was plainly a year when American voters wanted little to do with either the far Left or the far Right, when, or maybe because, the alternative was Richard Nixon.

One thing I wanted to do in California was increase our percentage of the black vote, in those days the Negro vote. I called Ed Sexton, a former Kansas state senator who headed up the Negro outreach program at the RNC. An old friend, Ed came out for a few days and helped me line up some Negro leadership. He found me people who remain friends to this day. I asked Henry Lucas, a San Franciso dentist and businessman, to be my statewide Negro chairman. A Los Angeles businessman, Richard Allen, became my Los Angeles County chairman, even though he started out as a Democrat. Both Allen and Lucas did outstanding jobs, as did a dozen others at a time when Republican popularity among Negroes was at a low point. One other Negro, LeRoy Jeffries, became my mentor in the Negro community. Both he and Allen taught me valuable lessons.

One day Allen came into the headquarters and told me he had just fired three of his people. I expressed sympathy, saying I knew how difficult it was to fire people.

"Not at all," he said. "Just remember, if you have to fire someone it's his fault not yours."

He was right, and I have not forgotten what he said.

Neither have I forgotten the tongue-lashing I got from Jeffries. He was in the public relations business, advising major corporations on how to deal with the Negro community. Early in the campaign he called together a group of about twenty prominent Negro businessmen who he thought could be helpful. After I finished talking to them in what I thought was sterling fashion Jeffries called me out of the room and lit into me. He was furious at my insensitivity. And I thought I'd been sensitive as hell.

"When you're talking to Negroes don't ever refer to them as 'you people.' It's insulting. You're separating them from the rest of the campaign. Talk about 'us' and 'we.' "

Thanks to the hard work of the campaign's Negro leadership Nixon picked up 19 percent of the Negro vote in California, a big improvement over 1968 and the Goldwater campaign in 1964.

While neither the Reaganites nor the Nixonites doubted my loyalty, some on both sides doubted my competence and both eventually sent in their spies to watch over me. National headquarters sent in Marvin Collins, a Texan and, incidentally, a friend of Rose Marie. Gordon Luce, a San Diego savings and loan executive, also vicechairman of the California Republican party and of the California Committee to Reelect the President, sent in a young lawyer named Dana Reed. Reed and Collins were pleasant, inoffensive gentlemen who didn't get in the way much or create problems, and didn't, as far as I know, send bad reports back to their superiors. Collins, especially, pitched in to help with the day-to-day work.

Unfortunately for him somebody at national headquarters had leaked a story that he was being sent to California to take over the campaign. It wasn't true. Marvin agreed that it wasn't true, as did the people at headquarters. But just to be sure, I waited three weeks before I managed to scrounge him up a desk and a telephone.

The fact is, thanks to Flanigan and some other good grass-roots politicians we had brought in—Bob Hatch, Bruce Nestande, Curtis Mack—we had put together a good organization not only at the top but, for the most part, all across the state, including precinct operations and telephone banks. Of course, with our resources it would have been hard not to do a good job.

We also had a reporting system and, because of some good advice from Bruce Nestande, a backup system. Nestande was a politically ambitious young man who had run for the state assembly twice and lost. He was working in the governor's office when, at Mike Deaver's request, I brought him into the campaign.

"Remember," Nestande told me, "they—the people in the campaign you are depending on—will lie to you. Not because they want to hurt you, but because they don't want you to think they have let you down. So you have to check up on them."

Nestande was talking primarily about volunteers, who make up the bulk of the campaign workers. With every good intention a volunteer will agree to do something, but things get in the way such as PTA meetings, baby's colic, or visits by the in-laws. So when you call and ask, "Have you finished polling your precinct?" the answer is seldom, "I haven't yet begun." It's usually, "I'm almost through. Just a couple more people to call."

At which point you get on the phone and call your backup or your field man and say, "You'd better spot check that precinct." After that you don't fire the precinct chairman—how do you fire a volunteer?—you give him a cochairman to make certain the job gets done.

Later Nestande, on his third attempt, won a seat in the state assembly, bucking the Orange County Republican organization and the money people, both of which had given up on him. He did it the old-fashioned way; he knocked on every door. Along with learning that people will lie to you, Nestande had also learned that the best way to get a vote is to ask for it in person. In these days of television, radio, and direct mail too many political "experts" have forgotten or never learned that basic political truth.

Because we were doing things right I paid no attention to a piece of mail that came in from headquarters one day in September. In fact, I never opened it until a few days later when a truck came and dumped a stack of paper 4-by-5-by-3 feet high. I didn't have the vaguest idea what it was although I soon found out it had been air-freighted to us from Washington at some astronomical cost.

Rose Marie called my attention to one of these long cardboard tubes that people use to send big pieces of paper or large pictures in. It had arrived about a week earlier. Inside was a chart, 4-by-5 feet, a sample of the thousands sitting in the parking lot. They were to be distributed in large quantities to all our headquarters around the state. Every day volunteers were to fill in dozens of little blank squares and telephone the results to national headquarters, completely by-passing the state organization.

"This," I said to anyone who would listen, "is a lot of doggy doo-doo [I am not sure how President Bush spells this—it could be dewdew, duedue, dodo, doodoo, or a combination of any two—in Vietnam they say "dhudhu."] I am not going to use these. They're a waste of time and money."

Besides, we already had our own, much simpler system in place.

The word of Nofziger's recalcitrance got back to Washington. I think I called and told them what they could do with their charts. More doo-doo all over the place. Next thing I heard, an earnest young man named Larry Mitten was being bundled aboard an airplane headed for California. His mission: force Nofziger to distribute the forms or, if worse comes to worst, distribute them yourself. I waited for him all a-flutter.

When he arrived he came gently into my office and introduced himself. I asked what I could do for him. Nothing, he said, he was just looking around. I took him to see Nestande who explained to him what we were doing. When he came back to my office I took him to a nearby deli and bought him lunch. Shortly thereafter he left for the airport and a flight back to Washington. I couldn't figure out why he had come.

A few days later Bob Mardian came by the office and laughingly told me what had happened. He and the young man had come out on the same plane and sat next to each other. They were probably in first class; it was that kind of campaign. Mardian asked why he was going to California. The gist of his answer was he was going to make Nofziger distribute the forms.

"Young man," Mardian said he said, "when you get to Nofziger's office throw your hat in first. If it doesn't come back out then you go in, but when you go in speak softly because otherwise he will throw you out the window."

I wouldn't have, of course, because I couldn't have. Even then I was getting old and fat, to the point that Nixon, when he came to California late in the campaign, smilingly told me to "lose some weight." On top of all that, it was only a mezzanine window. But that is beside the point. The point is that Mardian's warning made things easier on a lot of us.

Ten days later Fred Malek, the man in charge of all kinds of things in the national campaign, came to Los Angeles and asked me to meet him at the Proud Bird restaurant near the airport. I surmised he wanted to talk about the forms.

The morning of the meeting I had a stroke of genius. I hand-lettered a sign about 2 feet-by-18 inches and fastened it to a stick that I fastened to the pile of forms that still sat in the parking lot. The sign read, "Malek Memorial Monument." Somebody dug up a Polaroid camera and I took a couple of pictures.

At the restaurant I showed them to Malek, who had long been one of my heroes in the Nixon administration. On the day Nixon fired Interior Secretary Wally Hickel, Malek, who was heading the White House personnel office, went over to Interior and fired Hickel's five top aides. I was in the meeting in the White House when the deed was announced. I cheered. More of this sort of thing needs to be done in all administrations.

Malek looked at the pictures with interest.

"I want you to have them," I said. "And in return I'd like a favor. Please tell those people in Washington I'm not going to use those stupid forms and please will they get off my back."

"I'll do it now," he said. He found a phone and came back a few minutes later. "You don't have to use them," he said. Which, of course, I wouldn't have anyway.

There is a lull in every presidential campaign between the primary elections and the nominating conventions which usually are held in July or August. The president's party traditionally holds its convention last. To my way of thinking, the earlier the better. An early convention gives your troops a shorter time after the primaries to become restless and more time after the convention to prepare for the unofficial campaign kick-off day, Labor Day.

But in recent years, spending limits for the general election cycle have forced party leaders to move conventions closer to election day so the party's nominees can spend their money, now supplied by the federal government, more effectively over a shorter period. In 1972 the Republican Convention began on August 21, late for a first-time nominee but not a problem for a sitting president who was running at least thirty points ahead. During the postprimary lull the campaigns get ready for the national conventions and assess what must be done afterward. Volunteers take their vacations and nonessential paid workers are temporarily laid off without pay in order to save money. This was true with the California reelect campaign except that very few people were laid off. Money was not a problem.

Two months before the convention, on June 17, something happened that had only a minor effect on the campaign, but after the election had a major effect on the nation, on the president, and on many of his closest confidants and aides. The happening was Watergate, a third-rate burglary that was to become a world-class disaster.

Many of the important people in the national reelect campaign were in Los Angeles when the first story on Watergate broke. They had come to attend a strategy meeting at the Airport Marina Hotel. Mitchell was there and Magruder, too. Mitchell was his usual taciturn, unflappable self, but Magruder was antsy and huddled frequently with others from Washington.

I finally drew him aside and asked, "What in the hell is going on?"

After he told me, "Nothing," and I told him I didn't believe him, he finally came up with a story that he may or may not have thought was true but was good enough for him to think I would believe. He said several people had been caught breaking into Democratic National Committee headquarters and a couple were carrying money that had been traced back to Nixon headquarters.

"You damn fools," I broke out.

"No! No!" he said. "We're all right. We had nothing to do with it."

Because I didn't think anyone could be that dumb I halfway believed him, just as I did nearly a year later when he came to see me in my office in Sacramento, where I had moved after the election.

Watergate, he then assured me, was behind him. He had testified before the grand jury and was free and clear. He had come to California, where he had lived before joining the Nixon White House staff, because he wanted to run for secretary of state. Could I, he asked, get him an appointment with Governor Reagan so he could tell him of his intentions?

I called Deaver, who in those days took and returned phone calls—at least mine—and asked if he could find a few minutes for Magruder to see the governor. He did. Magruder then flew back to Washington where a few days later he confessed to his role in Watergate. He never did run for secretary of state.

But at the Airport Marina Hotel the concern was about what Mitchell as campaign chairman would say at a press conference scheduled that afternoon. Cliff Miller, a California public relations executive who served as a PR adviser to the White House, was called in to help. It was wasted time. The story hadn't yet filtered out to the West Coast and Mitchell was not asked a single question.

Any relief Mitchell and the others felt was short-lived, of course, because the story played all during the summer and fall, especially in Washington. Fortunately for Nixon, probably because McGovern was such a bad candidate, the nation had yet to take it seriously and it never interfered with either the convention or the election.

Late in the fall campaign a little side bar to the drama played out at our L.A. headquarters. The *Washington Post* had discovered that a young man named Donald Segretti had been hired by Nixon's scheduling secretary, Dwight Chapin, to play political pranks on the McGovern campaign in the same way Dick Tuck had been hired by Democrats to play pranks on Nixon in 1962 and 1968 and on Barry Goldwater in 1964.

The difference, Chapin was to find when the story broke, was that

Tuck was a favorite among political reporters, most of whom were Democrats who enjoyed seeing Republicans in general, and Nixon in particular, made the butt of Tuck's pranks, but resented a Nixon operative playing pranks on McGovern. What had been pranks when pulled by Tuck became dirty tricks when pulled by Segretti. And, in all fairness, Segretti pulled some stunts that crossed the line from pranks to dirty tricks. But then, over the years, so had Tuck.

Segretti had been hired by Chapin unbeknownst to anyone in the reelect organization. This was why I received a frantic call from Magruder at the Republican National Committee. He asked if I had someone in Wisconsin messing around with the Democratic primary campaigns. I assured him I did not, thinking that things were beginning to get a little out of hand, what with Nixon's people all trying to be heroes and not telling each other what they were doing. It turned out that it was Segretti who was messing around in Wisconsin.

A couple of days after the Segretti story broke Rose Marie came into my office and said, "There's a man downstairs who wants to see you but he won't give his name."

"Tell him to go away."

She came back shortly. "He finally sent his name up in a sealed note."

I opened it. "Segretti," I read aloud. "Who in the hell is Segretti?"

"Shhhh," she admonished.

Then I remembered. "Tell him to come up."

A moment later a little old man appeared, greying, scrawny, about five feet four, nervously smoking an unfiltered cigaret. He told me he was Donald Segretti's father and, when I asked, showed me some identification. His son had been hiding out since the first story broke, and no, he hadn't seen or heard from him and no, he didn't know where he was. But the press was annoying him and upsetting his wife who was ill. He didn't know what to do. Neither did I. What he really wanted was a little comfort and some sense of not being abandoned.

After he left I called Gordon Strachan, a Haldeman assistant, and told him of my visitor. He thanked me but didn't offer any advice. The old man came back several times. I saw him twice more but he never seemed to want anything except reassurance. When he left the third time I told Rose Marie that I didn't want to see him again. I was getting nervous.

"He probably isn't, but it's always possible he might be setting me up," I said. "All I need is for some reporter to see him come in here and write a story about how Segretti is communicating with the White House through his father and me. Besides, there's not a damn thing I can do for him."

To protect my backside I checked around to see if the younger Segretti had been involved in any way in the California campaign. He hadn't, but our headquarters in Torrance turned up a card that listed him among its volunteers. The people there wanted to destroy it.

"Don't," I said. "I'd rather see a story about him being one of our volunteers than one about us destroying evidence that he had worked in our campaign."

Fortunately, no stories appeared and nobody ever wrote or testified about our little role in the great Segretti caper.

After the nominating convention we went back to work on the campaign and tried to ignore national headquarters which kept its plethora of campaign aides busy interfering in what is done best at the state level, namely identifying your candidate's supporters and planning a get-out-the-vote effort. As is usual in a presidential campaign, we were involved in an activity that upset many in the party and almost all of the lower-level candidates.

We were working to get to the polls those Democrats who would vote for Nixon, regardless of their stand on members of Congress and the state legislature. Politics is a selfish, me-first business. You help others only when you have your own race wrapped up, and sometimes not then. Our job was to win California for the president. And in California if Republicans are to win a statewide election they must have Democratic votes.

That is not always the case, however, in races for Republican-held congressional and legislative seats. In those cases all the incumbents want—and they want it fervently—is for Democrats to stay home on election day. So we had a lot of protests from candidates and party workers, but we also had our orders from Washington to find and activate our Democratic vote. As a sop to Republican candidates we promised to give them the names of pro-Nixon Democrats so they could go after their votes too.

Our state chairman of Democrats for Nixon was James Roosevelt, son of Franklin D., a former congressman and an old friend whom I had covered when he was serving in the House. Once when he was considering running for mayor of Los Angeles, he asked if I would be his press secretary, but I couldn't do that. Friendship is one thing; working for a Democrat is something else, even in a nonpartisan mayor's race.

The selection of Roosevelt was a stroke of genius on someone's part; Democrats could follow the son of the revered president and not have to vote for the radical nut who wanted the federal government to give $1,000 to everyone in the country, George McGovern. Roosevelt had not abandoned his New Deal liberalism, but he was a marine combat veteran of World War II and believed that America ought to win its wars, whereas McGovern was advocating peace at any price, on our knees if necessary.

Late in September Nixon began a campaign swing around California accompanied by Haldeman. When he saw me Haldeman asked, "How much are you going to win by?"

"By more than you did in 1968," I said.

"You have to do better than that," he grumbled.

"What about a million votes?"

"That's better."

Those were confident words on my part because I really didn't have a feel for how things were going. I knew we were doing all right, but the McGovern campaign was a mystery to me. Since Washington had refused to show us any polls all we knew was what we read in the papers. But what really had me uneasy was that there was almost no sign of the McGovern campaign. During the California primary McGovern had had a smart, savvy crew and it showed in his victory over Hubert Humphrey. But they went away and apparently never came back. During the last month before the election I called around the state almost daily fruitlessly trying to find signs of McGovern activity. I worried about a last-minute blitz or a last-minute dirty trick (even Democrats are not above this sort of thing) or a last-minute charge that we wouldn't have time to disprove.

Then it finally dawned on me. There was nothing there. McGovern had a few really good people, but they were spread too thin to be effective. It was almost as if the votes he had gotten in the primaries were all he was going to get in November. He was too far left for most Americans.

Beyond that, his party was in tatters with even the AFL-CIO refusing to support him. But still, you never know. The great middle of the American electorate is as fickle as the weather in March. Which is one reason you always have to be a little leery of even reputable polls. Another reason is that people lie to poll takers, especially when polling is done on the phone and they don't have to look the pollster in the eye.

Two weeks before the election Nixon was comfortably ahead all across the nation, and he decided to spend the night before the election in San Clemente and fly to Washington on election day. But first, he would land at Ontario, a city thirty miles east of Los Angeles, where he expected a large and enthusiastic rally.

Ordinarily White House advance men took care of presidential appearances. But this was to be Nixon's homecoming rally as well as the end of the campaign and Washington wanted us to turn out fifty thousand supporters. We tried. We advertised the president's appearance on the radio. We distributed thousands of fliers. We put our organizations in the eight counties of southern California to work advertising his appearance and lining up buses to bring supporters from as far away as a hundred miles. With all this effort you'd think that from a population of about 12 million people you could drag fifty thousand out to see the president of the United States. Well, you've been wrong before.

Crowd sizes are difficult to estimate. Over the years I've found that most reporters tend greatly to overestimate the number of persons attending a rally or watching a parade. They get their estimates from a police official who hasn't the vaguest idea but hazards a guess anyway. Or they ask the candidate's press secretary, who lies to them.

So fifty thousand is a lot of people and that's how many we told the press attended the Ontario rally. For the most part they believed us. Better than that, so did Nixon. In his memoirs he refers to "the overflow crowd at the Ontario airport" and two paragraphs later recalls thanking that crowd "for making it probably the best rally we have ever had."

It was a good rally and President Nixon was emotionally up for it. But it certainly was not the best rally of his career; there weren't even close to fifty thousand people in attendance. I figured about nineteen thousand—the temporary stands which would only hold about twenty thousand, were little more than half full and it was easy to walk through the loosely packed crowd standing in the infield.

The next day was election day and we put our volunteers and paid

staff to work getting our vote out. When it was all over I had the
pleasure of writing Haldeman announcing that we had won California
by more than a million votes. That was my reward, my sole but very
satisfying reward. Today, many years later, I still know one thing:
George McGovern made me look good by so badly screwing up his
campaign. I will always be grateful to him and to the delegates to the
Democratic Convention for choosing such a lousy candidate.

As the campaign drew to a close I began giving thought to what I
would do next to make a living. That bugaboo seemed to come up after
every campaign and every time I quit a job. I knew I didn't want to go
back to Washington, primarily because I couldn't get any job in the
Nixon administration that I wanted. In a phone conversation with Chuck
Colson, as yet unconvicted and unsaved, I explored briefly the possibility of becoming chairman of the Republican National Committee. He
told me bluntly to forget it; the job had been promised. And so it had
been—to George Bush.

Bob Dole, who had been busting his tail for Nixon since the start of
his administration, had served as chairman since early in 1971. But
Nixon decided he wanted Bush even though Bush was said not to be
particularly interested. Dole was summoned to Camp David and told his
services as chairman were no longer needed.

With the chairmanship out, and thus, eventually, the presidency, the
question for me became: What now?

Fortunately, or so I thought, that question was answered almost
before I had a chance to ask it. Immediately after the election I was
contacted by Ed Reinecke, California's lieutenant governor and Reagan's heir apparent. I'd known him since his years as a congressman. He
was a conservative and had quickly become the darling—after
Reagan—of the big conservative majority in the California Republican
party. He was personable, handsome, intelligent, and a CalTech graduate. His downside, as I was to discover, was that he had no political
smarts, was not a good administrator, and was a difficult person to work
with. But I didn't know all this in late 1972.

Reagan had already said he would not seek a third term. Mainly, I
think, he was tired of the job, tired of dealing with the petty personalities in the legislature, tired of commuting to Los Angeles on most
weekends so his wife could socialize with their rich friends, tired of the
small-town atmosphere of Sacramento.

Reagan was also boxed in a little. In 1966, when he was running against Pat Brown who was seeking a third term, he had called for a two-term limit for governors. It had been my idea and was purely a political ploy. Reagan wasn't much enthused but he understood what I was trying to do. Brown brushed off the proposal and so did the press.

After Reagan was elected he did submit a two-term limit proposal but never pushed it and it was soon forgotten. Philosophically neither Reagan nor I at the time believed in term limitations. Reagan still doesn't. I do. I used to think, and Reagan still thinks, that if the people in a certain district want to elect some bum to the legislature for ten or twenty terms or as governor or president for three or four, that is their business.

But I believe now that it isn't, because the votes of the bum elected to the Congress from New York are going to have an effect on all Americans. And if we elect an aging president to a fourth term, who knows how he will deal with a major crisis while he lives or how well the vice president, picked on a whim, will perform?

I used to believe that the wondrous thing about this country and this people was that we managed to survive and keep most of our freedoms regardless of whom we elected or how often we reelected them. Today, I'm not so sure. I worry about a system that reelects 98 percent of its incumbent congressmen and I'm glad a two-term limit on the presidency keeps an incumbent from growing too old and too tired and keeps the people from reelecting a man out of affection, without regard for the future.

Some want to limit a president to one six-year term. Not me. I can't help but wonder if the nation could have survived six years of Jimmy Carter. Give me two terms of four years each and if that's too long I'll settle for one four-year term. Most presidents don't get much done of any value in their second terms anyway. A president like Reagan, by the end of his first term, has gone from being the outsider determined to change things to becoming an integral part of the establishment—more a part of the problem, if you will, and less a part of the solution.

With Governor Reagan not seeking a third term conservatives saw Reinecke as his logical successor. After all, Reagan personally had picked him to serve out the remainder of the term of former Lt. Gov. Robert Finch.

In those days California governors filled constitutional office vacancies by appointment without the concurrence of the state senate. But Reagan, who didn't enjoy either hiring or firing, had a problem. Several people in his administration wanted the job. So rather than pick one and hurt the feelings of the others he took a typical Reagan "out." He decided not to name anyone from his administration. After looking around he offered the post to a veteran San Diego congressman, Bob Wilson. Wilson, a staunch Nixonite and never part of the Reagan organization, was surprised and flattered, but quickly decided not to leave the Congress.

While he was trying to figure out what to do next Reagan received a call from his brother, Neil. Neil barely knew Ed Reinecke but did know he was a conservative. So Reagan called Reinecke. Reinecke said he was interested and almost before anyone could say "Bob Finch" Ed Reinecke was the new lieutenant governor and next in line to succeed Reagan. In the statewide elections of 1970 Reinecke, whom the voters knew to be Reagan's boy, was elected to a full four-year term.

As I have said, Reinecke was personable and intelligent, a mechanical engineer, and seemingly an all-around good fellow. But he turned out to be a weak lieutenant governor. (That's kind of like being a weak vice president: it's hard to conceive of any other kind.)

When he contacted me, however, he was still Reagan's fair-haired boy, or so I thought. His political godfather at the time was Burt Raynes, the CEO of the Rohr Corp. of San Diego that manufactured airplane parts and light rail cars.

At Reinecke's request he and I flew to Phoenix to meet with Raynes who was on vacation and we discussed the possibility of my running Reinecke's campaign. They asked what I would cost. Having overcharged the Nixon campaign I figured I could do no less for the Reinecke campaign. Five thousand bucks a month, I said. They never blinked. In fact, they wanted me to agree to a two-year contract and go to work immediately. We compromised. I went to work the first of the year and at Raynes' insistence signed a two-year contract in February. Raynes also guaranteed to find the money to pay campaign expenses during the first year. It proved too good to be true.

In early January Bonnie and I moved back to Sacramento. My mission was to make Ed Reinecke California's next governor, my very own mission impossible.

Before accepting, I called Ed Meese to see if Reinecke was still

viewed by Reagan and those around him as heir apparent. Though
Meese said yes, I thought I detected a lack of enthusiasm, but I put it
down to his inate caution. Foolishly, maybe greedily, I didn't press him.
I should have because Ed's attitude, I'm now convinced, was really the
beginning of his and Reagan's disillusionment. As time went by it was
easy to see why. In spite of himself, Reinecke was his own man. He
wanted to be on the Reagan team but never quite figured out how to
join it.

Arriving in Sacramento, I found cheap office space near the capitol
and hired a young woman named Diane Graham as my secretary. She
had worked for me in the governor's office and again in the reelect
campaign. A smart, competent woman, as time went on she evolved
into a women's libber and eventually found her new philosophy incom-
patible with secretarial work or much work of any kind.

But in early 1973 all was sweetness and light. I perceived my job that
year as primarily a public relations task; keep Reinecke ahead in the
polls, make him appear unbeatable in a primary and thus discourage
any serious Republican opposition. That seemed all right with the
lieutenant governor and with Raynes. In addition, I planned a series of
fund-raising events to supplement the money Raynes had guaranteed
and bring together Reinecke's supporters from the various areas of the
state.

As I look back, it's easy to see why some who had tabbed Reinecke as
Reagan's successor walked away from him. But I'd have been a bit
happier if they'd warned me sooner. I'd have probably gone to work for
him anyway but I'd have spent a lot of time doing what I didn't think
needed to be done—shoring up his relations with the governor's office
and fatcat supporters who, both Reinecke and I initially expected,
would also support him. Instead they sat on their hands.

Raynes had never been part of the Reagan team, but he wanted to be,
so as he watched the kitchen cabinet and the high-level members of the
Reagan administration quietly sneaking away he followed. I suspect,
too, that he may have had a hint from Reagan's people that they were
going to hang poor Ed out to dry. The funny thing is, they didn't have to.
Ed proved fully capable of doing it all by himself.

By mid-1973 Raynes had left the Reinecke campaign without so
much as a "so long" or a parting wave. He only took one thing—his
checkbook. One thing he didn't take was any more phone calls, either

from Reinecke or me. He also left me a souvenir, a signed copy of my contract which I hope to sell someday for what it proved to be worth. In spite of his desertion, the campaign limped along. And in December Reinecke was where I wanted him to be, ahead in all the polls. I was pretty pleased about that.

In late fall a wealthy Reinecke supporter offered us an oversized billboard at a major Los Angeles intersection. We took it. It featured a picture of Reinecke and the words, "Reinecke for Governor—His Own Man." I figured that if the Reaganites weren't going to help we would have to divorce Reinecke from them, at least a little bit. In short order I had a call from Mike Deaver, Meese's assistant.

"Who's responsible for the slogan?" he asked.

"Me," I said.

He muttered something and hung up. I guess he wanted it both ways. It was okay to abandon Reinecke; it wasn't all right to point it out, even subtly.

Because I thought things were going well I thought Reinecke thought so too. Wrong again.

In mid-December Reinecke decided we should go to Palm Springs and discuss the campaign. I don't know why people in government always have to go somewhere else to have meetings and seminars, but they do. They must enjoy spending other people's money. For this meeting we stayed at a little old motel owned by a little old Republican couple, Dave and Annie Margolis, strong Reagan and Reinecke supporters.

Right off Reinecke demanded to know why he didn't have chairmen in all fifty-six counties. I told him the plan had been to build his popularity in 1973 so as to discourage any serious opposition and in that we had succeeded—he was the clear leader for the Republican nomination. That didn't satisfy him. Neither did my explanation that picking chairmen two years in advance didn't make much sense. You can't organize volunteers that far ahead and stay organized. There ain't nuthin' for them to do and volunteers with nothing to do often go away and don't come back and if they don't go away they pester the campaign management for something to do even when there isn't anything.

Next I went on to the campaign organization. I had drawn up an elaborate chart showing what personnel was needed, who reported to whom, and all the rest of the nonsense that nobody ever pays much attention to. I figured the chart was made to order for Reinecke who after all was an engineer and therefore would like complicated things. Not this time.

He blew his top, said the chart was too complicated, said he wanted a simple one. I think to this day that had I given him a simple chart he would have demanded one with more details. That day he was suffering from whatever it is in men that compares to PMS in women and I was the guy he was aiming his wild hormones at. In any event, he had obviously come to fight—with me. I still don't know why. I had stood with him when Reagan and his people had walked away, when Raynes had reneged on his contract and refused to pay my salary, when without the money we raised his campaign would have been dead.

On Monday, back in Sacramento, I drafted a friendly letter of resignation and messengered it over to Reinecke, thinking he would respond in kind. Then I called our campaign chairman, Cliff Anderson in Pasadena. He had talked to Reinecke so he knew of my letter. He asked me not to say or do anything until a statement could be worked out that would be in the best interests of both Reinecke and Nofziger.

I agreed, ignoring the advice of Burt Williams, a public relations man who was doing some volunteer work for me. He warned that if I didn't get a statement out first Reinecke would put one out that would hurt me.

"They wouldn't do anything like that," I assured him.

But a couple of blocks away they did. The first I knew of it was when reporters began calling asking for my reaction to Reinecke's statement. I didn't take their calls. After all, I had been promised by Anderson that nothing would be put out that Reinecke and I didn't agree on.

Then a letter from Reinecke was delivered accepting my resignation, but no copy of the press statement. When I finally got a copy I found it was filled with lies and other untruths and said so a day later in a letter to Joe Drachnik, who had become Reinecke's chief of staff on my recommendation. I asked him why they had set out to make an enemy out of a friend and why they had not lived up to the agreement between Anderson and me. I told him that when I called Anderson to protest, his first words were, "I didn't sandbag you," meaning someone else certainly had.

Thus ended my association with Ed Reinecke, which was just as well, because he was later indicted and convicted on charges of lying to the Congress. His conviction eventually was overturned, but well before that he had lost the Republican primary and any chance of becoming governor of California. Thus also ended my chance of helping to elect another California governor and, for all practical purposes, Reinecke's political career.

I struggled through the next year and a half doing some political consulting, some fund raising, some writing, and a lot of penny-pinching. In many ways it was a time of drifting. I should have found a job, worked at soliciting new business, or put Bonnie to work. Actually, she began selling real estate, something a lot of politicians' wives do, either out of boredom or because their husbands aren't making enough money. In our case it was probably both.

In retrospect, what I was doing was just waiting—waiting for Reagan to run for president. I had thought since 1966 that he could be president. I had wanted him to run all out in 1968 instead of in the reluctant, quarter-hearted fashion that he consented to. Now, at the start of 1974 I thought 1976 would be his year and so did people like Deaver, Meese, and Pete Hannaford.

Ed Meese, God bless him! What a good friend, then and over the years. He made it a point of staying in contact with me after I left the governor's office. He remained a friend and ally, as did his predecessor, Bill Clark. A small example: After Reinecke was convicted he resigned as lieutenant governor. That left Drachnik without a job. Meese was willing to hire him, but before he did so he called me to see if I had any objections. Although I had been less than happy at Drachnik's part in the resignation fiasco I knew he was competent and had no problems with him going to work in the governor's office.

At the beginning of Reagan's first term Meese had been his legal affairs secretary and had turned out to be a solid, sound, and sensible assistant. At the end of 1968 when Clark resigned as executive secretary, i.e., chief of staff, Meese succeeded him. A kind and decent man, Meese kept the staff he inherited from Clark, including Clark's long-time aide, Mike Deaver. He later promoted Deaver from assistant to the chief of staff to assistant chief of staff, in effect making him the number two staffer in the governor's office.

A few years later Deaver was to repay his two mentors by urging the president to fire them. He never succeeded, although he, along with

Nancy Reagan and Jim Baker, made life miserable enough for Clark so that he left the administration. Meese was another matter. Under that pleasant and unflappable demeanor he is a bulldog, as his enemies and detractors have found out. He never quits. And nobody has ever yet run him off.

This might be a good time to set a little bit of the record straight. In his ghost-written book, *Behind the Scenes*, Deaver asserts that Clark was always a little afraid of Nancy Reagan. Not so. Clark learned early that he did not have enough time to serve adequately both Ronald Reagan and his wife. To make sure Nancy was properly taken care of he assigned that task to Deaver. And as it turned out, Clark's action served all three of them well until he went to the White House, nearly fourteen years later.

After Clark left the governor's office Meese kept Deaver on the same assignment for the next six years. He really had no choice. By this time a special, almost mother-son relationship had developed between Nancy and Deaver and she would not have settled for anyone else. Deaver, in turn, had developed into much more than a purse carrier for Nancy. He became the Reagans' chief advance man, helper, close personal friend, and adviser on many subjects, some of which were beyond his ken. He served them well in the early years, less well later when he attempted to manipulate them for his own purposes. This is not unique in politics or government or, for that matter, anywhere else. Jim Baker, Reagan's first presidential chief of staff, is a master at it.

But back in the early and middle 1970s we were all part of the same clique that had one goal—to do what was best for Ronald Reagan. We were loyal to Reagan. We were loyal to each other. And by mid-1974 we had pretty much decided that Ronald Reagan should be and could be the next president of the United States.

6

Reagan's Big Try

RONALD REAGAN'S CAMPAIGN for president in 1976 really began in 1974, before he left the governor's office. But, early on, President Nixon almost derailed it. Under threat of impeachment he resigned. And Gerald Ford, the nation's first ever appointed vice president, became the first president who had never been elected either president or vice president.

For a while Reagan debated not running. He was a strong party man. His inclination was to support the person in office, whether Nixon under fire or Ford, the president by fluke. But the people around him wanted him to run. After all, hadn't Ford, shortly after being sworn in, announced he would not seek a full term? Nobody really believed Ford, but his statement gave those with Reagan an excuse to continue our campaign planning.

As far as I know, in 1974 Reagan never told any of us, including Deaver, that he would run. His style was to keep his plans to himself, not tie himself down until he felt he absolutely had to. He liked to give his supporters full rein to charge ahead, but not personally get out in front until he could see what was out there. This always worked well for him, not that he always won, but he never walked into a political ambush. In running for office Reagan was a careful, cautious man.

With Reagan's second term as governor ending, Deaver put together a series of planning meetings that left out some old Reagan people and brought in some new. F. Clifton White and Thomas C. Reed, the two principal players in the abortive effort of 1968, were left out, primarily, I think, because Deaver hardly knew them—they were outsiders by the time Deaver had become an insider.

Two others Deaver ignored may well have cost Reagan the nomination—the men who ran Reagan's gubernatorial campaigns, Stuart Spencer and Bill Roberts. Deaver was feuding with Spencer and didn't want him around. Reagan, as usual, stayed aloof from the organizing of the campaign, which he pretended wasn't going on, and any internal feuding.

Spencer wound up running the Ford campaign, although a series of other men, Howard (Bo) Callaway, Rogers C.B. Morton, and James A. Baker III, chaired it. None, however, had any great political smarts, which left the serious job of beating Reagan to Spencer. For example, when Reagan had a chance early in the campaign to win Florida, Spencer sent in Bill Roberts, who cut Reagan into little pieces. As a result, Ford, after narrowly escaping in New Hampshire, won Florida handily.

While ignoring a number of those who had helped make Reagan governor, Deaver brought in others, including John Sears, Jim Lake, and Peter Hannaford. Lake and Hannaford had joined Reagan late in his second term, but both were dedicated to him and eager to see him run. Lake ran the campaigns in New Hampshire and Vermont and later became campaign press secretary. Hannaford, a fine writer, became Reagan's chief speech writer and scheduled a number of briefings to bring Reagan up to snuff on key issues.

Lake, a former grocer in Delano, California, had been bitten by the political bug while helping in the congressional campaigns of Bob Mathias, the former Olympic Decathlon champion. But at heart Lake was a Reaganite, so when the job of heading California's Washington office opened up Lake applied and Meese hired him. Thanks to Meese's sponsorship he quickly became a Reagan insider.

Hannaford had come to the governor's office in 1974 as communications director. An advertising and public relations man in Oakland, he had run once for Congress in a highly Democratic district and had lost. As a writer, researcher, and idea man he quickly became a valuable part of the Reagan organization.

Sears, a lawyer, had been the self-proclaimed boy wonder of the Nixon campaign of 1968 and liked to take much of the credit for Nixon's nomination. The truth was, Nixon had been a shoo-in from the beginning. He had spent the years since his 1962 defeat for governor of California piling up political IOUs, solidifying his national base, and gaining a reputation as his party's foreign policy expert. His two eventual opponents, Reagan and Nelson Rockefeller, entered the race much too late.

After Nixon was nominated Sears was demoted to the campaign of Nixon's vice presidential nominee, Spiro Agnew. John Mitchell, Nixon's campaign manager, former law partner, and close friend, neither liked nor trusted him, feelings I grew to understand and appreciate. Regardless, Sears was a bright young man with a line of political patter that made him seem even brighter. After the 1968 election he worked briefly in the Nixon White House until Mitchell, by then attorney general, forced his resignation.

Sears came to the Reagan organization on the recommendation of Bob Walker, the man who dreamed up the Eleventh Commandment. Walker had known Sears in the 1968 Nixon campaign and persuaded Deaver to invite him to some early organizational meetings. Deaver became enamored of Sears, whose line of political chatter impressed almost all of us, including the Reagans. Thus, in mid-1975 when Deaver recommended that Sears be named campaign manager there were no objections, even though he was the kind of person who ordered chicken instead of steak for his main dinner course.

When Reagan left office at the start of 1975 the immediate question was what would he do to make a living. Ford had craftily offered him a cabinet post, but Reagan had smartly turned it down. Some of his wealthy friends told him they would have him named to corporate boards, but nothing ever materialized. Another possibility, going back to acting, didn't have much appeal.

So, what to do? Deaver and Hannaford made the decision for him. They went from the governor's office directly into the public relations business in Los Angeles and the first thing they did was sign Ronald Reagan on as a client. It was a good deal for all three of them.

Deaver set out to do what he did best, look after the Reagans' personal interests, leaving Hannaford to run the business. They quickly turned Reagan into a miniconglomerate, signing him up to make speeches at $5,000 a whack, a lot of money in those pre-Carter inflation days, syndicating a daily three-minute radio commentary, and eventually closing a deal with King Features for a twice-a-week column.

All in all there was more than Reagan could comfortably do. So, though he liked to write his own radio commentary, Hannaford wrote some of his columns and articles and farmed out others to me. He paid me fifty bucks for any radio commentary I wrote and once paid me $200 for an article signed by Reagan defending the right to keep and bear arms. It was a pretty radical right-wing piece and I was a little surprised when Reagan accepted it without a change.

Reagan made a lot of speeches, many on behalf of the party and its candidates. I had always assumed his political speeches were given free and therefore I was upset when several candidates for whom he'd spoken and raised money returned the favor by endorsing, supporting, and working for Ford.

It wasn't until 1977 that I discovered a reason. I ran into a conservative congressman from Minnesota, Tom Hagedorn, for whom Reagan had spoken and who, in turn, had supported Ford. I was still a little irritated with him.

"How come," I asked, "you supported Ford when Reagan raised money for your campaign?"

"Lyn," he said, "we paid him."

I was flabbergasted and annoyed. I had not figured that Deaver was that dumb and/or greedy. Besides, like me, he had complained about those whom Reagan had helped helping Ford. Unbelievably, he had not understood that if you take money for helping someone it isn't a favor and you have no right to expect a favor in return.

As soon as I saw him I informed him of this little truism and, as far as I know, he quit charging for Reagan's political speeches.

In June of 1975 our little group decided it was time to put a show on the road, which we did immediately after the Fourth of July. The campaign organization consisted of John Sears, Jim Lake, and me, operating temporarily out of Sears' law offices in Washington, D.C. The first thing we did was get a post office box so people could send us money. And shortly the money began to trickle in.

We'd been operating only a few days when Bo Callaway dropped by to see Sears. Callaway had just resigned as secretary of the Army to take over as manager of Ford's fledgling campaign. Somewhere between August of 1974 and July of 1975 Ford had forgotten his promise not to run for a full term. Bo's mission was to try to bring Sears aboard the Ford campaign. Sears turned him down, a decision he probably regrets to this day.

Callaway was a patrician (whatever that may mean) Georgian who had served briefly in Congress and had been euchered out of the Georgia governorship in a race in which he won the popular vote but lost the governorship because he failed to win a majority of the counties. An old Nixon hand, he had been named secretary of the Army as a reward for faithful service.

Callaway was also an old friend and I took to needling him in what I thought was a friendly way, with what I thought were humorous memos. One had to do with Crested Butte, a Colorado mountaintop that Bo was attempting to develop into a ski resort. Some of his problems with the project had hit the papers and I clipped one story and sent it to him with the notation, "You have crested too soon."

He didn't think that was funny. In fact, as I discovered eventually, he didn't find humor in any of my notes. During the late summer when he was looking for a campaign press secretary he told one reporter, who later told me, "I want someone to do to them what Nofziger is doing to me."

Actually, I wasn't doing anything to him; I was just having fun.

Bo eventually left their campaign to be followed by Secretary of the Interior Rogers Morton, who was followed by James A. Baker III, who presided over Ford's ultimate defeat at the hands of Jimmy Carter. Baker is unique in recent American politics. He parlayed Ford's defeat, his own defeat two years later when he ran for Texas attorney general, and George Bush's defeat by Ronald Reagan (and never mind his minor role in Reagan's 1980 general election campaign) into positions as Reagan's chief of staff and, later, secretary of the Treasury. And he almost became Reagan's national security adviser, but that is another story.

Those first weeks of the incipient Reagan campaign were a lot of fun. Sears knew what he wanted to do and he set about doing it. And early on we lucked into a finance chairman of sorts.

One day a man came in, saying he'd been sent by our silent partners in the West, Deaver and Hannaford. His name was Jack Courtemanche, he wanted to help elect Ronald Reagan president, and he didn't need any money; he would work as a volunteer. Our kind of guy.

When he had gone Sears turned to me and asked, "Did you notice how much he looks like Herb Kalmbach?"

I said I did. Kalmbach was a fine man, a southern California attorney who had been one of Nixon's chief fund-raisers. Once, when I was running the Nixon reelection campaign in California I was summoned to Washington. I flew first class. After we landed I saw Kalmbach, a much more important part of the campaign than I, leaving the plane from the coach section. I hid.

"Well," Sears said, "since he looks like Herb let's put him to work raising money." Which we did.

Looking back, given that Reagan was running against a sitting president and not many Republican fatcats thought he could win or that he should even run, Courtemanche did a good job.

In the meantime Reagan and Deaver and Hannaford were sitting in West Los Angeles pretending they were really no part of what was going on in Washington.

But Reagan was increasingly visible as he continued to speak around the country, write his syndicated column, and air his radio commentary. It has always been interesting to me that Reagan's opponents in 1976 and 1980 didn't use any of those radio programs or writings against him. They were either a lot more mellow than I remember, or the Fords and Bushes and Carters just didn't think it worth their while.

During this period Reagan continued to mull over whether he should really take on a sitting president, even one as lacking in luster as Ford. I think if the political people around him—Sears, Lake, Deaver, Dick Wirthlin, and Nofziger—had come to him and said, "We think you ought to call it off; we're convinced you can't win," he would have dropped the idea. But we never said it and the polls never indicated it. Indeed, Reagan was about the only exciting figure on the political scene, and the media, which relishes a good political fight, did nothing to discourage him.

Sears knew that, partly because of Reagan's coyness, the campaign needed a chairman, one of national stature, to give it legitimacy. He settled on Paul Laxalt, a conservative freshman senator from Nevada. Laxalt had served a term as governor of Nevada and had declined to run for reelection. He had also turned down an offer from Nixon to be secretary of the Interior. His term as governor had coincided with Reagan's first term and the two men had become friends. They worked together to try to preserve Lake Tahoe, the big mountain lake that straddles the California-Nevada border and is threatened by all the evils that come with civilization and overdevelopment.

Though only in his second year in the Senate, Laxalt was one of its most popular members. He is a careful, cautious politician, and before he leaped into a campaign against a sitting president of his own party he wanted to be sure Reagan was going to be a candidate. But Sears couldn't give him that assurance. So Laxalt asked to talk to Reagan. Reagan said he hadn't made up his mind, but, yes, he was letting "Sears and the fellas" explore the possibility. And, yes, he wasn't real happy with Ford. But, no, he wouldn't decide until sometime in the fall.

It was classic Reagan, but Laxalt had watched him long enough and knew him well enough to realize that Reagan's failure to say "no," while not quite a "yes," still was better than a "maybe." That was good enough. He agreed to take the chairmanship of the Reagan exploratory committee.

That decision was a ten-strike for Sears, for Reagan and, in the long run, for Laxalt, because the road he chose led to a long, close personal friendship with the man and woman who in 1980 were to be elected the president and become the first lady of the United States. Not bad for a sheepherder's son from the boondocks state of Nevada and only a generation removed from the French Basque Pyrenees.

As the campaign moved into the fall of 1975 it became ever more evident that it still needed one other thing to get it off the ground—a candidate. Reagan was still dilly-dallying. I'd been pushing hard to get him to announce, because without him, too many conservatives, such as Margaret Brock, the grand dame of the California Republican party, were drifting off to the Ford camp. And money was a problem. We were raising some by direct mail but the $1,000 contributions were hard to come by without a candidate.

Even so, most of our people, excluding me, thought we could afford to wait, or if they didn't think so they at least kept their mouths shut. One reason was that Sears was not pushing for an early announcement date. I always suspected that he wanted one, but 1976 was not 1980 and he had not yet become familiar enough with Reagan to become contemptuous of him. That would come later. At any rate he held his peace.

Reagan had his own reasons for not announcing. He was making his living by writing his columns, taping his radio commentary, and speaking. All of this would end the minute he became a candidate. And not only for him, but also for Deaver and Hannaford, who were renting him office space, handling his business affairs, and booking his speeches.

Eventually, they were to solve their problem by joining the campaign as paid staffers, but Reagan couldn't. Although he took expenses while he was running, it would not have looked right for him to take a salary out of his campaign coffers.

Reagan had another reason, too. He really did want to be certain he was doing the right thing. This was an especially tough decision, deciding whether to run against a sitting president. He would be up against the party hierarchy and the party machinery, and he would be accused of splitting the party. Besides, what if he couldn't raise the money needed to run an effective campaign? What if the support we assured him was out there really wasn't? If his campaign turned into a fiasco it could ruin him politically and severely eat into the demand for his writing and speaking services.

So he waited until he was certain he was doing the right thing, waited until it became evident that he had a serious shot at the nomination.

There were three things to decide about his announcement: the date, the place, and what he would say.

Although some thought was given to a California announcement, Washington was the better place. The headquarters was there, and the national news media were there. We picked November 20 for the announcement date. November 22 was Sears' first choice but when it was pointed out, he agreed that an announcement on the date of John Kennedy's assassination would seem a bit tasteless.

Sears figured out well in advance what he wanted the candidate to say. There would be two themes. One would be an attack on the so-called "buddy system" in Washington, but the main theme would be anti-Bigness. Reagan would be against big government, big labor, and big business.

Reagan had no problem with the first two. He was traditionally against big government and big labor. But big business? He saw nothing wrong with bigness per se. After all, he had worked for years for General Electric and its longtime, legendary chief executive officer, Ralph Cordiner, was one of his idols.

But Sears, who can be very persuasive, finally convinced him that his voting support lay principally with small businessmen, blue collar and ethnic workers, and people who were suspicious and resentful of bigness, whether labor, government, or business. In Sears' view bigness meant oppressiveness to the common man.

Reagan announced on the morning of November 20 in the ballroom of the National Press Club. All went well. He read a two-page statement and handled the questions flawlessly. But he said little about the evils of bigness. Instead he attacked the Washington buddy system that was "increasingly insensitive to the needs of the American worker who supports it with his taxes." He made no direct attack on the president.

Following his announcement we took off on a two-day inaugural campaign swing that covered stops in Florida, New Hampshire, North Carolina, Illinois, and ended in California. In Florida the first untoward incident occurred. As Reagan was addressing a small crowd outside his hotel a man brandished a pistol that nobody recognized as a toy. Alertly, Secret Service men grabbed him before he could even holler, "Bang! Bang!"

The trip ended in California on a disappointing note. We had hoped to land at Hollywood/Burbank airport to the cheers of thousands of Reagan's adoring fans. Instead, despite the efforts of our advance team, only a couple of hundred showed up.

No matter, the campaign was off and running.

New Hampshire was our first and our number one target. It is small and insignificant with only four electoral votes. But it is the first state to hold a presidential primary with a law saying that no matter when any other state holds its primary New Hampshire must set its primary date earlier. Someday, I suspect, New Hampshire will hold its primary a year before the general election. Meantime, the media and, therefore, voters everywhere view the New Hampshire primary as a harbinger of things to come, meaning that it's important for a candidate to win it or at least do better than expected.

We were in good shape in New Hampshire by the time Reagan

announced. The credit again belongs to Sears. Shortly after recruiting Laxalt, Sears had scored another coup by talking Hugh Gregg into becoming Reagan's chairman there. Gregg, a former New Hampshire governor, was, more importantly, a moderate Republican. I don't know to this day why he agreed to take the position. He didn't need it and he had been wooed avidly by the Ford forces. Maybe it was the challenge.

In some ways Gregg was a difficult man; he figured he knew how to run his state better than us outlanders. For the most part he was right, but the one time he was wrong contributed mightily to Reagan's narrow loss to Ford. After the election, Gregg walked away from the Reagan organization, figuring rightly that Mike Deaver had screwed him. It was one of those little things Deaver is noted for.

At the time, Gregg spent his winters in Florida and not long before he had opened a fine restaurant in Sarasota. He asked, reasonably enough, that Reagan dine there if he were ever in the vicinity. Sure enough, Reagan showed up on a speaking engagement and Deaver had him eat somewhere else. It wasn't exactly a Bittberg incident but it was typical of Deaver who has never figured out that loyalty is a two-way street, even in politics.

As for Sears, despite his coups with Laxalt and Gregg, all didn't go smoothly for him. In his pride as a political salesman, he had persuaded himself that he could convince such liberal Republican governors as Bob Ray of Iowa and Bill Millikin of Michigan to join the Reagan campaign. He visited each man, each of whom listened politely to his pitch, snickered behind his back, and stayed firmly in the Ford column.

Still, by the time Reagan announced Sears had put together an effective campaign operation filled with top-notch people, only some of whom had been old Reagan enthusiasts. These included Keith Bulen, the former Indiana national committeeman, Charlie Black, Roger Stone, Martin Anderson, Jeffrey Bell, Don Totten, and my two cohorts from the ill-fated, half-assed 1968 attempt, Andy Carter and Frank Whetstone.

Then, in September, something occurred that seemed inconsequential but turned out to be a costly blunder in terms of the New Hampshire primary and therefore the nomination.

I walked into campaign headquarters late one afternoon and stuck my head into Sears' office. He handed me a sheaf of papers.

"Take a look at this and tell me what you think," he said.

It was a speech he had asked Jeff Bell to prepare for Reagan to give before the Executive Club of Chicago in September. Bell's claim to fame these days is that in 1982 he upset the longtime liberal Republican senator from New Jersey, Clifford Case, in a primary, only to lose the general election to that old Knickerbocker dribbler and Rhodes Scholar, Bill Bradley.

But at that time he was merely a leading young enthusiastic right-winger who had worked for a while for Reagan in Sacramento. Sears had brought him into the campaign as a researcher, idea man, and speechwriter. His idea for this speech was a doozy. In the interests of decentralizing the federal government, he had Reagan calling for a $90 billion cut in federal spending. Mind you, this was in 1975, well before the Carter inflation halved the value of the dollar.

To this right-winger the idea of cutting that kind of money out of the federal budget was pure genius. But I had one question: Where would the money come from? I took the speech back to Sears.

"It's great," I said, "if it can be done."

He assured me that the speech had been researched thoroughly and that, yes, it could be done.

I went away and in mid-month several of us went to Chicago to hear Reagan speak. He used 4-by-6 index cards instead of a teleprompter, and he did not set the audience, much less the world, on fire.

Reagan is the world's best teleprompter reader, but it takes him two or three times to get comfortable with a speech when using cards, even when he's printed them himself. Additionally, he was not familiar with Bell's speech-writing style. As a consequence, he stumbled or lost his place several times. Fortunately, or so I thought, the press virtually ignored the speech—the $90 billion proposal appeared to float right out the window and down the drain. But we weren't that lucky.

It turned out the boys on the bus were saving it for New Hampshire. And there they nailed Reagan on two counts. First, where was the $90 billion coming from? Some, it turned out, was going to have to come from privatizing the Post Office. The second count had to do with turning large segments of the federal government back to the states. How would the states finance these new responsibilities? Would they have to raise or add new taxes?

How about a state income tax? New Hampshire didn't have one and its residents didn't want one. Many had moved there from Massachusetts to avoid that very thing. As a result, Reagan spent his first weeks in New Hampshire crawling out from under the weight of the $90 billion fiasco, explaining that no, he wasn't asking the people of New Hampshire to increase their taxes, and no, he wasn't advocating abolition of the Post Office, and on and on. Fortunately, by that time Martin Anderson was aboard, and we turned to him to explain what the hell it was that Reagan thought he had meant.

Marty was a marvel. He made like he knew what he was talking about and, using his own unique brand of academic doubletalk, he was able to convince enough of the press to that effect, and so, eventually, they abandoned the story. But it was too late to repair all the damage. In retrospect, that single problem probably cost Reagan the thirteen hundred votes that made the difference between victory and defeat in New Hampshire.

Martin (don't call me Doctor) Anderson was unquestionably one of the two or three most important staffers aboard the Reagan campaign plane in 1976 and again in 1980. He was the domestic issues-and-policy man and he, more than anyone, shaped Reagan's domestic policy views in those areas where Reagan wasn't already in concrete. Although not a supply-side economist, he leaned that way, and in 1980, as Reagan increasingly adopted the Jack Kemp-Art Laffer-Jude Winiski approach to economics it was Anderson who figured out how to explain and justify it.

Common wisdom has it that Reagan was always a supply sider. Not so. While he always dreaded raising taxes he was, initially, a budget balancer, even if that meant raising taxes. Those who claim Reagan was rigid and unbending should remember that. In 1967 in his first term as governor there was no talk of cutting taxes to increase revenues; revenues were increased the old-fashioned way—by raising taxes.

Anderson had been one of the bright young men around Richard Nixon in the 1968 campaign and went on to the White House as deputy to Arthur Burns when Burns was counsellor to the president. A graduate of Dartmouth, who had been unaffected by the strange and far-out social policies that rule that hoary campus, he had written a book called *The Federal Bulldozer* that exposed the evils of the federal urban renewal program. And while in the Nixon White House, he had drafted the plan that resulted in the United States returning to the concept of all-volunteer armed services.

I envied Marty, not only for his brains but also because he could eat all he wanted, including candy and ice cream, and never gain an ounce.

After he left the Nixon administration he joined the Hoover Institution of War, Revolution, and Peace, the conservative monkey on the back of the liberals and radicals who make up the faculty and administration of Leland Stanford University in Palo Alto, California. There he sits to this day, a senior fellow who writes books and articles that generally defend Ronald Reagan and his conservative revolution.

In 1976 and again in 1980 Anderson took time off from Hoover to participate in the Reagan presidential campaigns and, for a little more than a year, to serve as Reagan's first assistant for domestic affairs. He was one of a small group sorely missed during Reagan's last six years in office.

Despite the $90 billion plan, Reagan ran well, if not quite well enough, in New Hampshire. He campaigned hard, visiting every village and farm and places in between. Hugh Gregg had been a first-rate choice as state chairman. He knew his state, he was not seen as a right-wing kook because he wasn't one, and his moderation helped mold the perception of Reagan as a reasonable man over the months of the campaign.

And, despite Gregg's presence, Reagan managed, with a lot of help from Sears and Lake, to retain the support of the state's two real right-wing kooks, Gov. Mildrim Thomson and Bill Loeb, the vitriolic and tremendously effective publisher of the state's biggest and only state wide paper, the *Manchester Union-Leader*.

Thomson, whose tight-fisted fiscal policies suited his state to a tee, had wanted to be Reagan's state chairman. He would have been a disaster. As a front man for Reagan he might not have hurt him with New Hampshire voters, but he would have made it difficult, if not impossible, for Reagan elsewhere to attract those middle-of-the road Republicans who believed Lyndon Johnson when he said Ford was too dumb to walk and chew gum at the same time.

Sears and Lake did a wonderful job of setting a political pick on Thomson that kept him out of the limelight during the campaign— except for the day they turned him loose to campaign with Reagan. On that day he lived up to our predictions. Among other things, he called for the use of nuclear weapons in combat and advocated the abolition of the Fourteenth Amendment. But to our vast relief, the news media paid no attention.

The primary, pitting Reagan, the party outsider, against Ford, the lucked-into-it president, went down to the wire. It was viewed by the pundits as a make-or-break primary for both.

The consensus was that if Ford wanted to keep the presidency he had to show that he could hold onto the loyalty of rank-and-file Republicans by winning New Hampshire. He already controlled the national party apparatus in most states, including California. There, Reagan's hand-picked state chairman, Paul Haerle, had violated a long-standing neutrality policy and announced for Ford.

At the beginning most experts agreed that Reagan could not beat a sitting president; all he had to do was make a good showing. But that wasn't good enough for us died-in-the-wool Reaganites. We not only wanted to win, we thought we were going to win. Our optimism spread to the point where most of the media also foresaw a Reagan victory. Only Hugh Gregg kept warning us that we probably wouldn't win. We thought he was just protecting his rear.

We went into the weekend before the Tuesday primary thinking we were on a roll. So when Gregg said he didn't want the candidate in the state anymore, because he wanted to make certain his organization was in shape and Reagan was a distraction, Sears acceded and we left. It was a massive blunder on the part of both Gregg and Sears.

Reagan's early departure spelled overconfidence to the New Hampshire voters, especially since Ford continued to campaign right up to election day. And he won by 1,300 votes.

It should, nevertheless, have been written up as a great victory for Reagan—the challenger, losing to a sitting president by such a tiny margin. In 1968 Eugene McCarthy lost to President Johnson by a much larger margin, yet the media termed it a devastating defeat for Johnson and Johnson quit the race.

But not so with Reagan. For two reasons. The press had decided that Reagan was going to win; and that he didn't made his loss, in their infallible eyes, an upset of major proportions. This was compounded by their knowledge that the Reagan people had expected to win. And when he didn't, when they saw our disappointment and chagrin at what we viewed as a major loss, they had little choice but to conclude likewise.

Sears immediately recognized the problem. At a meeting early the next morning he ordered everyone to adopt a positive attitude and talk about Reagan's great victory. It didn't work. We headed for Florida, the site of the next primary, like whipped dogs. I, for one, was totally unable to maintain an optimistic tone or even a smile. Reagan wasn't much better.

We had had high hopes in Florida, but New Hampshire helped turn it around for Ford. Our chairman there, Tommy Thomas, a big, bluff Panama City Chevrolet dealer who had once been the Republican state chairman, had early on predicted a two-to-one Reagan victory. Reagan never came close, losing to Ford by six percentage points.

Reagan got into trouble a couple of times in Florida, once when he suggested that "the industrial might of America" be used to keep the Social Security trust fund solvent. The press and the Ford campaign quickly translated this into a suggestion that the fund be invested in the stock market which to the old folks, such a large part of Florida's population, was not a very good idea. On another occasion, he referred to young, able-bodied free-loaders on food stamps as "young bucks." Liberal reporters, looking for a free shot at Reagan, accused him of meaning young black men—a racist slur.

Poor Reagan didn't understand. He tried to explain that when he was growing up in small-town Illinois in the 1920s any young man was a young buck. The super-race conscious press didn't want to believe him but they couldn't stir up any black protests and the story died. It was one more case of the press's determination to make Reagan fit the mold they had fashioned for him.

Something else happened in Florida that did not affect the Florida primary but was to play a major part in Reagan's comeback from an eventual series of five straight primary defeats. In New Hampshire Reagan had found serious public opposition to proposals pushed by President Ford to turn the Panama Canal over to the banana republic of Panama. In Florida and throughout the South the feeling was even stronger. Note that I did not say anything about giving the canal "back" to Panama. That is because Panama never owned it until Jimmy Carter, with Ford's support and the help of liberal Democratic and guilt-ridden Republican senators, gave it away in 1978.

Reagan was outraged at the idea of giving up the canal which he viewed as vital to the security of the nation. But, then, he outraged easily on issues of foreign policy that involved the United States knuckling under to another nation, whether Panama or the Soviet Union. In the past he had advocated "paving over North Vietnam and making a parking lot out of it" and later, when North Korea seized the American naval ship, the *Pueblo*, he had suggested giving the Koreans forty-eight hours to return it, "or else."

In Florida Reagan coined a phrase that became a rallying cry for those who wanted to keep the canal. "We built it, we paid for it, it's ours, and we're going to keep it," Reagan declared again and again. He dismissed Gen. Omar Torrijos, Panama's dictator of the moment and leader of the clamor for the canal, as a "tinpot dictator."

One day we took Reagan into a Florida television station that had offered each candidate half an hour of free time. We sat him at a desk with a plain, horizon-blue backdrop, and a single camera that zeroed in on his head and shoulders and stayed there, and Reagan spoke into the camera as only Reagan could. He talked about the wrong in giving away the canal, he stuck it to Secretary of State Henry Kissinger and, all in all, he made one of the most effective speeches of his political career. It was Reagan talking from the heart and nobody talks from the heart better than Reagan.

It was too late for Florida, where Gerald Ford was bribing the voters with such projects as new highways and a new Veterans Hospital. But the North Carolina primary, which came a few weeks later, was a different matter entirely. Tom Ellis, the intense, aggressive Reagan majordomo there, heard about the speech, obtained a tape, and ran it on stations all over the state, thereby almost single-handedly turning the campaign around.

But before winning in North Carolina Reagan had lost the first five primaries: New Hampshire, Massachusetts, Florida, Illinois, and Vermont. Within the campaign dejection was rampant. Sears had sneaked off to meet privately with Ford's campaign chairman, Rogers Morton, without consulting Reagan or any of his senior staff. His excuse, when the meeting came to light, was that we were broke and he wanted to be sure Reagan was given an honorable way out if that became necessary.

I've always thought he was preparing to dump Reagan after what he thought would be a loss in North Carolina and take a major position in the Ford organization.

Prior to the North Carolina primary there was talk about getting

Reagan out of the race since it appeared evident he couldn't win and was only embarrassing himself. Nancy, campaigning with her husband, was distraught and pushing for the candidate to quit. But for the most part the staff wanted him to stay in at least a little longer. In our hearts we knew he could still win if he could just gain some momentum by winning a few primaries, starting with North Carolina.

North Carolina was being run by the leadership of Jesse Helms' Congressional Club, Tom Ellis and Carter Wrenn, the first a right-wing zealot with a lot of far-out ideas, some pretty good, the other a man fat of body and face with squinty little eyes and a first-class political brain.

I had been in Washington at campaign headquarters while the candidate and his wife rested in a hotel in North Carolina. When I rejoined the traveling party I was met by Deaver who had signed up again and was doing what he did so well—taking care of the candidate, the traveling party, and the logistics. He took me to one side.

"Nancy wants the governor to get out of the race," he said. "You've got to talk her out of it."

That was funny. Deaver, her surrogate son, her confidant and adviser in most things, the man who had the patience to listen to her for hours on end, couldn't do it. So he asked Nofziger to try, Nofziger who was not known for any of the above, whom Nancy once had tried to have fired, who'd gone for months without being spoken to by her. Well, what the hell.

I wandered into the Reagan suite where Nancy, while maybe not lying in wait, nevertheless leaped on me immediately and eagerly.

"Ronnie has to get out," she told me. "He's going to embarrass himself if he doesn't."

She insisted that I talk to him.

I sat there listening—you cannot argue with Nancy; you can only agree or sit silently as she chews on a particular bone—trying to figure out how to tell her diplomatically that I didn't want Ron to get out, that I thought he could still win.

Lucky for me I never got a chance because Reagan came into the room. Knowing his wife and being no fool, he divined immediately what Nancy was talking about. He guessed wrongly, however, that I was agreeing with Nancy. Or maybe he used me for a foil.

"Lynwood," he said, "I'm not going to quit. I'm going to stay in this thing until the end. I still think we can win, but even if we don't I can't let down all those people who believe in the things we believe in and who want me to be president."

That was the Ronald Reagan I knew and loved.

"I don't want you to get out," I protested softly, hoping in my cowardly way that Nancy wouldn't hear me. "I was trying to figure out how to tell Nancy you should stay in."

I never again heard Nancy talk about her husband getting out of the race. Today, I'm sure that if he had yielded then, conservatives would never have given him a second chance in 1980.

We were in La Crosse, Wisconsin, on the night the votes were being counted in North Carolina. Reagan was speaking to a batch of outdoor sportsmen from an organization called Ducks Unlimited. Reagan identifies with people who use guns, at least for hunting ducks and geese and deer and other nonhuman critters.

While he was speaking, reporters began sidling up to campaign staffers, whispering the surprising news that Reagan was leading in North Carolina. I remember saying "Gloriosky!" or something more pungent like "Hot damn!" After five straight losses it was a little hard to believe, especially with all the experts predicting loss number six and the end of the Reagan run.

When Reagan finished speaking we spirited him back to the hotel before the press could get at him. I went to the pressroom and told the reporters I would bring Reagan down shortly to comment on what seemed a sure victory. Wrong again!

Back at the suite I asked the candidate how soon he wanted to talk to the press. He didn't. He remembered what had happened in New Hampshire. There, too, he had run in front in the early returns and sometime around 10 P.M. had gone to a crowded ballroom and in a roundabout way claimed a victory that two hours later slipped away. He didn't want to chance a repeat.

"When all the votes are counted, then I'll talk to the press," he said.

Every now and then you can't budge Reagan, ordinarily the most reasonable of men. So I trotted back to the pressroom and apologized to an unhappy bunch of reporters and photographers. Then I went back to the suite where candidate and staff were preparing to leave for the airport and California.

"You have to promise me one thing," I said. "Don't answer a single question when we leave."

He agreed, and we made it to the plane with several "no comments." Airborne, the pilots on our chartered plane kept radio contact and appraised us of the vote count. With 90 percent of the vote in Reagan strolled to the back of the plane—the press section—and calmly claimed the victory. And suddenly he was back in the race and Ford had a fight on his hands.

Several things led to Reagan's upset in North Carolina. Ford's planned giveaway of the Panama Canal was a key factor. So were Reagan's strong personal campaign and the support of Jesse Helms, North Carolina's conservative Republican senator. Also, North Carolina had recently been the site of perhaps the worst speech Gerald Ford ever gave, which made it very bad indeed. It talked about women as home-makers, so condescendingly that even women who liked being home-makers wanted to throw up.

Finally, over the preceding weeks, voters had begun viewing Reagan as an underdog fighting the entire Republican establishment. And nobody likes an underdog better than the American voter.

Back in California we huddled over what to do next. We had one major problem: no money. From the beginning we'd run on a shoestring and it was becoming pretty frayed. Our friends in Wisconsin were convinced that if Reagan were to come back for a couple of days he would win their primary, and they might well have been right. But we didn't have the money. Or at least that's what Sears said. I've always had a hunch that if he had really wanted Reagan to go he would have found a way.

But before we did anything else, we made a significant change in assignments, one that involved me in a major way. At the time I thought it was made for the good of the campaign. It took me a little over three years to figure out that Sears was trying—successfully—to push me to one side and that any benefit to the campaign was purely incidental.

Why? It wasn't that I was trying to usurp his campaign leadership. I wasn't. Neither was it that I was not a competent press secretary. In all modesty, I was. I never asked him why, because since early in the campaign we had not been friends. One reason was that Sears liked to make decisions by himself, then ask for approval, and then carry out the decision, regardless of whether anyone else liked it.

But the main reason, I think, was that Sears was jealous of what he saw as his perogative as campaign manager to talk to the press. He didn't like sharing it with me. He knew most of the political press, but so did I. He cultivated them, but so did I. And I had two advantages: I had been one of them while he never had, and neither had any of the other staffers; and also, I knew Reagan a hell of a lot better than he did. On the other hand, he had two advantages over me: he was running the campaign and he was by far a better bs-er. You'd have thought he'd be satisfied with that edge.

There was a third reason, too. He and Jim Lake had become very close. Lake worshiped Sears as a political genius. And at this point in the campaign Lake had little to do—the states in which he worked had had their primaries. Lake, futhermore, liked to deal with the press and got along very well with them. He posed no threat to Sears because he deferred to him in all things.

When Sears and Deaver, who also had become a Sears worshiper, suggested that I drop off the traveling party to take charge of California I thought only positive thoughts. They pointed out that California was crucial to us, our campaign there wasn't going well, and I was the only member of the staff who had run statewide campaigns in California.

I said fine, whatever would help the campaign was all that mattered.

"And by the way," I added in all naivete, "I think Jim Lake should be the press secretary. He likes the press and they like him."

Sears and Deaver liked the idea and quickly implemented it, which is not surprising since they had planned to name Lake to begin with.

So, almost before I had time to think, I was back running California again. Rose Marie as usual came along to make sense out of what I was trying to do.

California headquarters was a dilapidated old building on the northwest corner of Wilshire Boulevard and Bixel Street. Ford headquarters was right down the street, manned in part by old Reaganites who had joined Ford before Reagan announced because they thought he wasn't going to run. Ours was my kind of headquarters—cheap, and looking like it. There was no way anyone could complain that we were spending scarce dollars on fancy headquarters.

It was also handy for volunteers. And it had two other advantages. It was just across the street from Pete's Grandburger, which since has made way for progress, but then made the best, juiciest hamburgers in Los Angeles and maybe in all the civilized world. The headquarters itself had a glass outside door which was a two-way mirror. We could look out, but people walking by saw only a mirror. We could sit inside and make obscene gestures or watch as they stopped to comb their hair, squeeze a pimple, or adjust a bra. In between we ran the campaign.

During that first week back in California I had one of the worst days of my political life. Sears, right again, had decided that Reagan's only chance to overtake Ford was to go on national television with a speech that would raise enough money to carry on the campaign and also rally undecided conservatives to his banner. Reagan had entered the race so late that many who ordinarily would have supported him were committed, or kind of committed, to Ford. Others were supporting Ford because they didn't think Reagan could beat him. And still others because they were uncomfortable with the idea of Reagan or anyone else running against a sitting Republican president. These were attitudes Reagan had to change.

From the beginning Sears' campaign strategy had been to win the early primaries and then coast, and he had spent accordingly. He had not prepared for the need to come from behind. So he hadn't set aside a penny for any contingencies, including television.

There were three financial heroes in the campaign of 1976. One was Joe Rodgers who during Reagan's second term as president was ambassador to France. He earned that appointment one night in the early spring. The campaign was broke. It needed around $100,000 to get it off the ground, where it sat because of overdue bills. In desperation Deaver called Rodgers, a Nashville building contractor and developer, for help. He raised the money overnight.

Another was Jimmy Lyon, a Houston banker and a Reagan supporter since the abortive campaign of 1968. We needed another $100,000 to put Reagan on national television as per Sears' plan. We had gotten NBC to sell us the time, but not surprisingly, in view of the lousy record campaigns have for paying their bills, they wanted their money in advance. Jimmy loaned it to the campaign.

Wonderful! Except for one thing. We needed $23,000 to pay for the studio in which to film the speech and to build the fancy set our Hollywood-based television consultants felt was necessary. We didn't have $23,000. For no particular reason the job of finding the money fell on me. Lyon did not feel he could lend any more and you couldn't blame him.

While members of Reagan's old California kitchen cabinet could have supplied the money without any difficulty they were fearful of doing so. Even though Loren Smith, the campaign's legal counsel, assured me a loan would be legal, William French Smith, a member of the kitchen cabinet and a lawyer (who, however, knew little about election law) warned them not to. In desperation I called Mike Curb, a wealthy young record producer and our California chairman. I explained the problem. He didn't hesitate.

"I'll get you the money," he promised.

He called back a short time later. He had just talked to Holmes Tuttle, the unofficial honcho of the kitchen cabinet.

"Holmes tells me not to do it. It's illegal," he told me.

I assured him that Loren Smith thought it wasn't.

"I'll get you the money," he said again.

And he did. And I got something else also, a call from Tuttle who screamed at me that I was going to be responsible "for sending this fine young man to jail." I just listened, which is about all anyone could do when Holmes, who was really a kind man, was hollering at you.

Needless to say Curb did not go to jail and Reagan taped his speech on schedule. Over the next couple of weeks $1.5 million dollars poured in, and the campaign was solvent again.

I don't know to this day if Ronald Reagan realizes what he owes Joe Rodgers and Jimmy Lyon and Mike Curb. What he owes is an awful lot. Without those three his 1976 campaign would have collapsed. He never would have had the opportunity to capture the hearts and souls of the rank-and-file of the Republican party during the 1976 National Convention. And without their support then there is little chance that he would have run for president in 1980. That contest in all likelihood would have been between Jimmy Carter and George Bush. The Lord works in mysterious ways His wonders to perform.

We ran the California primary on a shoestring in 1976. But our slim staff, supplemented by volunteers, worked hard and we found the money as time went on to hire some field men for pittances, and sometimes less. And throughout the state the old Reagan people, who had stayed loyal while the opportunists and faint of heart and little faith drifted off to the Ford campaign, rallied around, determined to hold California for their hero. In a way it was a come-from-behind effort since Reagan had been deserted by his hand-picked Republican state chairman, Paul Haerle, and his hand-picked national committeeman, Dr. William Banowsky, both of whom seized the first opportunity to endorse Ford.

But our two state cochairmen, Elsa Sandstrom, also the national committeewoman, and Curb worked hard and effectively. She concentrated on the women's vote and Curb, a political novice, cheerfully did whatever was asked of him. Years afterward, Curb, who was elected lieutenant governor in 1978, became a controversial figure in California Republican politics and I was asked on occasion why I had always supported him. I had and have one answer.

"He has always been there when Reagan needed him."

People like Curb are rare—at least in politics.

One decision I made early on was to produce our own paid media for the California campaign. It had been the weak spot in the national campaign. I called Jack Easton who had handled press for me in the Nixon campaign and he found the small advertising agency run by Charles Martin who, in turn, came up with a bright kind of oddball named Tom Kasten. Martin was to produce our spots and buy the time for them. Easton conned Martin into producing for cost and placing the spots for an 8 percent commission, about half the going rate.

We had some fun with these and a couple of near disasters and we wound up with a bang. Kasten proved to be innovative, sensitive, and competent, a wonderful combination. But I just never got used to him carrying a purse.

Early on we struck gold. Up in San Francisco lived an old Reagan antagonist named George Christopher. Reagan had beaten him badly in the 1966 Republican gubernatorial primary and Christopher hated him for it. But by 1976 Christopher disliked Ford more than Reagan. It had to do with Christopher's Greek heritage and the unsolved nastiness between Greece and Turkey over control of the island of Cyprus. Ford was on the Turkish side and Christopher was unhappy and I knew it. I called and asked if he would cut a radio spot for Reagan. He would.

I sent Kasten up to San Franciso where he taped him for an hour. When he came back he put together a spot that was so good it made you want to cry. It was George Christopher talking about his roots before anyone ever heard of "Roots" and about other people who had come to America and California for a better life and how Ronald Reagan understood them and their dreams. If there had been a contest for best radio spot of the year it would have won hands down.

In May Reagan came home to California to campaign. I asked him to hold one speech to about twenty-seven minutes so we could film it and put it on television. Reagan did his usual good job, but when I saw the film I went through the roof. Martin's cameraman was drunk, or thought he was being smart, or was incompetent, or was determined to screw us. Everything was fine except that while Reagan was making one of his major points, the camera left him and focused on a Boy Scout standing on the stage as a member of an honor guard. The kid was yawning. It was better than picking his nose, but not much. The great communicator, though not yet so labeled by the press, was putting the kid to sleep.

What to do? We couldn't edit the tape without cutting out what Reagan was saying. We had already bought time around the state for the speech and we needed it. It was Kasten who came up with the solution.

"Why don't we leave the audio but cut out the video and where the video is blank we can run an insert that says 'Technical Difficulties?' " he suggested.

It worked like a charm. We showed that film up and down the state and, unbelievably, no matter what station ran it or at what hour there were always technical difficulties in the same spot. No bored Boy Scout or crazy cameraman was going to screw our Ronald Reagan!

Toward the end of the campaign I had a bright idea that nearly backfired. I thought it would make the candidate happy if we shot a spot using Reagan's daughter, Maureen, who was attractive, had professional acting experience, and wanted to help her dad.

I broached the idea to the candidate who was pleased. I broached the idea to Maureen who was delighted. But then we ran into difficulties. She didn't want to use our director. She was involved at the time with an old leading man named Gene Nelson whose star had faded, and she wanted him to direct the spot. What the heck! I didn't really care. Nelson had done some directing and if this would make Maureen happy it was fine with me. They shot the spot. Unfortunately, they only wounded it. It was awful. It featured Maureen cuddling her toy poodle and saying at the end, "Isn't that right, Flopsy?" or Mopsy or whatever the mutt's name was.

It might have been passable if we'd been wooing the young Beverly Hills matron crowd. But we weren't. We were wooing Middle America and mommies and daddies of Middle America would have gotten sick and voted for Gerry Ford. At least that was my opinion. But I wanted another so I called Dick Wirthlin, Reagan's pollster, who is a man with a good level head. I asked him to come take a look. He watched it a couple of times and shook his head.

"It will cost us votes," he said. "I wouldn't run it if I were you."

"You've confirmed my own opinion," I said. "And I'm sorry about that, but I'm going to have to call the candidate."

It was not something I looked forward to. I knew he wouldn't be happy, and he wasn't. I didn't blame him. Maureen was his daughter and he certainly didn't want to hurt her feelings. For that matter, neither did I. I'd first met her in the 1966 campaign and we'd become friends when we both worked on a special election campaign in early 1969. I liked her then and I still like her, even though she gets mad at me from time to time to time.

I tried to explain to Reagan how bad the spot was. He didn't want to understand.

"I want it to run," he said.

"It's going to cost you votes," I warned.

"Run it," he ordered in very un-Reaganlike fashion.

"Can I show it to you first?" I asked. It was Saturday afternoon. He was home for the weekend.

"I'm not going to be home," he grumped.

Clearly, he had his mind made up and didn't want to be swayed by the facts.

"What about tomorrow," I asked.

"It's Sunday," he grouched. He has always hated to give up what he thinks are his rightful days off. A lot of us feel like that.

"I know," I said. "It won't take long. We can do it in less than an hour."

Reluctantly, unhappily, he agreed. It wasn't often I pushed like that so he must have figured I really had a problem.

I rented a machine to show the tape and the next morning around 10 A.M. I lugged it into the den of the Reagan home. He and Nancy were both there. I set the machine up and the damn thing wouldn't play. After fiddling around for fifteen or twenty minutes, taking up valuable Reagan loafing time, I found the trouble. The cord plugged in at both ends and I hadn't plugged it into the machine. That remedied, I ran the tape. And ran it again. Reagan just sat there.

"Well?" I asked, finally.

He looked at Nancy. "What do you think?"

She is a smart lady. "Don't get me in the middle of this," she said.

After a moment Reagan said, reluctantly, "You're right."

"I tell you what," I said. "I'll find a couple of places to run it where not very many people will see it and then if she asks us we can say we ran it and that way you're off the hook."

He liked that. He always liked ideas that got him off whatever hook he might have been on. I thanked him for letting me come, unplugged my rented machine at both ends, and went away.

We ran the spot in Palm Springs in the wee small hours. Maureen to this day has never asked me about it. As I said, she isn't dumb. She knew as well as I what would play in Peoria.

As we labored to keep Ford from taking Reagan's home base, Reagan himself was marauding effectively through the rest of the nation, winning more primaries than he was losing and gaining rapidly on Ford in terms of delegates. He swept Texas, picking up all one hundred delegates. Ford helped by being photographed trying to eat a tamale with the husk on. Not the thing in TexMex land. The Texas Reaganites, feeling their tacos, refused to put the state's senior Republican, Sen. John Tower, on the delegation because he refused to pledge for Reagan. Which isn't hard to understand, seeing as how he was supposed to run the Ford operation at the National Convention.

Reagan also upset Ford in Missouri, thanks to the superior politicking of the state chairman, John Powell, and the old pros from New Mexico and Virginia—Anderson Carter and Kenny Klinge. In Missouri the Reaganites, in a kinder and gentler mood than the Texans, gave a seat on the delegation to Gov. Kit Bond, a Ford supporter.

Reagan's biggest disappointment came in Michigan, Ford's home state. Nobody really thought he would win it even though late polls showed him running close, but Ford eventually clobbered him by nearly a three-to-two margin. Michigan was also the site of a doublecross that has bugged me ever since.

One day John McGoff, publisher of a string of small daily and weekly papers in Michigan and owner of the *Sacramento Union*, called me. A conservative, he was involved in a public controversy over the source of his financial support which came from South Africa.

The gist of his call was that he wanted to endorse Reagan in his newspapers, but felt that in fairness to his editors he couldn't do it unless Reagan would meet with them before the Michigan primary. His problem, he explained, was not so much with Ford as with Ford's secretary of state, Henry Kissinger, whose policies regarding South Africa he strongly opposed. He knew, of course, that Reagan had been attacking Kissinger constantly and effectively.

(As an aside, two years later Paul Laxalt and I ran into Kissinger in a Washington hotel and though I had known him casually in the Nixon White House I hadn't seen him since so I introduced myself.

"I remember you," he said. "You're the guy who chopped me up in the 1976 elections."

"Not me," I said truthfully, remembering that Bo Callaway had had the same complaint. Paranoia, however, is not unheard of in politics.)

I heard McGoff out and enthusiastically told him I would do my best to set up the meeting. The thought of a batch of newspapers coming out against Ford in his home state was intriguing even though newspaper endorsements of candidates carry little weight these days, if they ever did.

I found Deaver in Michigan with Reagan and recommended strongly that he set up the editorial meeting. Deaver agreed and juggled the schedule to find a couple of hours for Reagan to meet with McGoff's editors. And, sure enough, the weekend before the Michigan primary all of McGoff's papers came out with strong endorsements— of Ford. I wrote McGoff telling him I didn't appreciate being lied to. He wrote me back saying there had been a misunderstanding. I did not respond and he will never get another chance to test my understandability.

In California we were coming down to election day and I was confident Reagan would win. The Ford people must have felt the same way because they took a desperate gamble. They based it on a remark Reagan had made in Sacramento in response to a hypothetical question, which, being hypothetical, he should not have answered. He had said that as president, if Rhodesia (now Zimbabwe) asked, he would send a contingent of American troops there as part of a United Nations force to fight guerrillas.

The Friday before the election Ford headquarters in California notified the news media that on Saturday morning they would hold a press conference featuring three United States senators, including Howard Baker of Tennessee who later supported vigorously Jimmy Carter's giveaway of the Panama Canal and still later became chief of staff for the ever-forgiving and sometimes forgetful Ronald Reagan.

At this moment, however, Baker was merely part of a particularly vicious effort to sink Reagan's California campaign. The highlight of the senators' press conference was to be a preview showing of the newest Ford television spot.

This information came to us on the news wire. All major campaigns subscribe to at least one of the wire services. Since the news media, which these days take it upon themselves to set political ethics standards for the nation, deem it unethical for a campaign to put a spy in the rival camp, the best way to keep track of what both your enemies and friends are doing is to lease a news wire. It's surprising what the self-important people in any campaign will tell reporters to convince them they are really important.

Being naturally curious, I sent a couple of our people to the press conference with a tape recorder. They came back all excited and played me their tape of the spot. It was a strong and distorted attack on Reagan's alleged hawkishness. It wound up with the line: "Governor Reagan couldn't start a war; President Reagan could."

Funny, nobody talked about dirty campaigning in those days.

At first hearing the spot was devastating. The Ford campaign planned to run it the Sunday and Monday before the primary in the belief that we would have little time to respond effectively. In fact, we weren't even supposed to know about it until it appeared on the air and that would have made it much too late. It was reminiscent of the famous Lyndon Johnson spot of 1964 which, although it only ran once, lives in infamy. It pictured a little girl picking daisies while the announcer counted down from ten. At zero the little girl disappeared in a mushroom cloud. The implication, of course, was that Barry Goldwater would propel us into a nuclear war.

But now Goldwater, twelve years later, was part of the Ford team. Like many other conservatives who stay in Washington too long he had become part of the Washington political establishment; he was no longer an outsider. And so, even though the Goldwaters and the Reagans were personal friends and even though Reagan had campaigned heavily for him in 1964, he had cut a particularly virulent anti-Reagan radio spot which the Ford people used in Nebraska until Nancy personally called him and complained. Reagan won Nebraska anyway by a lopsided margin, but things were never the same between Goldwater and the Reagans.

In looking back, the odd thing about the Ford California spot is that it didn't discourage me; it excited and challenged me. I knew almost instantly what I wanted to do and because California had been turned over to me more or less carte blanche I could do whatever I wished without consulting anyone in the national campaign. Or at least I did what I wished without consulting anyone.

I called Dick Wirthlin again—my level head in that campaign. I told him this was reminiscent of the 1964 Goldwater spot and I didn't think we had any choice but to go on the attack. He agreed, just cautioning that I should not mention Goldwater in our response, which I hadn't intended to do anyway.

The first thing I did was marshal our forces. I called in Easton and Martin and members of our campaign staff. We had a lot to do in a hurry since time was short.

Every now and then, in politics as in life, we all do something well, something we're proud of. For me this was one of those occasions.

We quickly put together a spot for radio. We didn't have time to do one for television and newspaper ads would have been a waste of money. Memory fails me as to who thought up the idea for our spot, but I suspect it was Kasten. The ad urged voters to watch for the Ford spot and to look at it closely, because, our announcer said, "We think it will tell you more about Gerald Ford than it does about Ronald Reagan."

Easton, with the help of Kay Valory, Kathy Wilson, and others, began a full-fledged counterattack on the Ford spot, which had yet to run on a single station. They called in our surrogate speakers and offered their comments to radio stations, called a press conference for Rep. Phil Crane, the right-wing Illinois congressman who was in Los Angeles, and in general did everything they could to stir up the media, and through the media the Republican electorate.

It worked. Reporters came out to the headquarters and I denounced the spot on the spot. They got hold of Reagan who reacted, properly, more in hurt than in anger. They called Ford who defended it in a lame and surly fashion. One television station called and asked if we were preparing a TV spot to respond. We explained that we didn't have time, but then, as a favor, we let them come out and film us going through the phony motions of putting together a TV spot. They ran it that evening, demonstrating once again that television is never above manufacturing a good news story.

We had a hell of a lot of fun and we aroused a hell of a lot of righteous indignation around the state and Reagan beat the hell out of Ford the following Tuesday. Some Fordites later claimed that the spot hurt us in the Ohio primary which was held the same day. I didn't believe them then, I don't believe them now. Reagan lost in Ohio primarily because Sears failed to take the necessary steps to get Reagan delegates on the ballot in all Ohio congressional districts.

But California was a great success and it kept Ford from locking up enough delegates to win the convention. Still, he was very close.

With the end of the California primary, Sears was left with a familiar dilemma: Where now to put Nofziger so he wouldn't be around to get in Sears' hair? He still wasn't sure enough of his own position to try to dump outright any of the old Reagan hands. That wouldn't come until the 1979–80 campaign.

Somebody lent us a cabin at Lake Tahoe and the senior staff met there to go over campaign strategy. Sears' strategy regarding me was to ask me to go to Kansas City and begin putting together the apparatus for our operation during the Republican National Convention which would be held there in August. I went willingly and cheerfully, figuring once again that I was being asked to do an essential job, still unaware of Sears' motives.

I'd already been mixed up a bit in the convention. National conventions are run by the Republican and Democratic National Committees, but a national committee is under the thumb of the president when they're both of the same party. Likewise, presidents pick, or at least approve of, the national chairman of their party. Thus, Ford, as president, controlled the Republican National Committee through Mary Louise Smith, his personal pick as chairman. Mrs. Smith, of grandmotherly age and sanctimonious manner, was a longtime Republican activist out in Iowa where she had served as state chairman and national committeewoman. She was a liberal Republican, pro the Equal Rights Amendment, as was Betty Ford, and pro just about everything else that was anathema to the conservative wing of the party. And she was strongly anti-Reagan. I had known her from my days as deputy chairman of the national committee and I didn't particularly like her and I imagine she felt the same about me. We didn't have much in common.

Mary Louise—nobody ever called her Mary Lou or Mary—was sitting over at Republican National Committee headquarters doing what Ford wanted her to do—sticking it to the Reaganites. And I had to try to persuade her to do some unsticking. I didn't have much luck, but I tried.

She had, for instance, decided that members of the Ford administration had nothing to do with the Ford campaign, even though she knew they would be in Kansas City working for the president, and therefore there would be extra tickets, passes, and housing for them. She had given our supporters the worst seats in the house. Wherever possible, which was everywhere, she gave the edge to the Ford campaign. And why not? If Reagan had been president and I had been in her shoes I'd have done the same thing. But that didn't mean I had to like it or wouldn't try to do something about it.

Fortunately for us the man running the convention for the party was Ody Fish, the national committeeman from Wisconsin, whom I also had known at the RNC. Ody was husky and bald and competent and fair. He could never give me all I wanted but, even though he was no Reagan supporter, I always felt he tried to treat us equitably.

I remember in particular one incident. Deaver had made friends with Joe Canzeri, a short, bouncy, competent aid to Ford's appointed vice president, Nelson Rockefeller. Rockefeller, among other reasons, had come to help keep some of the wavering Ford delegates in line. He asked for two extra floor passes, which are limited in number because they allow the holders to move around the floor of the convention politicking with the delegates.

Instead of sneaking him two passes and saying nothing, which he could easily have done and probably should have, Fish told him he would have to get the approval of the Reagan people. Canzeri asked Deaver for help, and Deaver, trying to be a nice fellow and not understanding much about politics or that the passes would be used against us, asked me to approve their issuance. I told him no, unless we also got two more passes.

Shortly afterward Fish called and asked if he could issue the passes to Rockefeller. "Sure," I said, "if I get two more."

"But, Lyn," he grumbled, "he's the vice president."

"Yeah, and he'll be working the floor against us."

Ody sighed and did the only thing he could honorably do, now that he had called me—he gave two passes to the vice president and two to me. I'm only sorry I never had a chance to repay him for his fairness.

But that was later. Weeks before I was off to Kansas City to try to figure out what needed to be done. As usual, Rose Marie came along to make sure I did it. In the meantime Sears, who undoubtedly and with some justification was worried about my ability to handle the task, reached out to New Jersey to an old Nixon hand named Douglas Hofe who came to Kansas City to help. In fairness to Hofe, I wound up helping him, although I've always taken the credit for having "run" the Reagan 1976 convention operation.

What I did do was keep the operation running smoothly. Whenever Doug or someone else ruffled a feather, I went and unruffled it. And sometimes it seemed as if things were ruffled all over.

The job was largely a mechanical one. We had two places and the route between them to worry about. They were the Alameda Plaza Hotel, the Convention Center, and in between. They were not close, but then none of the good hotels was close to the center. At the center we had to get a large trailer and set it up as an operational headquarters that Sears and other key political operatives would work from. Sears, who was always afraid that someone else might know more than he did or even be smarter, had made the convention job more difficult by keeping F. Clifton White out of the campaign, even though White's connections with Reagan went back to 1966.

Clif White knew more about running conventions and putting together their mechanics than Sears or I will ever know. His time in politics went back to Tom Dewey and he was in many ways the father of modern convention communications techniques that include phones at every delegation position, walkie-talkie communications among operatives on the floor and between the floor and the trailer, special phone lines to the candidate and other important persons, and all kinds of stuff like that there. Although he was not with us, some members of the Clif White network were and some, like Frank Whetstone, who came down from Cutbank to help set up the trailer, were invaluable because they had much more experience in these areas than either Hofe or I.

The Alameda Plaza Hotel was a midsized luxury hotel in a nicer part of downtown Kansas City. It was managed by a man named Phil Pistilli who had a silly, rather naive notion with which I totally concurred—it was his hotel and we were there at his sufferance. Somehow he didn't like to be told what he had to do and how he had to do it, so at the beginning there were problems. We found it worked much better if we sat down and explained our problems and asked for his help. It's amazing how much more you can get done sometimes if you treat people decently. It's a lesson many advance men seem to have trouble learning.

Besides setting up the communications network and the trailer other things had to be done. A motor pool had to be established to pick people up and move them about. I put my old partner, Bob Tuttle, now a Reagan advance man, in charge of that.

There was also the matter of demonstrations. When people go to conventions they like to act like children and one way they get to do so is to participate in demonstrations at key times. One of those is when your candidate is nominated and seconded and another is when he makes his speech to the convention. It was our job to help our delegates revert to their childish ways by supplying signs, noisemakers, and other paraphernalia.

Our man in charge of demonstrations was James Stockdale, an innovative, smart, hardworking politician originally from South Dakota. He did the usual, passing out noisemakers and making other arrangements for the demonstration that was to accompany the nomination of Reagan. But then he did the unusual. He kept that demonstration going for forty-five minutes, a world's record, despite the best efforts of the convention chairman, Rep. John Rhodes of Arizona, to gavel the Reaganites into silence.

There was method to Stockdale's madness. By keeping the demonstration going, it was past prime time when Ford's nomination and subsequent hoopla began. I always thought that wasn't very nice of Stockdale.

Stockdale also put together a group of children to demonstrate for Sen. Richard Schweiker, Reagan's choice for his vice presidential running mate, as Schweiker made the rounds of state delegations. Stockdale called them "Schweik's tykes," which is why I think he organized them in the first place.

The choice of Schweiker was Sears' idea, and although it created consternation among Reagan conservatives and didn't even work, I have always thought it was a stroke of genius.

I was at campaign headquarters in Washington when the idea of Schweiker first came up. Sears broached it to me and others of the senior staff separately. That was Sears' style. He was a powerful advocate for his own ideas and was especially effective one-on-one. Like most people he was more interested in having his ideas approved than in having them picked apart.

His reasoning in this case was simple. The Reagan campaign was dead in the water and there were not enough delegates pledged to Reagan to win. Sears had been conning the political media for weeks, claiming that Reagan had more delegates than in fact he had. But soon he wouldn't be able to fool the press any longer, and he knew it. He had to find more delegates somewhere and after some thought he settled on Pennsylvania, whose delegates were not pledged by law to vote for Ford even though nominally committed to him. Additionally, Ford's Pennsylvania chairman, Drew Lewis, was rumored to be unhappy. His close friendship with Schweiker, Pennsylvania's senior senator, went back to childhood days. And they were both Schwenkfelters, members of a small Quaker-like religious sect.

Sears' premise was that if he could convince Schweiker, who had been supporting Ford, to come aboard the Reagan campaign then Schweiker, in turn, could convince Lewis and other delegates to come along. How to get Schweiker? Why, offer him the vice presidency, of course. But there were two problems. Would Schweiker take the bait and, if he did, would Reagan take Schweiker? That was number one. Number two was that Schweiker was known not as a moderate Republican, but as a liberal Republican, so liberal that even if Reagan accepted him he might drive away many of the conservatives who formed Reagan's base.

For, even though Sears didn't believe it, they did have somewhere else to go. Ford may have become an establishment Republican, but he had always been in the conservative wing of his party and was still far to the right of where Schweiker was perceived to be.

Sears discussed his plan with Reagan after putting together a package on Schweiker that showed him to be, if not conservative, at least not as far left as usually pictured. Reagan, aware that his chances of winning were dimming, went along with the idea. So, much to the surprise of many of us, did Schweiker, who flew secretly to California for a personal meeting with Reagan whom he had not met. Sears now had to move quickly, before news of the deal leaked. He swore all of us, including Schweiker, to absolute secrecy until the announcement. That turned out to be a mistake.

It meant that Schweiker, who abided by the secrecy pledge, could not discuss the situation with Lewis and others who were close to him politically before he announced. Thus, when on July 26 he was introduced at a press conference by Paul Laxalt as Reagan's running mate, they were caught with their pants down. And they, especially Lewis, were not happy. He took it as a personal affront—and properly so—that Schweiker had not consulted with him in advance. And yet, it was really not Schweiker's fault. He had been caught in the middle by Sears' demand for secrecy. That blooper created a rift between Schweiker and Lewis that was a long time healing and any chance we might have had of bringing Lewis into the Reagan camp vanished.

I did not know Lewis then but I came to know him pretty well and I'm convinced that under no circumstances would he have reneged on his commitment to Ford. I also believe that if Schweiker had been allowed to talk to him, Lewis would have respected the confidence.

Reagan had no trouble accepting Schweiker as his running mate. He quickly discovered they had much in common. Both had hearing problems; Schweiker was already wearing a hearing aid, something Reagan fought off until after he became president. I told him once that deafness was of great benefit to any president—he could shut off his hearing aid and not hear the lousy advice he was getting. In addition, both men were strongly anti-abortion and shared many of the same social concerns. And both were devout Christians. Reagan was a member of the Christian Church although for years he has attended the Bel Aire Presbyterian church whose pastor is the old UCLA all-

American center, the Rev. Donn Moomaw. Schweiker, as I've said, was a Schwenkfelter.

Once agreeing to be Reagan's running mate Schweiker gave Reagan his total loyalty, not only for the duration of the campaign but also between campaigns and during the 1980 campaign. He did not run for reelection in 1980, but, I think, hoped against hope that Reagan would pick him again. But that was not to be. By 1980 he had nothing to bring to the ticket except friendship and loyalty and that was not enough. It seldom is in politics, where winning always comes first.

Schweiker, a good soldier, went to work trying to bring Pennsylvania's delegates into the Reagan column. But he had no luck. Every time he thought he had one convinced Lewis went to work and unconvinced him. And Schweiker did create problems among the conservatives. In North Carolina, former Gov. Jim Edwards was so angry he jumped ship. Five years later he and Schweiker served together in the Reagan cabinet.

In Mississippi, Clarke Reed, who was more interested in backing a winner than in riding a cause, also deserted. Many others came close. Reagan personally met with some of them and attempted to calm them down. Schweiker also met with many of them but without much luck. So, in the end, Sears' bold gamble came to nothing.

But it did do one important thing. For the three weeks prior to the convention it changed the name of the game. The media spent less time counting delegates and more time focusing on the Schweiker gambit and wondering what Sears might do next. And it gave Sears time to figure out his next step, which proved to be as futile as the Schweiker ploy.

That, by the way, made a pariah out of Sears among most right-wingers. You would have thought the Reaganites would blame their hero for Schweiker, but they didn't. They blamed Sears just as, when Reagan became president, they blamed Jim Baker or Howard Baker or Mike Deaver or anyone but Reagan for Reagan's mistakes, both large and small.

There is something about Reagan. People want him to succeed, want him to do right and be right, and when he doesn't or isn't they blame somebody else. All presidents should be so lucky.

The right wing never forgave Sears. It strongly opposed his appointment as Reagan's campaign manager four years later and cheered when Reagan finally fired him. That included me, but for different reasons.

When Sears and the campaign entourage, including operatives from headquarters and field men, arrived in Kansas City the campaign, to all intents and purposes, was over. We were refusing to admit that Ford had won, but he had. The Schweiker gambit had failed, leaving Sears with one last desperate ploy—to change the rules of the convention in such a way as to force all presidential candidates, including Ford, to pick their running mates before their names were placed in nomination. Sears' hopes were that pro-Reagan delegates pledged to Ford would see this as a way to support their real choice, and second, that Ford would pick a running mate unacceptable to his conservative delegates who would then switch to Reagan.

But Sears overlooked one salient point, which was that it would have been difficult for Ford, who already had dropped Rockefeller, to pick a running mate more unacceptable to conservatives than Schweiker. That single fact enabled conservative delegates pledged to Ford to stick with him. But Sears pushed stubbornly ahead. He had no other plan and was not willing to discuss any other. Each morning during the week of platform hearings and the first days of the convention itself Sears went over the delegate count with the political staff. And each day the count came up short and each day he demanded that the operatives go find more votes, but there were none to find.

When Reagan arrived in Kansas City he, too, began making the rounds of the state delegations, but to no avail. In this it was like the 1968 convention. There were delegates who wanted to vote for him but were bound by law, or delegation rules, or their word to vote for Ford. Words of honor seem, somehow, to mean more to citizen-politicians who make up most of the delegations than they do to the pros.

The California delegation, which I had helped select, arrived, excited and determined to help. They, too, failed. Shortly after their arrival I was asked to address them about the state of the campaign—I still held out hope—and afterward there were questions. Bob Sholass, an old-line Reaganite from San Mateo, called out, "What should our demeanor be?"

Without thinking, I replied, "Da meaner da better."

The place broke up. Even today I am occasionally reminded of what might be my worst, but still is my most famous pun.

Things don't just happen at conventions. They are made to happen. Delegates sit in assigned seats and stay in assigned hotels. Delegates for the most part vote a certain way because the entire delegation has committed to do so or the delegate himself has committed to it as part of the delegate selection process. Convention speakers are picked in advance either by the national committee or the candidates' organizations.

When we went into the convention we knew that Senator Laxalt would place Reagan's name in nomination. But it had not been decided who would make the short seconding speeches. One member of the California delegation was Henry (Hank) Lucas, the black dentist from San Francisco who had chaired Nixon's reelection effort in California's black community in 1972. Henry, a tall, pleasant man who makes no apologies for being a black Republican, moves well in both black and white Republican circles. He was an integral part of the Reagan California organization. Shortly after the California delegation arrived in Kansas City Lucas sought me out.

"Who's going to make the seconding speeches?" he asked.

"Ain't been picked," I said.

"A black lady from New York named Gloria Toote ought to be asked to make one of them."

"I hear she's a nut."

"No," he protested, "she's not a nut. She's a first-class lady. She just won't do what the leaders of the delegation want her to do."

"Is she pledged to Ford?" I asked.

"She's not pledged to Ford," he assured me. "That's one of the problems they have with her."

The idea intrigued me. A black woman seconding Reagan was a tofer—two for the price of one—a black and a woman. On top of this she had been an assistant secretary of housing and urban development in the Nixon-Ford administration, was an attorney, and, Henry assured me, "a first-class speaker."

"I'd like to meet her," I said.

In a little while Henry brought her around. She was a petite woman, maybe forty, one of those people whose age you just have to guess at.

There are few people that I think more highly of. She was definitely interested in seconding Reagan but she had never met him and wanted to before she committed.

"I've gotta get this cleared first," I said. "I don't have the authority to designate you all by myself, although I think I can fix it."

I went to Sears. He couldn't have cared less. He was concentrating on just one thing, finding votes for his vice presidential selection scheme. After all, if Reagan won the nomination the national press, which liked and respected Sears anyway, would crown him as the reigning genius of Republican politics. I think that thought is what really motivated him during the entire campaign. That, and the belief that if he elected a president he could control a president.

Since Sears didn't care, I asked Deaver to set up a meeting between Gloria and the candidate. It was love at first sight, which is easy to understand. Anybody who has ever met Reagan likes him, from the redneck, beer-swilling, blue-collar worker right on up the ladder as far as it goes. Even people such as Tip O'Neil, who as Speaker attacked him meanly and personally from time to time, liked him. Hell, even I like him. So it wasn't surprising that Gloria liked him.

Neither was it surprising that he liked her. He likes almost anybody, especially if he senses that they like him. And Gloria is easy to like. She says it like it is and looks you in the eye when she says it. In contrast, Sears looks almost anywhere else when he's talking to you, a mannerism that always annoyed Reagan, who complained once that he— Sears—"won't look me in the eye, he looks me in the tie."

So it was agreed that Gloria would make a seconding speech. And I was tickled, not only because she was black and a woman and had captured Reagan's fancy, but also because, by using a member of the New York delegation, we were sticking it a little bit to Rockefeller and his hand-picked state chairman, Richard Rosenbaum. Rosenbaum had just finished turning thumbs down on Sears' request to let Reagan address the New York delegation. Clearly he didn't want to risk any defections, but his refusal left a bad taste in the Reagan camp as well as among some of his own delegates.

Rosenbaum is a hard-nosed pol but he is also a party Republican. In 1976 he was doing what he thought best for his candidate and his state party's real leader, Rockefeller, from whom, I suspect, he was taking orders. In 1980, after Reagan won the nomination, and again in 1984 he campaigned strongly for Reagan. He is the kind of politician other politicians understand and admire.

Gloria wound up seconding Reagan's nomination twice, in 1976 and again in 1980. Interestingly, the networks, which in those days pretty much covered the conventions from gavel to gavel, managed to find other things to do both times Gloria spoke. Either they found nothing significant in a black woman from Harlem standing up in support of the man they thought of as a right-wing, trigger-happy, semiracist cowboy from California, or else they found more of significance than they wanted to deal with or wanted the American people to think about.

After Reagan was elected Gloria hoped to be and should have been appointed to a high-level position. Reagan wanted that, too, but it never happened. High-level people in the Reagan White House, many of whom had never supported Reagan until after he was nominated in 1980, blocked every effort made on her behalf. In fairness, it wasn't because she was black. They didn't like her because she was tagged as a troublemaker. What government doesn't have enough of, of course, is troublemakers.

Reagan could have made it happen, just like he could have made a lot of things happen if he had stayed on top of them. But presidents have much more on their minds than taking care of their own—I'm sorry, but that's the way it is—and while they may follow up once or twice on a request such as finding Gloria an appropriate position, their underlings can delay and delay and eventually thwart even a president if they know what they are doing. And the people running Reagan's White House in the early days knew what they were doing, and what some were doing wasn't always what Reagan wanted or in his best interests.

Shortly after the convention opened I received a call from an old friend, Bob Dole. He began as usual by kidding around, joking in particular about who the vice president would be. Ford had already said he would not pick Rockefeller and several names including those of Dole, Howard Baker, and John Connally were being mentioned. There was also speculation about Reagan but he had said categorically that he would not take the job if it were offered.

There was little chance anyway of Ford offering it. He was hurt and angry at Reagan for having had the temerity to challenge him. Before Bryce Harlow died he told me Ford had absolutely refused to discuss the possibility of picking Reagan. And yet if he had and if Reagan had accepted—and Reagan said afterward to several people that if Ford had insisted he could not have turned it down—he almost surely would have been elected to a full term. For, in fact, too many disappointed Reaganites sat on their hands during the general election when they should have been out campaigning for their party's nominee even if his name was Ford.

But even as Dole and I kidded I thought I detected a note of seriousness, so I asked if indeed he wanted to be Ford's running mate. He did.

"What do you want from me?" I asked.

"Well," he said, "Ford will probably meet with Reagan after he's nominated and will probably ask him about vice presidential possibilities. If he does maybe you could get Reagan to say something nice about me, or at least not say anything bad."

I told him I would be glad to speak to Reagan, which I did, asking if Ford brought up Dole's name please to say something nice. He assured me he would. Later I asked Deaver to remind Reagan and, subsequently, he assured me he had.

And sure enough Ford did visit Reagan on the night he won the nomination, and sure enough he did ask what Reagan thought of the various vice presidential possibilities, and sure enough Reagan did say nice things about Dole, and sure enough the next morning Ford picked Dole as his running mate.

For as long as I live I will not forget the night they nominated Ford. I was in the headquarters trailer during the balloting. After Ford had gone over the top delegations, as is customary, began trying to switch their votes to make it a unanimous vote for Ford. But to the chagrin of the Ford people many of the Reagan delegates wouldn't switch and it began to look as if Ford would not get the unanimous support of the convention which his victory, good politics, and custom all entitled him to.

One of the delegations that would not switch was California, the largest, which once again had become my responsibility. I called Bob Nesen, the delegation chairman, and asked him what the trouble was.

"They just won't do it," he said.

"Make them," I told him. "Tell them they're embarrassing Reagan."

And it was true. There was no way Reagan could leave the convention without the party being united. He would look like a sore loser and a prima donna and any plans he had for the future would be severely damaged.

"They won't do it. I've tried," Nesen iterated.

"Let me talk to Holmes."

Holmes Tuttle, member of the delegation, was the strong man and untitled leader of the California Republican party. When Holmes wanted someone to do something that person usually did it. He came on the phone.

"They won't do it," he said.

"Please try again," I asked. "I'll call you back in a couple of minutes."

When I called back nothing had changed.

"Maybe I better talk to them," I suggested.

Holmes allowed as how that would be a good idea.

When I reached the delegation it was plain that the word was out that I was coming and why. Good friends were glaring at me angrily. Many had been crying. I spotted Reagan's close personal and totally nonpolitical friends, Bill Wilson and Alfred Bloomingdale, and went over to plead with them not to embarrass the candidate.

"We came here to vote for Reagan and we're going to keep voting for him," Wilson declared, in less than friendly tones, his eyes watering.

I was trying to figure out what to do next when John Rhodes, the convention chairman, took matters into his own hands. He knew that the party could not leave the convention divided, so he did the only thing he could do. He pounded his gavel.

"The vote is unanimous," he declared, thus unifying the party for all the world to see, and getting me off the hook at the same time. To my mind that was one of Rhodes' proudest moments, a moment that Ford, Reagan, and the party in general should have been grateful for.

Heading back to the trailer, all at once I began to cry, not just a few tears but real sobs. I couldn't figure it out. In the back of my head I was calm and rational but still, there I was, crying like a girl. I stopped and got hold of myself, but every time someone offered a word of condolence I started to cry all over again. When I reached the trailer I went straight to the small lavatory and wept. For five minutes. Then I went out and poured myself a large glass of gin and after that I was all right.

For many Reaganites that was the end of the 1976 campaign. True, there was a lot of sentimentality the next day, with Reagan giving a farewell talk to staff and members of the California delegation and anyone else who happened to drop by. Nancy stood next to him and shed a few genuine tears. I lent her my handkerchief—clean—so she wouldn't spoil her makeup. Reagan thanked everyone and promised it was not the end. He quoted from a Scottish ballad about a wounded knight:

> I am wounded. I am not slain.
> I will lie down and rest a while,
> and then I'll rise and fight again.

It was prophetic, but most of us didn't believe so at the time and I think that probably included Reagan. After all, he would be sixty-nine before he got another shot at running. And that, most of us agreed, was too old.

One event soured the day a little. While Reagan was speaking, Clarke Reed, the Mississippi national committeeman who had deserted Reagan, walked in. He was about as popular with the Reagan people as a pig at a debutante ball. In fact, one of our field men, Kenny Klinge, had to be restrained from hitting him. Reed was sobbing and crying and saying what a terrible mistake he had made—almost enough to make someone who didn't know what a phony he was feel sorry for him. Four years later, after Reagan had won the nomination without Reed's help, he put on the same act and got even less sympathy.

In many ways the highlight of the convention came that night when Ford, at Bryce Harlow's suggestion, generously invited Reagan to join him on the platform. Reagan responded and in a brief, off-the-cuff speech upstaged the nominee and won the hearts of the delegates. I have no doubt, although Ford and his people would never admit it, that if the delegates could have voted after Reagan's speech he, not Ford, would have been the nominee.

Although a couple of books have placed me on the scene during Reagan's finest convention hour, the fact is I missed it. For me the convention had ended the night before. I had no desire to face the smirking, joking winners at the last session of the convention. I had fought too hard to be in their shoes, pretending sympathy for the fallen. Besides, I was tired. So I went to bed and never even saw it on television, which I still regret. It would have been fun watching Reagan there at the last, winning the hearts and minds of the Ford delegates.

Reagan flew to California the next day along with Deaver and Hannaford and others. Before they left I talked with Deaver and we agreed that I would close down the campaign, see that the bills were paid and the reports filed.

It was hardly a romantic job but I wanted it for reasons I didn't explain to Deaver. I wanted to make sure that all the staff people were paid what they had coming and were treated fairly; and just as important, I didn't want Sears and some of the people I thought were more loyal to him than to Reagan controlling the assets of the campaign after it was closed down.

At about the same time I received a call from Bob Dole, who had been nominated, asking me to work for him. I should have said yes, but I was still going through the throes of the emotional letdown I had suffered the night Reagan lost. I told him I didn't want to work full-time and we let it go at that.

In the meantime, Ford had gathered his political hierarchy at Vail, the Colorado resort, to plan the fall campaign. Reaganites noted with righteous indignation that neither Reagan nor any of his people had been invited—not Laxalt, not Sears, not Deaver, not anyone. I was told later that one of the more brilliant minds in the Ford organization had asked Reagan's lawyer and later attorney general, William French Smith, if Reagan should be invited and Smith had said no, Reagan was tired and wouldn't come. Now, Bill Smith was a lot of things, many of them good, but politician he wasn't. And maybe Reagan wouldn't have gone, but he should have been asked, regardless of what Smith thought, and so should half a dozen of Reagan's top staff. But none was, and there we sat, wondering how Ford and his people could be so stupid as to figure he could win without the Reagan people.

Of course they eventually did involve many of us, while others, such as Sears and Deaver and Hannaford, never participated. Our campaign staff had quickly scattered. Deaver and Hannaford went back to their public relations business in Los Angeles. Reagan went back to his radio commentary and his speeches. Others just went back home.

To my surprise, Reagan, who is seldom bitter, went to California a bitter man, convinced that Ford had stolen the nomination from him. I've never agreed with that premise, though I do think he would have been the nominee if Sears had not taken him out of New Hampshire the weekend before the primary, or if he'd worked to organize some key states such as Ohio and New Jersey instead of vainly depending on his powers of persuasion.

Likewise, while I'm certain he would have beaten Jimmy Carter, I'm still not sure that things didn't work out for the best in the long run. The nation needed a Jimmy Carter in order truly to appreciate a Ronald Reagan.

Several things, added together, could have given Reagan the nomination. If he'd gotten into the race earlier he would have kept the support of many activists who drifted away to Ford. And we would have raised more early money, because people generally prefer to wait until their candidate enters the race before they contribute their hard-earned bucks. There's nothing quite so disappointing to a political activist as seeing his candidate drop out of the race and, as a result, watching his money and his time go right down the drain.

In addition, Reagan would surely have done better in Ohio if Sears had acted in time to get a slate of delegates in every congressional district. His Schweiker strategy, brilliant in concept, would have worked better if he had trusted Schweiker to take Drew Lewis into his confidence before he announced.

But all that is hindsight. Reagan lost. He lost, but he went home a hero to most Republicans. And while the Ford people often complained—and some still do—that he didn't do much to help in the general election, he did most of what he was asked. He campaigned extensively, if not exactly enthusiastically, making about twenty-five speeches for Ford and speaking for other candidates as well.

Because the Ford people wanted one particular appearance by Reagan I managed to get even with California Republican chairman Paul Haerle on behalf of Reagan's California loyalists. Haerle, as you may recall, had been on Reagan's staff in Sacramento and then asked for and got Reagan's support when he wanted to be party chairman. Haerle repaid that favor by violating a cardinal rule of the California GOP that said the state chairman must remain neutral in a contested primary. He declared early and often for Ford.

Needless to say, Reagan and some of the rest of us weren't happy. But there are two sayings everyone in politics should learn. One is an old Kennedy family motto: Don't get mad; get even. The other was given to me by a newspaperman friend, John Pinkerman, after I had lost an in-house power struggle while working for the Copley News Service. "Just remember," Pinkerman consoled me, "if you sit by the window long enough they all come by."

According to my wife Bonnie, neither saying is fitten for a good Christian lad to adopt, but believe me, if you turn the other cheek in politics you wind up with at least two bruised cheeks.

In any event I'd been waiting at the window for Haerle for nearly two years when my opportunity finally came by. I was working in the Ford-Dole campaign and one day Stu Spencer called me into his office. There was to be a Salute to Ford fund-raising dinner in Los Angeles and Reagan was reluctant to attend. Today Spencer would get through to Reagan a lot easier than I. But not then. Then Spencer was the guy who'd deserted Reagan for Ford, and the Reagans were not happy about it. You really couldn't blame Spencer, however. Deaver and he were feuding and between Deaver and Sears, who was afraid of any kind of rival, they wouldn't let Spencer near the Reagan campaign.

Anyway, Spencer asked me to call Reagan. I said I would on one condition. If I could get Reagan to attend he would have to see that Haerle, even though he was the state Republican chairman and big in the Ford campaign, was told he could not come. Spencer agreed, and as I remember, not particularly reluctantly. Stu has always understood these things.

It fell upon Leon Parma to inform Haerle. Parma, a longtime friend and golf-playing buddy of Ford, was also his California cochairman. It was a dirty job, but Parma did it. Reagan went to the dinner; Haerle did not. And I continued in the campaign with renewed enthusiasm.

I'd come into the Ford campaign shortly after I'd turned down Bob Dole. Spencer had called from Vail and asked if I would work part-time for Dole and part-time for the overall campaign. He said they didn't want me full-time with Dole because they didn't want the media talking about "the man who shot the bullets"—Dole—and "the man who supplied the ammunition"—me.

So it wound up that Charlie Black and I took turns going out on the campaign trail with Dole. Black had come out of Jesse Helms' organization, had helped found the National Conservative Political Action Com-

mittee (NCPAC), and was the unofficial leader of the conservative wing
of the national Young Republican organization.

When I wasn't working for Dole I was heading a little group Spencer
had asked me to put together to run an attack operation against Carter.
Spencer hadn't detected much enthusiasm for that sort of thing in the
campaign communications arm run by Bill Greener, Sr. Stu and I
discussed what ought to be done, then he sent me to see Greener and
find out what he was doing. What he wasn't doing I was to do. Greener
said he was doing all the things Stu and I had talked about.

When I told this to Stu he said, "Go ahead and do them anyway."

He let me hire three people and gave me a little office suite on another
floor of the campaign building and we went to work. I brought aboard
"our Bob" Tuttle and another Reagan advance man, Paul Russo, and
one of my favorite right-wing nuts, Maiselle Shortly, who had vowed
she would never work for Ford, but couldn't stay away from the action.

We put out a lot of stuff on Carter in the next several weeks, all of it
accurate, none of it friendly. Toward the end Spencer asked me to put
out a campaign tabloid newspaper we called *Heartland*, which attacked
Carter from the standpoint of the religious right. It turned out to be an
effective publication, but it would have been better if Jim Baker, the
campaign chairman, hadn't made me take out some of the more sensa-
tional material. Jim was a timid man back then, too.

Dole was a good campaigner and enjoyed the campaign trail. But he
was not very well known, even though he was in his second term as a
senator and had served two years as Republican National Committee
chairman. Even so, it wasn't uncommon to have someone introduce him
or refer to him as Senator Doyle, which tells you how important vice
presidential nominees are in the eyes of many people.

It took a while for the Ford people to give Dole an organization of his
own and make him an integral part of the campaign. He made up his
own schedule with almost no coordination from Ford's people, and
brought in his own chairman from Kansas, Dave Owen, who didn't have
much to do. The Ford campaign eventually supplied him with a scheduler, a tour director, and a press operation headed by Larry Speakes who
wound up eventually as President Reagan's chief spokesman. Speakes
rode the Dole campaign plane but his relations with the media were
poor. They complained that he wasn't always truthful. As a result Black

and I spent a large amount of time on the plane dealing with the press. Also riding the plane was Noel Koch who had been a Nixon speech writer and was performing the same function for Dole, and, when she wasn't campaigning on her own, Dole's relatively recent bride, Elizabeth.

Elizabeth Dole is a smart, attractive lady from North Carolina who was graduated from Duke University and Harvard Law School. The thing to remember about Elizabeth Dole is that she does not like to be called Liz or Liddy, a childhood nickname. She likes being called Elizabeth. She is a good campaigner and a good politician and if her husband never gets to be president or vice president maybe she will.

I wrote a short, funny speech for her shortly after she and Bob were married. Between my words and her delivery she was a big hit when she went off to Kansas to let the home folk see who it was their Bob had married. We've been friends ever since, although she got mad at me once when she was Transportation secretary and I returned the favor when I was being tried on charges of violating the Ethics in Government Act.

The low point of Dole's campaign for vice president came when he debated the Democratic vice presidential nominee, Walter Mondale, who eight years later lost a presidential run against Ronald Reagan every bit as badly as his mentor, Jimmy Carter, had done four years earlier. Dole came out of the debate thinking he had won and early press reports had him no worse than even. It took about a day for liberal writers to decide he really hadn't won because he had said a terrible thing. He had called the Democratic party the war party. And, as is customary with Republicans, as soon as the Democrats and the liberals began whining about being unfairly maligned a goodly number of so-called moderate Republicans (read "self-righteous Republicans") jumped into bed with them.

Dole, of course, had every right to say what he said and he should have been supported by his party's leaders and elected officials up and down the line. If the Democrats can malign Herbert Hoover for fifty years because of one little ten-year-long depression that Franklin Roosevelt only ended by getting us into World War II, then Republicans have ever right to label as the war party the party whose presidents were in office when the United States, in the twentieth century alone, went into World War I, World War II, Korea, and Vietnam, to say nothing of the

Bay of Pigs and the invasion of the Dominican Republic. Compared to these Grenada, Panama, and Iraq were hardly blips on the radar war screen. And they hadn't even happened then.

After the Ford-Dole ticket lost to Carter-Mondale, Fordites liked (unfairly) to blame Dole for the loss. But Dole did well for the ticket in the farm states and the West coast where he did most of his campaigning. In addition it was Ford, not Dole, who freed the Poles in the debate with Carter, and it was Jim Baker, not Dole, who wound up a narrowly lost campaign with nearly 2 million bucks still in the bank.

But it was a tough loss for Ford and I was sorry to see it happen. I was not a Ford fan, but mainly because I was a Reagan fan. Any Reaganite would be hard put to be a Ford enthusiast. The fact is, after I'd worked in the Ford-Dole campaign for a week I went to Spencer and told him I just couldn't work up any enthusiasm and maybe it would be better if I went home. But he told me to hang around, that he could use me.

Among other things, he needed a visible Reagan hand in the campaign and the only other high-ranking Reagan campaigner to come in was Jim Lake who was helping Clayton Yeutter with the farm vote. But, by the end of the campaign I was involved both physically and emotionally. You can't work for a man and a party in which you believe without rooting for them to win and, while Gerald Ford never got a real chance to prove what kind of president he could be, I knew then and I know now that he would have been better than Jimmy Carter because in the long run he had a better feel for the America people than Carter would ever have.

7

CFTR

PAVING THE WAY FOR 1980

THE 1976 REPUBLICAN National Convention had ended and Gerald Ford was his party's nominee. The disheartened Reagan delegates and campaign staffers had dried their tears and were rapidly departing Kansas City. As the Reagans, along with the California staff, took off in their chartered plane for Los Angeles, Frank Reynolds of ABC television described the scene with a catch in his voice and a tear in his eye. Reynolds was nobody's conservative, but he was an honest man and over the course of the primary campaigns a genuine bond had grown up between him and the Reagans.

Despite my own affection for Reagan and disappointment at his defeat I didn't see him off. It didn't seem to make much sense. There was work to do in the aftermath of the convention—returning cars and walkie-talkies, and dismantling all the stuff we had so arduously man-

213

tled in the previous weeks. But before Reagan and entourage departed I did something that was to have a major impact on Reagan's future—I got Deaver to agree that I would be in charge of closing down the campaign. It was important that he agree because he would tell Reagan who would not object unless he had already picked someone else.

I'm sure Deaver didn't give it much thought because, like almost everyone else, he just wanted to go home. He showed no curiosity about why I wanted one more drudge job. He probably thought I needed a salary, but that never occurred to me, and I didn't take any pay, which may surprise the money-hungry Deaver even today.

My reason was simple: money, the leftover campaign money, which I wanted for the future of the Reagan movement. Reagan's nationally televised speech at the end of April had money pouring in during May and June, and we literally had no place to spend it except on the convention.

So all that money was just sitting in a bank—about $1.5 million after all our bills were paid. And I didn't want Sears or one of his cronies controlling it. I didn't like Sears, didn't respect him, didn't trust him; I'm confident the feeling was mutual. And I didn't want him to have any say in how it was to be used.

Kathleen Lawrence, who had worked in campaign finance, took care of the details of closing down the campaign and she and I jointly made the decisions on any payments we deemed controversial.

Through part of this period I was also working for the Ford-Dole campaign. But by the time it began in earnest we pretty much had the Reagan campaign shut down, the proper papers filed with the Federal Election Committee, and the leftover money tucked safely in the bank. All that was left was to pay late bills and dicker with the FEC over how much of the money we could keep. Eventually Reagan wound up with roughly a million bucks.

The FEC is just about the most useless and most not-quite-honest subdivision of the federal government. Its staffers are forever twisting and misreading their own rules and regulations hoping to chisel a little more money out of a defunct campaign or put a politician in his place. The members of the commission, a bipartisan group, mostly incompetent, aren't much better. About all that can be said for them is that they treat Democrats every bit as rudely as Republicans.

With the election over, kicked away by a bumbling Jerry Ford and his timid campaign manager, Jim Baker, the question that arose in Reagan's inner circle was what to do with Reagan's campaign money? Under the law it was his. He could have paid income tax on it and put the remainder in his pocket. Or he could have tried to return it to his contributors, a nearly impossible task. Or he could have given it away to any person or any organization he chose. He did none of these things.

Shortly after the election the Reagans, Deaver, Hannaford, Meese, and I met to decide what to do with it. None of the Easterners was there, nobody whose loyalty was to Sears, not Reagan. We went over the options, one of which was to use it to form a political action committee, the option I favored.

I had given the situation a lot of thought, based on the belief that Reagan would not run again. Too old. Nor was I alone in this belief. Among others, it was shared by Deaver, who was closest to the Reagans not only physically but also as friend and confidant. On several occasions during the next two years he was to confide to Meese, Hannaford, and me over breakfast that he thought Reagan was too old to run again.

On my part, I thought that at age sixty-four he had had his shot at the presidency and had missed. By the time he could run again he would be sixty-eight, an age which in general is a little long in the tooth to be seeking the presidency.

But though I thought Reagan would not run again I was convinced he could continue to be an effective force in the Republican party and a strong advocate for his philosophy of government. He was, after all, the unquestioned leader of the conservative wing of the party, now the dominant wing.

At our meeting we concluded that the best way to keep Reagan effective was to form a political action committee (PAC) with Reagan as chairman. The leftover money would serve as seed money—a million bucks buys a lot of seed—and using Reagan's name we could raise a lot more.

The PAC would finance Reagan's political activities—his speeches, appearances, travel—and allow him to support candidates who shared his political views. And it could be used to sponsor political education programs and campaign schools. My dream was to use it to build a political power base that would effectively carry on the Reagan philosophy long after he had retired to Rancho Cielo in the mountains above Santa Barbara.

We called the PAC "Citizens for the Republic," a name I suggested because it had the same initials as Reagan's campaign organization, Citizens for Reagan. We called it CFR for short, but not for long. CFR, it seems, also stood for Council on Foreign Relations, a nonpartisan organization peopled largely by the important and self-important denizens of the Eastern liberal establishment. Ain't no blue-collar workers ever been invited into membership, other than some labor leaders who have graduated to wearing business suits and using proper grammar.

After receiving dozens of letters of objection, I decided we would become a four-letter acronym—CFTR, Citizens for THE Republic. It worked like a charm. We were immediately reaccepted as genuine, bona fide right-wing kooks by all of Reagan's right-wing kook supporters. Of course, this all happened after our meeting which wound up with one final decision: Reagan would be the PAC's chairman and I would run it on a day-to-day basis as executive vice chairman.

It was natural for me to run CFTR. First, I was the only one of us who needed a job. Deaver and Hannaford had gone back to their PR business with Reagan as their major client, and Meese was setting up a school of criminal justice at the University of San Diego. I had abandoned my business—such as it was—in Sacramento during the campaign and Bonnie had sold the house and moved into an apartment in West Los Angeles because, while I often came into L.A., I never seemed able to get to Sacramento.

Besides, I was the only one seriously interested in politics beyond what Ronald Reagan was doing or might do. Meese had been in government but had never really been active in politics except as an issues person and an adviser to Reagan. Hannaford, true, had once lost a race for Congress in a highly Democratic district, which spoke well for his courage but less well for his political judgment. Deaver had the most political experience of that trio. He had been a field man for the Republican State Central Committee before joining Governor Reagan's staff and he later took a leave of absence to direct a tax reform initiative that was to be the crowning achievement of Reagan's second term, except that it lost.

Still, I had vastly more political experience than any of them. I had been Reagan's press secretary in his first run for governor, had been deeply involved in his abortive run for the presidential nomination in 1968, had directed the last month of Max Rafferty's run for the U.S.

Senate in late 1966, had been part of the political operation in the Nixon White House, had run communications at the Republican National Committee, had directed California in Nixon's reelection campaign in 1972, had done a variety of things in Reagan's 1976 campaign, and had wound up working in the Ford-Dole campaign. By this time, I was primarily a politician, which the others were not.

On top of this, I knew and understood Reagan and knew and got along with the other three. In those days, before Deaver had sold out first to Sears and later to James Baker, we made a pretty good team with Meese the senior adviser, Deaver and Hannaford taking care of the Reagans, and me running Reagan's PAC.

With the formation of CFTR Rose Marie returned from Texas to make certain it ran properly. Angela (Bay) Buchanan, later President Reagan's first United States treasurer, came out from Washington to be the comptroller, deal with the FEC, and keep us honest and out of trouble. Joan Sweetland also came out to do secretarial work and lend a good political head. By the first of 1977 we were up and running.

CFTR is perhaps the only PAC that ever opened its doors with a million bucks in the bank. That made things a lot easier for us. We were able to hire people and get a direct mail fund-raising program off the ground without ever having to borrow a nickel. One of my first tasks was to get Ronald Reagan's name back. Let me explain:

In direct mail fund-raising a good name is literally worth its weight in greenback dollars. By a "good" name I mean a name that, signed to a fund-raising letter, will bring in a large number of contributions. At the start of 1977 the best name in America for raising money among conservatives was Ronald Reagan.

Early in his political career Reagan had talked about starting a "prairie fire" that would sweep the nation. He had lit the match in 1976 and now in 1977 the fire was burning strongly. He had supplanted Barry Goldwater as the conservative leader. Regardless of his age, they wanted to follow him all the way to the White House. While many around Reagan may have given up on the idea, the people, his people, had not. Anything they could do to advance his cause they would do.

That included giving money. And that is why Reagan's signature was so much in demand by conservative direct mail fund-raisers. They were clamoring for the use of his name. Unfortunately, a few people in the Reagan campaign who had no authority to authorize its use had done so.

That meant that letters could be going out without Reagan's permission, or at the same time as we were mailing Reagan-signed letters to raise money for CFTR. It meant that Reagan's name could be overused and its value diminished very quickly. I had to put a stop to that even though I would be viewed as a miserable son-of-a-bitch by some people who, if not our friends, should at least have been our allies. But better that I, not Reagan, be viewed as the MSOB.

Surprisingly, I only had serious arguments in two cases. One was with the Congressional Club of North Carolina, the PAC of U.S. Sen. Jesse Helms, which has raised and spent millions in the last twenty years keeping Helms in office and helping elect other conservatives. In this case Reagan himself had given permission, and that was proper because if Reagan had lost North Carolina in 1976 his campaign for president would have been all but over, not only then, but probably in 1980 as well.

The problem was the Congressional Club wanted to use Reagan's name first whereas I was determined that CFTR would use it first, since it was Reagan's PAC. Senator Helms himself called me to argue the point and threatened to go to Reagan. He never did, after I explained that I was the designated Keeper of The Name. But he wasn't very happy.

The other case was even more difficult. It concerned a mailing by conservative fund-raiser Richard Viguerie on behalf of John Harmer, an old California ally of Reagan's and a friend of mine. Harmer had served in the California State Senate and in 1974 had run for lieutenant governor and lost. Undeterred, he ran for the U.S. Senate in 1976, finishing third in the primary and deeper in debt.

In early January I heard a rumor that Viguerie was planning a mailing for Harmer using Reagan's signature. I called Viguerie and asked who had given him permission. He said he had been assured by Harmer that Reagan had. I called Harmer. Yes, he said, Reagan had given him permission. When, I asked. In August, he said.

"That was five months ago," I protested. "You should have used it then." He insisted that he should be able to use it now.

"John," I said, "if I told you last August you could use my car and you came around and drove it off six months later, I'd think you'd stolen it. It's the same with Reagan's name. We're not letting it be used and you just can't use it."

"If I can't use it you'll be responsible for me going bankrupt," he warned.

"Don't put that monkey on my back," I responded. "I didn't ask you to run for the Senate."

He hung up and didn't speak to me for several years.

One thing I wanted to do was help the conservatives take the party mechanism away from the moderates. The contest in 1977 for chairman of the Republican National Committee was between Richard Richards and Bill Brock. The Reagan people were supporting Richards. He had been the Utah state chairman and had worked the West for Reagan in 1976. Brock was not one of ours. A two-term senator from Tennessee, he had been defeated for reelection in November. I thought that Brock wanted the chairmanship in order to keep his political career alive. I had never viewed him as a particularly strong senator and did not think he would be a strong chairman. Wrong again. He turned out to be extremely competent, one of the best chairmen in my time in politics.

In winning the chairmanship he proved once again that the RNC does not necessarily represent the rank-and-file of the party. Reagan and I met with him after he was elected and Reagan asked him to appoint a Reaganite, Charlie Black, as the RNC's political director. Black had headed up Reagan's field operation and was recognized as one of the better young politicians in the party. Being a smart pol and not wishing to offend the party's most popular leader, Brock agreed.

But Brock was slow to move and we had an exchange of correspondence, each letter less cordial on both our parts, before he finally came through. I think he always intended to make the appointment, but wasn't in any hurry, and then got his back up when I pestered him. On the other hand, if I hadn't, who knows?

Black stayed at the RNC until we began putting together Reagan's run for the 1980 nomination. Then, like most who had worked for Reagan in 1976, he quit and joined the new Reagan campaign.

After CFTR was organized we set up a steering committee with Paul Laxalt as chairman and just about everyone who'd done anything in the campaign as a member. If you are going to have a steering committee it should either be very small, with the few members pretty much committed to agreeing with whatever you want done, or else so large that there is hardly ever agreement on anything so you're free to do what you want. We went the large route, and it never interfered with what I wanted to do.

We officially opened CFTR right after the first of the year 1977 in Santa Monica, about three miles from Reagan's home and the same distance from his office, but he never visited us unless urged.

Reagan is full of contradictions. On the campaign trail he works the fences and the crowds better than anyone I have ever seen because they're there and because he knows that's what he's supposed to do. And he does a fine job at cocktail parties and receptions. But he never seems to remember that the people who work for him, both paid and volunteer, largely do so because they love and admire him and that they would be ecstatic if he would just drop by and says thanks once in a while. Which he almost never does of his own accord. It's not that he's indifferent to people or that he takes them for granted. The fact is, in some ways he's a little shy; he tries not to intrude, even on people who want to be intruded upon.

Reagan's office in West Los Angeles was located in the Deaver and Hannaford suite. So we were close, but not too close. At their request we put Deaver and Hannaford on our payroll as public relations advisers— a complete waste of money except that it bought friendship and cooperation from the people who dealt with Reagan on a daily basis and controlled his schedule and speaking engagements.

My plan, hardly etched in stone, was to keep raising as much money as possible, primarily through direct mail, using not only the list of Reagan contributors but also testing other identifiably conservative lists. With the money I wanted to run campaign schools in the off years—the years with no elections—and concentrate on helping Reagan-like candidates in the election years with maximum contributions. I never figured it made much sense to give $500 to someone who needed to raise $500,000 or $5 million to get elected. But $5,000 in a primary and another $5,000 in a general election could be of significant help. That is the maximum amount that a PAC can legally contribute to a United States House or Senate campaign. All states have their own laws regarding how much can be contributed to in-state races.

That first year we concentrated on putting on campaign schools in Los Angeles, Chicago, Salt Lake, Kansas City, Philadelphia, and Atlanta. They went well. A number of people have told me that they first got actively involved in politics because of our schools. Reagan was always the chief drawing card. Devotees at each school could see and hear the great man up close, maybe shake his hand, maybe get an autograph. And Reagan enjoyed it. These were not curiosity seekers at some business convention; these people loved him, admired him, still wanted him to be president, and intended to work toward that end.

I still wonder if it wasn't these schools and the other political gatherings we pushed him to attend that helped rev him up for one last try at the presidency. Of course there were other reasons, too. He still thought he had been cheated out of the 1976 nomination. Further, he was convinced that if he had won he would have beaten Jimmy Carter. The thought of getting his own shot at Carter certainly pushed him toward his eventual decision to run again. I'm sure that Nancy, too, wanted him to run again. They had come so close. And there was no doubt in her mind or her husband's that he was the best man, better than Ford, better than Carter.

By early 1978 we all thought he'd decided to run again. Not that he told us, because he didn't. He had a thing about throwing his hat into the political ring too soon and his idea of too soon was a lot later than mine. For me, the earlier the better. You can raise money more easily with a declared candidate. You can organize more easily and plan better.

But there were practical personal reasons why Reagan did not want to be seen as a candidate any earlier than he had to. They boiled down to one thing—money. Although the Reagans lived well they did not live lavishly. They were certainly not as rich as the people they associated with—the Holmes Tuttles, Alfred Bloomingdales, Bill Wilsons, Earle Jorgensons, and others with really deep pockets.

In order to maintain their living style Reagan had to work—make speeches, do his radio commentary, and write his column. And that was fine. He liked doing them. And he did them well. The ones he personally wrote were in longhand on yellow legal pads. THE speech, however, which he was forever changing and polishing and adding new jokes and anecdotes onto, he fiddled with on 4 x 6 inch cards.

When he first began making speeches he used 3 x 5 inch cards but we got him to change to the 4 x 6s because you could get more on them. For a time when he was governor, we put his speeches on 6 x 10 inch cards for the same reason, but he was more comfortable with the smaller ones and eventually reverted to them. He didn't write the cards in longhand, which in his case is small and cramped; he printed them in capital letters for easier reading while standing at a dais.

Reagan's handwriting is not easy to read. It looks as if he'd been switched from a left-hander to a right-hander as a kid, something commonly done to children before the social scientists decided such switches were damaging to childish psyches. Reagan denies he was switched even though he chops wood left-handed and wears his six-gun on his left hip and draws it with his left hand. At least he did in the movies.

During 1977 and 1978, nothing really challenged Reagan and he needs to be challenged to stay on top of his game. He is one of those who never does well in practice but is hell on wheels when the game begins. Sure, he was writing and speaking, but this was easy work. And Deaver, seeing him coasting along, mistook a lack of intensity for aging. He was not alone. Many members of the media who interviewed him in those days came away with the impression that Reagan wasn't as sharp as in 1976.

Fortunately, a last chance to win the presidency was all the challenge Reagan needed. By the time his campaign began in earnest in late 1979 he was charged up both physically and mentally and by campaign's end there was no doubt that he was up to the demands of the presidency.

Certain by early 1978 that Reagan would run in 1980, we began making plans. For one thing, I changed my approach to making contributions to candidates. I became more interested in making friends and picking up brownie points for Reagan than in helping elect a select few. That year we gave to almost any Republican to the right of Lowell Weicker, the nominally Republican senator from Connecticut who made Ted Kennedy look like a moderate and Charlie Manson like a nice guy. We wanted broad party support for Reagan come 1980. So we contributed about $800,000 to campaigns that year and bought a lot of friends for him. What we sought was enough political support to create an impression of inevitability about a Reagan candidacy.

One move I made backfired. I should have known it would, but sometimes my inate Republicanism gets the better of my political instincts and suspicions.

Shortly before the November 1978 elections I had a call from the campaign chairman for Sen. (Chuck) Charles Percy who was seeking reelection and was in deep trouble. A pompous moderate, which appealed to the political writers, Percy came from Illinois where he had beaten Paul Douglas, one of the grand old men of the Democratic party, and had once fancied himself destined for the presidency. But by 1978 Illinoisians, tired of his pomposity, his self-righteousness, and his liberal Republicanism, were preparing to chuck Percy.

His campaign manager sounded distraught.

"Mr. Nofziger," he said, "I know you [meaning Reagan and his friends] don't think much of Senator Percy, but he's going to lose unless something happens. I know Governor Reagan is going to be out here next week to talk at a fund-raiser for the state party. Senator Percy will be there. I can't ask you to ask Governor Reagan to endorse him but would it be possible for him to say something nice about the senator? It would mean a great deal."

"I don't have any problem with that," I told him, truthfully. "I can't promise you Reagan will endorse him but I'm sure he'll agree to say some nice things. After all, we're all Republicans."

He thanked me profusely and I called Reagan and related the conversation. Reagan without hesitation agreed to help, even though Percy had campaigned rather nastily against him just two years earlier.

And help Reagan did. At the fund-raiser he spoke glowingly of Percy and endorsed him, to the disgust of many conservatives who, nevertheless, forgave Reagan, as they always did, for this bit of apostasy.

Percy was reelected narrowly and the next day credited Reagan for his victory. But a day later, remembering that he was a moderate and Reagan was a right winger, he backed off. And less than two years later he contributed $500 to John Anderson's third party campaign for president.

The story continues. When Reagan won the presidency he pulled ten new Republican senators into office with him, enough to give Republicans a majority in the Senate and make Percy chairman of the Foreign Relations Committee. Percy took advantage of his new clout to demand that the president appoint his daughter, Sharon Rockefeller, the very liberal Democratic wife of the very liberal Democratic governor and later senator from West Virginia, as chairman of the Corporation for Public Broadcasting. She got the job, even though we knew—and she proved us right—that she would oppose Reagan's policies. Politics is a strange business—no hard and fast rules, few loyalties, no lasting gratitude.

In the spring of 1978 I flew to Texas to see James A. Baker III, a

Houston society lawyer. Baker had run Gerald Ford's losing campaign in 1976.

On the surface Baker is an impressive man and during my stint in the Ford campaign I had been impressed enough to want him on Reagan's side if he should decide to run in 1980. I told Baker that I thought Reagan would run and that we were trying to get some preliminary commitments from people we thought might eventually support him.

He told me he was probably closer philosophically to Reagan than to George Bush (not true) but that he had a long personal friendship with and commitment to Bush and would have to support him if he ran. I appreciated his forthrightness and later that year when Baker was running for Texas attorney general—and losing—I didn't object when he asked Reagan to come to Texas and do a fund-raiser. But there were some candidates even Reagan couldn't help.

Reagan also went to Texas to help Bill Clements in his successful race for governor. Clements, a wealthy oilman, spent something over $10 million buying the governorship and most of that he fished out of his own very deep pockets. At Tom Reed's request Reagan met with Clements and later did a fund-raiser for him that raised more than a million dollars.

The meeting with Clements also involved Mrs. Clements, Nancy, Reagan, Reed, and me at the Reagan's home. Eventually I grew to like Clements, but our initial meeting was not propitious. Always a bull in a china shop, he stuck his nose in where it didn't belong. A staunch Reagan supporter running for Congress in Texas was involved in a Republican run-off with George Bush, Jr. I had sent a $1,000 contribution from CFTR to the Reaganite which upset the Bush people immensely. Papa George himself had called Reagan to complain, which I thought strange since he had never supported Reagan and was prepared to run against him in the next presidential primaries.

Reagan, who didn't like to get involved in primary fights, had asked me about the contribution and I had explained that we were supporting one of his supporters, something that seemed perfectly logical to me. Then Clements butted in, telling Reagan it had been a big mistake for CFTR to make the contribution. I held my tongue, Reagan kind of nodded, and Clements then suggested that CFTR should also give a thousand to young Bush.

"We can't do that," I said. "We're not going to play both sides of the street."

Clements iterated his point. This time neither Reagan nor I said anything and the conversation turned to other things. After the Clementses left I brought the matter up.

"We just can't give to both sides," I said.

He agreed, and I left. A couple of years later he made it up to young Bush by making his daddy vice president, which beat the heck out of a $1,000 contribution.

There are a couple of kinds of people I find it difficult to understand in the business of politics. I don't understand or like people who give to more than one candidate for a single office, and I don't understand people who don't like to get mixed up in primaries. In my opinion, people who give to opposing candidates at best are whores; by contributing to both candidates they think they will be assured of access to the victor. At worst they are gutless wonders who either knuckle under to pressure or are fearful of saying no. Corporate officers and their lobbyists are chief among the whores. They also give to incumbents, regardless of party or politics or philosophy. Like Ado Annie, they just "cain't say no" to the Bill Clementses of this world.

As for people who don't like to mix in primaries, well, Ronald Reagan is one of those. And, though I understand his approach, I don't agree with him. He reasons that he, Reagan, wants to be a unifier, wants to be sure that he can be of effective help to the primary winner in the general election, and that he can't be if he has been involved in a bitter primary fight. But if all Republicans felt that way no Republican candidate would ever be able to put together an organization or get a penny in contributions. On that ground alone, Reagan cannot justify his decision to run against Ford or his requests to other Republicans that they work for him in his primary campaigns.

My view was that if we wanted to mold the Republican party after Ronald Reagan we had to help Reagan-like candidates in the primaries. But Reagan was the chairman of CFTR so we pretty much did as he wanted. I remember only one other time in 1978 that we got into a congressional primary and that was vindictiveness on my part.

It involved a race in South Dakota where a Vietnam POW named Leo Thorsness was running against the state treasurer, David Volk.

Thorsness was the more conservative and a genuine hero of the Vietnam War. He had been awarded a Congressional Medal of Honor. I sent $500 to Volk.

I first met Thorsness and his wife, Gaylee, in early 1974 shortly after he had been repatriated. Many released war prisoners had been flown home through Travis Air Force Base, about an hour's drive from Sacramento. The Reagans usually drove over to welcome the boys home. They found these occasions extremely emotional and they and members of the governor's staff wound up close friends of many of them, including Thorsness.

The day I met him he had come from South Dakota to seek Reagan's advice about running for the U.S. Senate against George McGovern, who had run for president in 1972. McGovern seemed ripe for defeat. He not only had been trounced in 1972, including losing his own state, but also had disclosed to the whole world, including South Dakota, what kind of a left-wing extremist he was. And South Dakota was a state with a Republican majority.

Asking Reagan's advice on running for office is a little like asking mine on how to get into the movies, something the people around Reagan recognize, but nobody else seems to. So after Thorsness talked to Reagan the people in Reagan's office sent him to see me. I relished the idea of a genuine war hero whipping the peacenikishness out of McGovern. Thorsness had almost no money so I volunteered to help for expenses only. The first thing he had to do was win a three-way primary against two better-known opponents.

The man who had largely persuaded Thorsness to enter the race was Jim Stockdale, a skinny, redheaded, youngish, chainsmoking, beer-swilling country lawyer who preferred being a penniless politician to practicing law. Stockdale had run South Dakota for Nixon in 1972. He knew it like the backs of his hands, and was convinced that Thorsness could be elected. I flew to Sioux Falls to meet with Thorsness and Stockdale who, it was agreed, would run the day-to-day campaign. I would serve as the campaign consultant and come in every couple of weeks. I would also try to raise enough money at least to pay my expenses.

Stockdale and I agreed that Thorsness should run, not as a prisoner of war but as a man who understood South Dakota and would represent it in Washington better than McGovern. I explained to Thorsness that the prisoner of war thing would be there in a subliminal way, but I wanted him to keep using his cane, which he really didn't need anymore, as a semisubliminal reminder to the voters.

My friend, Dick Wirthlin, called me early on and advised me against getting involved. Thorsness can't win, he told me, and quoted polling figures that had him trailing badly, with only 17 percent support among Republicans. I thanked him but said, regardless of the figures, Thorsness was a good candidate for a number of reasons and properly handled could win.

The June primary proved me right. Thorsness did what the early polls said he couldn't do. Not only did he win, but he garnered more than half the Republican votes cast. Given this victory he should have been elected senator in November.

But something happened to Thorsness after the primary. He thought he'd won it by himself. He forgot that Stockdale had put together a good organization, that a woman named Lynn Solum had written effective radio spots, that an earnest young man named John LeBoutellier had come from New York to help raise money, and that the strategy he had followed—to run as a South Dakotan, not as an ex-POW—had been laid out by Stockdale and me.

I met with Thorsness in late June and I could see he was nervous. Columnist Jack Anderson had recently written a couple of nasty columns about me, and Leo was fearful that they would hurt him. I've always thought the McGovern people fed Anderson the stuff because McGovern himself had begun attacking me as one of the bad guys from the Nixon administration.

Actually, Thorsness was more than nervous, he was downright scared and clearly uncomfortable with me around. I learned from him, then, something I should have known all along: there are different kinds of courage. Leo was a brave flier and a brave prisoner, doing things in battle and enduring things as a POW that make me shrink to think of. But he lacked political courage. Having won the primary against long odds he was afraid something might happen to cost him the general election. And he was right. Something did happen. In fact, several things happened.

By the time I had arrived home from our June meeting I realized that Thorsness wanted me gone. And since I was working for expenses only I figured I ought to accommodate him. So I wrote a letter of resignation, which he accepted with alacrity. He followed up by firing Stockdale and Lynn Solum and bringing in a new campaign manager who ran him as a POW whom people ought to vote for because they owed him. Not surprisingly, he lost.

By 1975 Thorsness was holding a minor job in the Ford administration. Although a professed Reagan supporter he quickly found his way into the Ford campaign as a surrogate speaker. He often campaigned wearing his Medal of Honor ribbon, which probably netted Ford an extra two votes during the preconvention campaign.

Now, in 1978, he was back in South Dakota running for Congress and Stockdale was working for me as CFTR's political director and Dave Volk was an old friend of his. Stockdale approached me about sending money to Volk and after debating the matter for about two seconds I said, "Sure, let's do it."

So we sent him $500 which isn't a lot, but is more in South Dakota than in places like California or Ohio. In return Stockdale got a commitment from Volk that he would support Reagan if he ran for president. In the meantime, unbeknownst to Stockdale and me, Thorsness had called Helene von Damm, Reagan's personal secretary, and asked if he could see Reagan when Reagan went to Sioux Falls in May to speak at a party fund-raiser. Helene thought it was a reasonable request and put him on Reagan's schedule without telling me.

As luck would have it Volk received his check from CFTR a day or two before Reagan arrived in Sioux Falls. Naturally he put out a press release because the check would be seen as tantamount to an endorsement from Reagan. Thorsness was outraged and when he saw Reagan he complained bitterly. Poor Reagan was somewhat nonplussed since I had neglected to tell him I had sent the check to Volk. I apologized when Reagan returned home, but he did not appear particularly upset. Like me, he doesn't enjoy whiners, and, besides, I explained that Thorsness had supported Ford.

The icing on the cake was the headline in the *Sioux Falls Argus Leader*. It read:

THORSNESS SEES REAGAN
VOLK GETS THE MONEY

Despite CFTR's contribution to Volk, Thorsness ran a repeat of his Senate race, winning the primary and losing the general. Needless to say, he was not involved in the Reagan campaign of 1979–80. And somehow, even though he sought one, he never got a job in the Reagan administration.

In May of 1978 I received a significant phone call, one that would affect Reagan's campaign and his ensuing administration. It was from Drew Lewis, who as Ford's campaign chairman in Pennsylvania in 1976 had been key in preventing Dick Schweiker from stealing the Pennsylvania delegation for Reagan. When I got on the phone he started to explain who he was.

"I know who you are," I said. "What can I do for you?"

"I think Reagan is going to run for president in 1980, and I want to be involved," he said.

I explained that Reagan hadn't said he was going to run. He said he understood, but he still thought he would and he still wanted to be involved. I was delighted. He is an excellent pol and was the strong man in the Pennsylvania Republican party. His involvement would just about assure Reagan of the Pennsylvania delegation.

Lewis said he had never met Reagan so I suggested that, first off, he should talk with him and then maybe we could meet in Washington in the near future. I gave him Reagan's phone number and called Reagan to say that Lewis would be calling and please take the call, which he did.

A few weeks later we met in Washington in Dick Schweiker's office. Also there were Lewis's political associate, Rick Robb, Dick Schweiker, and Paul Laxalt. Not there was John Sears. By this time neither Laxalt nor I wanted much to do with him. Neither of us thought he was essential to the next Reagan campaign.

Lewis turned out to be easy to deal with. He just wanted to be involved, either in the national campaign or in Pennsylvania.

"I'll do whatever you want me to do," he said.

I like a man like that. Too many people come into a campaign with the idea of running it, or demanding to be part of the "inner circle." For the most part you don't need those people because they are more interested in being important than in winning. Lewis, because he was competent and wanted nothing but to help elect Reagan, wound up in the inner circle, and eventually became Reagan's first secretary of transportation.

Later that summer I had lunch at the Capitol Hill Club in Washington with Rep. Philip Crane of Illinois and his administrative assistant, Richard Williamson.

Crane is one of the more conservative members of the House of Representatives. He is handsome, articulate, and a fine speaker. He had traveled the country extensively during the middle 1970s, rallying the conservative troops. Along with Reagan and Rep. Jack Kemp of New York, he was one of the most articulate and visible expounders of conservatism. And he was ambitious. Some among the so-called New Right leadership in Washington were encouraging him to run for president in 1980 and he was doing nothing to discourage them.

The purpose of my lunch with Crane was to find out how serious he was about running. Crane waited until Williamson had gone to the men's room to tell me. Sure, he said, he was interested in running, but he had no intention of doing so if Reagan was going to run again.

"I am like an acorn compared to Reagan's mighty oak tree," he said frankly. That told me what I wanted to know and, back in California, I reported the conversation to the Reagans and Deaver, Meese, and Hannaford.

But between then and mid-July Crane had a change of heart. Some leaders of the Eastern New Right establishment, led by Paul Weyrich and Richard Viguerie, persuaded him that he had a shot at winning the Republican nomination. They should have known better, but they let their resentment at never having been admitted to the Reagan inner circle get the better of their normally good political judgment. Viguerie promised to raise most of the money Crane needed.

These Eastern conservatives did not know Reagan very well and, more importantly, had never really grasped the fact of his across-the-board, across-the-country voter appeal. They had also convinced themselves that conservatives, given a choice between a candidate they looked upon as old and tired, and a young, dynamic conservative would choose the latter. Like I said, they just did not understand Reagan's appeal.

Reagan had business in Washington in late July and Crane asked for a meeting, which took place in Paul Laxalt's office on July 25. Rep. Dan Crane, Phil's brother who lost his seat in 1984, came with him, as did another Illinois congressman, Rep. Edward Derwinski, who, I learned later, had been kind of snookered into coming and was not a Crane for president supporter at all. Laxalt and I also sat in. None of us knew what was on Crane's mind although there had been rumors that he was becoming serious about running. Crane was nervous but came right to the point: "I'm going to run for president."

He went on to say how much he admired and respected Reagan and assured him that he would support him if Reagan ran and won the nomination. Reagan sat quietly until Crane was through, then told him that whatever he did was up to him and that he, Reagan, had not yet decided what he would do.

I'm sure Crane was surprised by Reagan's calm reaction and his refusal to be drawn into any kind of discussion or argument. Crane announced a few days later but his early entry did him no good. His campaign never got off the ground. He was unable to raise substantial sums and his campaign organization eventually fell apart.

Although he didn't show any particular emotion at Crane's disclosure Reagan was privately irritated, as he had every right to be, if only because Crane had assured him through me that he would not run. But Crane's announcement had no effect on Reagan's base. And Reagan's refusal to be critical of Crane made it easy for his few supporters, including Viguerie and Weyrich, to endorse Reagan after Crane dropped out.

In retrospect it is interesting that Crane never received consideration from Reagan for the second spot on the ticket. It was not animosity; it was just that when it came time to think about a Reagan running mate Crane had literally fallen off the screen.

By the time Crane had cast his die it was obvious to Reagan insiders that he was serious about running again. But a lot of wrinkles had to be ironed out before a campaign could be up and running. The biggest question was, who would run the campaign? And who wouldn't?

On the surface and to most political reporters Sears was the logical choice since he had run the 1976 campaign that had seen Reagan come within a gnat's eyelash of unseating a sitting president of his own party. But among Reaganites there was much antagonism toward Sears. Most did not think he was a conservative. Many thought he had not run a good campaign in 1976. Some were suspicious of him because of his secret meeting with Rogers Morton; others because of his role in picking Dick Schweiker. Still others thought he was arrogant or secretive or more interested in John Sears' career than in Ronald Reagan's.

Whatever the reasons, many people who had supported Reagan in

1976 urged Reagan not to rename him to the top job for the 1980 campaign. And on at least two occasions Reagan assured groups that Sears would not run his campaign if he decided to run again. But when it came right down to the nub he changed his mind, not an unusual thing for a politician to do, especially if the presidency is at stake.

8

Electing Reagan President

REAGAN'S CAMPAIGN FOR the 1980 Republican nomination for president began in turmoil long before the candidate himself was ready to announce.

By early 1978 we had no doubt that Reagan would run again. At CFTR we were operating on that premise, trying to keep the 1976 Reagan organization in place, and wooing possible supporters.

The turmoil was among the political people around Reagan, largely the leadership of the 1976 campaign. By now Sears was carrying on an active vendetta against me although he would never face me about his concerns. Instead, he told others that I had leaked false and defamatory information about him to Jack Anderson. This was a bald-faced lie and when I bearded him he refused to discuss it.

For my part I now had little use for him and thought he would be a negative in the campaign. In my opinion he had failed us in the clutch in 1976. A secretive man, he made decisions and then asked for confirmation of his brilliance. He was fearful of sharing authority and gathered around him men who shared his belief in his genius. Others he pretty much ignored and, as time went on, tried to eliminate entirely.

Laxalt shared my views, if not my reasons for them, and urged Reagan to pick someone else to run his campaign. His idea was to have Sears run the Northeast, which Sears refused even to consider—he was not about to take a lesser position. His ambition was not so much to elect Reagan as to build his own political stature by having elected him. That Reagan several times assured groups that Sears would not run his campaign, if he decided to run again, did not deter him.

Deaver, although a Sears fan, recognized that he was unpopular among Reaganites and initially sought to find an advisory role for him, one in which he would not have day-to-day control. But Sears would have none of that either. He hinted at going to work for Sen. Howard Baker, the moderate Tennessee Republican who had supported the Panama Canal giveaway and had hinted that he would be a candidate. Fearful that Sears might indeed go elsewhere, Deaver knuckled under and persuaded Reagan that the only way he could win was to put Sears in charge.

So it was that when we launched the Reagan exploratory committee in early March of 1979 Sears was firmly in control. He named Jim Lake press secretary and put his other crony, Charlie Black, in charge of the field operation. Both were well qualified. Deaver, as usual, was the majordomo, taking care of the Reagans, worrying about logistics, and serving as the deputy campaign manager and general manipulator of people and things. Ed Meese was the overall issues man while Marty Anderson was again in charge of domestic issues and Richard Allen headed up foreign affairs. Angela (Bay) Buchanan was the treasurer and business manager. As for me, Sears, in another stroke of near genius, decided that I should be the fund-raiser, the one position where he was confident I would fail. But what the hell, somebody had to do it, so I accepted without a fuss.

Actually, for a campaign without a candidate or a finance chairman the money came in quite well. But Sears and Black were far better spenders than I was a raiser.

From the beginning I complained, vainly, that money would be hard to come by until Reagan announced. It was and is a fact that most people don't like to spend money foolishly and many view as foolish giving to a campaign that has no candidate. But this truism never sank in, because the foursome—Sears, Deaver, Lake, and Black—didn't want it to sink in; they wanted me out. I was a mote in John Sears' eye, an albatross around his neck, a burr under his saddle, a thorn in his side, and more.

I put together a pretty good fund-raising staff including one of the best I know, Wendy Borcherdt, along with Kathy Wilson, who had worked for me in 1976, and John Erthein, who had raised money for CFTR. Helene von Damm, Reagan's personal secretary, went East to shake the money tree in that part of the country, and Charles and Mary Jane Wick, friends of the Reagans and a couple of fireballs, worked on some money-raising proposals. But with no candidate the money just wasn't there.

In midsummer Black asked if, when I went to Texas to raise money, I would check on the political operation. I said sure, and did. Why not? We were all in it together, or so I thought.

But on August 24 I had a rude awakening. In midmorning Deaver came to my office and sat down. Without preamble he said that fund-raising wasn't going well.

"I'm going to take it over," he said.

Surprisingly, I wasn't surprised. I had felt from the beginning that Sears would try to get rid of me. I just didn't know how or when.

"Have you told Ron?" I asked.

"Yes," he lied.

"And what am I supposed to do?" I asked.

"We'd like you to run Texas and California," he said.

By "we," I took him to mean himself and Sears. Sears, the man in charge, didn't have the courage to face me; he had sent his flunky to do his dirty work. I don't know if Deaver really thought I would accept the demotion, but he probably did. In his book, without going into explanation, he says he fired me. Maybe he thinks he did, but I suspect that in his book as in life he was twisting facts to make himself look good. For my part, I knew now why Black, another Sears flunky, had asked me to do some political work in Texas.

"Mike," I said, "I won't do that. Reagan will carry California regardless of who runs it and in Texas it's not a matter of whom you pick; it's whom you don't pick that's important."

Deaver went away and I called in Rose Marie, told her what had happened, and asked her to say nothing. I drafted a brief sentence of resignation—to Paul Laxalt, again the campaign chairman, but not actively involved. I merely said I was leaving to pursue other opportunities. I drafted another memo to my staff, urging them to stay on and help win one for the Gipper. Rose Marie distributed it after I left.

But before that, as Deaver was leaving for Sacramento, he stuck his head in my door. "I hope you'll stay," he said. It didn't sound to me like he thought he'd fired me.

I went home and late that afternoon Bonnie and I joined my unhappy ex-staff for drinks, nachos, and recriminations at Tampico Tillie's, a Mexican restaurant in Santa Monica.

The next morning, Saturday, Reagan called.

"I don't want you to quit," he told me. "We've been together too long."

I remembered when he'd said the same thing in early 1968 and I thought he meant it this time, too. He added that he was leaving for the ranch and would get together with me when he came back. As always with Reagan, time at the ranch came first.

On Monday morning Meese called. There had been a meeting at the Reagan residence. Present were Reagan, Meese, Sears, Deaver, Black, and Lake. I learned later that only Meese and Reagan, who didn't count in such matters, wanted me to stay on. That made sense since the other four had conspired to get rid of me. I had had no problems with any of them but Sears, but during that period he dominated them totally. I was an example of what could happen if you stood up to him.

Meese told me that Reagan wanted to see me and would I go to the residence. I went. Reagan greeted me pleasantly but he no longer was prepared to ask me to stay in the campaign. Instead he asked if I would take over as chairman of CFTR in a paid capacity. I explained to him that Curtis Mack, an old Reagan hand whom Rose Marie and I had chosen to succeed me as executive vice chairman, was doing a fine job, that I wasn't needed, and that CFTR couldn't afford me.

We parted on friendly terms, and not long afterward I called him to tell him I'd had a partial change of heart.

"I'll take the chairmanship," I told him, "but on a nonpaying basis."

I didn't talk to him again until I went back to the campaign the following June.

Deaver took over the fund-raising and, despite his cocksureness, didn't have any more luck than I had had. When Reagan finally announced in November, the money began coming in, but still not as fast as Sears and Black could spend it.

Ironically, immediately after Reagan announced, Sears, Lake, and Black forced Deaver out, telling Reagan if Deaver didn't go they would. Deaver took the Reagans off the spot by resigning, which is said to have upset Reagan, but didn't make me feel at all bad.

Marty Anderson had already resigned and returned to the Hoover Institution. Sears had forced him out by setting up a parallel but less conservative operation in Washington, thus by-passing Anderson's Los Angeles shop. Meese was slated to be Sears' next victim, but when Sears made his move on him Reagan had finally had it and, much to Sears' chagrin, it was he and Lake and Black who went and Meese who stayed. Sears went back to Washington and resumed his avocation of convincing the news media that he was a political genius, which he and they still believe.

A few days after I left the campaign an unhappy Rose Marie also left. She undoubtedly would have been fired anyway, as Kathy Wilson already had been. It was no time in the Reagan campaign to be known as a Nofziger person.

Rose Marie found us office space in the inappropriately named Paradise Building, a small office building in Westchester near the airport, and we went back into the political consulting business. L. Robert (Bob) Morgan whom I had known from the 1972 Nixon campaign, was also officed there. I had asked him to come from Chicago to handle the direct mail fund-raising for the campaign. Needless to say, he shortly was dumped. Nobody fired him; they just ignored him and gave the work to someone else. It was a typical Sears ploy.

The news of my resignation had been out only a day or two when I had a call from Mike Curb, by now lieutenant governor of California. Still in his thirties, Curb had made millions in the record business and had ambitions to be governor—at least. He has yet to make it, but he is still young and still rich.

He wanted to know how things were and then offered me a consulting contract. He needed a consultant like a hole in the head, but he saw a friend in trouble and set out to help. I was and am grateful.

A couple of weeks later Truman Campbell, chairman of the state Republican party, hired me as a consultant. That let me go to Fresno a couple of times a month for the next nine months, a thrill I still haven't gotten over.

Shortly thereafter, Edward Rollins, executive director of the State Assembly's Republican Caucus, also signed me on as a consultant. I did two things for him. By his own admission I kept him sane. And by the common agreement of members of the legislature I reduced him to being the second worst-dressed person in Sacramento.

One night in late February of 1980 I received a call from Dick Wirthlin who was in New Hampshire with the Reagan campaign. Like Meese, Wirthlin had hung on in spite of Sears' antagonism. Wirthlin's loyalty, like Meese's, was to Reagan. As a result both he and Meese were seen by Sears as threats to his absolute domination of the campaign. Calling from the New Hampshire campaign headquarters at the Highway Hotel in Concord, Wirthlin was guarded in what he said.

His question was: "If Sears were to leave the campaign would you be interested in coming back?"

"I can't," I said. "Not until after the June primary. I've got clients I just can't walk away from now."

I was terribly disappointed. I would have given at least one eye tooth to rejoin the Reagan campaign, without Sears. It was my last chance to help make Ronald Reagan president, and I knew it, but I couldn't run out on my clients.

The next day the good news broke. Sears had been fired. It was primary election day in New Hampshire, and the story was that— miracle of miracles—Ronald Reagan had summoned up the intestinal fortitude to do what he found hardest, fire someone. Actually, he fired three people: Sears, Black, and Lake. I cheered.

I had been convinced for a long time that concerning Sears, Deaver had been 180 degrees out of whack. It wasn't a question of Reagan not being able to win without Sears and company, but a question of whether they would drag him down to defeat.

At the time he was fired, Sears had kicked away a sure victory in the Iowa caucuses, giving George Bush a surprise win. By election day in

New Hampshire, he and Black had virtually bankrupted the campaign, forcing the new campaign manager, Bill Casey, to lop off dozens of staff members and take other draconian steps to keep the campaign afloat.

While I was still cheering, I had a call from the *Los Angeles Herald-Examiner*, asking if I would like to do a background story on the upheaval in the Reagan organization. They wanted to use it the next day. I was delighted, especially since it merited a page one banner headline. I did a lot of getting even in that piece.

Reagan, of course, won New Hampshire and between then and the first of May proceeded to clean everybody's clocks pretty thoroughly. The "big mo" Bush had boasted of coming out of Iowa had been reduced first to "slo mo" and eventually to "no mo," and the other major contestants, Bob Dole and Howard Baker, had dropped out. Reagan was now a shoo-in for the nomination.

Therefore, I was surprised when in early May I received a call from Deaver to whom I had not talked since the day he decided to show me how easy it was to raise money. Deaver has always either underestimated the difficulty in raising money or overestimated his own ability to do so. In 1985, just before he left the White House, he told me he had taken on the job of raising $50 million for the Reagan Presidential Library.

"That's a tough job," I commented.

"No," he said, "it'll take me about three months."

Two years later he had made and spent, largely on legal fees, several million, been indicted and convicted of three counts of perjury, and claimed to be a recovering alcoholic at peace with himself. But he still hadn't raised the fifty million.

I was of a mind not to take Deaver's call; he was not a friend and I had nothing to talk to him about, but curiosity won out and I agreed to meet him.

Although the Reagans had acquiesced when Sears had forced his resignation, hurting him deeply, Deaver had stayed close to them. He and they seemed to be connected by a kind of psychological umbilical cord, as we psychologists like to say. He had served them as a personal aide since early in Reagan's first term as governor. Once, in a Mexican airport, Mrs. Reagan discovered that she had left her purse behind. Deaver, in his haste to retrieve it, ran right through a glass door, but was not seriously hurt.

Now, I figured, he wanted to talk to me about the campaign. I knew also that whatever he had to say would be at the Reagans' request.

His first order of business was to apologize abjectly for having been part of the cabal that had forced me out of the campaign. It was a grievous mistake, he admitted, and added, "I will never forgive myself for what I did to you and I will always owe you."

Foolishly, I told him to forget it, which he did shortly thereafter. That taken care of, he got down to business.

"You have to come back to the campaign," he said. "You have to take over as press secretary."

The Reagans, he assured me, wanted it.

"What about Ed Gray?" I asked.

Gray, who had been brought in to head the campaign press operation, had served a lengthy stint as press secretary during Reagan's second gubernatorial term. I had initially brought him into the governor's office as an assistant press secretary and he had taken over as campaign press secretary after Lake was fired.

But, according to Deaver, he was having a difficult time handling the national press. This, I found out later, was an understatement. It wasn't that reporters disliked him; they were contemptuous of him. Gray is essentially decent and hard working, but he had no experience dealing with the national political press.

It didn't take much persuasion for me to agree to return immediately after the California primary election in early June. Reagan was my first, and in a way, my only political love. I had been there at the beginning of his political career and I wanted badly to be there when he was elected president.

Deaver said he, too, would be returning to the campaign. I welcomed that. He not only handled the Reagans well, but he also ran a good road show for those traveling with the campaign. But Deaver had never really been gone. He had too much emotional capital invested in the Reagans to walk away. Besides, he had to know that he was responsible for his own demise, having insisted that Sears be brought in in the first place.

By the time I returned to the Reagan camp, Bush's campaign manager, James A. Baker III, had withdrawn him from the California primary and the race for the Republican nomination was over. All that was left was for Reagan to accept the nomination, pick a running mate, and beat Jimmy Carter. He had to beat third party candidate John Anderson, too, but that was a foregone conclusion.

By August when Reagan and entourage rolled into Detroit for the National Convention about the only thing left on the agenda was who would be his running mate. The platform was well in hand with Marty Anderson in control of domestic issues and Richard V. Allen in charge of foreign affairs. Nothing in the platform would contradict what Reagan believed.

For the life of me I still don't know why we waited so long to decide on the vice presidential nominee. In Detroit, Dick Wirthlin finally brough in a list of three names that his polling showed would be assets—former President Gerald Ford, George Bush, and Sen. Howard Baker. Reagan was not enthused about any of them, but he agreed with Wirthlin that of the three Ford would make the strongest candidate and the strongest vice president. He didn't like either of the other two. Ever since the New Hampshire campaign, during which Bush had handled himself badly in a row over who should participate in a debate, Reagan had thought him a wimp. As for Baker, he had not forgiven him for supporting Carter's give-away of the Panama Canal.

His personal choice was his good friend, Paul Laxalt. Unfortunately, Laxalt brought a very small constituency to the table, one that would support Reagan anyway. Further, there was a geographical disadvantage since Nevada neighbors California, and a philosophical disadvantage since Laxalt is every bit as conservative as Reagan and would do nothing to bring in the party's moderates and liberals. Finally, Nevada is the home of legalized gambling and local option legalized prostitution, which might have alienated the Christian Right, for as governor Laxalt had done nothing to outlaw either.

Several other names had been on a preliminary list: Rep. Jack Kemp of New York; Don Rumsfeld of Illinois, a former congressman and secretary of defense; Sen Richard Lugar of Indiana; Rep. Guy Vanderjagt of Michigan; and William Simon, former treasury secretary. With the exception of Kemp none had any significant national following.

In hindsight Reagan could have chosen just about whomever he wanted and still have won. Bush's selection of Sen. Dan Quayle eight years later would seem to indicate that a vice presidential choice does not have to have a national constituency, be viewed as a leader in any given field, or even be deemed a worthy successor to the presidency.

But not many presidential nominees are bold enough to take the chance Bush took with Quayle. In Reagan's case I'm sure it never occurred to him to go against the advice of Wirthlin and the rest of his advisers.

Since Wirthlin's polls showed that Ford brought the most to the ticket, it was decided that Reagan should sound him out. Unbelieveably, Ford was interested, and the dickering began. But after two days of negotiating Ford's conditions for coming on the ticket remained unacceptable. He saw himself not as a vice president but as a co-president. He wanted to run the White House and control the government while Reagan met the dignitaries and attended the funerals.

Ed Meese, who took part in the negotiations, wrote down Ford's demands and showed them to me. Among others things Ford, or at least those negotiating for him, was demanding that the White House staff report to the president through him—Ford would decide who on the staff would and would not see the president. He also wanted to pick the secretary of state and secretary of defense, although he generously offered Reagan a veto. But in turn, he wanted veto rights on Reagan's other cabinet picks.

"He wants us to give away the store," I said.

"Exactly," Meese replied, "but we're not going to do it."

As the negotiations continued it began to look, to me at least, as if Ford and his advisers were planning to stall right up to the last minute, hoping to leave Reagan no choice but to select Ford on his terms. But I was wrong. With time growing short Marty Anderson and I decided to go to the candidate and tell him that it was time to forget Ford and go with Bush, whom those around Reagan viewed as the lesser of two evils, lesser, that is, than Howard Baker.

As we were speaking with Reagan word came that Ford was on his way down from his suite. When he arrived he and Reagan immediately went into a bedroom where Ford told him he would not accept the vice presidency, that on reflection he did not think it was the proper thing to do. Of course, he was right.

It is easy to see why the idea was intriguing to Ford and just as easy to see why he finally rejected it. But, in retrospect, it is hard to see why any of the Reagan people including Reagan himself and, in honesty, me, thought it was feasible. In every respect, it was a lousy idea. It would have been extremely difficult for Ford, a former president, to run on a Reagan platform, backing Reagan stands that might have been contrary to issues he had endorsed as president—for example, the Equal Rights Amendment. And equally difficult for a former president to play second fiddle, despite his second fiddle-playing past. Also, to put in direct line for the presidency a man who had been rejected by the people might well have cost votes, despite Wirthlin's polls. At the least, it would have given the Democrats another issue.

Most important, it is doubtful that Reagan could have won, even against Carter, if it became known that he had agreed to share the presidency with Ford. It clearly would have signalled, even though falsely, that he felt incapable of handling the job by himself.

Ford's decision nullified any chance he might have had of being the only man to hold the presidency twice without ever having been elected. He would certainly have been the only man to hold the vice presidency under two different presidents.

After Ford had left, Reagan, without hesitation, said he would go with Bush. He asked Drew Lewis to call Bush's suite. When Bush came on the line, Reagan took the phone and asked if he would like to be his running mate.

It was Jim Baker who answered the phone. He said later the people in Bush's suite thought it was just a courtesy call from Reagan to tell Bush personally that he was going with Ford. As a result, Bush was slow to take the call. When he did and heard Reagan's offer, he gave a joyful "thumbs up" sign to those in the room. Baker later told Lewis he himself let out a whoop and jumped up and down.

Reagan is a man who can make a decision, justify it in his mind, and never look back. He's had a few regrets, but not many. One was when as governor he signed a bill liberalizing abortion. He always felt he'd been snookered on that one, because the bill's sponsor, a Democrat, had assured him it would only apply if the mother's life was in danger or her health threatened. Reagan learned too late that just the normal process of having a baby can be interpreted by abortion proponents and proabortion doctors as endangering the life and health of the prospective mother.

But in the case of George Bush, Reagan had, and has had, no regrets.

Bush, he decided, was not after all a wimp. And he set out to be Bush's friend, immediately making him an integral part of the team. One of Reagan's strongest points was that he was never an excluder, always an includer. Who else but Reagan would one day name as his chief of staff a man who opposed him when he ran for president and before that had fought him on the Panama Canal issue—Howard Baker?

Bush turned out to be a good choice for Reagan, politically and personally. His broad background in politics and government made him a worthy opponent of Jimmy Carter's vice president, Walter Mondale. Personally, he was likeable and determined to be a team player. He had no trouble modifying those areas where he had differed with Reagan and he knew that as the vice presidential candidate his job was not to make policy but to support Reagan.

If he differed with Reagan he kept it to himself, and while his good buddy, Jim Baker, was the biggest leak in the White House, Bush himself never leaked. Additionally, he brought a special asset, his wife Barbara, a lady not only of great charm but also with good political instincts, who knew how the game was played and played it well.

On another matter entirely, but of general interest and pertaining to the campaign, Ronald Reagan is not a racist, not a bigot. I have never heard him make an anti-Semitic remark or heard him say "nigger." When the accusation is made, he defends himself vigorously, telling about how his father refused to stay in a hotel that wouldn't take Jews, how one of his good buddies in college was a black football player, how as a baseball announcer he took organized baseball to task for not allowing Negroes to play.

Most of his time in politics he just didn't think in terms of race; it was no big deal to him. But after he became governor he set up a minorities office. Honchoed by a black, its field staff consisted of blacks and Hispanics. The first head of the office, a black man named Bob Keyes, later publicly accused Reagan of being a racist. Reagan was so embittered by this that when Keyes, dying of heart disease, placed a call to him he refused to take it. The second head of the office, Mel Bradley, worked in the White House throughout Reagan's two terms.

Neither is Reagan a sexist, although, despite feminists, he has always been a gentleman, opening doors and pulling out chairs. Some feminists think such courtesies are belittling, but to Reagan they are signs of respect.

Once when he was governor, he and I and Nancy Reynolds, by then an assistant press secretary, were walking to an airplane. Since I was carrying a portable typewriter and a briefcase, Nancy volunteered to carry the typewriter. When Reagan noticed, he insisted on taking it from her. A lady should not carry anything heavy, except her purse, if a gentleman, even though a governor, is available. I said nothing. If Nancy wanted to carry my typewriter or if Reagan, thinking it was hers, wanted to carry it, it was all the same to me.

Reagan never swears, never uses foul language, and never tells dirty jokes around women, although he knows some doozies.

But during his time as governor it was rare that a woman advanced beyond secretarial rank, and equally rare for a member of a minority to hold a high-ranking position. These weren't deliberate slights, they were merely matters of indifference. He did better as president, but that was because those around him were more conscious of the need. Over the span of his two terms, four women and one black were members of his cabinet. And, at the very end, as a political favor to George Bush, he named a Hispanic as secretary of education.

One of Reagan's more famous gaffes involved his black cabinet member, Samuel Pierce, secretary of Housing and Urban Development. Pierce brought some black mayors to see the president and as Reagan was bidding them goodbye he shook Pierce's hand and said how nice it was to meet you, Mr. Mayor. In Reagan's defense, Pierce, a New Yorker, had never been part of the Reagan team and Reagan barely knew him. Another time Reagan, meeting with the Congressional Black Caucus, hospitably passed around the jelly beans for which he was famous. "The green ones," he noted innocently, "are watermelon."

There was little effort by the Reagan campaign to win minority votes, as that term is commonly understood, in either 1976 or 1980, but then, too, there were few black Republicans.

In the general election of 1980 the campaign aimed largely at ethnic Europeans, mostly Roman Catholic, heavily blue collar, family oriented, traditionally Democratic, and traditionally union. At the time, many believed their party and their parents' party, the Democratic party, had gone soft on communism, soft on crime, soft on defense, soft on patriotism, and soft on family values. It had embraced women's lib and homosexual sex, and opposed the death penalty and a national defense buildup. Big labor, with the exception of the Teamsters and a few small unions, went along with the party policies, leaving its members ripe for plucking. And pluck them Reagan did.

Some effort was also spent on Hispanics, a large, family-oriented voter bloc that votes about one-third Republican, and on picking up the emerging Asian vote and the Jewish vote that had been inching away from the Democratic party in recent elections.

But the attempt to win the black vote was at best sporadic, and for good reasons. First, there was no indication that a major effort would add significantly to the pro-Reagan vote. And more important, almost no money was available to spend in the black community.

In politics there is an old saying that you hunt where the ducks are. That is, you go after those votes you have a shot at getting before you go after the votes that you probably aren't going to get anyway. That is especially true today with campaign expenditure limits. Since 1976, federal law has limited both the raising and spending of presidential campaign funds. For Reagan in 1980, and again in 1984, that meant spending precious little money on the black vote.

Democrats have pushed for federal financing of elections because the party with the most members benefits—i.e., the Democratic party. Concerning the black community, Democrats can get away without spending much more than Republicans because Republicans have no money with which to build a base in the black community. Democrats, who are smarter pols than Republicans, had this figured out from the beginning. Most Republicans still haven't figured it out.

If there had been significant numbers of registered Republicans in the black and Hispanic communities there would probably have been black and Hispanic members in the Reagan political inner circle. I haven't figured out yet why there were no women. Except that there never had been, and Reagan probably figured, if he bothered to figure at all, that that's the way it was supposed to be.

In the beginning Reagan and Carter seemed evenly matched, with third party candidate John Anderson well behind. Anderson was an Illinois Republican who gradually moved leftward and finally clear out of the party.

In their book, *Blue Smoke and Mirrors*, Jack Germond and Jules Witcover say Anderson initially ran in order "to make a statement."

That is a major reason why he didn't do better. As I said earlier, there is only one legitimate reason to run for office and that is to win. If that is not your intention you are deceiving the people you ask to finance you, support you, and vote for you. And you're not going to run a good campaign because your campaign is not about winning.

Some pols, to hear them tell it, go through entire campaigns without making a mistake. Others I know of actually make very few. I have trouble getting through a day without making one. I made a lulu in early September.

We had a huge press following Reagan, close to two hundred counting television cameramen and technicians. They filled the back half of our Boeing stretch 727 and nearly filled a follow-up 727. For the most part, those on the second plane were technicians, campaign staffers who were not needed on the campaign plane, reporters, and others who covered the campaign only sporadically.

The people on the second plane had a lot more fun than those on the main plane. For one thing they didn't have to worry about disturbing the candidate. And since they knew no story was going to break on their plane, there was a lot more drinking and a lot more fooling around. I made it a point to ride that plane from time to time, usually after the last event of the day. It was good to mingle with people who couldn't help but feel neglected and for the most part my appearance was appreciated. Besides, it allowed me to relax, too.

One night I was strolling the aisle drinking Bombay gin, a bottle of which was always kept aboard for me, and chatting with various and sundry. It was generally understood that this kind of casual conversation was off the record, or so I thought. I stopped to talk to a couple of reporters for British papers and the conversation turned to a false rumor that had hit Wall Street that day—that Reagan had had a heart attack. I had no proof, but I was convinced the rumor had been started by the Carter campaign. They were the only ones who might gain from it.

"If they want to start a rumor about Reagan, I'll give you one about Jimmy Carter," I said jokingly. "When Jimmy was at the Naval Academy he almost got thrown out for contracting a dose of clap."

The reporters laughed, I laughed and thought no more about it until several days later when it suddenly ceased to be funny. One of the reporters, David Blundy, who worked for the *London Times*, wrote the story, except that he quoted me as saying "Carter has the clap." The *Washington Post* picked it up and ran it in one edition that went to outlying areas, then killed it. The UPI also picked it up, but most editors, recognizing that it was a nonstory, never ran it. Still, it gave Robert Strauss, a fine gentleman who was stuck with being Carter's campaign chairman, a chance to wax indignant.

And wax he did, he even overwaxed, saying among other things that my remark "raises concerns about these people and what kind of people are on that plane." He added that "Nofziger has put his foot in Reagan's mouth," which was accurate.

I was chagrined, knowing that the candidate didn't need this kind of thing, didn't need to have me become an issue. I sought out Spencer and asked if he thought I should resign.

"Just forget about it," he said. "It's not important. It'll go away."

He was right. It did. The political press refused to play it up, for which I was grateful. But it remains one of my sidebar stories of the campaign, thanks in part to an old friend, Bill Fleishel, the staff artist at the Republican National Committee. I had occasion to visit the RNC shortly after the incident, and Bill quickly designed a large campaign button that read: "Clap for Carter."

I liked it. I thought it was funny. I had a couple of hundred made and on election night I distributed them to members of the staff and the press. After the election I went to talk to Carter's press secretary, Jody Powell, about the mechanics of running the press office. As a peace offering I gave him a "Clap for Carter" button. He accepted it with good grace and a smile, but I don't think he thought it was as clever as I did.

I learned one lesson from this episode and relearned another for the nth time. First, never, even in fun, credit someone with having acquired a loathsome disease unless you can prove it. And second, never never talk to a reporter without setting the ground rules. If you don't, and he writes a story, you have only yourself to blame. If you do, and he writes the story anyway, you have a moral right to punch him in the eye, especially if he's smaller than you are.

Most reporters will abide by mutually agreed on rules. But some will push a little too far, others will stick it to you for reasons of their own, and still others you always have to be very careful with. A press secretary should never forget that he—or she—is in charge of news emanating from a campaign or an office. As such you can set reasonable rules of conduct for reporters in interviews and at press conferences. And if they are not obeyed you can shut them off. A press secretary can never let the reporters take charge if he is to retain their respect and serve his principal properly. Most reporters know that and don't resent it.

Once in a while, a reporter will deliberately misinterpret what you have said while still quoting you accurately. You want to be careful of these people. In August of 1982, after publicly opposing a tax bill supported by President Reagan, at President Reagan's request, I spent two weeks helping to pass the bill. For a day or two reporters wondered why I had changed my mind. In a meeting with half a dozen of them I was asked that question by Helen Thomas who has covered the White House for many years for UPI. I laughed and replied that I was just like a woman; I had a right to change my mind.

It was a nonserious reply and the reporters ignored it. All but David Hoffman, a reporter for the *Washington Post*, who the next morning quoted me up high in his story. His quote was accurate but he implied that I had said it seriously, giving a few feminist columnists of both sexes a chance to attack me as a male chauvinist. When I wanted to defend myself Rose Marie rightly talked me out of it. As for Hoffman, I'd always thought he was a self-righteous sort, filled with his own importance. His story did nothing to change my opinion.

But back to the campaign. My memories of the general election campaign of 1980 are episodic. I guess everybody's are. As a rule, people remember only what was important to them. One minor event illustrates what I'm driving at. It revolves around the question of who called George Bush when Ronald Reagan decided to ask him to be his running mate. In his book Deaver says Reagan made the call. In *his* book Peter Hannaford says Chuck Tyson did. And my memory was that Drew Lewis placed the call, so I phoned and asked him.

"I did," he said, "and you gave me his number."

I don't remember that little part of the incident because it wasn't important to me. Apparently it was to Lewis.

Blessed be the reporter who goes into a campaign knowing he is going to write a book afterward. Reporters like the late Theodore White and the still living Lou Cannon of the *Washington Post*, syndicated columnists Jack Germond and Jules Witcover of the *Baltimore Sun*, and Rowland Evans and Robert Novak, are such reporters. Bless them for keeping good notes, for interviewing along the way and afterward, and for generally doing thorough jobs of research. While they are not always right, overall their accuracy is amazing.

One reason total accuracy is impossible, even for the best reporters, is that their sources are not always accurate. Before the convention in 1976 when Reagan's chances were rapidly diminishing, Sears regularly overstated the number of delegates Reagan had and, for the most part, the media accepted his figures. Sears' reason might not have been honorable but it certainly was understandable.

People also tend to remember what casts them in a good light and forget what does not. In addition, many a politician or campaign staffer has an ax to grind and some do not hesitate to do it at the expense of others.

In his book Deaver spends paragraphs saying how much he admires his old mentor, Ed Meese, but never mentions that he tried, and failed, to enlist another former mentor, Bill Clark, in an effort to persuade Reagan to fire Meese.

Deaver rose to power as the protégé first of Clark and then of Meese, both of whom assigned him to be the governor's office liaison with Nancy Reagan and to take care of the Reagans' personal needs. From there he went on to become the Reagans' confidant and adviser. I think of him as Reagan's Iago, always whispering advice in Reagan's ear that would serve him, not Reagan. Others have referred to him as the Reagans' Rasputin.

But Reagan over the years listened to advice from anyone who had physical proximity to him, including me. During the 1966 campaign he listened attentively to his drivers and his security aides. This practice continued into the governor's office until these worthies were instructed by Bill Clark to keep their opinions on matters of government and politics to themselves.

In another instance of faulty memory, Helene von Damm, in her book, *At Reagan's Side*, never checked with me before she wrote that in 1976 I was angry over the selection of Senator Schweiker as Reagan's running mate. She meant well, but in fact I thought Schweiker's selection was a stroke of genius.

Even Nancy Reagan errs. In her book, *My Turn*, she says I was with the Reagans the night that Ford was nominated, but, in fact, I was in the campaign headquarters trailer or on the floor of the convention the entire evening.

None of these mistakes changes the course of history, but they illustrate the need for those who would write even recent history— including me—to be careful.

Another problem for those who write recent history is that no two persons, much less ten, remember events alike.

In any case, I was due to return to the Reagan campaign immediately following California's June 7 primary but Reagan was making a trip to the Middle West around the first of June and the press operation was in such turmoil I was asked if I could go along. It was no time to just say no.

The campaign party was to leave from Los Angeles International Airport. The first person I met there was a big, shaggy, gray-haired cameraman from CBS, Bob Dunn, who had also covered the 1976 campaign. "Where's your Mickey Mouse tie?" he asked.

"Oh, Lord," I said, "I didn't bring it. I'll wear it next time." And I did. And thereafter. I digress to say that there was a special relationship between me and the TV camera crews. I did my best to help them and they did their best to make life easy for me. Also, most were less liberal than the TV reporters. The reporters might give Reagan bum stories but the pictures were invariably flattering.

But back to Mickey Mouse. During the 1976 campaign a member of my staff, Elaine Glick, gave me two identical Mickey Mouse ties. Embroidered in them was a caricature of the famed Revolutionary War painting, "The Spirit of '76." Mickey carried the flag, Goofy played the drum, and Donald Duck the flute. I had worn the ties frequently in 1976 and to my surprise they had stuck in people's memories.

So I dragged them out for the second trip and then wore them all during the campaign. Reporters with nothing better to write about mentioned from time to time that I wore Mickey Mouse ties and quoted my answer when I was asked why.

"Politics," I said, "is a Mickey Mouse business."

Nine years later I almost got into deep doo-doo with a similar answer about another situation.

I had been indicted for allegedly violating the federal Ethics in Government Act. Before the trial a television reporter asked if there was any significance to my wearing a Mickey Mouse tie during this period.

"It's a Mickey Mouse law," I said, after deep thought.

As soon as the reporter left my office I called one of my lawyers, E. Lawrence Barcella, and told him. He was not happy. He was afraid the smart-alecky remark would be used against me in court. In desperation, Barcella called the reporter and worked a deal whereby the remark did not appear. Because he did a decent thing, which too many people in the news business see as a sign of weakness, that reporter must remain nameless. But I will always be grateful to him.

My association with Mickey Mouse did not end with the campaign. My friend, Curtis Mack, who was running Citizens for the Republic, had the bright idea of getting a black bow tie embroidered with white silhouettes of Mickey on each wing. He gave it to me in time for the Reagan inauguration.

Naturally, I wore it, and just as naturally the society reporters wrote that I wore it. Some people now recall that it had blinking lights on it. So much for memory. Still, ever since I have been stuck with Mickey Mouse.

Going back to the campaign meant putting together a staff. We kept on most already there: David Prosperi, later an assistant secretary at Transportation and Interior; Joe Holmes, who died of cancer early in the White House years; and Robin Gray, who worked first in press at the White House and later as executive assistant to John Herrington at the Department of Energy.

More important than any of these was Jan McCoy, one of the most respected political press people in the nation. Our relationship went back to 1964 when she was working press in northern California for Nelson Rockefeller and I was a political reporter. She worked for me in the campaigns of 1966 and 1976, and among the press she was the most popular member of my staff, because she was competent and busted her tail to be helpful. She would also have a drink with you, or two, or three.

After the election she became administrator of the South Pacific Trust Territories. Today she is a South Pacific legend, entirely worthy of a movie or a musical comedy.

I also called on other staffers from the 1976 campaign: Matt (the Gnat) Lawson, who was too smart ever to come into government; Dana Rohrabacher, who spent nearly eight years as a presidential speechwriter and now is a congressman from California; and Rose Marie. After the convention we brought on Ken Towery, a Pulitzer Prizewinner, who had once worked for Sen. John Tower, and a fine writer and editor named Mary Catherine English. Two young women who had worked with me at the national committee—Laura Genero and Anne Graham—came on primarily to travel with the Reagan offspring. Their experiences with the three younger Reagans—Maureen, Mike, and Ron (Patti boycotted the campaign)—would make an interesting book if they could bring themselves to speak to each other long enough to write it.

I tried to hire Ed Rollins away from the California Assembly Republican Caucus but Carol Hallett, the caucus chairman, put up such a fuss that I backed off and didn't bring Ed aboard until we took over the White House.

I also brought back a young man named Richard Miller to handle radio. Miller later started his own public affairs business, got involved in helping raise money for arms for the Nicaraguan contras, and was caught in the toils of the Iran Contra affair. With a wife, a baby, and not much money Miller pleaded guilty to one Mickey Mouse count and was left dangling for two years until Oliver North was sentenced, at which time he received four hundred hours of community service and a $50 fine.

Because he didn't have the resources to fight a railroad job by independent counsel Lawrence Walsh, Miller, whose real crime was that he wanted to help his president, is now a convicted felon who has lost his right to vote and to own a gun.

Immediately following the convention, Bill Casey moved the campaign to Arlington, Virginia, just outside of Washington. All the old excuses were there: Washington was where the media was and the East was where the vote was. The fact is, East was where Casey, and Timmons, and a number of others lived and they snowed many of our Westerners into going along with the move. The media, needless to say, will go wherever a major presidential campaign is headquartered, including Hawaii or Alaska. And the advent of the jet airplane means a candidate can campaign wherever and whenever he wishes from wherever he wishes.

Anyway, we all moved back to the Washington area, and some genius—probably Deaver—found the Reagans a lovely farm home only forty-five miles from the headquarters. It was owned by the governor of Texas, the wealthy Bill Clements, and earlier had been known as "Atoka," the country home of Jackie Kennedy. It was just down the road from a farm owned by Virginia Sen. John Warner, at that time Elizabeth Taylor's seventh husband.

It was nice for the Reagans, especially the candidate, who could go horseback riding whenever he wished. It also meant that anyone who needed to see him had to drive for nearly an hour. In addition, the media had a lovely time staking out the place and the Secret Service had a delightful time guarding it.

Reagan's fall campaign took off on Labor Day with a bang and a bomb, so to speak. It began with a picnic rally at Liberty Park, a waterfront park on the New Jersey shore with the Statue of Liberty as the backdrop. It was meant as an ethnic rally and featured the father·of Lech Walesa, who was just emerging as the champion of freedom in Poland. The crowd was enthusiastic if not huge, and the first official day of the campaign began on a high note. It ended on a low note with the sharks in the press tasting blood and circling for the kill.

What happened was partly my fault. We had left New Jersey and were headed to Detroit in our chartered Boeing 727 on which Mike Deaver—nominally in charge of the traveling party but actually manager of the traveling campaign—had installed such electronic gadgets as telephones and news wire machines. Over one of these came the news that President Jimmy Carter was opening his campaign for reelection in Tuscumbia, Alabama, which the story identified as the birthplace of the Ku Klux Klan. I found that most interesting and suggested that the candidate might consider asking why Carter had picked such a place. The idea was quickly shot down by everybody. I had no objections; indeed, I agreed.

That should have been the end of it, but it wasn't. I had forgotten one thing: Ronald Reagan has a brain like a steel trap; it retains just about everything he hears. Unfortunately, from time to wrong time it leaks out something that it shouldn't. So here we were at the end of a great day of campaigning, and Reagan was giving his last speech of the day—off the cuff, in my opinion, his most effective mode of speaking. A minor tragedy of Reagan's years in the presidency was that his staff conned him into speaking from notes, instead of from the heart, even when speaking to small groups of supporters who didn't want to hear a prepared speech but just wanted to hear him say he was glad they were there and he loved them.

But this time a prepared text would have been a lot better, because Reagan, waxing enthusiastically eloquent, all of a sudden remembered our Ku Klux Klan discussion and it was too much for him to resist. He threw in that Carter was opening his campaign "down there in the city that gave birth to and is the parent body of the Ku Klux Klan."

As soon as he said it Reagan knew he had made a mistake. So did the rest of us. We cringed. When Reagan finished we headed straight for the security of the motorcade, dodging reporters as we went. In his hotel suite, after admitting that he blew it, Reagan explained that a woman in the crowd wearing a Jimmy Carter mask had triggered his remark.

It made for a bad twenty-four hours but it resulted in one of the key moves in the campaign. We kept the candidate away from the press and I spent a hectic hour on the campaign plane the next day turning aside press questions. Frankly, I had no answer and I had not been helped when one of our staffers in an effort to be helpful, said that Reagan's remark had been planned. Likewise, I was not helped when an anonymous staffer, obviously not one of my admirers, said the remark had been my idea, without explaining that we had unanimously rejected it.

In his book, *Reagan*, Lou Cannon says, "Nofziger made matters worse, blaming the press for overplaying the story and declining to tell of his own contribution to Reagan's blunder." (Lou—I was saving it for the book.)

So-called blunders, of course, can be subjective things. One man's blunder is another man's stroke of genius and a third person's "so what." Reporters love to charge politicians, especially Reagan, with blunders and gaffes. They feel superior criticizing a man they don't think is very smart, yet has risen far above them. And because Reagan mostly handled himself so well in dealing with the public and the press, reporters who, for the most part, didn't like his politics in the first place, often tried to "get him." As a result, so-called blunders that might have been overlooked in a liberal politician were pounced upon when committed by Reagan.

Cannon, for instance, declared Reagan blundered in appearing at the Neshoba County Fair in Mississippi a day before speaking to the Urban League in New York. Perhaps, if Reagan had had a right to expect substantial black support, but that was not the case. Reagan, whether or not he went to Neshoba, would in no way get more than 10 percent of the black vote, while his appearance at the fair shored up his Southern base at a time when it needed shoring. Many Southerners had not forgiven Reagan for picking Schweiker four years earlier and others were not happy with his choice of Bush, a perceived moderate, just days before.

Reagan went to Neshoba at the insistence of his Southern field man, Kenneth Klinge, and over the opposition of Dick Wirthlin and Nancy Reagan. Klinge loves to tell how, when he joined the traveling party at the stop before Neshoba, I found him and told him to get on at the rear of the plane because if Nancy saw him she was going to have his rear. But all was forgiven when Reagan, who had to slog through red clay mud to get to the speakers' stand, was greeted by a large and enthusiastic crowd.

Another so-called blunder Cannon cited was Reagan's trip to the devastated wasteland known as the South Bronx. Jimmy Carter had gone there four years earlier, had promised to rebuild it, and in the ensuing four years had done nothing. Ron McDuffie, a black staffer, came to me to urge that Reagan visit the same spot and say that if he were elected things would be different. I thought it was a great idea, persuaded all involved, and we went. But the press conference we scheduled never came off. Reagan was quickly surrounded by angry denizens who seemed to materialize from the ruined buildings. Secret Servicemen immediately hustled him to safety behind a barricade where, between heckles and jeers, he tried vainly to make himself heard.

Finally, in frustration, he shouted, "I can't do a damn thing for you if I don't get elected." From that moment on he was in control and the evening TV news turned the event into a major campaign plus. It was a harrowing experience, the most harrowing of the campaign. But it was not a blunder.

It would be nice to report that Reagan lived up to his promise to help the South Bronx, but he never did.

McDuffie came up with another bright idea that I persuaded the campaign to adopt—a visit with Jesse Jackson in Chicago. He went. It was a blunder. The conversation went nowhere and afterward Jackson scooted out and told his version of the meeting while Reagan was still struggling through the crowd of Jackson supporters who just happened to be bunched around the doorway.

All these mistakes pointed to a major flaw in the traveling campaign. A number of equals was aboard—Deaver, Anderson, Allen, Nofziger—but nobody was first among equals, nobody whom everybody could look to for the final judgment, no guru, no big daddy.

Shortly after we left Michigan Deaver came to me and said, "I've asked Stu Spencer to come aboard and he's agreed."

"Hooray," I responded, or something like that.

I was delighted. Spencer is a major asset to any campaign. Deaver left me with the impression that the idea was his. He is not dumb, and it was clear that the campaign plane needed a political thinker, one whose job was to sit back and look at the big picture, one who had the respect of the candidate and those around him. Spencer filled that bill. There were other good politicians aboard, but none had his depth of experience and none commanded the across-the-board respect that he had in the party and the press, and from the candidate and his wife. And none was so unflappable. So hooray, indeed, for Deaver if Spencer was his idea. But, if one believes Cannon, it was Nancy Reagan's idea. Deaver, as usual, was the faithful servant, carrying out her wishes.

It was a reunion for the Reagans and Spencer. Nancy and Ron had been bitterly resentful of Spencer's decision to go with Ford in 1976. Since he and Bill Roberts had run both of Reagan's gubernatorial campaigns, they felt he should have been a Reagan person. But Spencer had gotten crosswise with Deaver, or vice versa, and was looked upon as a nonconservative by the ideologues around Reagan. He was also viewed with suspicion by some as a man who used the press for his purposes, not the candidate's. And he had been ignored by Sears when he was putting the 1976 campaign together. Had Reagan insisted when he left the governor's office that Spencer be part of his political inner circle the odds are good that he, not Sears, would have run Reagan's 1976 campaign, and probably with a different result.

Now, however, Sears was long gone, Ford was out of the picture, and Nancy, recognizing that victory was more important than old grudges, asked Deaver to bring Spencer into the campaign.

On board Spencer was a calming influence, and much more. He had contacts that no one else had and he utilized them to win the endorsement of two prominent black leaders, Hosea Williams, whom Reagan called Jose, and Ralph Abernathy, who had succeeded Martin Luther King as head of the Southern Christian Leadership Conference.

Without seeming to, Spencer took charge of the traveling campaign. He didn't interfere with others' duties, but the things he wanted done usually got done and the things he didn't want done weren't. He was a key figure in deciding that Reagan should debate his opponents.

Reagan debated twice during the campaign, once with Jimmy Carter and earlier with John Anderson. He won neither on points but because he held his own he came out the victor. It's probably fair to say that impartial viewers for the most part judged him a clear-cut victor over Carter, thanks to one thing he said and one thing Carter said.

There are a couple of rules regarding political debates that presidential candidates violate at their peril. One: it is almost always a mistake for an incumbent to debate unless he thinks he's going to lose. The reason: by debating, the president brings the challenger up to his level and thereby risks losing that peculiar mystique known as presidential stature. Americans tend to look on presidents as something special, just by virtue of their office. Unless he overwhelms his debate opponent, the president loses that aura. Moreover, while presidents undoubtedly have more facts at their disposal than challengers, they are more vulnerable because they have four years of stupid mistakes and silly proposals and assinine statements at which their opponents can shoot. Besides, since they always take credit for all that goes right during their terms, they can legitimately be blamed for all that goes wrong.

Two: if you're running ahead you should think twice before debating. You have little to gain and much to lose, as Bill Timmons, the campaign field director, and Dick Wirthlin kept pointing out.

Fortunately for the candidates, presidential debates aren't really debates but kind of joint press conferences with opening and closing statements. That minimizes the advantages that would ordinarily go to the better debater.

I am ambivalent about debates. As a politician, I believe you should only agree to a debate if you think it will help your candidate. Sometimes it's better to demand debates and then set conditions you are confident your opponent will refuse. Chances are people will think you're brave and your opponent a coward.

But as a voter I like the idea of televised debates, although they can be almost as boring as professional basketball playoffs. For one thing you get a chance to look each candidate in the eye. You get to watch his mannerisms and see how he reacts under pressure. You get to see how he responds to stupid, or arrogant, or downright insulting questions. You get to see if he can take it as well as give it. Sometimes you find out more about a candidate than he thinks he's revealing. Gerald Ford freeing the Poles, Jimmy Carter consulting with Amy, Mike Dukakis being unindignant over the suggested rape of his wife—all these things might affect my vote. And the candidate's closing statement can tell you how well he memorizes lines, or whether he can ad lib effectively in the clutch.

But what's sauce for the voter isn't necessarily sauce for the candidate. When the subject of debates arose in the fall of 1980 most of the Reagan people were not interested. They didn't want to give Anderson credibility and they pretty much thought Reagan would beat Carter anyway. While the old Reagan hands were confident he could hold his own, many of the latecomers had their doubts.

Our initial ruse to keep from debating was to demand a three-way debate, because we knew Carter was adamant about not including Anderson since most agreed that Anderson would take more votes from Carter than from Reagan. Anderson, of course, was eager to debate either or both of the other candidates. He didn't remotely have anything to lose.

In his book, Deaver says it was Baker who persuaded Reagan to debate Anderson. I can find nothing to verify that and every indication points to Reagan having made the decision without the help of Baker, whom he hardly knew. Remember, Reagan had absolute confidence in his ability to deal with anyone on a one-on-one basis and to handle questions from the press or the audience. He had done it and done it well throughout his political career.

So Reagan agreed to the Anderson debate and it came off in Baltimore on September 21. It didn't excite anyone, but by holding his own Reagan proved once again that he was not to be underrated, for the political press generally agreed that Anderson was smarter, more knowledgeable, and every bit as articulate.

Nevertheless, no one in the campaign leadership circle was inclined to have Reagan debate Carter. Wirthlin, relying on his polls, and Timmons, listening to word from the field, were actively opposed. From their vantage point at campaign headquarters, Reagan looked like a winner without a debate. They were fearful that the days Reagan would have to take off to prepare would kill his momentum.

But out where the president was campaigning it looked as if the momentum had already stopped. Both the Carter and Reagan campaigns (Anderson was no longer a factor) seemed dead in the water, a situation that favored the incumbent. Those of us in the traveling campaign—Spencer, Deaver, me—were uneasy. One night in mid-October we pulled into Sioux Falls, South Dakota, for a campaign appearance. The next morning, crawling out of bed, it suddenly struck me: We were going to have to debate. Having received this message from on high I decided I should share it with Spencer. I wandered down to his room. His door was open and he was packing. Before I could open my mouth he looked up and said, "I think we're going to have to debate."

"Damn you," I said. "That's what I came to tell you."

We decided to say nothing further until we'd had a chance to talk with the Reagans and Deaver. As the traveling group was preparing to leave for the airport Deaver came up to me.

"Why don't you ride with the candidate," he said. "Nancy's got an interview and is going in another car."

I climbed in with Reagan and off we went. "Lynwood," he said after a moment, "I think we're going to have to debate."

Damn, I thought, now he's going to get on the plane and tell Deaver and Spencer and they're going to think I brought it up when I'd agreed to say nothing until we were all together. I told him that Spencer and I had come to the same conclusion and would he please let Spencer bring the matter up on the plane, which he did.

Aboard the plane we decided to wait until we arrived in New York, where Reagan was going to address the annual Al Smith Dinner, and then confer with the entire senior staff. Those not traveling would come up from Washington.

The morning after the dinner, which as usual I never attended, thus missing another sterling Reagan performance, the staff met with the Reagans in their suite. Nancy looked serious and remained silent during the ensuing discussion. I suspect she knew that the die had already been cast, that her husband would debate. While she had confidence in his ability she had a right to be concerned. A lot hinged on this decision, such as who would be elected president of the United States.

Again Timmons and Wirthlin stated their opposition and their reasons for it. And they were probably right. But the rest of us, with the exception of Baker, favored a debate. He straddled the fence, not risking being on the wrong side, no matter which side that might be. It was an interesting stand for a man who, if Deaver is right, persuaded Reagan to debate Anderson, unequivocally a better debater than Carter.

Finally it was Reagan's turn. "I think I should debate," he said.

And after much dickering between Baker for the Reagan side, and Baker's close personal friend, Robert Strauss, for Carter, it was agreed the debate would take place in Cleveland on October 28, a week before the election.

There are those who say Reagan is lazy. He isn't. He merely refuses to bother with things he doesn't think are important. But when things are truly important he pays attention and works. So it was with both debates. They were vitally important and he spent hours preparing for them. I only attended one preparation session, and I found it boring.

Besides, by early October I was feuding with Casey because I thought he'd lied to me. When I had returned to the campaign in June we had agreed that I would not only handle press relations but also oversee campaign public relations, although Casey questioned, legitimately, whether it was possible to do both jobs well. He then proceeded to make it nearly impossible by refusing to give me adequate headquarters staff. His reasoning, lack of money, made sense and I didn't argue. But in early October he informed me that he was thinking of talking to Robert Gray, who headed the Washington office of the public relations firm of Hill and Knowlton, about handling public relations. I protested that I could handle the job if he would let me hire staff. It turned out I was too late. He had already brought Gray aboard. Gray, in turn, brought in several hirelings who, of course, went on the campaign payroll. They did an effective job but that did nothing to lessen my resentment toward Casey.

I got over it eventually; there were enough Democrats and non-Reagan Republicans to fight, without feuding with a man who, regardless of his faults, was a staunch Reaganite. Besides, maybe it was a legitimate misunderstanding. Casey was a low-voiced mumbler whom everybody had difficulty understanding and maybe I'd said yes once to a mumble that called for a no. I'd like to think that, anyway; nobody served President Reagan more loyally than Bill Casey.

The debate with Carter was the icing on Reagan's campaign cake. He did no better than break even on points, but points are irrelevant in presidential debates. Public perceptions are what matter. They, not reality, are the real reality in politics. And in perceptions Reagan had it all over Carter.

In the first place Reagan is a master at using the camera to his own advantage. Carter is not. Reagan is tall, handsome, debonair. Carter is not. Reagan comes across warm and friendly. Carter does not. Reagan has a great smile. Carter has a mouthful of teeth. Carter pulled a boo-boo out of which no number of debating points could get him. Reagan did not.

Carter, who is seriously afflicted with sanctimonious pomposity compounded by self-righteous humility, decided to go after the children's vote. He related a conversation he claimed to have had with his daughter, Amy, in which she said the most important issue facing the nation was the nuclear arms race. It was deep thinking for a child of twelve, too deep, and the audience laughed, and Carter's credibility plunged. I laughed, too. I was sure Carter had just won one for the Gipper.

Reagan then proceeded to win one for himself. Carter was beating him about the head pretty heavily on his early stands against government-paid medical care. He made one minor misstatement, and Reagan looked over at him with a mixture of condescension and sorrow.

"There you go again," he said sadly, implying, of course, that Carter was lying.

It was a ten strike and we all knew it. From that moment, unless Reagan really screwed up, the election was won. He had just called the president of the United States a liar in front of the entire nation and Carter had had to sit there and take it.

We went out of Cleveland feeling better than at any time since the start of the campaign. We finished up on a high note, campaigning in Michigan with Reagan's new friend, Gerald Ford, in Peoria with his new friend, House Minority Leader Bob Michel, on the West Coast and points I don't remember with other new friends I don't remember. We wound up with a major rally in San Diego, the city that more than any other loves Ronald Reagan.

Then we flew to Los Angeles; the Reagans went home and the staff went to the Century Plaza Hotel where we all would await election returns the next night.

But I don't like election days. For me they are let-down days and I am short tempered and irritable. The fun has been the fight. I get emotionally up and stay up for that time. The long, long days, despite their tiresome tediosity (new word meaning tediousness) are somehow exciting. So are the long hours on airplanes between stops, eating too much, drinking too much, sleeping too little; the sudden surges of activity, jousting with the press, coping with the screw-ups; the ups and downs of the campaign and the campaign plane and the candidate and his wife. You don't have enough energy left to work up to a let-down.

But on election day it's all over. There is nothing more to do, nothing more you can do, except wait. And even after the results are in and you've won, if you have, the excitement for me is gone. I wish it weren't so.

On election day I was stopped by David Blundy, the reporter who had written that I said Jimmy Carter had the clap. He started to apologize.

"I have nothing to say," I said and turned away.

I was immediately sorry. I knew I should have accepted his apology. What he had written was really no big deal. I determined that if I saw him again I would apologize for my rudeness. But I never did and I never will. He was killed while covering the fighting in Nicaragua.

Reagan clobbered Carter, and Anderson was never in the race. Both men called Reagan before 6 P.M. California time to concede. Carter's call dragged Reagan from the shower, but he didn't seem to care. The long campaign had ended with a bang for Reagan and whimpers from Carter and Anderson.

I recalled the time I had told Bill Roberts nearly fifteen years before that "someday he [Reagan] might even be president." And I recalled the first time Reagan had won office fourteen years earlier. Then we had all looked at each other and asked, "What do we do now?" There was no such question this night.

We knew what we were going to do. With Ronald Reagan leading the way, we were going to turn the country around.

9

The Reagan White House

POLICY AND PEOPLE

I'VE WORKED IN the White House twice. Three times if you count one unpaid two-week stint in 1982. Would I work there again? Sure, under a president I liked and a chief of staff I had confidence in and with the authority to do what had to be done. Would I stay around very long? Probably not. For a lot of reasons, including that I don't believe anyone should stay in government very long, because eventually you go from being part of the solution to being part of the problem.

Ronald Reagan, when he was young in politics and still naive enough to recognize and separate truth from the nonsense Washington's pundits pass off as wisdom, believed a person should come into government for a couple of years, try to make it run more effectively, and then go home. This, he believed, was a citizen's responsibility, like voting or paying taxes.

Of course, that was long ago when he still called himself a citizen-politician. He hasn't called himself that in recent years, and for that change I'm truly sorry. The power and pomp of the presidency does that to the best, the most dedicated and sincere of men.

Which doesn't mean there aren't good people with long service in government, either as bureaucrats or appointees; there are, but they're not the majority. If this sounds as if I'm not a fan of big government I've made my point. And the time I served in the Nixon and Reagan White Houses did nothing to change my mind. To liberals and to most Americans who never give the matter much thought, government is a necessary good. But to a few of us, government is a necessary evil. We render unto Caesar, but reluctantly. Ronald Reagan used to be one of us, but by the time he left the presidency he also had left us.

For my part, I become impatient with government. Too many checks and balances. Too many things that should be done that the rules and regulations won't let you do. Too much crap up with which you shouldn't have to put. And too many people who forget too soon just why it was they came into government.

Nevertheless, I was enthused when I finally decided to accept a position in the Reagan White House. I knew that in the first days and months of a new administration you can have an impact on what direction it will take. That is exciting.

During the 1980 campaign I had served as Reagan's press secretary. It was not a new job. I had held that position in Reagan's 1966 gubernatorial campaign, for twenty-one months during his first term as governor, and for a while in his 1976 presidential campaign. But I did not want to be his presidential press secretary. That job I'd have once given my left whatever-was-available to have, but two things had happened since. First, I'd grown if not wiser at least older, and these days press secretary is a younger man's job. Second, in recent years too much personal nastiness has entered the relationship between press secretary and media. And it ain't no fun being in a constant pissing contest with the people with whom you have to work every day, and if you can't have fun you ought not to take the job.

Because of these feelings I decided to return to California as soon as convenient. That proved to be December 1. In the interim, I continued to accompany Reagan as he shuttled between California and Washington, during which period a couple of incidents occurred.

I remember a meeting in the New Executive Office Building between Reagan and a group of Reagan loyalists from the House of Representatives, people such as Tom Evans of Delaware, John Rousselot of California, and Jack Kemp of New York. Their mission was to persuade the president-elect to name one of theirs as director of the Office of Management and Budget. We all make mistakes and these guys were about to make a dilly—they wanted Rep. David Stockman for the post.

Reagan had already said he would not name a Republican congressman to a cabinet position, ostensibly because he did not wish to weaken Republican strength in Congress, but really because a couple of Republican senators, John Tower of Texas in particular, wanted cabinet positions, and Reagan wanted to keep them out without alienating them. But he knuckled under to this request because he owed them. His excuse was flimsy: the OMB position was not cabinet level. That was technically true, though Reagan annointed both Stockman and his successor, James Miller, with cabinet rank.

Stockman at the time was viewed as one of the staunchest Reagan Republicans in the House. Yet he repaid Reagan for his appointment by betraying him, not once, but twice. Unlike Judas, he never kissed him, but he got the silver anyway—two million bucks to put one of his betrayals between the covers of a book. Before that he gave a freebee to a *Washington Post* reporter named William Greider who sold it to *Atlantic Monthly*.

In Stockman's favor, he did come into the administration determined to balance the federal budget, more so, it turned out, than Reagan. In the early days, Reagan gathered his cabinet and senior staff from time to time to go over a list of cuts Stockman had proposed. But Stockman didn't win very many because even those who profess to be conservatives can usually find a reason not to abolish a government program.

One that Stockman lost was a HUD program called UDAG (Urban Development Action Grants) which funded projects the federal government should have kept its hands off of, such as hotels and convention centers. Supporters of UDAG had done a good lobbying job on the Reagan conservatives sitting around the cabinet table, including the president.

Nobody spoke in support of Stockman until I finally piped up: "I thought we came here to keep people's noses out of the public trough." The president glared. The room remained silent. And UDAG lasted until 1988 when Carol Crawford at OMB managed to "zero fund" it out of existence.

UDAG was not alone. Many other programs that could and should have been abolished weren't. Reagan gets the end blame for this, but blame spreads to those around him who either came to believe that such boondoggles were legitimate, or didn't want some Democratic congressman to get mad, or didn't have the courage to fight for the things we came to Washington to fight for.

In these early days one of the good people in White House personnel was a former prep school headmaster named Ed Curran. For his good work two things happened to him. One, he was named to head up a little piece of government lodged within the Department of Education called the National Institute of Education. Two, he was fired after being led inadvertently down the garden path by one, Lyn Nofziger.

Curran had taken a careful look at his little bit of turf and decided most of it could be abolished and the rest assigned elsewhere. And he so informed the secretary of education, a liberal education bureaucrat named Terrel Bell who should never have been appointed. Bell blew up at him.

"If I'd known you were going to feel this way I wouldn't have hired you," he said.

Curran, who figured his loyalties were to Reagan, not Bell, called me. "How do I get to Reagan?" he asked.

Though I had left the White House I had a special number that, put on an envelope, ensured it would get to the president. I gave the number to Ed. He sent his recommendation to Reagan who gave the letter to Mike Deaver who sent it to Bell who fired Curran. So much for trying to help Reagan cut the size of government.

Curran was then given a job as deputy director of the Peace Corps, working for Lorette Ruppe, who had gotten her job through Vice President Bush. Mrs. Ruppe, nobody's conservative, didn't have much use for Curran and his desire to save the taxpayers' money, so she isolated him. Curran hung in, but was never allowed to play a meaningful role. Mrs. Ruppe stayed, too, because every time Reagan's personnel chief, John Herrington, tried to fire her Bush intervened.

What happened to Curran was a loss both to him personally and to Reagan. His was just one instance where Reagan appointees who had no use for him thwarted those who wanted to carry out his philosophy of government. If Reagan had ever, instead of never, paid attention to personnel matters his administration would have been more successful.

Another useless little piece of government was the Institute of Museum Services. I received a call one day from Senator Tower. He wanted Lilla, his wife, to head it. I arranged it, and why not? Tower had always been an anyone-but-Reagan Republican, but his antagonism was personal and political rather than philosophical. Besides, winners can afford to be magnanimous, and we had always beaten him.

A few months after Lilla was appointed Jim Baker called me. "I've got a dirty job for you," he said. "We're going to abolish the Institute of Museum Services and you have to tell Lilla Tower."

Baker, never noted for his courage, was not eager personally to cross Tower. Now most people, including me, viewed Lilla as a little nutty and a lot difficult. But I called her and she accepted the news calmly. Sure, she said, she understood. Which maybe she did, but she hied herself up to Capitol Hill and lobbied for her lousy little institute—and won. Baker caved and the institute survived.

Immediately after the election there was a meeting between President-elect Reagan and the governor of Texas, William Clements. Clements is outspoken, pugnacious, totally lacking in diplomacy, and rich. When the Reagan campaign moved to Arlington in the summer of 1980, an estate owned by Clements was rented for the Reagans. Somehow Reagan forgot the place was only rented and one day, looking out a window, he found that a good-sized pine tree was obstructing his view. Always the man of action, he located an axe and chopped it down. This, it was later discovered, was Clements' favorite tree.

But Clements' visit was not to protest the chopping. He came to discuss who should be the next secretary of defense. It was usual to have a staffer sit in on Reagan meetings, primarily to keep track of what was going on but also to make certain that Reagan, nice man that he is, didn't, in a fit of niceness, give away the store. On this day Deaver and Meese were elsewhere so I sat in.

Reagan and Clements knew each other slightly and he and I were not strangers. I had participated in a meeting with him after the Republican National Convention to decide on the chairmanship of the Texas Reagan for President campaign. Ernie Angelo, the Texas national committeeman and Reagan chairman before the convention, wanted to retain the post, with Clements serving either as cochairman or honorary chairman. There was only one problem, Clements wanted to be chairman, with Angelo as cochairman.

Bill Casey, Reagan's national chairman, decided to go to Texas to see what he could work out and asked me to go along. We met with Clements and Angelo and Clements came to the point.

"I want to be the chairman," he said, "and if I'm not I won't take part in the campaign."

Nobody ever accused old Bill of being a team player. We had no doubt that he meant what he said. Casey looked at me. I looked at Casey. And, with my silent concurrence, he sacrificed Ernie Angelo on the altar of expediency. Angelo, a longtime Reaganite, took his beating, stayed in the campaign, and made it work, despite the general dislike of Clements by most Texas Reaganites. Oddly, by campaign's end, he and Clements had developed a real liking for each other, which made me feel less guilty over our doublecross.

Now, at the Reagan meeting, Clements, as is his wont, launched right in. Caspar (Cap) Weinberger, he told the president, should be named secretary of defense, although John Tower coveted the post. Clements and Weinberger had served together in the Nixon-Ford administrations, Clements as deputy secretary of defense, Weinberger in several high-level posts, the last of which was secretary of health, education and welfare.

Reagan agreed that Weinberger, who had worked briefly as Reagan's California director of finance, was indeed qualified to head up any federal department.

After Clements left, Reagan turned to me. "I didn't want to say anything to Bill because I didn't want him to think I was stealing his idea," he said. "But last night, lying in bed trying to figure out who should be secretary of defense, it suddenly hit me. Cap should be it. But if Bill wants to think it's his idea that's fine with me."

As far as I know, Reagan has let Clements think Weinberger was his idea to this very day. That kind of generous heart is worth almost any pine tree in the world. And if I'm spoiling one of Bill Clements' pet delusions, I apologize.

It was James Addison Baker III who offered me the job in the White House that I couldn't turn down. On the morning after he was elected,

Reagan named Baker his chief of staff, surprising and disappointing a lot of us who figured that Meese had a lock on the job.

When Baker approached me to serve as assistant to the president for political affairs, a post he was creating especially for me, I naively thought it was because he thought I was the right person for the position. But when he also brought into the White House a large gaggle of his liberal, moderate, and non-Reaganite cronies to fill important staff jobs, I figured out his real reason. I was a sop to the conservatives who had fought and bled with and for Reagan right through to the presidency and who now were feeling a tiny bit betrayed. And a lot ignored. And with some justification.

Well before the campaign ended I had told Deaver and Meese and anyone else who would listen that I was not interested in being White House press secretary, that I wanted to go back to California where the sun shone and there was no snow in the winter. I had spent fourteen years hoping to help in the making of a president—more exactly in making a president of Ronald Reagan; I had never envisioned serving in his administration.

I iterated my position to Meese a few days before the campaign ended and told him I would stay on until November 15 to give him time to find a replacement. I dealt with Meese because he was in charge of the transition and had expressed the hope that I would stay on. He accepted my informal resignation but the day after the election asked if I couldn't stay longer. I reluctantly agreed to stay until December 1 on the condition that I not stay beyond that date because Bonnie and I had plans to drive to California in early December.

Meese was as good as his word, so on November 28 I sat down with Reagan to say goodbye one more time. It was a brief meeting. I said I was quitting. He asked why. I said I didn't want to be his press secretary anymore. He asked why again, and I said I was tired of following him around. He said he understood and added, "There'll always be a job for you in my administration."

We shook hands and I left. That was before Baker decided he needed a prominent right-wing Reaganite on the White House staff, one to whom he could point and say, "I brought him aboard."

He was later to throw the "I-hired-you" in my face as if I were supposed to be grateful. In fact, my presence did more for him than he could, or would, do for me. But I also think he thought that, in my gratitude, I would become a member of his team. It only took him a little while to figure out that I came, as always, to serve Ronald Reagan.

Even though I had said my official goodbye to Reagan in California, I traveled to Washington with him a day or two later to pack, pick up Bonnie, and head for California. It was during this brief interval that Baker came to me with his proposal. Although the idea intrigued me, initially I turned him down. But after talking that night to Bonnie and the next day to Meese, who urged me to reconsider, I told Baker that I'd like to think about his offer and would call him when I got to California.

We arrived home on December 20 and almost before we walked in the door the phone was ringing. It was Baker calling from Jamaica, wanting to know my decision. I said I would take the job.

In mid-January we flew to Washington with the Reagans on Air Force II which President Carter had put at their disposal. They were shocked when they saw me. I had grown a beard. I still have it. I like it, even though once in 1981, when the *Washington Post* ran a color photo of me on the cover of its Sunday magazine, the little son of Steve Studdert, an old Reagan advance man, asked him, "Daddy, is that the devil?" Steve never told me how he responded.

By this time I had asked Ed Rollins to be my deputy. Rollins is a short, stocky man, shiny bald on top and with a full beard. He is as good a politician as I know, a conservative Republican, and to top it all off, he was (and is) my friend. He had spent the presidential campaign trying to elect state legislators in California because the lady he was working for, Carol Hallett, the Republican leader in the State Assembly, balked when I tried to bring him into the campaign.

When I left the White House early in 1982 Rollins succeeded me. Two years later he was picked to run the Reagan reelect campaign and shortly thereafter, as a favor to Don Regan, went back to the White House for a nine-month stint, running both the political and the intergovernmental affairs shops. Over Reagan's two terms he did as much or more than anyone to advance the president's cause, despite limited support from Baker and Regan and, unfortunately, the president.

Before the inauguration, I also brought aboard another assistant, Harvey Lee Atwater, a still-in-his-twenties South Carolinian who had run part of the South for us. Lee was hanging around transition headquarters hoping to latch onto a decent position when I returned to Washington. I didn't know him, but Baker asked that I interview him.

He put no pressure on me to hire him, but I did anyway. One reason was that I thought Baker wanted me to, and at that time I thought I could work with him.

It turned out to be a good move. Lee in many ways was a character—rock guitar player, collector of horror movies, jogger, Friday cigaret smoker, and a man of boundless energy who couldn't sit still. He was also smart and knew how to get things done. And, like Rollins, he was a good politician. When I left the White House Rollins made him his deputy and, as such, took him to the Reagan Reelect Committee. When Vice President Bush was looking for someone to put his 1988 presidential campaign organization together he picked Atwater. The job Atwater did for Bush earned him the chairmanship of the Republican National Committee.

Lee had one other quality that endeared him to me. Like Rollins, he did not forget his friends.

Lee died in the spring of 1991 from brain cancer. He was thirty-nine.

Two more came into the political shop with titles of special assistant to the president—Paul Russo and Morgan Mason. Both began working for me almost by accident.

Russo had been an advance man for Reagan in 1976 and 1980. He came into the White House working for Max Friedersdorf in congressional relations but soon got crosswise with Friedersdorf who fired him. Russo came to see me and since I still had slots to fill I brought him on board.

Mason, the son of actor James Mason, had volunteered in the campaign in early 1979 and soon became a protégé of Mike Deaver. Mason first worked as deputy to the chief of protocol, Lenore Annenberg, who eventually fired him. Deaver asked me if I would split Morgan's pay and services with him and I agreed.

Even before Reagan was inaugurated I made my first mistake as a member of the White House staff, but I did it knowingly, and not caring. Actually it was my third or fourth mistake. The first was taking the job and the second and third were trusting Jim Baker. This mistake was to settle for an office in the Old Executive Office Building, that magnificent Victorian horror right across West Executive Avenue from the White House.

For those unfamiliar with Washington, West Executive Avenue is a one-block long, one-way street that separates the Old EOB from the

West Wing of the White House. These days it is closed off, guarded at both ends, and for official use only. The problem with officing in the old EOB is that, while it is only about a hundred feet from the West Wing, it is sometimes clear across the country in terms of keeping track of or being involved in what goes on there. The West Wing houses the Oval Office, the cabinet room, and the offices of the chief of staff, the National Security adviser, and other high-ranking staffers. People fight and bleed for West Wing offices since occupancy signifies power, and proximity to the Oval Office signifies importance, which most White House staffers find it difficult to do without.

Since I had not sought my job and did not intend to stay beyond a year I felt the need for neither. I was preparing to ask Baker for the northeast corner suite on the first floor of the Old EOB, occupied by Herb Klein during the Nixon years, when Baker beat me to the punch.

"You don't really need one of those little offices in the West Wing," he said. "Why don't you take Nixon's old hideaway office in the old EOB?"

He wanted, of course, for me to think he was looking after my interests when in truth he didn't want me in the West Wing, which, if I *had* wanted in, he would have had a tough time keeping me out since, in terms of service to Reagan, I outranked just about everyone there. But as soon as I saw the office I knew I wanted it. It had all the comforts of home except a fireplace—a private bathroom with a shower, and a kitchen complete with refrigerator and ice maker. It also had a door to the outside that led down a flight of steps leading directly to West Executive Avenue.

I remembered President Nixon using those steps in the seventies. But when I moved in I discovered I couldn't use the outside door because under the new security rules a guard had to be stationed at any door leading to the outside, and I didn't rate my own private door guard.

But there were advantages to being in the old EOB. For one, my entire staff was housed in a string of adjacent offices, whereas those in the West Wing had their staffs in the old EOB, which made things a little awkward.

On moving into our new offices I found that at least some of the Carter people were pig dirty. My bathroom was unfit for human use. I called the General Services Administration and complained. The woman who came to clean explained apologetically, "We wanted to keep it clean but they wouldn't let us in."

The people who cleaned the office had the same complaint. Along with the general filth, great flakes of paint were peeling from the walls. Baker had dictated that no one order new carpeting or renovation work, but I went ahead and had the carpet replaced and the walls painted.

But no matter how clean and comfortable the Old EOB, unless you fight daily to discover what's going on in the West Wing, you tend to be isolated: you miss out on the hallway gossip, and you can't stick your head in somebody else's office to ask a question or pass on a bit of information. Telephone calls, no matter how urgent, may not be returned right away, and you have to set up an appointment to see someone just for a second. So you deal more in memos, which were the bane of my times in government.

Early on, Deaver asked how often I would need to see the president. I said once a week for half an hour. Had I been halfway smart I would have insisted on scheduling that half hour. But I didn't and as a result didn't see the president as often as I should have to get in my two-cents worth.

Indeed, many of my meetings with the president were at somebody else's insistence, sometimes the president's. I soon learned that any staff member wishing to see the president had to be cleared by Deaver. This I viewed as insulting since I had had direct access to Reagan long before anyone knew who Deaver was. Sure, someone had to be gatekeeper for a president or he would be pestered to death, but I had never abused my privilege—well, maybe once or twice when he was governor—and Deaver knew it.

I was remiss for two other reasons in not insisting on regular weekly meetings with the president. One was that it left Rollins in a difficult position when I resigned because I had not paved the way for him to develop his own relationship with the president. And, more importantly, I lost the opportunity to speak my piece on policy matters, to remind the president from time to time why we were there and who our base constituency was. I did not give him the political advice and information he needed and had a right to expect but would never ask for. Bill Clark always said that if Reagan had all the facts he would make the right decisions. I should have remembered that.

Of course, Meese was there, and Martin Anderson on domestic issues, and Dick Allen and later Clark on international issues, but one more voice—mine—speaking from a political and a "remember-our-promises" point of view wouldn't have hurt.

Something to remember: In Washington the pressures on any president, but especially a Republican president, come from the Left, from the Eastern liberal establishment. (Yes, Virginia, there is an Eastern liberal establishment, made up in part of the *Washington Post*, the *New York Times*, most of the reporters who cover Washington, the network anchormen, the academic elite from the Ivy League—and those who wish they were from the Ivy League—the liberals and radicals in Congress, and the radical and peacenik think tanks that abound in Washington. And some people in the White House, any White House.)

President Nixon knew this and took constant steps to counteract the Left's pressures. Through various staffers he arranged for public support for actions he took or planned to take that would arouse the ire of the Left. For instance, a Nixon televised speech always drew large numbers of supporting phone calls and wires, and not just by chance. Nixon's political organization saw to it. This allowed the White House spokesman to announce heavy and enthusiastic support for whatever it was Nixon had said or done.

Efforts also were made constantly—in speeches, newsletters, appearances on television and radio—to have members of Congress support Nixon publicly. Not to mention the support solicited from important individuals and organizations in the private sector. High-level members of the administration were ordered to join in, even if the particular issue had nothing to do with his or her expertise. And, finally, the Republican National Committee and party leaders at every level were utilized to build up the president and tear down his political enemies. The RNC became, for a while at least, the hatchet-wielding arm of the White House.

This constant, intense PR effort had much to do with the extraordinary success Nixon, a not particularly loved president, had in dealing with a Democratic Congress and the liberal Washington establishment until Watergate.

Although there were people around who knew what Nixon had done and how he had done it, the Reagan White House during its entire eight years made only sporadic attempts to mobilize the full force of the Reagan constituency to back up the president. Several reasons explain this failure:

1. Reagan had unlimited confidence in his personal persuasive powers both with individuals and groups, and liked to exercise them.

2. Reagan's various chiefs of staff and congressional relations aides shared his belief. As a result, not enough back-up pressure was brought on his behalf. Over the years the president wore out his welcome with many congressmen because he went to the well too often. Any president should deal with individual members of the House and Senate carefully and sparingly. Call a congressman for help rarely and only in dire need and he's honored and flattered. Call him every time you need a vote and the familiarity breeds a certain kind of contempt.

3. When Chuck Colson first put together the Nixon White House office, now called Public Liaison, his purpose was to persuade outside organizations that were friendly to or needed help from the administration to rally their members on behalf of the president. In return Colson would try to help them in their dealings with the administration. By the time Reagan became president, the Public Liaison office was taking the approach that if the White House, mainly the president, promised to heed the complaints and requests of outside organizations and pressure groups, then, maybe, they would support him in his time of need. Long lines of special interest supplicants were brought in to meet with Reagan. These often included liberal and anti-Reagan Democrats who frequently left the White House to voice to the news media their differences with and contempt for the president.

Successful politics is based on a system of rewards and punishment. Members of Congress and leaders of pressure groups soon learned that most in the Reagan White House—the president himself—didn't believe in punishment; you could oppose and even betray the president with impunity. When Rollins threatened to punish the Republican congressmen who refused to support the president, Baker publicly reprimanded him. He was more interested in having recalcitrant Republicans think he was a good guy than in staunchly supporting either the president or members of his staff.

4. Reagan and his various chiefs of staff pretty much ignored the Republican National Committee and Republican organizations around the country. None of the chiefs of staff backed up efforts by the political office to utilize party resources for the president in his dealings with the Congress or in his efforts to take the issues to the people.

Ronald Reagan was a successful president and perhaps a great one, but the tragedy is he could have been even more successful had his chiefs of staff understood and been willing to use all the resources at their command.

White House meetings tend to be long and long meetings bore me. So I didn't go to many, instead sending Rollins, who is a goo-goo at heart and doesn't mind long and boring meetings. Besides, the meetings gave him a chance to know first hand both the issues and the players—the cabinet members, senior White House staffers, and high officials from the various other parts of government. That helped him and it helped our shop, even though my purpose was to keep from being bored. When Reagan became bored in meetings he dozed off, or so Deaver told the media, but I left. So, I noticed, did Deaver.

Besides, in those early days there was plenty to do without going to meetings, some of which I had not expected. One added responsibility had to do with personnel: hiring and firing, finding jobs for Reagan supporters, including Democrats, trying to keep out the anti-Reaganites, including Republicans, and trying our best through the appointments process to keep the administration on the track Ronald Reagan had laid out during the campaign and over the years.

We won some, we lost more, and many victories proved to be temporary. It was amazing how many anti-Reagan Republicans managed to sneak in through the back door when I wasn't looking and later on walked boldly through the front door. One reason we moved into the personnel area was that Pendleton James, Reagan's first head of personnel, tended to confuse his priorities and put competence first when looking for people to fill upper level jobs. I recognized the need for competence, although I'm sure some will argue that point, but other qualifications came first.

For instance, had the prospective appointee supported Reagan? Was he or she a Republican? Eventually a young woman named Becky Norton Dunlop joined the personnel staff and my office was able to back off. She was tougher than either Rollins or I and a more dedicated conservative.

One day shortly after Reagan took office F. Clifton White dropped by for a visit. He left the president with one bit of advice: "You can't win a revolution with mercenaries."

Becky Dunlop instinctively knew this. But over the years it became obvious that Reagan never got the message.

One personnel fight I won was of no great importance except for its symbolism. Baker wanted to appoint Ann Wexler to the president's bipartisan Commission on White House Fellows, a rather insignificant appointment. Ann is a smart, competent politico, but she is a very liberal Democrat who had run Jimmy Carter's White House political operation. I was outraged. I told Baker he couldn't do it. Our argument raged off and on for a week until he finally caved in.

"But," he said, "I'm going to appoint Bob Strauss and you can't stop me."

I should have tried because Strauss, like Baker a Texan, had been Carter's campaign manager and a Democratic National chairman. Instead I said I didn't want to, and it was the right decision. Throughout the 1980s Strauss was of significant help to Reagan, which would not have been the case with Ms. Wexler.

Another I lost but had the last laugh anyhow. It had to do with naming an administrator for the Small Business Administration. Baker wanted to appoint Michael Cardenas, a Hispanic who had been active in Fresno Republican politics. I knew him from the Nixon reelection campaign. In 1976 I had asked him to help Reagan, but he declined, saying he did not want to become involved with either candidate. Shortly thereafter he signed on with Ford. Five years later I had not forgotten or forgiven. I called Baker again.

"You can't appoint this guy," I said. "He's incompetent and besides he lied to me."

Baker was adamant. "We need Hispanics," he said.

"We need loyal and competent Hispanics," I countered, "and he ain't one of those."

I had to fall back on the competency pitch because my loyalty pitch was meaningless to Baker. My usual line was that loyalty was the first requisite and only after that came competency. The exception was if we were determined to hire a Democrat.

Then I advised, "Hire a dumb one because a smart one can hurt us."

In Cardenas' case my arguments went nowhere, and eventually Cardenas was appointed. Less than a year later he was fired—for incompetence. He blamed me because he and I had tangled a time or two over his refusal to act on White House—meaning me—requests. But this time I was innocent. They fired him before I could get to him.

One thing you learn about Jim Baker if you work for him or around him for any length of time is that he is among the slickest of political operators in a town where slick operators come a dime a dozen, or even cheaper. At this writing he has slicked his way up to the most prestigious cabinet job going, secretary of state, in the administration of his second best buddy, George Herbert Walker Bush. His best buddy is himself, James A. Baker III. The president runs a poor second, as he may eventually discover.

In the meantime, it seems appropriate that a guy with III after his name is working for a fellow with two middle initials. If nothing else, they are doing the country club set proud.

This might be the right time to take a close look at the man who claims to be President Bush's best friend and wants to be his successor.

I first met Baker in the presidential election of 1976. A Texas society lawyer, he was also the political protégé of an ambitious Texas politician named George Bush. He had come to Washington at Bush's suggestion to work in the Ford administration as an undersecretary of commerce. Handsome, debonair, polished, he impressed members of the Ford White House as intelligent and competent. Actually, he impressed me the same way after I joined the Ford campaign, so much in fact that I welcomed him into the Reagan campaign four years later and never protested when Reagan named him chief of staff. Some things I would do differently if I could.

On May 7, 1976, as the Reagan presidential campaign was threatening to overtake Ford, the president's inner political circle recruited Baker to take over as the campaign's chief delegate hunter. This eventually allowed him to take credit for rounding up enough delegates to beat Ronald Reagan. And why not? Taking credit, deserved or otherwise, is commonplace in politics. Twelve years earlier, John Sears was taking credit for rounding up the delegates who nominated Richard Nixon.

Immediately after the Republican convention, Ford named Baker campaign chairman, replacing Rogers C. B. Morton, who was dying of cancer and had nearly kicked away the nomination for Ford. But, though Baker was chairman, the man in charge of day-to-day operations was Stuart Spencer. Spencer had been muscled aside by Tom Reed and Clif White in Reagan's abortive bid for the presidency in 1968. They thought he was too friendly with Nelson Rockefeller, who also was running. In 1975 the same thing happened to him at the hands of Deaver and Sears.

It is doubtful anyway that Spencer would have been willing to play second fiddle to Sears. Besides, only zealots such as Nofziger really thought Reagan could steal the Republican nomination from a sitting president, and Spencer is anything but a zealot. What he wouldn't have done—and didn't do—is sit on the sidelines; he is not a sideline sitter.

In any event Ford's first chairman, Bo Callaway, brought him in to run Ford's campaign. He responded by winning the nomination for Ford. After the convention he called me from Vail, Colorado, where Ford campaign bigwigs were meeting and asked me to come aboard.

Spencer's call caused me to change my mind about working for Ford. Earlier I had turned Dole down on the justifiable grounds that I was worn out. The real reason was that I was in no mood to work for Ford, whom I had not yet forgiven for beating Reagan. But, by now, I wanted to do what I could to help Dole, whom I looked upon both as a friend and as a smart, competent pol who might someday become president. Wrong again!

I always liked working with Spencer who, I think, has one of the best political brains in either party. This he demonstrated by leaving me pretty much alone to do my thing and rescuing me when I got into trouble. And he never lost his cool, which is more than I can say for most politicians, me included. I still think if Spencer has been left to his own devices Ford would have been elected.

When an incumbent president loses a close race there are always plenty of places to spread the blame, starting with the candidate. My own feeling is that Ford lost because of his blunders and Baker's timidity. Ford's biggest blunder, as mentioned, came in the foreign policy debate with Carter when he declared that the Poles were not under Soviet domination.

The day after the debate I called Spencer in California and urged him to get Ford to confess his error before it was too late. Stu assured me that Ford would, but he didn't. And by the time he finally did the nation had decided it preferred a man who lusted in his heart over one who apparently didn't understand the Cold War. In his book, *Marathon*, Jules Witcover examined the follow-up efforts to correct the Ford mistake, naming everyone who participated, or so it seemed. One name strangely missing was Baker's.

Normally, the campaign manager takes the lead in handling troubles that arise. But like the "man upon the stair" Baker not only wasn't there in 1976, but he wasn't there again fourteen years later to handle another political screw-up. In 1988, when his candidate, George Bush, ran into a firestorm of criticism for naming Sen. J. Danforth Quayle as his running mate, Baker quickly leaped out of the fray, proclaiming, "I had nothing to do with it. Don't blame me."

Despite Ford's boo-boos, he might still have won if he'd had a couple of million dollars to spend at the last minute in key states. And the fact is, he did. Federal Election Committee records show the campaign had at least $1.7 million left on election day. But Baker had refused to spend it. Perhaps he wanted to save it to pay late bills, although any experienced politician knows you worry about winning first and paying bills last.

He also may have felt that exceeding the budget would have made him look bad or resulted in a slap on the wrist from the FEC. Ford's losing, of course, made only Ford look bad.

A lot has been written about Baker since he appeared on the national scene, most of it favorable, as befits a man who cultivates the news media assiduously. Baker has always made himself available to reporters, feeding them inside information, often of the kind that makes others look bad.

Not until the 1988 presidential election did he come in for any serious media criticism. Reporters covering the campaign had decided that a good continuing story would be to accuse Bush of running a dirty campaign. Baker, as campaign chairman, was held responsible by many, which must have shaken him in light of the time and effort he had spent kissing up to them. Since then he has run afoul of the press several times: for owning bank stock while secretary of the Treasury; for planning to shoot a species of endangered mountain goat in Mongolia; for isolating himself as secretary of state from the career foreign service; for trout fishing in Siberia while Bush was sending American troops to Saudi Arabia.

The 1988 Bush campaign was not particularly dirty. But the media needed an issue against Bush when the public began to get bored with the attacks on Quayle. If, however, there had been dirt Baker would not have been responsible for it, because he seldom does anything overtly to warrant public criticism. And if there is blame to be placed he will see that it is shifted away from him. In 1988 his built-in scapegoat for the charges of dirty campaigning was the day-to-day campaign manager, Lee Atwater, who gloried in his reputation for playing political hardball.

I have already mentioned Baker's quick disavowal of involvement in the selection of Quayle. Another example came earlier, in 1983, when the media tried (unsuccessfully) to raise to the level of a Watergate scandal the fact that in 1980 someone had stolen a briefing book from the Carter campaign and passed it on to the Reagan campaign. Baker eventually wound up with the book, but he quickly tried to shift the blame onto the man who had brought him into the campaign, William Casey.

After Baker was named Ford's campaign chairman in 1976 he maintained a low profile as befits any shrewd operator who doesn't have confidence in his candidate. This positioned him perfectly to claim credit if Ford won or to evade blame if he lost. And evade blame he did, with Ford the fall guy and Baker viewed by press and politicians alike, including me, as a class act.

He came across as knowledgeable, sincere, and altogether a regular kind of guy—chewing tobacco, smoking a cigar, taking a drink, telling a dirty joke with the boys, and killing wild creatures just for the fun of it. One of his hobbies is wild turkey hunting. It has inspired my definition of fratricide: Jim Baker bagging a turkey.

In 1979–80 Bush and Baker, with a major assist from David Keene, who ran Bush's day-to-day operation, proved to be an effective team. They ambushed Reagan, or rather, John Sears, in the Iowa caucuses and headed for the New Hampshire primary where Bush fell into the famous debate trap Gerry Carmen, Reagan's New Hampshire chairman, and Sears had set for him.

That was the time Reagan challenged Bush to a one-on-one debate and then invited the rest of the Republican candidates to join in. Instead of welcoming them, Bush sulked publicly. He compounded the error by going to Texas on election day to jog in the sunshine while Reagan stayed to campaign in the snow.

This was a classic case of history repeating itself. As you recall, in 1976 Reagan left New Hampshire the weekend before the primary at the behest of his New Hampshire campaign manager, Hugh Gregg, who wanted to prepare his organization for election day. But Ford stayed, showed the natives he cared, beat Reagan narrowly, and went on to win the Republican nomination.

In 1980, Bush's New Hampshire campaign manager, the same Hugh Gregg, sent Bush home so he could prepare his organization for election day. Reagan stayed, showed the natives he cared, beat Bush handily, and went on to win the Republican nomination. Which proves that Jimmy Baker was no smarter than John Sears, and Hugh Gregg in 1980 was no smarter than Hugh Gregg in 1976. There was one big difference, however. In 1976 Reagan had a real shot at beating Ford; in 1980 Bush had all the chances of a snowball in hell of beating Reagan.

After Bush lost the nomination, Baker went home to Texas. He might have stayed to help Bush's vice presidential campaign, but that would have been demeaning to a man of his overweening ambition and self-importance.

Casey and I sought him out after the convention to ask him to come aboard in a high-level but unspecified job. He turned us down, but a few weeks later, unbeknownst to me, Casey made another run at him, and this time, apparently acting on Bush's and Spencer's advice, he came aboard and Casey put him in charge of debate negotiations.

Casey lived long enough to regret it because it led to Baker's appointment as Reagan's chief of staff, and he and Casey, who had become CIA director, soon fell out. Casey later told me that bringing Baker into the campaign was the biggest mistake he had ever made.

"You can't put the biggest leaker in Washington in charge of national security," Casey told Reagan, when Reagan suggested making Baker head of the National Security Council. What he didn't say, but what nearly everyone in the room on that occasion knew, was that Reagan shouldn't have made him chief of staff, either.

In that position Baker worked constantly to persuade the president to do what he, Baker, wanted done rather than carry out the president's wishes. In senior staff meetings, he constantly admonished that "we can't let the president do" whatever it was the president was thinking of doing, or "we have to make the old man do" whatever it was he didn't really want to do.

Typical was the 1982 tax increase, the so-called Tax Equity and Fiscal Responsibility Act (TEFRA), one of the great misnomers in congressional history. Rallying a "Gang of 17" from the administration and Congress, Baker persuaded Reagan to accept the tax increase on the promise that the Congress would give him three dollars in spending cuts for every dollar of tax increase. Of course it never happened; 27 cents was more like it. But Reagan, relying on Baker, wanted to believe the worthy gentlemen in Congress wouldn't lie to him, when he should have known better. It took several years for Reagan to realize he'd been had.

The TEFRA incident is a good illustration of a unique Reagan trait that served him well throughout his political career. Unlike most politicians, whenever he took a stand on an issue, he believed he was right. Even though he might flipflop on it, he did so on belief, not expediency. The late (and in my opinion, great) Jesse Unruh, the California Democratic Speaker of the Assembly when Reagan was elected California governor, remarked unhappily yet admiringly on this trait.

"The reason the people believe Reagan," he said, "is because Reagan believes himself. He sounds sincere because he is sincere, even when he should know better. Most politicians know when they're lying and so the people sense it. But in his own mind Reagan never lies and the people sense that, too."

So it was with TEFRA. It was 180-degrees out of phase with Reagan's belief in supply-side economics, but at the time Reagan truly believed it was the best thing for the country.

As chief of staff, Baker was not above trying to use Reagan for his own ends and Reagan sometimes complied. One such instance happened in late 1982. I had invited a number of old Reagan hands to come to a meeting about the 1984 presidential election, saying I wanted to make sure the election was a Reagan-Bush and not a Bush-Reagan campaign. I figured Baker would control the campaign and its staffing and I worried that Reaganites would be left out in the cold.

One of my "friends" gave a copy of my invitation to Baker. He was not happy.

So there I am participating on a panel at a meeting of political consultants when in the corner the phone rings.

"It's for you," I'm told. "The White House."

"You're kidding," I say. "Find out who it is."

"It's Jim Baker," he says.

By this time people in the room are laughing. They figure I have set this up as a gag. Not so. I take the call. It is Baker, calling from Air Force One. He is out of control, screaming and shouting about my letter and threatening dire consequences.

I interrupt. "I am in a room full of people. I can't talk and you're calling from Air Force One. Your line is not secure. Why don't you call me when you land?"

I hang up. The panel resumes. Three minutes later the phone rings.

"It's for you," the man says. "It's Air Force One."

The room breaks out in laughter. Nofziger is really trying to pull their collective leg. I take the phone. It's Ronald Reagan. I think I detect a chuckle in his voice.

"Lynwood," he says, his nickname for me which he wouldn't use if he were upset. "Lynwood, what are we going to do about this?"

("Oh, shit," I say to myself, "Baker has gone and complained to the president and asked him to call me and disinherit me or defrock me or something equally drastic.")

Out loud, but softly so the roomful of eavesdroppers can't hear, I say, "Mr. President, I wouldn't for the world deliberately do anything to embarrass you."

"I know it," he says equally softly. "What do you think we ought to do about this?"

"Nothing. If anyone in the press talks to me I'll say I misspoke. I'll say—truthfully—it was not an attack on the vice president. If they ask you about it, you should probably tell them the same thing. I'll send George a note of apology."

We say good-bye and I go back to my panel discussion. My reaction is: That big crybaby—meaning Baker—making that poor guy—meaning the president—do his dirty work for him.

The upshot of Baker's tantrum was that I wrote a letter of apology to the vice president and he wrote me a note of forgiveness. Baker followed up by ordering the invitees serving in the administration not to come to the meeting, and most of them didn't.

Then Baker went to Texas to shoot his brother turkeys and while there told a reporter that "we cut him [Nofziger] off at the knees." Which, of course, was untrue, as anyone who watches me walk can plainly see. People in the administration continued to talk to me, eat with me, deal with me. What more could anyone ask? And, for some reason, Reagan people ran the campaign of 1984.

That wasn't the first time Baker ordered people in the administration not to go somewhere. In late 1981 he did just that when conservatives held a luncheon in support of Richard Allen, the head of the National Security Council. Allen had been falsely accused of unethically taking money from a Japanese television reporter and gifts from Japanese friends. I ignored Baker's order and went. Not many from the administration attended, but I spotted Samuel Pierce, secretary of Housing and Urban Development.

"What are you doing here, Sam?" I asked.

"Dick Allen is a friend of mine," he replied.

Baker should have friends as steadfast and loyal as Sam Pierce.

Baker early set himself up as superior to others on the president's staff. Though he carried his White House pass in his wallet he ordered all other staffers to wear them on chains around their necks. Naturally, I didn't do it. One day a guard at the entrance to the Old Executive Office Building asked where my pass was. I took it out of my wallet and showed it to him.

"Wear it around your neck," he ordered.

"I won't do it," I said.

He asked for my name and I gave it to him. A little later George Sanders, who was in charge of that sort of thing, came to tell me that I had to wear my pass around my neck. I told him I wouldn't. He told me he would have to report me. I didn't know who he was going to report me to—certainly not the president who wouldn't have cared less—but I told him, nicely because he is a nice man, to be my guest.

The next day at the senior staff meeting Baker announced that everyone would wear his pass around his neck.

"I won't do it," I said.

He repeated: "Everyone will wear his pass around his neck."

I repeated: "I won't do it."

"Everyone but Nofziger will wear his pass around his neck," Baker said. We then went on to try to solve the world's more pressing problems. And I never did wear my pass around my neck.

A week or so later I noticed that Ed Rollins was wearing a beeper.

"Where'd that come from?" I asked.

He laughed. "Baker wants all the senior staff to carry one but he knew you wouldn't so they gave it to me."

I never will know how many of the president's calls I missed because I didn't have a beeper. On the other hand, Rollins went on to take my job when I resigned and then he ran Reagan's reelection campaign. Afterwards he married the prettiest girl in the campaign. It's amazing what carrying a beeper can do.

Baker's biggest coup came after the 1984 reelection campaign. In his book, Deaver says the idea was Baker's. But Don Regan told me it came from Don Regan. I believe Regan because he has never lied to me and, besides, it sounds more like him.

He said he went to see Jim Baker after the 1984 election and said, "Have I got a deal for you!"

He then proposed that he and Baker switch jobs, with Baker becoming secretary of the Treasury. Baker said he'd think it over. At the time Ed Meese and Bill Clark were still in the administration. They thought as little—or less—of Baker as Baker thought of them. In any event, Baker stalled until Clark, tired of the infighting and the active enmity of Baker, Deaver, and Nancy Reagan, quit as secretary of the Interior and Meese left the White House to become attorney general. This left neither in a position to succeed Baker as chief of staff, thus clearing the road for a no fuss, no muss job switch.

Deaver wrote that when he brought the proposal to the president he agreed at once. Which is probably true. He was clearly wearying of Baker waggling his index finger and lecturing him on what he should or should not do. But mainly, who was this and who was that didn't matter that much to him. After all, Baker had run two campaigns against him;

Regan was an apolitical Wall Streeter who had contributed to Jimmy Carter; and Howard Baker, who succeeded Regan, had been instrumental in the Panama Canal give-away.

Regardless, the switch made sense in some ways. Both men wanted the challenge of new jobs and on the surface both were qualified. Baker had long wanted a top cabinet position while Regan, no shrinking violet, wanted to wield and taste some of the power and glory he thought had been Baker's.

But, as it turned out, Regan usurped more of the power and the glory than he could handle. Worse, he never understood Nancy Reagan, never figured out where she was coming from, and eventually lost his patience a couple of times and hung up the telephone on her. Not smart if you care about retaining the friendship and respect of the lady's husband. Or if you value your life.

Regan's problem was not competence; it was a lack of political judgment combined with an arrogance that made his predecessor look humble and alienated nearly everyone.

My dealings with Regan were always good. Early in his stint as chief of staff he hinted that he would like me to return to the White House. I told him I wasn't interested. Around that time, he invited his friend, Ann McLaughlin, and me to lunch. I urged him to bring in an aide who would devote his time to Nancy. It never happened. The aide—Dennis Thomas—came, but Nancy was never his, nor anybody's else's, top priority. Regan found out too late, if at all, that while one may ignore sound advice one should never ignore the First Lady.

Baker stayed at Treasury through the drift of Reagan's second term. He left to enter Bush's presidential campaign when it became clear it would take either a minor miracle or a major screw-up to keep Bush from beating the Democrat, Michael Dukakis.

As a reward for faithful service Bush's first cabinet appointment was his old friend Baker as secretary of state. It was widely assumed—at least by Baker—that in that post he would serve as Bush's deputy president. But during Bush's first term, little has been heard of Baker in other areas of government and Bush has overshadowed him in foreign affairs.

One reason for Baker's success was that Ronald Reagan was not a hands-on manager. (That last may go down as the understatement of the decade.) Some critics call it a weakness. I don't think so. Reagan didn't hire out to the people of California or to the people of America to be the government's personnel manager or to oversee its assembly lines. He hired out to advance a philosophy of government, to set policy, and to try to implement both. He hired out to make the tough decisions that affect the people, the nation, and the world. He hired out to fight for the things in which he believed and against those things he opposed. He never worried about personnel problems that did not affect what he saw as his role.

And, though sometimes it created problems for him, he trusted the people who worked for him and believed, not always correctly, that they were loyal and shared his basic principles. In a cynical business a cynic he was not, although a little cynicism in the right place at the right time could have been helpful.

People who trust others to the extent that Reagan did are optimists. Certainly Reagan was. He not only trusted those who worked for him, but he also had confidence in himself, confidence in the American people, and confidence in the future. And that, at least in part, was why he was an effective leader.

I am convinced that Reagan beat Carter so badly because he instilled confidence in the voters and Carter did not. Late in his term Carter spent a week at Camp David knuckling his brow, cracking his knuckles, and generally contemplating the demise of the American Empire and all of Western civilization. When he came back to the Potomac swamp-lands he told the American people three things: (1) America was afflicted with a national malaise; (2) life and government had gotten so complicated that the presidency had probably become too big for any one man; (3) the nation's problems were so big and complicated they probably couldn't be solved.

Today I wonder why, in the 1980 campaign, we didn't make much of this. Maybe it wasn't necessary. Voters can sense fear and pessimism and defeat, and they react. This is especially true when the alternative candidate exudes optimism and boldness and a winning spirit, as Franklin Roosevelt did in the 1930s and 1940s and Reagan did throughout most of the 1980s. Reagan knew instinctively that he could handle the presidency, just as he had handled the presidency of the Screen Actors Guild and the governorship of California. And he had tremendous confidence in the people's ability to meet any challenge, solve any problem.

In speech after speech he talked about America as "a shining city on a hill" and he told audience after audience that he believed America had been placed by God between the two oceans for a special purpose—to be a beacon of freedom to all the world. He believed these things and his beliefs were contagious. In the campaign of 1980, and even in the losing campaign of 1976, the Reagan troops marched into political battle expecting victory because their leader expected victory, and that spirit bred a feeling of uncertainty not only among Carter's people but also among Ford's.

It was that spirit—the Reagan spirit—that sparked both the White House and the nation in Reagan's first term. In spite of themselves many non-Reaganites who came into the administration found themselves supporting the president as strongly as those who had worked for him for years. They may not have always thought he was right, but then, neither did I. But the sneering, obvious in the first days, largely vanished. There were some, of course, such as Stockman, Darman, and Baker, who remained contemptuous, but they worked to hide their feelings.

What never did vanish, however, were the leaks that weakened and divided the White House—that often made Baker look good at the expense of Reagan or Meese or other old Reagan hands. One day I urged Reagan to do something about it.

"I would," he said, "if I knew who was doing it."

"I can tell you," I said, and ticked off Baker, Darman, David Gergen, Rich Williamson. As usual, Reagan shied away from problems involving staff.

I didn't name Deaver because I had never thought of him as a leaker. Later, I was not so certain. He ate lunch frequently, I learned, with the *Washington Post*'s Lou Cannon and became cozy with Larry Barrett of *Time* and Bill Plante of CBS, not exactly Reagan admirers.

Meese, almost as trusting as Reagan, had a difficult time believing that anyone would deliberately do a hatchet job on him. As a result, he was a sitting duck. It would have been fun if he'd ever said, "Let's go get even with those SOBs," but he never did.

I suppose optimism requires a certain kind of courage or maybe courage requires optimism. Whichever, Reagan showed both to extraordinary degrees on the day young John Hinkley shot him and three others. That day will live in my memory for reasons beyond those for which it lives in the memories of other Americans.

Even now I meet people who want to talk about my role that day as a spokesman for the wounded president. Many tell me my coolness and calmness in briefing the press held the nation together during those hours of national stress. That, of course, is not so, but I must admit it boosts my ego every time someone says something like that, even though outwardly I tend to shuffle my feet and shrug modestly.

The fact is, I didn't know I was supposed to be holding the nation together, or even that such a thing was needed. Neither did I feel that the president was dying. Actually, all the accolades should go to three people: Ronald Reagan, Alexander Haig, and an unidentified reporter.

Haig, a good man, an able man, and a guy you would want on your side in a fight, sought in his own way to calm the nation. And failed. Famously. From the podium in the White House pressroom, shortly after word came that the president had been shot, he told the nation that, as secretary of state, "I'm in charge here."

Unfortunately, he was wrong, and not only did the reporters know it but so also did half the viewing public. That blunder, which will haunt him all his life, left the press looking for someone else as a spokesman. I fell into that role.

It started out as a normal enough day and continued until I came back from a long lunch with a group of businessmen. I had just walked into my office when Joe Holmes, who had worked for me in the campaign, came in.

"Somebody took a shot at the president," he said. "I don't think he was hit but a couple of Secret Service agents may have been."

I leaped gracefully for the television set, a perk which every White House office has, and turned on Channel 7 (ABC) where Frank Reynolds was trying desperately and futilely to find out what was going on. After a moment he said it appeared as if Jim Brady, the president's press secretary, was one of those shot.

"I think," I said to no one in particular, "that I'd better go see if I can help."

When I walked into Baker's office Meese was there as were Karna

Small and Larry Speakes, the deputy press secretaries. Deaver, who was with the president when the shooting occurred, was at George Washington University Hospital, where Reagan and Jim Brady had been taken. He had phoned to say that the president had been shot. I told Baker that I was there to help if needed.

I still look back in amazement at how calm the people in the room were. No panic, no confusion, no tears or wringing of hands. Meese suggested that he and I go to the hospital. Baker said he and Speakes would also go. Baker's White House car was outside. I quickly got in front with the driver, leaving Baker, Meese, and Speakes to crowd into the back. Even in that time of stress I remembered where the comfort zone was.

By the time we arrived at the hospital the entrance had been blocked off to keep out the reporters and the curious. Baker decided immediately that I should handle the press at the hospital while Speakes returned to the White House to deal with reporters there. I told those standing at the barricade that as soon as we knew something I would come out and brief them.

Inside, the president had not yet been taken to the operating room, but shortly they wheeled him by on a gurney. He was conscious, aware of his surroundings, and recognized us as he went by. After he passed, Baker was ecstatic.

"He winked at me," he said, and repeated, "He winked at me."

I guessed that no one had ever winked at him before.

By this time, the president's good buddy, Senator Laxalt, had arrived and had spent a moment with him. Along with Meese, Baker, and me he had watched as Reagan was wheeled by. He reported that the president had told him, "Don't worry about me. I'll make it."

Good news for all of us.

I scrounged some blank forms from a nurses' station and began making notes and writing down the president's quips. When I later reported them to the press, the nation knew that everything would be all right.

I went outside and told the reporters that Reagan had been taken to the operating room, that he was conscious and had walked into the hospital under his own power.

Realizing that I would need a place in which to brief the reporters who were arriving on the scene, I buttonholed the hospital administrator who quickly found me an auditorium, about a block away, where a podium and microphone were already set up. I called the telephone company man assigned to the White House and relayed the urgent need for press phones at the auditorium. He had them connected in record time, for which he deserves a medal. I then asked the helpful hospital administrator if he could send along someone who could brief the press on the president's wound, operation, and condition.

I ruled out the president's personal physician, who ordinarily would have been excellent, because the press might think he was trying to minimize the severity of the president's condition. Neither did I want an operating surgeon because I thought they would be tired and emotionally involved. And I sure as hell was not competent, even if briefed, to do more than scratch the surface, and the wound was too deep for that.

I was told that a doctor on the staff, Dennis O'Leary, dean for clinical affairs, had had experience dealing with the press. He was young, personable, and articulate in a low-key way. I told him what I was going to need: an absolutely honest briefing in layman's terms. And I warned him to "be prepared to answer every stupid question those guys can dream up. There'll be a lot of them."

I held two briefings in the auditorium. Before the first one Meese, Laxalt, Baker, and I wandered into the hospital chapel. Baker, an Episcopalian, dropped to his knees to pray, as did Laxalt, a devout Catholic. Meese and I remained standing, but I think we all prayed. Truly, it was a time for prayer, for the president, for Brady and the other wounded, and for the nation.

Shortly thereafter Meese and Baker returned to the White House. There was nothing they could do at the hospital and the president was in no shape to give Baker another wink.

I didn't need O'Leary for the first briefing—the president was still in the operating room, as was Brady—and I only remember two questions.

One was, "What is the position of the vice president?"

"He remains the vice president," I replied, refraining from asking if there were any more stupid questions.

I had ended the briefing and was turning away when the angel the Lord had planted in the crowd called out, "Has the president said anything?"

"Oops," I said to myself, turning back to the podium. And out loud, "I almost forgot. Yes, he did."

I fished out the pieces of paper on which I had written the president's remark to Laxalt and his quips:

His way of assuring Nancy, "Honey, I forgot to duck."

His question to Meese and Baker on his way to surgery, "Who's minding the store?"

His plea to the doctors in surgery, "Please tell me you're Republicans."

These lines assured the nation that the president was going to be all right. They also said that here was a most unusual man, what Americans like to think they're all about, a swashbuckling people who laugh in the face of death and don't shrink from the teeth of danger. That day he fit well Rudyard Kipling's description of the American: "He greets the embarrassed Gods, nor fears/ To shake the iron hand of fate or match with destiny for beers."

Here was a man who for years had talked the good fight to all Americans, but none of them knew how he would react to the blows— until now—and now his courage made all but the most bitter Reagan haters proud to be Americans.

I wonder sometimes how the nation would have reacted if that reporter hadn't hollered at me and I hadn't read those lines. But in my heart I know. We're a tough people. We would have accepted the facts, demanded that the assassin be hanged, drawn, and quartered, and gone about our business. But I did make it a little easier on us.

At the second briefing I brought Dr. O'Leary along. And he was superb. He answered every stupid question as well as the relevant ones and he did it with grace and aplomb, maybe even two plombs. He was so good he became an instant celebrity for all of two weeks, a long time in TV America.

The briefings allowed me to correct some of the careless reporting that had gone out over the air as the urge to be first in some reporters overcame the vital need at this moment to be careful and correct. One early report had Brady dead, another had the president undergoing open heart surgery. They were not moments that the electronic reporting profession should remember with pride.

While the media and the briefings were concentrating on the president, Jim Brady was in the operating room fighting for his life. And Nancy Reagan was at the hospital worrying about her husband and comforting Jim's wife, Sarah. Nancy Reagan did herself proud that day. She was in firm control. If anyone ever wanted to make a movie of a courageous president lying gravely wounded, with his wife standing bravely by, Ronald and Nancy Reagan could play the lead roles. If Americans want examples of toughness and a certain gallantry in their women in times of terror and pressure they need look no further than Jackie Kennedy in Dallas and Nancy Reagan in Washington.

The president came out of the operating room at 5:45 P.M. The doctors had found the bullet, or at least a piece of it, in his left lung, which had collapsed. There had been a lot of bleeding and they had given him two liters of blood.

The doctors said he would need pain medication after he awoke and therefore he should not make any major decisions for two or three days; it would be nine or ten days before he could return to the White House. O'Leary passed all of this along to the press.

My notes—one of the few times in my political career I took and kept notes—tell me Vice President Bush, returning from Texas, landed at Andrews Air Force Base at 6:30 P.M. In the meantime, those at the White House had decided not to turn the reins of authority over to him, largely because Meese, Baker, and the others wanted to minimize the seriousness of the president's wound. To emphasize that he was still in charge they took a minor bill to him the next day to sign into law. Good thinking.

By thwarting the assassin's bullet and refusing for the next seven years and ten months to fall prey to mortal illness or accident the nation's oldest president laid to rest the superstition that presidents elected in years ending in zero are doomed to die in office. How come the libs never credit Reagan for that? Maybe because that's one superstition they'd hoped to see prolonged.

At 8:15 that evening Jim Brady came out of the operating room. His neurosurgeon, Dr. Arthur Kobrine, came into the little room where O'Leary and I and one or two others from the hospital staff were waiting. He was elated. Brady not only was alive, but he also had a chance to recover. When he had begun the operation, Kobrine said, he had been pessimistic. The x-rays had left him with almost no hope that

Brady would live and if he did Kobrine was sure he would be a vegetable.

But once he got inside the skull he found the wound, while terrible, was not as bad as indicated. The bullet, to all intents and purposes, had amputated the brain's right frontal lobe. There was a long shot possibility, he said, that Brady would be all right except for weakness in his left side. One point he made left room for optimism. In these cases, he said, if a patient continues to improve, no matter how slowly, there is no telling how far he will eventually return toward normalcy. But if the patient ever stops improving, he will not begin again. Almost exactly eight years later Kobrine and I ran into each other at Georgetown University Hospital. I had one question for him.

"Is Jim Brady still improving?"

"Yes," he said, "he still continues to improve."

By the time Brady came out of the operating room, the press had gone home or back to the White House and I had closed up the auditorium. I returned to the West Wing and sought out Baker to report on Brady and then to brief what press remained. Baker was reluctant for me to proceed, but agreed after telling me not to go on television. The next day, he added, Speakes would take over the briefings. After my briefing on Brady, I drove home.

Bonnie was there with Pat Connally, one of her dearest friends. I saw that she had been crying.

"What the hell have you been crying for?" I demanded with unforgiveable rudeness. "Nobody shot at me."

"I was thinking of all the times you were standing where Jim Brady was standing," she replied shakily.

I was instantly and truly contrite. "I never thought of that," I admitted.

Reagan is a great raconteur and after he recovered he liked to tell the story of the shooting. The bullet, he explained, ricocheted and came through a crack between the body of the car and the car door on the hinged side. It hit him in the side under his left arm just as Secret Service Agent Jerry Parr was shoving him onto the floor of the car and falling on top of him to protect him. As the car sped off, the two men crawled back onto the seat where almost immediately Reagan began coughing blood.

"Damn you," he said to Parr, "you broke one of my ribs when you jumped on me and it's punctured my lung."

Parr immediately ordered the driver, who was headed for the White House, to drive to George Washington Hospital. On the way he slid his hand under the president's coat and ran it over his back, feeling for blood, looking for a wound. There was none because the wound was hidden and wasn't bleeding much.

It wasn't until Reagan was inside the hospital and attendants had cut off his suit and his shirt that they found the wound. In the process they ruined Reagan's suit, for which the president, not known as a spend-thrift, never forgave them. He complained that it was new, which means it was probably under ten years old.

The finale to my part of the assassination story came a short time later. In the early 1980s, after Richard Nixon had moved from San Clemente to New York, he held a series of small dinners in his small dining room, seating eight. It was one way he had of keeping abreast of news, opinion, and high-level gossip. In return for an evening of some-times scintillating conversation Nixon provided an excellent meal pre-pared by his excellent Chinese chef and led and directed the conversation.

Two weeks after Reagan had been shot I was invited to one of the dinners. I was flattered. I still am. I went. Some important people would be there and some smart ones, too, which isn't always the same thing. I was invited, I knew, because of my role in the aftermath of the shooting. I had been on television as the White House spokesman on the scene and the *Wall Street Journal* and President Nixon, among others, had said some kind things about the way I had handled the job. In addition, I was one of the persons Nixon relied on to keep him informed about Reagan's condition.

I flew to New York, checked into a hotel, and cabbed to the Nixon townhouse. Nixon's son-in-law, Ed Cox, met me at the door and Mr. Nixon quickly came to greet me. Before taking me into the other guests he said quietly, "Stay around after the others have left. I'd like to talk with you."

Dinner was delicious and while I don't remember what it was I'm sure it wasn't chop suey. The multitopic conversation was also interesting but all I remember is that Mr. Nixon had good words to say about the way I had handled the shooting which embarrassed me a little and pleased me a lot.

After the other guests had departed, as per Mr. Nixon's request, I stayed. He smoked his pipe, I smoked my cigar, and we talked for about half an hour about a variety of things, but not foreign affairs. To Richard Nixon I am a politician, not a Henry Kissinger. Who knows what I might have done in Kissinger's place? Or he in mine? The thought is awesome to contemplate.

I remember one bit of that conversation and I have related it over and over because it symbolizes something and someday I will figure out what. The story has poignancy and also a bit of sound advice. We were talking about the assassination attempt and the president's recovery.

"Don't let him make any major decisions until he is entirely well," Mr. Nixon advised. "You don't make good decisions when you're sick. I was recovering from pneumonia when I made the decision not to burn the tapes."

I refer anyone who doesn't know what Nixon was talking about to the public library under "Watergate."

But Mr. Nixon needn't have worried. Nobody tried to push the president to resume a full schedule before he was ready, and if anyone had two people would have stopped him. Reagan himself is no martyr. Nor has he ever felt he had to prove something by working harder than he wanted to. But in this case, even if he had, Nancy would have stood in the way. Adamantly, as she always did whenever staff tried to overwork her husband. Nancy—and I say this with due respect—is a tough lady.

Nancy's courage in the face of the attempt on her husband's life was not surprising. Anyone who has observed her during her husband's years in politics—and after—knows that. From 1965–89 Nancy Reagan was like a lot of political wives, only more so, as Don Regan was to find out. That is, if you screwed up and in the process embarrassed her husband, or hurt him politically, or in any other way, or if she thought that you had, she got mad—at you. In fairness, it is hard to blame her. In equal fairness, her anger was sometimes misdirected, and her unforgivingness was sometimes more than was called for.

When you got on Nancy's special list life could become somewhat less pleasant. I know; I have been there. In fact, some in the all-knowing news media insist I never got out of there. Each time I quit working for Ronald Reagan, which I think was four times, those pundits who would have you, innocent reader, believe they have access to inside information wrote that Nancy had had me fired.

Some wrote that she blocked my appointment as press secretary after the 1980 elections. All of this is nonsense. I did not, as I have said, want to be the president's press secretary and so told Deaver, Meese, and Reagan. If this coincided with Nancy's wish, which it might well have, then we both lucked out. But no story has ever quoted her as saying she didn't want me to have the job, or that she didn't like the way I dressed, another of the alleged complaints she had against me.

Someday I'll figure out why they think I kept coming back, or why Reagan kept rehiring me, or why Nancy let him.

One thing about Nancy, you can tell when she's angry with you. You either get hollered at or get the silent treatment. To the best of my recollection Nancy was really angry with me only four times, including when she tried to get me fired in 1967–68, which was the second time.

The first was during the 1966 campaign. I noticed she hadn't been speaking to me for a few days and I didn't know why. So I asked the candidate, "Is Nancy mad at me?" "Well," he said, "she didn't like the remark you made about her perfume. You hurt her feelings."

Oops! The lady had been wearing a gardenia perfume, which I can't stand and I'd—kiddingly, I thought—made a remark about dime store perfume. I never made that mistake again.

I was truly contrite. "I'll apologize," I said. "I sure didn't mean to hurt her feelings."

"She'll be all right," he assured me. And she was.

The third time was during the 1980 campaign. I had let network television cover the candidate as he was making a television commercial on what the Carter inflation had done to the price of groceries. Nancy thought I shouldn't have and maybe she was right, although it didn't have any effect one way or another on the outcome. Anyway, when I boarded the campaign plane she lit into me in front of half the staff. One thing you learn: there is no sense getting into an argument with Nancy Reagan. You can't win. So I listened her out and walked on to my seat, angry but smart enough to keep still. Eventually she realized she'd been out of line but, rather than apologize personally, she sent Deaver to tell me she was sorry.

The fourth time was in August of 1991 when I wrote a column in the *Washington Post* criticizing the Reagans for the way they had treated three old Reagan hands, Ed Meese, Bill Clark, and Martin Anderson. She was not happy, but then, neither was he. Nor I. In a less than cordial telephone conversation he assured me that Nancy had not been involved in their rude removal from the board of the Reagan Library although many persons, including the three men, thought otherwise. And it would not be surprising if she had, especially with respect to Meese and Clark. Although she wept when Clark resigned as executive secretary to Governor Reagan, she later formed an intense dislike for him, as she made plain in her book, *My Turn*. She was more kind to Meese, but still highly critical, and voiced no opinion of Anderson.

Almost certainly, it was Deaver who attempted to poison the Reagans' minds against Clark and Meese. At various times he tried to persuade Reagan to fire both men on the incredibly spurious grounds that they were hurting his presidency. He enrolled Nancy in his efforts, but failed to persuade Clark to help him get Meese. Although neither was fired, Deaver and Nancy made life so unpleasant for Clark that he went off to be secretary of the Interior for a year.

The disaster of that move can be seen in Clark's successors as National Security advisers, a couple of very decent men named Bud McFarlane and John Poindexter, neither of whom really understood Reagan; hence, with all good intentions, they took him down the primrose path that led to the quagmire of Iran.

Jeane Kirkpatrick, then ambassador to the United Nations, was almost everyone's first choice to succeed Clark, but Secretary of State George Shultz kicked up such a fuss that Reagan decided not to appoint her. Even then McFarlane almost didn't get the job, thanks to last-minute maneuvering by Deaver and Baker. One day, while Clark, Meese, Cap Weinberger, and Bill Casey were hasseling over the choices, Deaver and Baker sneaked in to see the president. They had a great—for them personally—idea. They proposed that Reagan name Baker head of the National Security Council and Deaver chief of staff.

Reagan bought the idea. He wanted to reward his old friend and aide, Deaver, and he had begun to tire of Baker's never very subtle attempts to use him to build his own persona.

Why Baker wanted the job is hard to figure unless he saw it as a stepping-stone to the job he really wanted, secretary of state. To get that post he and Deaver, with Nancy's possible cooperation, would have had to muscle Shultz out, a feasible maneuver given Baker's great ability to con the news media and Deaver's equal ability to con the Reagans. Although Clark had recommended that Reagan name Schultz as secretary of state, Deaver brought him into Ron and Nancy Reagan's inner circle. Deaver might therefore also ease him out.

Why Deaver wanted to be chief of staff is easier to understand. On a number of occasions, recognizing his limits, he had said that he thought of himself as a good No. 2 man but lacked what it took to be a No. 1. He was right. But the power and the glory and the social prestige he had garnered as the White House aide closest to the first couple had clouded his vision and done wonders for his ego. By stepping into Baker's shoes, when he finally left the White House he would be even more famous and make even more money than he could leaving as Baker's deputy.

In any event, Reagan agreed and went to the NSC's situation room where Clark, Meese, and the others were meeting. His announcement brought near rebellion.

Casey set the tone, declaring, "You can't make the biggest leaker in Washington the head of the National Security Council", a comment well worth repeating. Weinberger threatened to resign, while Clark said he would withdraw his resignation. Reagan got the message and went back to the Oval Office where the two conspirators were waiting. When Reagan gave them the bad news Deaver reportedly threw a tantrum, accusing Reagan of being weak and disloyal. Baker took the news calmly and bided his time, which came when he and Treasury Secretary Don Regan cut their own deal to switch jobs. And this time no one was around to warn Reagan that it was the lousy idea it turned out to be.

I blame Deaver and Baker for the Iran disaster even though neither, so far as I know, had a part in it. But I'm confident that if they had not made life intolerable at the White House for Meese and Clark, they both would have stayed. Had they done so they would have convinced the president, if indeed they had ever let it get that far, that arms to Iran in return for hostages not only didn't make good sense but was in direct contradiction to what the president stood for.

I agree with Nancy that had even Baker and Deaver stayed at the White House they would have blocked it. Deaver's instincts would have told him this was something the president couldn't live with, and Baker's would have told him it was something he couldn't live with.

I'm willing to bet that Ronald Reagan was never given all the cons of the proposal, only the pros. Repeating Bill Clark, Reagan makes good decisions when he has all the facts and options; in this case I don't think he had them. And I don't think Nancy did, either. She has a unique sixth sense when trouble threatens her husband, but this time there were no scents at all.

Nancy Davis, the actress who became Nancy Davis Reagan, the first lady of California and the United States, never made it to the top as an actress. But when she latched onto Ronald Reagan, her career became Ronald Reagan, and if any one person besides Reagan is responsible for the success of his political career it is Nancy.

Like her husband, she could always act. In fact they still can and still do. When Reagan throws his glasses in the heat of a political argument, it's an act. When Nancy is nice to someone she dislikes, it's an act and a very good one.

The first time I saw Nancy act, and knew she was acting, I was impressed. I'm still impressed. During Reagan's first gubernatorial campaign, *Look* magazine, now defunct, but then still very much funct, sent a photographer named Stanley Trettick to California to do a layout on the Reagans. It was summertime and they were staying in a borrowed beach house up the coast from Malibu.

Trettick and I drove up so he could take pictures of the Reagans at play, or at least relaxing. When we arrived they were out on the beach. Trettick said he wanted pictures of them together. He got some beauties. Without hesitation Nancy began throwing every pose she'd learned at the studios. Trettick clicked away like mad; he never had to set up a single picture. Driving back to Los Angeles he raved about what "a natural" she was, how she instinctively knew what to do. I agreed. One should never destroy a young man's illusions.

Nancy wrote a book after leaving the White House, or rather a man named Bill Novak wrote it for her. But the thoughts were hers, as well as the experiences and the treatment of individuals. I found four mentions of me. Two were in passing. But it seemed to me that in the other two Nancy went out of her way to treat me with kindness and even some affection, which today she probably regrets.

While the book was being written Novak called to ask how I got along with Nancy. I said I thought I got along with her fine. "We don't have any problems that I know of," I said. "What did Nancy say?"

"She said the same thing," Novak replied. "I just wanted to be certain you both felt the same way."

But a certain amount of frustration and unhappiness comes through the pages in Nancy's book. I wonder if one of the reasons is that by early in Reagan's second term the people who had been around Reagan from the beginning—Meese, Clark, Deaver, Nofziger—were gone, as were other key loyalists such as Richard Allen and Martin Anderson. No one was left who knew the president to whom Nancy could turn. And when she turned to Don Regan, he, not understanding her, would have none of her. Thus Reagan was left with advisers who shared none of his background and Nancy was left with no one who could effectively add his voice to hers, or keep her on track as she sought to guide the president.

She did, of course, have her astrologer, but most of us had never been aware of her. A lot of us knew that the president was intrigued with astrology, but he always denied that he did anything more than read the astrological forecasts in the daily paper. During the years I worked directly for him I never saw any sign of a decision based on the soothsayery of some star gazer or chart writer.

Much, but not all, of the bitterness in Nancy's book is understandable, but none should have been aimed at Meese, Clark, and Deaver, all of whom also loved her husband. Meese and Clark, in particular, served her husband as governor and president well and faithfully. Deaver for a number of years was indispensable to the Reagans on a personal basis; it was only when he was given more power and authority than he knew how to handle that his advice became counterproductive.

Deaver's book and the Reagan's reluctance to contact him during his legal troubles created a rift that lasted until 1991. Deaver had a miserable few years which he blamed largely on an alleged case of alcoholism. He had been convicted of three counts of perjury, to which he claimed innocence but did not bother to appeal, and lost most of his business. Old-time Reaganites who might have come to his aid had long since been alienated by his arrogance bordering on disdain and, in many cases, by his refusal to have anything to do with them. Besides, if one were a friend of Clark or Meese, it was not easy to like or respect him. For my part, I didn't try. Still, Deaver needed both friends and business, and the Reagans helped. A contract to handle the dedication of the Reagan presidential library was a good start.

But that same library dedication, despite all its important participants and fancy opening hoopla, seemed to me to be not a beginning but an end—an end to the Reagan era.

The great political adventure that began with Reagan's speech for Barry Goldwater in 1964 and reached its peak with Reagan's election as president in 1980 is now consigned to the archives and the history books. Reagan's handpicked successor, George Bush, has dashed whatever hopes many of us had that he would carry on the Reagan legacy. He has proved that eight years of personal loyalty are not enough, that no man, including George Bush, can carry out another man's dream if he doesn't share it.

And the men who did share it—Meese, Clark, Anderson, John Herrington, and others of us—leaderless and in many ways abandoned, have gone on to other things. The Reagan revolution has ended where it began, with the pragmatists and mercenaries in full control. Meanwhile, back at the ranch, as the sun sets over the Pacific, it is plain that Ronald Reagan doesn't know it, doesn't believe it, or no longer cares.

10

Insider on the Outside

THE YEAR 1982 was an especially busy and hectic one, but I never dreamed that my activities then would, nearly five years later, have a disastrous effect on a solid chunk of the rest of my life. I couldn't know that a tiny part of what I did in all innocence—or ignorance—that year and, to a minor extent, in 1981, would in 1986–88 come close to sending me to prison. Or that it would also destroy our business and cost my partner, Mark Bragg, and me nearly $2 million in legal fees, and our partnership.

On January 1, 1982, that dire possibility was the last thing on my mind. Instead, I was counting the days until January 22 when I would leave the White House and return to the real world.

When I had entered the Reagan White House I had agreed to stay for just one year, after which Bonnie and I would return to California, but as the weeks and months passed it became clearer and clearer that the best opportunities to make money lay in Washington. At the risk of sounding greedy, money had suddenly become important to me. For here I was, fifty-seven years old, and suddenly it dawned on me that I had relatively few years left to provide for Bonnie in case something happened to me—the girls had long since flown the coop—or for the two of us in case it didn't.

One thing in life is true: ain't nobody else going to assume your responsibilities for you. It doesn't take a genius to know that nobody lives well on Social Security. I didn't want Bonnie to have to try. During 1981 several opportunities opened up: old friends Paul Wagner and Roy Pfautch suggested I join their companies; and the publisher of the *Los Angeles Times*, Tom Johnson, suggested I might write a column for their syndicate, while Neil Freeman, who had his own syndicate, made a similar proposal. But I had met Mark Bragg and I liked him. After some thought I agreed to his proposal that we go into business together.

During my last month at the White House he arranged for the Washington Speakers Bureau, run by Harry Rhodes and Bernie Swain, to line up speeches for me as soon as I had left the White House. He also hired a law firm to keep us legal and look after our interests, found an accountant, Dave Williams, an office manager, Beth Johnson, and office space. We decided to hire as my secretary Nancy Guiden, who worked for me in the White House.

I didn't pay much attention to White House business in January, aside from cleaning up odds and ends, writing my resignation letter, not the first one I had written to Ronald Reagan, and bidding goodbye to friends. On January 21, at the invitation of Larry Speakes, the acting press secretary in place of Jim Brady, I held my first press briefing since the day John Hinkley shot the president. A nonserious event, I punned and wise-cracked my way through it, and as I left the reporters tossed jelly beans after me. It was a delightful and touching send-off from people I knew and generally liked.

The next afternoon—Friday—we threw a goodbye party in my office suite. Most goodbye parties for Reagan senior staffers were held in the Roosevelt Room in the West Wing and were pretty staid affairs— hors d'oeuvres, punch, and a little wine. Our party was a bash. Booze was served. People from in and out of the White House and government came. Reagan dropped in uninvited. At the end, as Bonnie and I left to go to another party being thrown in our honor by our old friend Ron Crawford, we were followed down the hall by friends shouting out best wishes.

Early Saturday Bonnie and I flew to Phoenix for a speech and a short vacation. From there we went to San Antonio for another speech. A member of the audience told me afterwards that I had the makings of another Will Rogers. But I knew better. Will Rogers made that inane remark that he never met a man he didn't like, while I have never had that problem, as some may have noticed.

While I was gone, Mark furnished our new offices. I had specified only that I wanted a couch long enough to nap on and a rolltop desk.

We had decided that I would do an interview with "Sixty Minutes." Ten days after leaving the White House I walked into the offices of Nofziger and Bragg for the first time, followed by a CBS camera crew. Waiting for me was Morley Safer who did the interview. He was surprisingly gentle, for which I've always been appreciative. I don't know if it helped our business; I do know it never hurt it.

That was the beginning of a year that is largely a blur in my memory. The Washington Speakers Bureau kept me busy; along with the paid speeches were the political speeches, for which I never charged. That year I had well over fifty speeches and out-of-town appearances, including one sprint of ten in a two-week period. I survived largely by remembering a Reagan axiom: It is easier to change audiences than to change speeches.

One of the first things Mark wanted after we opened our doors was for us to have life insurance on each other. I wasn't worried about him dying, but he was worried about me, I guess because I was fat, fifty-seven, and his meal ticket. His worry was justified when the doctor found I had high blood pressure, for which he prescribed diet and exercise, to no avail.

On May 4 I suffered a stroke. I woke up at about 3 A.M. feeling dizzy. This puzzled me. Dizzy AND sober? I sat up, turned on the bedside light, and tried to shake it off. It refused to shake. I got up and tried to walk. Halfway across the bedroom the dizziness forced me to stop. At this point Bonnie did something unusual; she awoke.

"What's wrong?" she demanded.

"Nothing," I assured her. "Go back to sleep."

"Something's wrong," she insisted, alarm in her voice.

"It's all right. I'm just a little bit dizzy," I said, walking carefully back to the bed.

The next thing I knew she had called the emergency squad and in less than ten minutes they were there, taking blood pressure, counting pulse, and doing other odds and ends. Deciding something was wrong, they loaded me onto a stretcher, stuck me in the ambulance, and took me to Northern Virginia Doctors Hospital, with Bonnie following in her car.

In a few moments a young doctor was examining me and someone thoughtfully brought me a bucket into which up I could throw. George Bush should be so lucky. The doctor explained that the dizziness was making me nauseous. I knew something was. Eventually someone decided I should have a thing called a CAT scan. By this time I was so sleepy I didn't care what animal they wanted to use. I barely recall being bundled onto a gurney for the trip to the CAT scan machine, and once there, I slept through the scanning.

Morning came, or rather daylight, and I awakened to discover that Bonnie had summoned her doctor, Dr. Arthur Rubin, who was also my daughter Susie's doctor, and who quickly became, and still is, my doctor. I also discovered that I was having trouble using my right arm and right leg and that my speech, despite my sobriety, had a drunken slur to it.

Dr. Rubin told me I had had a stroke, which everyone else had surmised a few hours earlier and which seemed logical to me. Over the next few days he brought in another doctor to check my reflexes and coordination. And one day they took me down and hooked me up to a machine that ran a dye through my veins to see where, if anywhere, I had a blockage. I didn't have one. Not anywhere.

Most of this time they had me hooked up to a mobile contraption that dripped fluid into my veins and which I wheeled along beside me on my walks up and down the hospital corridors. After a couple of days a pretty young lady came to give me physical therapy. And Bonnie let me have a phone again. The president had called earlier but she wouldn't let me talk to him, or vice versa.

My friends, John and Lois Herrington, sent over a large, stuffed gorilla which scared the hell out of a couple of nurses who came in at night without turning on the light. And Lou MacIntosh, who had played the bagpipes at Susie's wedding, and would again at her funeral, came by and stood outside my window and skirled for a while. It was all right—being nearly tone deaf I love bagpipe music. After eight days I went home and by May 16 I was back in the office part-time.

Effects of the stroke lingered. My speech had cleared up on the second day and I seemed to get my basic coordination back within a week, but for some time my right foot would drag on occasion and for more than two years I could not carry a cup of coffee in my right hand without sloshing it.

The weekend after I came home from the hospital we moved. By month's end I was in California consulting with a client. The following week Mark and Pegge Gertzen, his fiancée, flew to Seattle to be married. While Mark was gone a letter I didn't write and don't remember seeing, but signed "Lyn," was sent to the White House. Four years later it was to rise up and bite me.

To repeat, I remember little of that year. I was on the road much of the time. Bonnie and I were house hunting and moving. Clients and potential clients were in and out of our offices. The stroke intruded. I only vaguely remember talking to our lawyers about what was legal or illegal. And we traveled to Japan.

In July the Braggs and the Nofzigers went to Japan at the invitation of the ruling political party, the Liberal Democrats, who aren't. The invitation had been arranged by Hiroshi Hitotsuyanagi, a high official of Nippon Electric Co., the only foreign client Mark and I ever took. We helped them sell fingerprint computers, one of which eventually figured in the arrest of Los Angeles' "Hillside Strangler." HH, as we called him, was a buddy of all the big shots in the Japanese government and in the party.

The party paid me $40,000 plus expenses for the four of us. It wasn't two million bucks, but then I wasn't an ex-president; I merely knew the president. For reasons only the Japanese know, they paid in American cash. I hope they didn't make Reagan tote $2 million in bills back with him. For those who might wonder, we declared the money, as the law requires.

In one meeting a Japanese legislator noted with a chuckle that the United States had become a colony of Japan. I had to agree. Economically, a colony provides the raw materials to the mother country which in turn exports manufactured goods to the colony. That pretty well describes relations between our two countries.

When we arrived in Japan we were whisked through customs, tucked in a limousine, and given a police escort to Tokyo's Okura Hotel, one of the town's fanciest. It was enough to make a fellow feel important. Our hosts had arranged audiences for me with the prime minister and several cabinet officers. The American ambassador, Mike Mansfield, an ancient but well-loved Democrat Reagan had left in the post because he had the strange and mistaken impression it might help him with other Democrats, gave a small reception for us.

We spent a week in Japan, including a day in Kyoto (Did you ever notice that Kyoto is an anagram of Tokyo? Do the Japanese know it? Does anyone care?), flew off to Hong Kong for a couple of days, and then back to the States, where shortly, and unexpectedly, I found myself back in the White House.

In August, much to the dismay of a lot of conservatives including myself, the president let himself be conned into supporting TEFRA. In short order, a group of conservatives, including Rep. Jack Kemp, one of the fathers of supply-side economics, met to plan opposition to the bill. Among those attending were two former senior White House staffers, Dr. Martin Anderson, the president's former domestic affairs adviser, and I.

The meeting made the morning papers. Within hours, Marty and I had calls from Deaver asking us to meet with the president. When we arrived the troika, Deaver, Meese, and Baker, was also there.

The first thing Reagan said, putting on his angry act, was, "You might at least have told me what you were going to do."

Marty and I allowed as how that was so, but explained that we didn't think he was really serious about supporting the measure. As Reagan began to explain his reasons Baker interrupted.

"Why don't you ask Lyn to come down and help us pass the bill?" he suggested to the president. Reagan seemed dumbfounded. I know I was.

But Baker persisted, and finally the president asked, "Would you?"

"Let me think about it," I said. "I'll let Jim know this afternoon."

I left, knowing that I had been sandbagged by Baker but knowing, too, that I could not turn the president down. It wasn't that he was the president, although that surely was part of it. The overriding reason was that I had a sense of loyalty toward him that came from having worked for him officially and unofficially for fifteen years, most of that time hoping against hope that I could help make him president. And now that he was president and said he needed me, how could I say no, even though what he wanted went against both his principles and mine. I couldn't. I stalled as a matter of pride and of pseudo-independence, and because I needed time to figure out how I would explain my flip-flop to my friends and to the reporters who were sure to make much of it.

Early that afternoon I called Baker and said I wanted to see him. We agreed on a time and I asked Mark to drive me to the White House. At the Southwest Gate we were met by a guard I didn't know. To facilitate my entry I did a dumb thing, I showed him my White House pass that I had kept when I resigned. He took it, asked us to wait, and returned to the guard house. It was five minutes before he came back.

"Your appointment with Mr. Baker is confirmed," he said. "But I'm going to have to keep your pass."

"Let's go back to the office," I said to Mark.

The guard was surprised. One doesn't normally walk away from appointments with the self-important people at the White House.

"Your appointment is confirmed. Mr. Baker is expecting you," he repeated.

"Tell him to stick it," I said. "Let's go, Mark."

"They don't want me very bad if they're going to confiscate my pass," I said between cuss words as we drove off. But pretty soon I began to chuckle. I wondered what Baker would do now.

When we arrived at the office the first thing Nancy Guiden said was, "The White House has been calling."

"If they call again tell them I've gone for the day," I said.

I went into our conference room where an autographed picture of Baker was hanging. You hang those things to impress clients. No other reason. I took it down, dropped it on the floor, and stomped on it, then I headed for home.

When I arrived Bonnie said, "The White House has been calling."

"If they call again tell them I'm not home," I said.

The White House operator did call again, about every ten minutes until we took the phone off the hook. When I arrived at the office the next morning the calls had already begun.

"Tell them I won't be in today," I said.

It was a slow, typical August day in Washington, and by noon I was considering going home. While trying to get up enough energy to leave I looked up to see Baker and Deaver coming through my office door. Baker marched over and tossed my pass on the coffee table.

"There's your pass," he said. "I didn't tell them to confiscate it but next time make arrangements to keep it."

"It seemed clear to me that you didn't want me very badly if you were going to take my pass," I told him.

"We want you. The president needs you," he said.

"Well, let me think about it some more," I hedged. "I'll call you this afternoon."

"We're going to lunch. Why don't you join us?" Deaver suggested.

"I have better things to do," I said rudely, not wanting to be friends with them and still irritated at Baker for sandbagging me and having my pass confiscated, which I still think he did, and at myself for letting myself be sandbagged, and for not having gone home before they arrived.

On their way out they walked through the conference room where Baker noticed the blank spot where his picture had been. He'd never been there before, but he ain't dumb.

"I see you took my picture down," he laughed.

"No," I lied, but we both knew I was lying.

They went away and later on I went to the White House and got in with no trouble. I met with Baker and said I would help, with the understanding that I would be in charge, that I have complete access to him, that if we couldn't resolve any differences we would take them to the president, and that I could draft what help I needed from anywhere in the administration.

In the middle of all this I knew I should call Jack Kemp and tell him, but it isn't easy to tell someone you're about to doublecross him, so I didn't. But I should have.

Helene von Damm, by now head of White House personnel, was on vacation so I took over her office in the West Wing. I asked Rose Marie

Monk to come up from Barbados, where she was working for an old friend, Ambassador Milan Bish, to help. Rose Marie not only knew the players but she also knew how I worked. For a short-term job like that she was indispensable.

We had less than two weeks to get the job done and only twelve committed Republican votes. The Democratic leadership had told the president he had to scare up between ninety and one hundred before they would give us the votes they controlled. They wanted to make damn sure the Republicans would share the blame for this dog.

Between Ken Duberstein, the president's assistant for congressional relations, and me, and with the help of a lot of other people in the White House and out, we got the job done—103 Republican votes. We did it with persuasion, friendly and unfriendly. We brought opposed Republicans in to see the president, exposed them to his powers of persuasion, and forced them to look him in the eye when they told him no, as some, including a few from California, had the guts to do. Without exception these dissidents explained that they were adhering to his philosophy, even if he wasn't.

We went after them in their home districts, persuading their supporters and money people to work them over. We threatened them, we cajoled them, we made commitments to them, we kissed their backsides. And every morning at seven o'clock, to the dismay of those who hate to get up early, I met with those involved to mark our progress and lay out our attack.

At the end of the first week Deaver asked Bonnie and me to spend the weekend at Camp David with the president—Nancy was out of town. We flew up in the presidential helicopter with the president and Secretary of State George Shultz, whom I had known, but not well, since my days in the Nixon White House. That night a few of us had dinner with the president, watched one of those golden oldie movies Reagan loves, and ate popcorn. On Sunday I played tennis, doubles, the first time in three years, and I was awful. I blamed it on creeping old age, but it kept bugging me until it finally dawned on me that my coordination had been affected by my stroke.

The following Friday the House passed the bill. To no one's surprise, except maybe Reagan's, Congress never did cut back on spending, and the president eventually realized he had been had. A year or so later when I mentioned this to Baker he said the president had "misunderstood."

I went back to my office and a few weeks later received one of the many form thank-you letters from the president that the White House sent out. I should have kept it but I threw it in the wastebasket. Knowing Ronald Reagan I hadn't really expected any thanks, but a form letter? It was the only thanks I ever received.

Like Reagan, I am a slow learner and it took me several weeks to understand that, while I'd known all along that I'd been had by Baker, it was even worse than I had initially thought. Baker, I realized, having decided the administration could not win the TEFRA fight, had brought me back to the White House where, if I were responsible for winning it, he could also blame me for losing it. I think he was surprised that we did win. Like Reagan, he never bothered to thank me.

What he didn't understand was that I knew I had to win and was going to do everything I could to assure victory. If I were going to betray my conservative friends I had to beat them, too. If they were going to despise me, they also were going to have to respect me. I remember that victory with as much satisfaction as I remember anything in my political life. Among other things, it ensured that Baker would never call on me again. The thought of someone else shining in public is more than he can stand.

For the next four years I split my time between business and politics, helping Republicans where I could. One person with whom I became friendly was Don Regan, then secretary of the Treasury. His assistant secretary for public affairs and congressional relations was Ann Dore McLaughlin whom I had known since the 1972 Nixon campaign. Competent, smart, and a good political hand, she had become Regan's political adviser.

Ann called me one day and asked if I could drop by and visit with the secretary. Of course I could, and over a period of time we met informally several times. I found Regan delightful. His self-confidence is overweening, but he was not afraid to ask questions and seek advice. One day he complained that Baker would never let him see the president.

"Don," I explained, "Jim Baker is just a staffer. You are a member of the president's cabinet. In fact, you are one of the three most important members. You don't have to ask Baker if you can see the president. Pick up the phone and call Reagan and tell him you want to see him. He may grumble but he'll see you."

Regan looked doubtful but I got no disagreement from Ann. I continued: "First of all the president is a nice man and if you ask to see him he won't say no. Besides, you and he will get along fine. When you see him tell him you want to come over every ten days or two weeks and brief him. He won't want to do it but he won't tell you no."

I can't guarantee that Regan followed my advice, but I do know that he and Reagan became buddies and that Reagan eventually welcomed him as Baker's successor as chief of staff. That did not happen, however, until after Reagan's reelection in 1984.

I was a volunteer in that campaign. Ed Rollins had been named to run it and he took with him his deputy, Lee Atwater, and his special assistant, Michele Davis, both of whom had worked in the 1980 campaign. Other Reaganites came aboard, including Bay Buchanan who again ran the business end and served as treasurer. Jim Lake, whom Reagan had fired along with John Sears and Charlie Black in 1980, returned as press secretary, a job at which he was very good. Black and Stu Spencer also joined up, and Rose Marie came aboard to help me.

My job was to do whatever needed to be done. I gave free advice by the bucketful to people who couldn't get in to see Rollins or Atwater and unofficially oversaw all the chairmen of all the special groups— minorities, business, blacks, religious, women. Once at Atwater's request I went to Alabama and held a press conference in the same hotel where the Democratic candidate, Walter Mondale, had just held one. It made Mondale so mad he forgot who was running for president and attacked me, much to Atwater's and my glee.

Rollins also asked me to represent him at the selection of California delegates to the Republican National Convention. He was concerned, and rightly so, that between Gov. George Deukmajian and Sen. Pete Wilson old Reagan supporters would be ignored. He was right. Both the governor and the senator had a tough time remembering that this was Ronald Reagan's delegation. Each attempted to load it with his own supporters. A couple of meetings had been held before I became involved but with the help of Trudy McDonald and one or two other Reagan supporters, we managed to infuse the delegation heavily with Reaganites.

Although I was friendly with both Deukmajian and Wilson neither was a political ally. As a state senator Deukmajian had refused to serve as a Reagan delegate in 1976, which I had not forgotten. Indeed, his refusal was one reason I had supported Mike Curb in the 1982 California gubernatorial primary, and Duekmajian had not forgiven me for that. Wilson, a moderate, had campaigned against Reagan in 1976 and I had gotten even with him by writing a nasty article about him in the *San Francisco Examiner*'s Sunday magazine.

One minor event during the fall made me wonder a bit about the Bush campaign, not the vice president but the people around him. I had traveled with him to California, followed him around the next day, and then attended his press conference. A television reporter spotted me and put out a story that I had been sent out to check up on the vice president and his campaign, which of course was not the case. Back in Washington the next day, Rollins greeted me at campaign headquarters with amusement. He told me about the television story and said he had just had a call from the Bush campaign. "They want you to go back out and hold a press conference to deny that you were checking up on Bush."

I laughed and told him it reminded me of the time Bill Scott had called a press conference to deny that he was the dumbest man in the Senate. Needless to say, I did not fly to Oregon, for which George Bush should be forever grateful.

An unusual event that year intruded on the campaign, but it was a welcome intrusion for the president politically and for me personally. It was the fortieth anniversary of the D-Day landings of the allied troops in Normandy. I had participated in that event and for years had told Bonnie that someday I would take her to France and England to show her where I almost cost the Allies the victory. This was the someday. Although I had had a call from the White House inviting me to join the president's party at Omaha and Utah beaches, a generous gesture on the president's part, I politely declined. As part of the president's entourage, you're trapped; you have no freedom to move around on your own. So Bonnie and I decided to go by ourselves.

We spent a few days in Paris and then drove to Normandy, where we visited the American cemetery just up from Omaha Beach. It was a moving experience, all the more so because I had been there. While we were looking around, some of the White House advance men found us—John Roberts and Mark Rosenker, both of whom had worked for me in the 1980 campaign, and Grey Terry—and gave us a tour of the area. That evening they joined us for dinner in the nearby city of Caen. It beat the hell out of being with the president.

Instead of staying for the D-Day ceremonies where Ronald Reagan gave the famous speech that Peggy Noonan told the world she had written, Bonnie and I headed for England. First we went to Bishops Lydeard, a village outside of Taunton, a small city in southwestern England. Forty years is a long time. Then an American hospital had been there. I asked the bartender in a local pub where it might be. He'd never heard of it. Finally we found an old man, about my age, I guess, who remembered and directed us to it. The Nissen huts, which had been hospital wards, similar to the Quonset huts in the Pacific, still stood, as did the old mansion which had been hospital headquarters. Fittingly, it was being used as a home for senior citizens.

From there we drove to Weston Super Mare, a resort city on the Bristol Channel. When the 413th anti-aircraft artillery batallion arrived there by train in the dark of an early November morning in 1943 the GIs asked the natives where we were and we thought they said "Western Super Man." But Clark Kent never fought in our war.

Again, I began to ask, this time about the old girls' school where Battery D, known as "dog battery," had been stationed. No luck. Most of the people we talked to only knew of the war secondhand; they had no idea American troops had been stationed there. I finally found a man who directed us to the general area; from there I found the spot. The girls school was gone and so were the Nissen huts. The only things left were the memories.

We proved two things on this journey: (1) You can go back again. (2) But things are never the same.

And if the United States ever rejoins UNESCO things will not be the same there, either. In the middle of Reagan's first term he withdrew the United States from the United Nations Economic, Scientific and Cultural Organization to the glee of conservatives and despair of liberals. UNESCO is one of those international organizations that always had one hand dipped in Uncle Sam's pocket while the other was shaking a fist in his face. America's withdrawal was one of those little victories conservatives won during the Reagan years, great for morale but not meaning a whole hell of a lot in the overall scheme of things.

Great bleeding outcries nevertheless erupted from the Third World countries that dominated UNESCO, largely because the U.S. not only was its chief contributor but also because we gave it a certain respectability.

As an example, early in the Reagan administration UNESCO was preparing to vote its opposition to the continued sale of infant baby formulas in Third World countries by large pharmaceutical companies. It had decided that breast feeding was plenty good enough. The State Department, though opposed, was still influenced by the wishy-washiness of the Carter administration and was going to abstain—a real stand for principle.

Learning of this, I called Marty Anderson. We put a meeting together and, still thinking we'd come to Washington to change things, forced the State Department to have the U.S. vote no. As far as substance went the vote didn't mean anything but it did send word that the U.S. was no longer going to be intimidated by the Soviet-dominated ragtags of the Third World or their allies in the State Department.

Not unexpectedly, someone leaked the story of our meeting to a reporter who called me. He wanted a story about how the White House was messing around in State Department affairs. I asked him who was at the meeting "since there are so many of them" and he gave me some names, including a couple of people who weren't there.

"I was never at a meeting with those people," I said truthfully, mentally chalking up another little victory for the good guys.

That minor episode was the beginning. By 1983 there were growing demands that the United States get out of UNESCO, among them the voice of our ambassador to UNESCO, Jean Gerard, a conservative New York Republican. That year I was asked to head the American delegation to the UNESCO meeting in Paris. At the last moment I was unable to attend, and on my recommendation a New York lawyer, Edmund Hennelly, was named instead.

Following the lengthy UNESCO session most of the delegates, Hennelly excepted, plus Assistant Secretary of State Greg Newell, recommended that the U.S. withdraw and the president agreed. To salve feelings he had Secretary of State George Shultz appoint a committee to monitor UNESCO and report back annually with a recommendation to stay out or rejoin.

I was asked to head the committee, which I didn't really want to do because I don't do those things very well, and so was relieved when Reagan's friend, Charles Wick, the head of the United States Information Agency, called and suggested that it wasn't a very good job and I could have more fun as vice chairman and why not let his buddy Leonard Marks be the chairman. That was fine by me even though Marks had headed the USIA under Lyndon Johnson and was a moderate-to-liberal Democrat who in his not-so-secret heart would have been happy to see the U.S. rejoin. I figured that among the right-wingers on the committee, including two tough ladies, Ursula Meese and Wendy Borcherdt, we could keep that from happening, and we did. Besides, the pro-UNESCO people in the State Department and on the committee all thought I was the eight-hundred-pound gorilla who talked daily to Ronald Reagan. And I did nothing to disabuse them.

Fortunately, Newell and his successor, Alan Keyes, were firmly on our side, too, as was Laura Genero, a deputy assistant secretary who had worked for me in the 1980 campaign.

Marks was always very nice to me—I found him a delightful and thoughtful individual. He took me to meetings with foreign ambassadors and otherwise treated me as an equal. We never once argued. I knew and I think he knew that as long as I was around his chances of getting the U.S. back into UNESCO were on the slim side, so why fight it. Today, the U.S. is still not a member, although I hear occasional rumbles.

Membership on the commitee gave me my first look behind the Iron Curtain when in October of 1985 Bonnie and I attended a UNESCO meeting in Sofia, Bulgaria. Sofia once must have been a beautiful city but in 1985 it was a dreary place, totally without humor. On the street no one would look us in the eye. Little or no food in the stores, no variety. But great yogurt. Bonnie tried to bring some home but the man at the customs counter at Dulles Airport took it away from us after I, patriotic citizen and coward that I am, declared it.

The hotel could best be described as modern drab. The room was tiny, barely large enough for two coffins. When the light bulb blew out we spoke to the microphones we assumed were hidden there and the bulb was replaced. Coincidence, I'm sure.

One day on a crowded street a man sidled up to me and offered to trade me a lot of Bulgarian money for a few bucks American. But fear got the better of greed and I fled. All of Bulgaria looked and felt like a prison; I had no wish to find out what a Bulgarian prison looked and felt like. All in all Bulgaria was a great place to make a person glad all over again to be an American.

But while all was going well on the foreign front, by mid-1986, trouble involving pay-offs and bribes was brewing at Wedtech. It was disquieting, but nothing more. We had done nothing wrong.

Then one day the stuff hit the fan. A reporter from the *New York Times* asked to see me. He had a copy of a letter written on our letterhead and signed "Lyn." It was addressed to Jim Jenkins, who in May of 1982 was an assistant to the president and Ed Meese's right-hand man. The *Times* man didn't tell me who gave him the letter, but it was either slipped to him illegally by someone in the U.S. attorney's office in New York or leaked by one of my friends in the White House.

I told him, "I never wrote that letter. I don't write like that. I don't ever remember seeing it."

He asked if it was my signature. I told him I didn't know but that it could be, except that I'd never seen the letter. He was interested because he thought I might have violated the Ethics in Government Act which prohibits high-ranking government employees from lobbying their former agencies for one year after their departure on matters of direct and substantial interest to the agencies.

When I saw the letter I was dumbfounded. By now I had been out of government for nearly five years during which much had happened. At the beginning we had hired lawyers to tell us what we could and could not do and therefore I couldn't conceive that I'd broken the law. But it wasn't long before I began conceiving.

After that first story the press scented blood—mine. Stories, relevant and irrelevant, accurate and inaccurate, fair and unfair, began appearing. TV reporters and cameramen parked outside my home and office. They'll admit I was always nice to them, even though I didn't tell them much.

In January, an independent counsel, a miserable little nobody named

James McKay, was appointed to look into our high crimes and misde-
meanors. We had already hired a law firm, Finley Kumble, which,
despite our best efforts to keep it solvent, went bankrupt a year later. But
a new law firm arose, harboring our lawyers, Paul Perito, Bob Plotkin,
Larry Barcella, son of an old newspaperman I had known when I was a
young newspaperman, and Sandra Wilkinson. One of the first things
Perito asked was, "Have you given or taken any unusual favors or
gifts?"

I laughed. "If you mean, have we been giving or taking bribes, the
answer is no."

Even with their help it took us thirty-nine months and $1.8 million
before we finally laid the case to rest. More than three years after it all
began a federal appeals court threw out my indictment, thus voiding my
three convictions. On January 10, 1990, Thomas Flannery, the judge
who had sentenced me to prison, signed the paper restoring my honesty,
my integrity, and my citizenship rights. I could vote again, possess a
gun just like Carl Rowan, and travel freely. Mark also kept these rights
since he had been found innocent of the single charge against him. That
charge, aiding and abetting, had no merit and was only brought by
McKay as a matter of spite.

But though vindication was sweet the cost was high. Our business
was destroyed, we had been literally paralyzed for three years, our
families had undergone untold anguish and embarrassment, and our
partnership was ruined.

I learned a lot from that experience, things that I never learned in
kindergarten, and some that I never wanted to learn. Such as:

1. Never let the bastards think they have you beaten.
2. Don't depend on lawyers or anyone but yourself to keep you out
   of trouble.
3. Faith, family, and friends will see you through this sort of
   ordeal. You need all three.
4. You find out who your real friends are. And are not.
5. How you play the game may be important, but it matters a hell of
   a lot more whether you win or lose.
6. The law is a ass and a idiot.
7. The Constitution doesn't mean what it says, only what lawyers
   and legislators and judges say it means.

8. The bad stories about you will outnumber the good ones.
9. People who need help don't hire people under investigation, on trial, or fighting convictions.
10. It ain't easy to get a jury of your peers in Washington, D.C., if you're a Reagan Republican.
11. Incompetence is no barrier to becoming a judge.
12. In the American judicial system justice is incidental to the jousting between the prosecution and the defense.
13. Partnerships have a tough time lasting out tough times.
14. Never let the bastards think they have you beaten.
15. Win or lose, life goes on.

And for me life has gone on, though at a different level and a different pace. In 1988 because of my legal problems, I was unable to participate in the presidential election, although Lee Atwater, a loyal friend, invited me to a number of small political meetings. And former Secretary of Education Bill Bennett asked me to join him at the Republican National Convention to help him with his speech.

When it was known I was coming I was invited to a small political gathering. As I walked in I was told that George Bush had just selected Sen. J. Danforth Quayle of Indiana for his vice presidential running mate. Unbidden the words came out: "What about Paula Parkinson?"

Just as quickly Mitch Daniels, an Indianan and former White House official, replied, "There's no problem."

Paula Parkinson was a lady lobbyist whose easy distribution of favors in 1981 had proved an embarrassment to several congresssmen, and rumors had included Quayle. Fortunately, it turned out he was more interested in playing golf than playing house.

But his selection, which came as a complete surprise, dominated the convention from that time on. After leaving the meeting I ran into Ody Fish, the national committeeman from Wisconsin who had run the 1976 convention.

"What are you saying, Ody?" I asked.

"Nothing," he replied. "I'm going to my room until I can figure out an answer."

He wasn't alone. Quayle, who has turned out to be a perfectly satisfactory vice president and a man of some principle, was either unknown or unwanted by most of the delegates.

As the convention ended and the presidential campaign swung into gear the Reagan administration began winding down. Even so I was surprised to get a call from Wendy Borcherdt who was running Citizens for the Republic, the old Reagan PAC.

At the time I was not the official chairman of CFTR, having resigned at the onset of my legal problems. But, because I had never been replaced I was, by common consent among the old Reagan hands, the unofficial acting chairman, the person Wendy turned to and consulted with and made any hard decisions that had to be made. Wendy was upset. She was being harassed in a nonsexual way by Jack Courtemanche, by now Nancy Reagan's chief of staff. Courtemanche had told her that the White House, implying the president, wanted her out and wanted him to take over CFTR.

It took me about one second to figure out why. CFTR had a million dollars in the bank and someone at the White House wanted it for the president's—or Nancy's—use when his term was up. After a long conversation we decided that she would tell Courtemanche to come see me. She did. He did.

We had a pleasant conversation. I told him he couldn't have CFTR. He said it was the president's PAC. I said, not now it isn't. He said if it hadn't been for Reagan there wouldn't have been a CFTR. I said if it hadn't been for me there wouldn't have been one either, to which claim he agreed.

I told him if Reagan wanted CFTR he could ask for it and he'd get it but that I was not going to stand by and let them fire Wendy and the other good people who worked there.

The conversation over, we parted on friendly terms. And I moved immediately to set up a small board of directors that could effectively block any further effort by Mr. or Mrs. X at the White House to take over CFTR.

I wrote the president a long letter explaining the situation. I think he never saw it because, very much unlike himself, he never responded. I called his chief of staff, Ken Duberstein, three times in an effort to talk to the president about the matter. Duberstein promised, but I never got in. I don't think that was his decision. Neither did I ever get a request from the president that I turn CFTR over to him, which he must have known I would do with all deliberate alacrity.

Unfortunately, and to my dismay, all our efforts to have CFTR work with Reagan after he left office were blocked by his chief of staff, Fred Ryan, for unknown reasons. I suspect Reagan doesn't know either. What I have been told is that Nancy was behind the failed highjacking. If so, I wish she had talked to me. CFTR would have been a great asset to her and her husband, without firing Wendy, one of the most loyal of all Reaganites.

The entire incident was so unlike Reagan that I think to this day he knew nothing about it. He is, in most ways, a kind and thoughtful man.

This is best illustrated by an incident that took place the day he left office. His daughter, Maureen, informed him that my daughter, Susan, had entered Georgetown University Hospital for treatment of lymph cancer. The last call Ronald Reagan made from the White House was to the hospital in an effort to talk to Susie. He couldn't reach her; he did talk to Bonnie. This bit of kindness was typical.

And yet, so was his refusal to cope with problems involving people, even his close associates. In mid-1991 the chairman of the board of the Reagan Presidential Library, Lodwrick Cook, informed Ed Meese, Bill Clark, and Marty Anderson that their terms on the board were up and they would not be reappointed because, he excused, they were not fundraisers.

When the action became public Reagan said the decision was his. I don't believe it. On his own Reagan would not fire or let be fired three of his oldest and strongest supporters. He had stood behind all of us in the past when the need arose, just as we had stood behind him. He is too old to change.

Reagan's career is winding down. And it is sad that whoever is pulling the strings now did not see fit to let those who had fought and bled with him over the years be with him as the curtain comes down. He deserves at least that. And so do they.

11

Troubles and Trials

"IT'S A LOUSY system."

I said that about the American justice system in November of 1990 as a member of a panel speaking to an audience made up largely of prosecuting attorneys from Los Angeles and southern California. Funny, but that's the last time I've been invited to talk to a group of lawyers. Certainly, Larry Barcella, the lawyer who invited me to talk, and one of my lawyers at that, has not asked me to speak again. But, what I said then I meant then and still mean today. It may be, as we like to claim, that the American justice system is the best in the world, but it lacks a lot of being good. I know. I am one of its victims.

Before I go into detail let me first mention two of the foundation stones of that system. One is the grand jury. The other is the United States Constitution. The first is a fraud. The second doesn't mean what it says.

Does this mean that I am bitter, that I have a grudge against our justice system? Indeed it does. I have been there, I have dealt with it, and I find the word "justice" to be a misnomer.

Oh, sure, the system does a fair job of putting dangerous criminals in jail, but it doesn't do a very good job of protecting the innocent, or those with few resources, or those who may have inadvertently broken the law. Its defenders say the so-called "adversary system" that pits prosecutors against defense lawyers and is fundamental to the way the overall system works ensures that the truth will win out. Utter nonsense!

Prosecutors want to put someone in jail regardless of the truth. Defense lawyers want to keep their clients out of jail—if they can pay their bills—regardless of the truth. Judges, who above all ought to be interested in the truth, are most of the time more interested in legal technicalities than in seeing justice carried out.

I believe this even though in late 1989 the United States Court of Appeals for the District of Columbia ruled that I had been wrongly indicted on four counts of having violated the Federal Ethics in Government Act and overturned the three convictions an all-black jury had levied against me.

Some members of the unbiased press, by the way, like to write that my convictions were overturned "on a technicality." They never say that I was indicted on a technicality under a law that even my judge agreed "lacked clarity" and was later changed by Congress to conform with my lawyer's interpretation of it.

Some will say the fact that the appeals court ruled in my favor is proof the system works. These are people who have never been trapped by the system, harassed by it, persecuted by it, bankrupted by it. The appeals court decision merely proves that if you have the money, if you have the will to fight, and if you have competent lawyers you can sometimes retain or regain your freedom.

But sadly, a decision in which one court or another finds you innocent never answers the poignant question put by former Labor Secretary Ray Donovan after he was cleared of trumped-up racketeering charges: "Where do I go to get my reputation back?"

That is a valid—and unanswerable—question, one that the justice system doesn't give a damn about. Nor do the news media. The prosecutors who have indicted and tried you, the reporters who have dutifully dredged up and/or reported every irresponsible and untruthful charge against you merely go on to their next victim.

They couldn't care less about what an unfair or trumped-up indictment does to a person's family, to his business, to his assets, to his future. This is all irrelevant to the blind lady of American justice, and for the most part to the prosecuting attorneys and reporters and editors who join initially in the attack on your honor, your honesty, and your integrity.

In several respects I was luckier that many persons who are caught in the toils of the law. In my younger days I had been a police reporter and I had seen prominent citizens arrested for minor crimes, minor, that is, in terms of the penalty to be extracted for their commission. These were crimes like exposing oneself—flashing—in public or perhaps making a pass at a plainclothesman in the park men's room. Today it might be for sexual harassment. Regardless, the arrested person's lawyer, usually the family lawyer who didn't know much about criminal law, would urge him to plead guilty, pay a fine, maybe serve a brief probationary period, and "get it behind you; even if you're innocent you don't need the publicity of a court trial."

So the man would do it and thereafter in the court records he would be listed as a sex offender. And as such, if police were rounding up known sex offenders to see if they could find who molested that little seven-year-old girl, the man who pleaded guilty, even though he may have been innocent, would find himself down at the police station in the lineup with the winos and bums and honest-to-goodness genuine pederasts.

And sometimes a lawyer would persuade his client, especially if he was short of cash, to plead guilty to a felony. "Get it over with, get it behind you, get on with your life," was the well-meaning advice. Often unsaid were the words, "and besides you can't afford to fight this and I don't work for free."

Overlooked was the fact that even though the person didn't go to prison, or went only briefly, he was now and would be for the rest of his life as much a convicted felon as the convicted rapist, or murderer, or bank robber. In most states a felony conviction means you lose your right to vote, or to serve on a jury, or to own a firearm. You also lose your right to travel freely because many countries will not allow convicted felons inside their borders.

I knew all these things; a surprising number of people don't.

I had another advantage many people don't have. I had money, not a great deal, but enough to pay my legal bills. Lucky for me, too, because defending yourself against the unlimited resources of government, especially the federal government, isn't cheap. Unless $1.8 million is cheap.

And finally, I had what was most important of all. I was not alone. My family stood by me. My friends stood by me, and I will always believe that my God stood by me. Regarding Him, one day early in my ordeal I stumbled across in the book of Nehemiah a verse that I took to apply directly to me. It read, "Nevertheless, we made our prayer unto our God, and set a watch against them [their enemies] day and night, because of them."

It made sense to me. I prayed to my God, and hired good lawyers.

The government's main tool for bringing people to trial is the grand jury. Only grand juries can indict. The grand jury originally was devised as the citizen's bulwark against the overweening power of government. It has since become a tool of prosecutors for implementing that power.

The way it works now, grand juries are rubber stamps for prosecutors. Larry Barcella, a former federal prosecutor, makes no bones about it. "I could indict a ham sandwich," he proudly proclaims.

Probably convict one, too, if my judge and jury are accurate samples of our justice system.

Grand juries are made up for the most part of average—very average—citizens, who wish they were somewhere else and, because they aren't, take refuge in various types of reading material, knitting, or sleeping until it is time to vote the indictment. The prosecutor, meanwhile, is having a field day, bullying unfriendly witnesses, heckling, threatening, distorting as he sees fit and making his case without opposition.

Unfair as it may seem, and is, neither witnesses nor targets of the investigations are allowed to have their attorneys with them inside the jury room. If they need to consult with them they must stop the procedures and meet them in the hallway or a nearby room. More than one woman called to testify against me in front of the grand jury came away in tears, indignant and bitter because of the abuse to which she had been submitted.

On occasion a grand juror may arouse himself or herself to ask a question. This happened to my friend, Ed Rollins, who later was forced to testify against me. This particular grand juror didn't like his answer so she flat out called him a liar. In that room, he had no recourse to the insults.

If a person is the "target" of a grand jury investigation he can refuse a request by the prosecution to testify. Some persons don't. Mike Deaver was convicted on three charges of perjury without being guilty, I'm convinced, of anything except arrogance and stupidity. Over his lawyers' objections he testified at different times before a grand jury and a congressional committee. And nobody answers the same way each time to a question which each time is put a little differently. Deaver's answers conflicted just enough to enable his Reagan-hating special prosecutor, Whitney North Seymour, to hang a trio of perjury convictions on him. I always thought they got him unjustly. It's hard to know what he thought since he didn't appeal and took refuge in the claim that that old devil, the demon rum, made him do it.

I'm smarter than Deaver. I listened to my lawyers. One, Paul Perito, told me, "Testify before the grand jury if you wish, but if you do go find yourself some new lawyers." I took the hint.

They—my lawyers—also told me, "If you're subpoenaed to testify before a congressional committee we are going to ask you to take the Fifth Amendment."

When I protested, they explained that any testimony I gave to a committee could open up new avenues for the independent counsel both in his investigation and in the trial. I agreed to do what they wanted. They notified a couple of committee chairmen—Democrats, naturally—who were making noises about calling me to tell them I wouldn't talk. They didn't call me.

It should be pointed out here that most members of Congress are publicity hounds and they will do anything to get their names in the paper or be mentioned on television newscasts. This includes screwing up Justice Department investigations, harassing innocent persons, exaggerating or outright lying about the part a person might have played in something under investigation, and in other ways making life difficult, embarrassing, or downright unlivable for decent American citizens, especially if they are important or well-known members of the other party. If you want examples you need look no further than Robert Bork or Clarence Thomas.

I said at the beginning that one thing you learn as you run the gauntlet of the American justice system is that the Constitution does not mean what it says. A good example is the First Amendment. On the one hand it has been stretched to permit the exhibition of pornography and pornographic acts onstage in the name of art and freedom of expression. In the name of free speech you can also burn the flag, although I doubt that you can burn a cross.

On the other hand, the First Amendment has been shrunk by Congress and the courts to where in some cases you can't talk to old friends or business acquaintances or ask a girl who may not like you for a date. At my age I won't worry about that latter, but the first example is deeply disturbing.

Who was it—Justice Holmes?—who said freedom of speech doesn't mean you can cry "fire" in a crowded theater? Unfortunately, in my case it meant much more—or less.

The First Amendment reads, in part, that "Congress shall make no law . . . abridging the freedom of speech. . . ."

Pretty clear, isn't it? Well, no. It isn't. Congress from time to time makes laws blatantly abridging freedom of speech. Cowardly or ignorant or uncaring presidents sign those laws and the courts uphold them.

I was indicted, tried, and convicted on three charges of exercising my nonexistent right to free speech. And when my indictment and convictions were thrown out it was for reasons having nothing to do with freedom of speech. As in George Orwell's *1984* we live in an age of Newspeak, where words and phrases and sentences mean whatever the courts want them to mean, nothing more, nothing less.

The law under which I was convicted did not exactly do Congress proud. Where it was not vague, it clearly circumscribed freedom of speech by making it illegal for a select few persons to talk business with persons in the agency where they formerly worked for a year after leaving the federal government. In other words, having worked in the White House, I could not talk to anyone in the White House about things in which they had a substantial interest. Through intuition or extrasensory perception I was somehow supposed to know what those things were. The reason was that persons in government, in the minds of the honorable ladies and gentlemen who serve in Congress, are susceptible to pressure, bribery, or kickbacks.

Congress, in passing the law under which I was indicted, assumed that those leaving government were dishonest, even though they might have been honest when they took their jobs, and that those staying in government were also dishonest, or at least weak. Clearly, we need better persons to serve as presidential appointees and bureaucrats. It might help, too, if we had better types in Congress and on the bench. It occurs to me that bench warmers in athletics are second stringers and that the same is true in our justice system.

I'll bet you thought that when Congress passes a law it applies to everyone equally. Well, think again. In its wisdom Congress exempted from this particular law government workers of lower grade levels who left government, members of the judiciary, AND members of Congress. Apparently none of these could offer a bribe or bring pressure as effectively as a former presidential appointee. What was illegal for me to do was perfectly legal for a member of Congress. One of these honorable creatures could leave Congress one day and the next day, as a lobbyist, walk back on the floor of the House or Senate and lobby his former colleagues on any issue or bill of his choosing. Anyone here for term limits?

January 10, 1990, if not the the most memorable day of my life certainly ranks in the top five. On that day I won back something most Americans take for granted: My freedom.

On that day in a federal district court in Washington, D.C., Judge Thomas A. Flannery dismissed a four-count indictment that had been brought against me two years earlier for allegedly violating the Federal Ethics in Government Act. The dismissal was "with prejudice," meaning that the indictment could not be reinstated.

Flannery was the same judge whose rulings against me on key points of the law nearly two years before had been largely responsible, I still believe, for my conviction on three of the four counts. These convictions, like the indictment, were now behind me forever.

Flannery was also the judge who had sentenced me to thirty days in prison and a $10,000 fine on each of the three counts of which I had been found guilty. Now, after having been overruled by a federal appeals court and rebuffed by the Supreme Court, which refused to review the appeals court's decision, he was being forced to eat his rulings and his sentence. It like to broke my heart.

But it wasn't Flannery's discomfiture that gave me the most satisfaction. It was the knowing that we—my lawyers and I—had finally stuck it once and for all to James McKay and his girl Friday, Lovita Coleman.

McKay, whom I found to be self-righteous and sanctimonious, was the independent counsel who had investigated me, had me indicted by a typically subservient grand jury, and had tried to put me in prison. Lovita Coleman was a black woman lawyer who had served neither wisely nor well as his chief assistant.

McKay, a Democrat, had gone through a long career as an unknown, run-of-the-mill civil lawyer in a city—Washington—overladen with unknown, run-of-the-mill lawyers. My case was a chance for him finally to get his name in the papers. My conviction was to give him a chance to be known as "the man who got Lyn Nofziger."

Lovita's record was a shorter version of McKay's. She had gotten by largely by being the daughter of William Coleman, a liberal Republican who had served as a secretary of transportation in the Ford adminis-tration.

McKay was a relentless, vindictive prosecutor who used thirteen lawyers, six FBI agents, three IRS agents, and unlimited federal funds to seek any possible violations on my part of any and all federal criminal statutes. I have often wondered if his own record could withstand that kind of scrutiny. Twice, before my trial, fearful that he could not get a conviction, he offered a deal. The first time he offered to let me plead *nolo contendere* (no contest) to one charge and to drop any charges against my partner Mark Bragg. The second time he offered to let me plead guilty to one charge. Both times I told my lawyers to tell him that if he wanted a conviction he would have to get it the old-fashioned way; he would have to earn it.

I told Mark, "Sorry, but there's no way I can plead guilty even if it means you go to jail, too." It was about then, I think, that he decided to get his own lawyer.

Well, McKay did his best, I'll give him that. He persuaded Flannery to make two key, but flawed, rulings. One was that it did not matter whether I knew I was breaking the law; all McKay had to do was convince the jury that I had broken it, even if in all innocence. The second ruling was that my lawyers could not bring up, under threat of being held in contempt of court, the fact that I had sought the advice of counsel before talking to people in the White House within a year of the time I had resigned as assistant to the president for political affairs.

Once the trial got underway McKay quickly figured out how to motivate the jury of twelve members and six alternates that heard my case. Seventeen of them were black. The one white member, a little old lady, was dismissed during the trial because she couldn't stay awake. It was a dull trial. I had the same problem, but I fought it better.

Asked about her dismissal, Plotkin said, "It was the snoring that finally did it."

Actually, it was my partner's lawyer, Rick Ben Veniste, who demanded that she be dismissed. I still don't know why. Asleep she wasn't any worse that the other eleven jurors were awake. It was an interesting jury, if not one that instilled confidence. The forewoman had a brother in prison on a bank robbery conviction. Another member was on probation for misdemeanor possession of drugs and for shoplifting. A third was illiterate. In that case, however, Flannery decided that if he had been good enough to serve in the army he was good enough to serve on my jury. And who cared if he understood what was going on?

McKay motivated this motley group in a simple yet effective way. He recognized that for the most part black Washington residents would be Democrats or at least anti-Reagan because Reagan was viewed by most blacks as anti-civil rights. Knowing this, McKay decided he didn't have to prove me guilty; all he had to do was take advantage of the jurors' antagonism toward Reagan and transfer it to me. They, in turn, would find me guilty, regardless of the facts.

So daily during the trial he reminded them that I was Reagan's "best friend" or "closest associate" or "most trusted adviser." Though none of these compliments was true it didn't matter. They were code words the jurors clearly understood—words that told them that while they might never be able to get Reagan here was their chance to get Reagan's good buddy.

And so it was. They took full advantage of the opportunity, finding me guilty of three of the four charges and showing their objectivity by deciding I was innocent of the fourth, but only because McKay could not prove I had signed the damned letter that started the whole travesty.

All of the charges involved what my lawyers called "lobbying before my time" or, in other words, communicating on behalf of clients with people I knew in the White House before I had been gone a year. My first batch of lawyers had believed that while I could not have any dealings with the people in the White House political office, which I had

headed, I could deal with the rest of the people in the White House—
the Ed Meeses, the Bill Clarks, and others. In fact, in 1983 the White
House ethics office ruled that that was the case.

Unfortunately for me, the ruling came a year too late. In my case the
court ruled that in 1982 I could not talk business with anyone at all in
the White House because they were so weak and dishonest they would
do what I wanted them to, regardless of the merit of my request.

I was the first person ever convicted under this particular law, and the
last, because in 1989 Congress changed and clarified it, effective in
1991. It's still not a good law, unless you favor rigid limits on free
speech and free association for some categories of people.

During this period my involvement with the justic system taught and
retaught me some valuable lessons, as well as the truth of the old saying,
"Too soon old, too late smart." Among other things I learned that:

1. The mills of the American justice system not only grind fine but
also exceedingly slowly.

2. Prosecutors aren't interested in justice; they are interested in
convictions.

3. The price of justice in America isn't cheap.

4. Defense attorneys have no faith in the integrity or impartiality of
prosecutors, judges, and juries. With cause.

5. Some members of Congress go out of their way to use the troubles
of others to get their names in the news media and otherwise make
political hay.

6. Many members of the news media do not care if what they write is
accurate. Neither do they care about the effect their stories have on a
person's family or fortune or future.

7. Freedom is worth any price.

I also learned that the law attempts to reduce all those convicted of
crime to the lowest common denominator. Though all along Judge

Flannery had left me free on my own recognizance it meant only that he didn't think I'd run. Nevertheless, his attitude was a pleasant contrast to that of Lovita Coleman who told my lawyers before the trial that she intended to bring Mark and me into court in handcuffs. They talked her out of that degrading idea but I will never, if it means going to hell, forgive her for wanting to subject me to that sort of debasement.

Her intent clearly was to demean and embarrass me before I had ever been tried or found guilty. Again, I'm sure it was another instance of a Reagan-hater taking her hatred out on a person she thought was close to him. There is room in our justice system for this sort of vindictiveness, but there shouldn't be.

My legal troubles began in all innocence shortly after I resigned from my job in the Reagan White House. My initial intent had been to return to California but I had been persuaded that I could do better financially by staying in Washington. Jim McKay called it "cashing in" on my connections with people in the administration and he was right.

But I was not alone. Every lobbyist, every person involved in government relations in Washington, cashes in on his connections. Everyone of us as we go through life cashes in on his connections and his experiences. That is the way life works, not just in Washington but everywhere. McKay, who cashed in on his connections in order to become my prosecutor and persecuter, tried to make something sinister or unethical out of it.

Early on, a man named Steve Denlinger came to see Mark and me. Later he was convicted of pocketing $10,000 he'd been given to bribe a government official. But at this time, he represented an organization called the Latin American Manufacturers Association, a group of small businesses operated by Americans of Hispanic heritage. One of its members was a manufacturing company called Welbilt, later to become Wedtech.

LAMA hired us for $5,000 a month, half the minimum we were charging larger corporations and organizations. Our job mainly was to help Welbilt, which was being run by men named John Mariotta and Mario Mareno, both of whom later went to jail on bribery and sundry other charges. At the time they were trying to get an army contract to manufacture small engines. They wanted us to help them.

In retrospect it is funny—ha, ha funny, that is—to recall that we took them on not because we needed or wanted their business, but because we thought we ought to help them in dealing with the federal government, because they needed the kind of help we could offer.

One reason Welbilt especially excited us was because it was located in the South Bronx, a devastated section of New York City, parts of which looked as if they'd gone through a bombing raid. Recall that at my insistence Reagan had gone there during the 1980 campaign and had promised its denizens that he would rebuild it. He never did, which is too bad because, even after thirty-five years in and around politics I have never discarded the naive idea that candidates should keep their campaign promises, even the small ones.

When we discovered that LAMA included Welbilt and that Welbilt was located in the South Bronx I saw an opportunity to help make the president's promise come true. How was I to know that that kind of well-meaningness could send a man to prison?

Mark was also excited about doing something for the good of the country and the administration. Late in the summer of 1982 we went to New York to see if there was any way we could become involved more generally in helping rebuild the South Bronx. It was a wasted trip.

I never did visit Welbilt but Mark did, several times. He couldn't say enough nice things about it; he became so enamored with it that one time when it was having trouble meeting its payroll he told me he had loaned it 50,000 dollars.

When Mark and I went into business we were careful, or so we thought. As I have said, we hired a CPA and we hired the law firm of Anderson, Hiby, Nauheim, and Blair. We were brought to them by Martin Artiano, a young lawyer who had been a campaign advance man and had joined the firm when income tax troubles kept him from getting a job in the Reagan administration. I had known the senior partner, Stanton Anderson, when I was still a reporter and he was serving as executive director of the National Young Republican organization. I thought they were good people.

But it was their advice that got us into trouble. It was they who led us to believe that we could deal with all the White House offices except political affairs. As if to emphasize their opinion, Anderson that spring asked me to speak to Meese on behalf of one of his clients, the Fairchild Corporation, at the same time I was to talk to him about the army contract for Welbilt. Later, but well before I had been gone from the White House for a year, I set up a meeting at the National Security Council on behalf of Anderson and attended the meeting with him. For that meeting I was indicted, tried, convicted, fined, and sentenced to prison.

Nobody, including McKay, ever said "boo" to Anderson for leading me down the garden path, and Anderson, in turn, never raised a finger to share the blame or explain that I had set up the meeting at his request while he was the lawyer supposedly advising me on what I could and could not legally do. Nice fellow, Stanton Anderson, a man to trust and rely upon, a man who will stand by a friend.

That was one of the four counts on which I was indicted. Two others arose out my efforts to help Wedtech, one for the meeting with Meese, the other for a letter I never wrote to Meese's assistant, James Jenkins, and am confident I never signed. I couldn't believe the fourth count. When my lawyers told me I was in trouble over it I busted out laughing.

"Believe it," said Bob Plotkin, "They're going to indict you on this."

And they did.

It must be understood that the Justice Department had given McKay an unrestricted license to hunt me down. Ed Meese, by then the attorney general, had recused himself from the case because of his involvement in Wedtech so the license was issued by his deputy, one Arnold Burns, who later turned on Meese. Under it McKay was not limited to the Welbilt/Wedtech situation; he had carte blanche and he took full advantage of it, looking for anything that would give him a shot at me. And he found one more thing, the thing I had laughed at.

In August of 1991, as you may remember, I was suckered into going back to the White House for two weeks to help pass TEFRA, a terrible tax increase measure that Jim Baker, Howard Baker, Bob Dole, and others had conned the president into supporting. The bill was passed and I deservedly take much of the blame for it. In the process I twisted a lot of arms and got a lot of help from a lot of people. One of those was a man named Jesse Calhoun, the head of a maritime union known as MEBA, the Marine Engineers Benevolent Association, which was a client of ours.

Calhoun had supported Reagan in 1980 and Reagan, in turn, had promised to increase the number of civilian crews on noncombat navy ships, something the navy didn't want and fought. At the time we were passing TEFRA the administration had done nothing to keep its promise to Calhoun.

After TEFRA was passed I sat down and wrote thank-you letters to all who had helped, including one to Calhoun. On a copy of that letter I typed words to the effect that the White House should help its friends, and sent it to Jim Jenkins, in whose files McKay found it. That note, it turned out, was another bit of illegal lobbying and for it I was indicted, tried, convicted, fined, and sentenced to prison, a real menace to society.

So those were the four counts on which I was tried. Actually, there were two more at the beginning but they were so ridiculous that McKay, knowing he couldn't win them, dropped them before we went to trial. In addition, Mark was indicted on one count of aiding and abetting me.

From the time the first stories broke in early November until McKay was appointed as our independent counsel it had been two months. It was another six months before he indicted us. During that six months he had subpoenaed more than twenty thousand pieces of paper from our office, been through our personal and corporate income taxes, been through thousands of papers at the White House, grilled our past and present employees, former members of my White House staff, friends, enemies—anyone he could find who willingly or unwillingly could say something bad about me.

At my lawyers' suggestion I agreed to talk with him twice. It was a mistake. I thought initially he wanted to find out what this was all about, what kind of person I was, how had this happened. None of that was of any interest to him.

Flanked by Lovita Coleman on one side and a woman FBI agent taking notes on the other, he started going through piles of papers, asking me about each one. Most were irrelevant, most I had forgotten about. None of it made much sense.

Part of the deal was that the grand jury would not be told of the meetings. Of course it was. Integrity not being McKay's strong suit.

The letter to Jenkins concerning Wedtech was the thing that opened the way for McKay to go exploring. It didn't matter that I protested that I didn't remember it, knew I hadn't written it, and didn't think I'd signed it. It was the opening wedge in McKay's broad campaign to get Lyn Nofziger. One thing he did was demand that I take handwriting tests, which were administered by the FBI. I thought—and still think—that that might be forcing me to testify against myself, but the lawyers said I had to, so I did. It didn't make any difference. The handwriting experts couldn't tell whether I had signed the letter. And eventually, because they couldn't say that I had, the jury had no alternative except to find me innocent of that charge. And in finding me innocent it had to find Mark innocent because that's what he was supposed to have been abetting me on, even though he was off on his honeymoon at the time.

But, if it hadn't been for that letter there probably would never have been an independent counsel assigned to my case and the chances that I would ever have been indicted in the Wedtech case are remote indeed. Nor would the Fairchild or MEBA incidents ever have come to light.

Immediately after Mark and I were indicted I had one change of heart. I decided to let friends form a legal defense fund on my behalf. I had refused to let them do it before the indictment, despite many urgings, including those of my partner. I was still hoping against hope that McKay would turn out to be a reasonable and decent person.

But with the indictment I knew we were in deep financial trouble. Already we had lost most of our clients and no more were coming aboard. And the legal bills were running $50,000 a month and higher.

There were good friends on that committee, Ed Rollins, Ed Allison, Ron and Caroline Robertson, Kathy Wilson. Over the next year they raised almost exactly $400,000. More than 1,500 people contributed sums ranging from $13,000 on the high side to two $1 bills on the low side. John Wolfe in Columbus, Ohio, sent $10,000 and said, "If you need it there's more." Ed Hennelly up in New York sent $5,000 and the same message. But how do you ask for more? Bernie Swain and Harry Rhodes at the speakers' bureau did the same.

A former president of the United States who understands the meaning of loyalty and friendship sent me a check for $500. It came from Richard Nixon. And I cashed it. Another check, unsolicited, came from Mervyn Dymally, a liberal, black Democratic congressman from California.

Beth and Judy and Nancy Giuden and some other of my lady friends put together a fund-raiser at the Mayflower where some good friends— Ed Rollins, John White, Bill Bennett and, yes, Sam Donaldson—said some nice things about me. A lot of right wingers changed their minds, at least temporarily, about Sam that day.

California friends also went to work on my behalf. In Sacramento Esther Greene put on a fund-raiser. Down on the San Franciso Peninsula

Hank McCullough lent his home for another one, and Bertha Nelson and a raft of other ladies from San Franciso pitched in to help. And in Los Angeles Ginny and Henry Braun opened up their Pasadena home for another fund-raiser put on by Bay Buchanan.

David Keene, who every spring runs a conservative gathering known as CPAC, invited Bonnie and me over one night, presented us with a check for $2,000, and said nice things about me. Afterward people crowded around giving me checks and cash. I'm certain I never got all their names and addresses, for which I'm truly sorry.

I wrote nearly two thousand letters during that period to everyone who contributed or helped and for whom I had an address. That was the least I could do. I can never repay even the smallest donor. Money came in from old friends, from people I don't particularly like but now I think I have to, and from total strangers. If Jim McKay didn't do anything else he showed me how many friends I have. And I'll bet mine outnumber his, any day.

Six months after the indictment and a year after the appointment of McKay, in January of 1988, Mark and I went to trial. Mark is kind of an easy panicker, and by this time he had gone out and hired his own lawyer, Richard Ben Veniste, who had been one of the Watergate lawyers. It cost him, meaning us and eventually me, a lot more money and I'm not sure it accomplished anything since the finding that I was innocent of the one charge automatically got him off.

Some of my black friends urged me to hire a black lawyer as part of my legal team if for no other reason than to impress the jury. A close friend, Gloria Toote, who is a black woman lawyer, offered to come down from New York and be that black lawyer at no charge. But Bob and Larry thought the inclusion of a black would look phony and turned down the idea. It's hard to know who was right. McKay had a black woman lawyer on his team, Lovita Coleman, and in retrospect I think I ought to have pushed harder to have one with us.

I'm sure some murder trials, some divorce cases, some rape trials are interesting, especially if they involve the rich or famous. Mine was a terrible bore. There wasn't a flamboyant lawyer in the batch, although Ben Veniste tried hard. To stay awake I wrote doggerel, everything from limericks to couplets to quatrains to sonnets. Shakespeare would not have been proud of me. Hell, Edgar Guest would not have been proud of me. But they helped pass the time.

SMILES AND TRIALS

Somehow We Need to Improve the System

Picking a jury's a bore.
Too many just don't know the score.
So the sound that you hear
As the panelists appear
Is Nofziger starting to snore.

So Much for the First Amendment

The Bill of Rights ain't worth a damn
It don't apply to me
Fer if it did one thing I know
Is I'd be walkin' free

The First Amendment guarantees
That I kin speak out free
But Congress passed a law that sez
It don't apply to me

It passed a law that sez that I
Cain't ask the government
To he'p me if I'm needin' he'p
They cast it in cement

It passed a law that sez that I
Ain't as good as congressmen
'Cause they kin lobby soon as they
Get private once again

But me, I got to wait a year
And if I get it wrong
Some little nerd like Jim McKay
Will try to ping my pong

It just ain't right; the Bill of Rights
Was meant fer every man
T'was wrote so folk like you and me
Won't wind up in the can

But congressmen and lawyers, too
Don't care fer you and me
The laws they make are just fer them
—Or I'd be walking' free.

Sitting Through Jury Selection

To sleep, perchance to dream.
Don't wake me up. I'll scream.

Ode to the Bailiff

The bailiff is gray and bluff and hearty
The sort you like to invite to a party

If I ever have a party I think that I'll
Ask him to come and visit a while

So I can tell him I'm a great supporter
Of the way he calls the court to order.

My Peers Bring Tears

This is the jury of my peers
That will decide my fate?
These are my peers?
Then all these tears
Are for how low I rate.

We all are equal under law—
But these can hardly read and write
Within the law
What ghastly flaw
Lets these decide my plight?

It matters not; the die is cast
These will decide my fate
The die is cast,
The time is passed
It's—dammit all—too late.

Among Other Things

Things that do disgust us
Include the bar of justice

What a Bad Boy Am I

I listen carefully to every charge
And wonder why I'm still at large
No one as criminal as me
Should be allowed to roam so free.

Keeping a Straight Face Isn't Easy

Plotkin insists that I be serious
Sane and low-key and never delirious
He worries, I guess
About jury and press
And the prosecutor most nefarious.

My Lawyers

Larry Barcella
Is a regular fella,
And Robert Plotkin
I like a lotkin.

Back and Forth the Lawyers Go

Back and forth the lawyers go
Back and forth and to and fro

To the bench and back again
Muddling things we think are plain
Unknowing things we think we know
Still back and forth the lawyers go
Another day goes by in vain
While we, the sane, go slow insane.

Elizabeth Is Nervous

Elizabeth is nervous as she can be
I wish that I could smile at she
But Plotkin says I cannot do it
So though it hurts I will eschew it.

This Old Duffer

Why should this old duffer
Any more be forced to suffer
The arrows and slings
Of a fate that brings
Times that are rough and rougher.

Once Again Flannery II

The judge is ruling against us today
It's morning, he's not quite awake
It takes him a while to remember
The rest of my life is at stake.

Waiting

This is a day of waiting and wait
Starting early and ending late
Like me, my patience is also tried
Come on, jury, decide! decide!

God Save the U.S.A. Anyway

"God save the United States
And this honorable court,"
The bailiff says when we begin
This daily, indoor, legal sport

"God save the United States"
With this request I do agree
But save this court? I must say
That supplication's not for me.

A Thought

I'd rather live in the Okefenokee
Than make my home in the federal pokey.

A MEBA Is Not a Microbe

Now we take the MEBA charge,
Perhaps it's my most heinous crime.
I wonder why I'm still at large?
There is no reason or no rhyme.

You see, I asked that Ronald R
Live up to his given word
Which had not been done, thus far
Apparently I erred. I erred.

I erred in seeking to get done
The things that Ronnie said he'd do
Forget such promises, my son,
Or wind up in the doggie doo.

Doing right in politics
Or keeping to one's given word
Is just for stupids from the sticks
At least that's what the charge inferred

Doing right is doing wrong
If you work in Washington
And thus doth end my saddest song
Profit from its words, my son.

Those Drips Are Leaking Again

They're leaking lies on Meese and Mark
To try to paint us dirty, dark,
In the hopes the jury sees
A picture of us colored "sleaze."

A Skinny Old Nag

Lovita she is mighty skinny,
And her laugh is like the whinny
Of a thirsty old dray horse
That knows it has not one recourse
But to whinny for its dinny.

A Legal Word

"Redact" is a legal word for "edit"
Who was it, I ask, who first said it?
I don't like the word "redact"
I do not, and that's a fact
And I think Webster should shed it.

Where Is the Talent?

What did Talenti
Ever inventi
To pay the renti?
He can't say
For he's absenti.

I Wish They Spoke English

"Refresh your recollection"
Is awful lawyerese

"Refresh your memory," you dolts,
Is proper, if you please.

Dear Lord, Forgive Me

As a Christian I should pray
For Coleman, Garland, and McKay
But I can't turn the other cheek
For people who of evil reek

Intestinal Fortitude Appears to Be Lacking

If Flannery had any guts
He'd tell McKay that he is nuts,
He'd throw this case right out the door,
He'd sweep it up forever more,
And then sit back and tut his tuts.

L'Envoi

The jury tells of its verdict.
The judge sets the sentencing date
My friends are weary and weeping
While I stand and I ponder my fate.
For the long, long trial is over.
It's done and it's finished, caput!
We never wound up in the clover
Pray the same for a prison striped suit.

Whatever Vicky Wants Vicky Gets

I dream of Vicky Frances Leake
And in those dreams I hear her speak,
Telling me what I must do,
Telling me just who is who,
And I respond with answers meek.

For Vicky has the upper hand
She is a power in the land

So if her favor one does seek
T'is best to turn the other cheek
And cave to Vicky's each demand.

For though this ain't some foreign strand
Where bullies come and kick the sand
Into some weakling's face,
Nonetheless it is the place
Where Vicky's wish is my command.

The reason why is simply this:
Something has really gone amiss.
I've been convicted of a crime
And it may be I'll do some time
Far from this place of idle bliss.

And my probation officer
Is Vicky Leake and it is her
Who'll recommend what I should get:
Probation, jail, or freedom. Bet
I'm Vicky's slave to keep from stir

So, Vicky, in my dreams or out,
You should not have the slightest doubt
That be it night or be it day
I will do just what e'er you say,
For that's what this is all about.

If you say jump, I'll ask, "How high?"
If you insist I'll touch the sky.
To Flannery please say good things
So I can soar on freedom's wings.
Jailbirds don't get a chance to fly.

To Be Continued

This is not the end of ends
But merely the end of the beginning,
For take it from me, my friends,
We'll hang in until we're winning.

There is a certain unreality to being prosecuted on felony charges when you've spent your life viewing yourself as a reasonably honest person. That may have been why I had a hard time taking the trial seriously. Daily, before the trial resumed, I chatted with members of the press, most of whom did pretty decent jobs of covering it. Many, many people came to the trial to lend moral support, some all the way from California. Black friends such as Richard Allen, Jim Woods, Leo Taylor, John Wilks, Jim Denson, and others. Democrats such as John White. People who had worked for me. People I had helped get jobs. People I had worked for.

They would come in between sessions and I would go to the railing that separates the audience from the players and welcome them. That is, I did until Barcella and Plotkin made me quit it. One of them, I think it was Plotkin, told me I was acting more like an official greeter than the defendant in a trial and that the jurists might resent me not taking the case seriously. That may be the real reason why they convicted me, but I doubt it.

Bonnie and my daughters, Susie and Glenda, were there daily. So were the ladies from my office, Beth Johnson and Judy Jackson. Kathy Wilson, a friend who worked at AID, was there almost as often.

Our lawyers had scrounged a couple of vacant offices down the hall from the courtroom for our use during recesses and noon breaks. We ate lunch there most days, salads, sandwiches, cookies. Kathy Millar brought in Chinese food one day but Beth, who runs a catering service on the side, brought in most of it. I gained weight, lots of weight, mainly eating cookies. At the end of each day another friend, Claire del Real, picked us up in her Jeep station wagon and drove us back to our office. If it hadn't been for the damn trial we'd have had a hell of a good time.

I was found guilty on February 11, 1988. I knew before the jury came in what the verdict would be. I had watched those sullen faces over a period of weeks and not óne juror would look me in the eye. As we went into the courtroom to hear the verdict I told Bonnie and Susie and Glenda, the girls both grown, that I didn't want one tear. We were not going to give McKay and his band of witch hunters, or the jurors, that satisfaction. And we didn't.

Outside the court I was stopped by a young reporter who on the basis of his question should go on to a great career in television.

"How do you feel about your conviction?" he asked.

"You asshole," I said, "how do you think I feel? You want me to tell you I'm happy?"

I did not hit him, one of my many regrets.

Immediately after my conviction I was ordered to report to a preselected probation officer with whom I would have to deal until my sentencing, which was set for April 8. Her name was Vicky Frances Leake. She was an attractive, dark-haired woman who appeared to be in her midthirties. She was pleasant but firm. She wanted to know my life's history, and asked me to bring her proof that I had indeed been graduated from high school and college, had an honorable discharge from the army of the United States, and was really married to the woman I had been living with since 1947. She also wanted to see back income tax records and a financial statement.

She sent me to a little room to urinate in a little bottle with a little man watching to see that I didn't cheat. This was to ascertain whether I was a user of illegal drugs. The thing that scares you about this procedure is the good chance that your sample is going to be switched with someone else's—say, Marion Barry's. Then what?

But the topper was when Vicky told me: "I want you to write a letter to Judge Flannery suggesting what you think should be a proper sentence."

I looked at her in amazement. "Hey, remember me?" I asked. "I'm the guy who pleaded not guilty."

"I know," she said, "but I want you to do it."

I realized then that she was just following policy, so I didn't argue further.

"I'll write the judge," I said, "but I won't suggest any punishment, because that would be an admission of guilt and I won't do that. As you know, we are going to file an appeal."

I asked her then if she told all her "clients" to write the judge and if they did, did they actually suggest realistic sentences? Yes, she said, she did require the letter from all of her wards, but gave no details.

So I wrote to Flannery. And I told him I couldn't help him because I hadn't done anything wrong and therefore he'd have to figure out my sentence all by himself. Which he probably would have done anyway.

Vicky also went out to the house to see Bonnie, I guess to see whether we were fitten people or whether the house was clean or whether we were growing marijuana in the sun room. In the course of the visit

Vicky asked Bonnie what my sentence should be, perhaps thinking she might suggest a life term. Instead, Bonnie got mad at her, told her I was innocent and should not have been convicted. Which I thought was darn decent of her.

Federal officers also questioned my brother and sister out in California. I still don't know why. I'd always been nice to them.

Barcella and Plotkin gave me some good advice after my conviction. But, then, in their minds they'd been doing that all along. This time they told me that if I would repent publicly, beat my breast a bit, mea culpa a bit more, and promise never to do it again the judge would probably let me off with a fine and probation.

"Hey, fellas," I said, "I pleaded innocent. We're appealing this case. If I do what you say that's an admission of guilt. Ain't no way I'm going to admit guilt."

"We're not recommending that you do," Plotkin said. "We're just telling you it's an alternative."

"Not to me it ain't," I said. "We're going to fight these bastards as long as there is a place to fight them."

That night I told Bonnie, "We're going to fight these SOBs all the way to the Supreme Court if we have to, if it takes every cent we have. We started out living in a two-room apartment and eating a lot of spaghetti and we can do it again if we have to."

Bonnie agreed immediately and completely. And fight 'em we did.

But first we had to wait and see what my sentence would be.

I had not made things any easier for the judge. I had refused to admit guilt. I had called the law under which I was convicted "a lousy law." I had refused to suggest punishment in the letter I had written at Vicky's order.

And early on, as the trial was getting underway, I had made an often quoted but totally misunderstood remark that could only hurt. I'd told the press that the crimes I was charged with were like running a stop sign. They took this to mean that I viewed the charges against me as no more serious than running a stop sign. McKay, too, although my lawyers took pains to disabuse him of that interpretation, found it fitted his purpose to continue the misunderstanding when talking to the jury, and to heck with the truth.

In fact, truth seemed to be something that McKay was largely unfamiliar with and uninterested in. The truth in this case was that my lawyers had explained to me that Flannery and McKay were interpreting my alleged crime the same way running a stop sign would be interpreted; they didn't have to prove intent, they just had to prove I had done it. The misinterpretation of my analogy stuck, however, not only with the media but also, I'm sure, with Flannery, who seemed as unconcerned as McKay about the thing called "fairness."

During the period before my sentencing well over a hundred persons, many, but not all, at my request, wrote letters to Flannery telling him all kinds of nice things about me. Even though they were true, they didn't do any good. I don't think he read them. I think he had his mind made up from the beginning that he would send me to prison as an object lesson to all the other potential criminals around the president.

On the day of sentencing, but before he passed it, I was allowed to address him. An honor, indeed. I read a prepared statement, once again protesting my innocence and refusing in any way to apologize or express regret. It was not the one I wanted to read; Plotkin and Barcella thought that one was too blunt, too antagonistic, but if I had to do it again it's the one I would read.

And then the sentencing.

That could have been the end. Some well-meaning friends advised me not to fight it; just go serve my time and get it over with. Afterward, they said, it would soon be forgotten. But my time and experiences as a police reporter served me in good stead and I refused.

Also there was one other incident that I had not forgotten. A loyal Republican contributor came to me in 1983 and asked me to help him get appointed chairman of an obscure federal commission. I said to him, as I always say to people who want presidential appointments, "Is there anything in your background that you don't want out, anything that won't stand the light of day, anything that might keep you from getting this job?"

"Nothing," he said.

Through my efforts he was approved for the position. But before he was officially appointed he came to me, embarrassed, and said, "There is something."

"Oh shit!"

He explained that several years before he had bought an out-of-state Cadillac real cheap. It turned out the car was stolen. He was charged with transporting stolen property across state lines. His lawyer, a family friend, advised him to make a deal and plead guilty. He got off with probation and a fine. He was aghast, or at least seemed to be, when I told him he had been convicted of a felony and that there was no way he would get the appointment. He couldn't understand it. He hadn't gone to prison and in his mind he was an honest man who'd made a dumb mistake. I sent him down to the White House to see the White House counsel, Fred Fielding, who told him what I had told him, "No way, Jose." (Not his real name.)

My point is, instead of fighting to prove his innocence he took the easy way and the cheap way out. But eventually, as it does nearly every time, the easy way and the cheap way rose up and bit him in the fanny. That was not going to happen to me. No way, Jose! (Not my real name.)

My lawyers announced that I would appeal, which we did. It was decided that we would bring in another expensive lawyer—all lawyers are expensive—Andy Frey, a specialist in appellate work. The way the appellate court works is that the presiding judge of the court appoints a three-judge panel to hear a case. After the panel decides, the losing side can appeal to the full court, which may, but doesn't have to, rehear the case. After that decision is reached the loser can appeal to the Supreme Court which may, but doesn't have to, hear the case. I was determined to go all the way to the Supreme Court, if necessary. So, it turned out, was McKay. He had nothing to lose. It wasn't his freedom or his money or his reputation (in the latter instance he didn't have one) at stake.

My three-judge panel was made up of two judges who had been appointed by President Reagan and one named by President Carter. They heard oral arguments in late November, about seven months after my sentencing. Andy Frey argued for my side. The American Civil Liberties Union, about which I have had a slight change of heart, presented an effective friend of the court brief on my behalf. I owe them and one day I will repay them, even at the risk of hearing bad words from my fellow conservatives.

Arguing for the independent counsel was Richard Friedman. I remembered him well. As my trial was beginning he slipped over to the defense side of the courtroom and sat next to my daughters. I saw him and immediately went to them.

"This is one of the bad guys," I said. "Don't say anything to him, and don't say anything around him. He's trying to put me in jail and anything you say he'll try to use against me."

He looked at me with an embarrassed smirk, but moved back to where he belonged. He turned out to be an ineffective arguer, or maybe he knew he didn't have much of a case.

In late 1988, while the court still dawdled, friends began talking to me about the possibility of a presidential pardon. Some even talked of petitioning the president. The idea of getting out from under was appealing and the lawyers saw nothing wrong with a pardon per se. But the more I thought of the idea the less I liked it. A pardon is just that. If you haven't done anything wrong there is nothing to pardon. If you accept a pardon you are admitting guilt. I didn't want to do that.

I came to the conclusion that I would rather risk ninety days in prison while continuing to maintain my innocence than accept a pardon and thereby tacitly admit my guilt. I also had the feeling that it really wasn't fair to the president. If he pardoned me some would accuse him of favoritism. If he didn't he would be accused of disloyalty and heartlessness.

So I wrote him a letter telling him I didn't want a pardon; I wanted to continue to fight for my innocence in court. A pardon would make that impossible. At the end I said I hoped a side benefit of my decision would be to make things easier for him.

He called me a few days later and thanked me for my letter and agreed with my decision. "And, yes," he said, "you have made things easier for me."

I have thought since that my decision might also have made it easier for him not to pardon others, mainly Oliver North and John Poindexter. If so, I am truly sorry. Their cases were entirely different from mine. I wish he had pardoned them and two or three of those lower down the ladder who did what they did in all innocence, thinking only that they were helping their president.

After oral arguments, another seven months ground slowly by before Judge James Buckley, writing for a two to one majority, handed down the decision that overturned my convictions and threw out the indictment. Buckley, a Reagan appointee, was supported by the other Reagan judge, Steven Williams. The third judge, a black New York liberal named Harry Edwards, who had been appointed by Jimmy Carter, wrote a stinging but meaningless dissent. Like the members of the jury he apparently had difficulty judging a Reagan Republican on the merits of the case.

Not surprisingly, McKay asked the full appeals court to rehear my appeal. In vain. The court refused his request. But four of the learned judges, all Carter appointees, wrote that McKay's next step should be to the Supreme Court. McKay took the hint. In vain. Moving with a speed unusual for a unit of the federal justice system, the high court in early December 1989 refused to hear my case and sent it back to district court for disposal.

My lawyers warned me that McKay next might seek a new trial. I screamed double jeopardy. They said it ain't necessarily so. But they also thought McKay was finished. McKay shortly came to the same conclusion, apparently not wanting to make a martyr out of me, for which Joan of Arc will be forever grateful.

At any rate, it was over, all but the shouting. And that came a month later, on January 10, when Flannery handed down the final decision in the case of the *United States of America vs. Franklyn C. Nofziger*. David had whipped Goliath again, and is damn proud of it.

But after that sort of ordeal things never really do get back to normal. During the three years of paralysis, brought on by the news stories, the investigation, the trial and sentencing procedure, and the appeals process, the rest of the world had continued to go around.

My older daughter, Susie, had died of cancer in May of 1989 and my regret is that she never lived to see her father vindicated.

A presidential election had been held and it was the first in more than twenty years in which I hadn't had a role.

A new administration had taken over and even though it was Republican I was no longer an insider. True, I had friends on the inside but the feeling was different and the relationships were not the same.

I began getting mail addressed to Miss Lyn Nofzinger or Knofziger or Notsiger and when my secretary called and left word that Lyn Nofziger was calling, their secretaries said, "How do you spell your last name, Lyn?" Her name was Beth. Fame and infamy, it seems, are equally fleeting.

But what the hell. From 1966, when I left reporting to go to work for Reagan, through 1986 I'd had a good run. I'd served in two White Houses and five presidential campaigns. I'd been involved in what goes on in this nation in a way and at a depth that most people never dream of. I'd had twenty years of fun and excitement and on occasion had even had a chance to have an impact on what was happening. It would be hard to ask for anything more.

Even though as a reporter I'd covered national politics and presidential campaigns out of Washington, D.C., for eight years, my real involvement in politics began with Ronald Reagan's first gubernatorial campaign in 1966. Fittingly, my political career ended to all intents and purposes about the same time his did. I might have asked for a more positive ending, but without argument, the timing was pretty good.

Index